MAKING LAMANITES

MAKING LAMANITES

*Mormons, Native Americans,
and the Indian Student Placement Program,
1947–2000*

Matthew Garrett

THE UNIVERSITY OF UTAH PRESS
Salt Lake City

The Defiance House Man colophon is a registered trademark of the
University of Utah Press. It is based on a four-foot-tall Ancient Puebloan
pictograph (late PIII) near Glen Canyon, Utah.

LIBRARY OF CONGRESS CATALOGING-IN-PUBLICATION DATA
Names: Garrett, Matthew, 1978- author.
Title: Making Lamanites : Mormons, Native Americans, and the Indian Student
  Placement Program, 1947-2000 / Matthew Garrett (winner of the Juanita
  Brooks Prize in Mormon Studies).
Description: Salt Lake City : The University of Utah Press, [2016] | Includes
  bibliographical references and index.
Identifiers: LCCN 2016005203| ISBN 978160781569-3 (paper : alkaline paper)
  ISBN 9781607814955 (ebook)
Subjects: LCSH: Indians of North America—Education—History—20th century.
  Church of Jesus Christ of Latter-day Saints. Indian Student Placement
  Program—History. | Indian foster children—Education—United
  States—History—20th century. | Indian students—United
  States—History—20th century. | Indians of North America—Ethnic
  identity—History—20th century. | Indians of North America—Cultural
  assimilation—History—20th century. | Church work with Indians—Church of
  Jesus Christ of Latter-day Saints—History—20th century. | United
  States—Ethnic relations—History—20th century.
Classification: LCC E97 .G37 2016 | DDC 970.004/97—dc23
LC record available at https://lccn.loc.gov/2016005203

To Jenny

CONTENTS

List of Tables   viii
Acknowledgments   ix
A Note on Terminology   xi

1. Introduction   1

2. Reimagining Israel: The Emergence of Mormon Indian Theology
    and Policy in the Nineteenth Century   11

3. Turning to Placement: The Navajo Nation, Helen John,
    and the Pursuit of Education, 1880s–1940s   36

4. The Institutional Rise of the Indian Student Placement Program,
    1947–1972   58

5. The Placement Experience: Entering Mormon Homes and
    Communities   91

6. The Placement Experience: Becoming a Lamanite   128

7. Rival Ideologies and Rival Indians: Self-Determination in the 1960s
    and 1970s   169

8. Decline of the Placement Program, 1972–2000   204

9. Conclusion   235

Notes   251
Bibliography   303
Index   327

TABLES

2.1. Church Population, 1830–1845   25
3.1. Reasons for Enrolling   56
4.1. Expanding Enrollment by Region, 1960–1967   84
6.1. Perceptions of Placement Students   160
8.1. Student Enrollment and Percent Change, 1969–1976   214
8.2. Eligibility Requirements and Projected Student Enrollment, 1979–1989   226
8.3. Projected Student Enrollment, 1989–2000   232

ACKNOWLEDGMENTS

A work of this nature is always a reflection of the energies of many people. I have been fortunate to benefit from the efforts and support of quite a few individuals and institutions. Much of this project began at Arizona State University under the tutelage of preeminent scholars Donald Fixico and Peter Iverson; the university also offered funding in the form of graduate assistantships, scholarship fellowships, and the Millett research award. Additional thanks are due to my graduate studies advisors at the University of Nebraska, Victoria Smith, John Wunder, and Wagonze Mark Awakuni-Swetland.

A great portion of this work relies heavily on research conducted by other scholars. I owe a debt to Armand Mauss who not only provided an intellectual framework through his well-known publications, but who also left a rich archival collection at the Utah State Historical Society. Several others unknowingly aided my work as they gathered dozens of interviews that assisted this project. Brigham Young University (BYU) Redd Center director Jessie Embrie conducted and otherwise oversaw the collection of dozens of interviews; several Latter-day Saints (LDS) Church Archivists likewise generated the ever-helpful Moyle Oral History collection at the LDS Church Archives. I am indebted to a number of archivists there and elsewhere. I am grateful for the support of staff at BYU's L. Tom Perry Special Collections library, Utah State Historical Society, and especially to those at the LDS Church Archives. Special thanks are due to Ron Watt, Bill Savage, and Allan Morrell who repeatedly worked to open and review restricted materials whenever possible. Special thanks also go to Tona Hangen who generously shared two dozen interviews she conducted as part of an earlier research project.

In addition to academics, I owe special gratitude to the dozens of individuals who shared their stories with me; without such support this project could not come to fruition. Many opened their homes and shared with me their intimate feelings and stories; I am humbled by their generosity and trust and hope this work honestly reflects their feelings. Their names, along with dozens more who answered my queries in the *Navajo Times* or in social media, are scattered across the next few hundred pages and this is ultimately their story.

Finally, I am very grateful to my friends and family who supported my efforts. Special thanks are due to close colleagues who read all or portions of the manuscript and offered useful feedback, specifically Paul Hirt, Elyssa Ford, Adam Tomkins, Cody Marshall, Patricia Biggs, Kristen Youngblood, Jed Rogers, Randy Beeman, Kirk Russell, and Margaret Jacobs. I am most of all grateful for my supportive wife who served as motivator, editor, and sounding board for the better part of a decade.

A NOTE ON TERMINOLOGY

It is fitting to begin this book with a brief discussion of the difficulty in selecting terms to represent people when no such unity exists among those very people. As is typically the preference of most Native people, this work strives to identify them by tribe whenever that information is available. However, when referring to Native American individuals or groups with unknown or heterogeneous ancestry, one of several pan-Indian terms is generally employed: Native American, Indian, and Native. All three are used synonymously in this work with regret that there is no single term agreed upon by all such people.

When referring to people of European American ancestry the term *white* is typically employed here for the purpose of simplicity; however, the chapter discussing early Mormons who often migrated directly from Europe more often employs Euro-American. People who are members of the Church of Jesus Christ of Latter-day Saints, white or not, are generally referred to as Mormons or Latter-day Saints. Both are used synonymously with similar awareness that there is no universal preference among that population. Likewise, the name of the church is often stated as Mormon Church, LDS Church, or simply the church. When Native Americans have converted to the church and claimed an identity as a Lamanite, that term is freely employed.

Debate over nomenclature also impacts the very title of the Indian Student Placement Program. While in its earliest years church leaders referred to it informally as the outing program, two quasi-official titles later emerged: the Lamanite Student Placement Program and the Indian Student Placement

Program (ISPP). Caseworkers and administrators used the two interchange-ably, even in print, with slight preference for the latter. For consistency's sake alone, the latter is universally employed in the following pages.

Finally, the words "some," "many," and "most" are unfortunate but necessary devices throughout this work when describing the opinion of participants in the ISPP. Often an exact number is unknown and an esti-mate is generated from the available interviews and research. In such cases, one of those three terms is employed to reflect incrementally different pro-portions ranging from just more than a few ("some") to a majority ("most") with space still allotted for a wildly unknown "many." The imprecise lan-guage is unfortunate but necessary due to the general lack of hard data. Hopefully the reader will accept the limitations of the documentary evi-dence and trust in the selection of the appropriate term.

1

INTRODUCTION

My parents never took many pictures, but while rebuilding their attic floor in the summer of 2007 I found a handful of faded photographs from several decades ago. I vaguely remembered the dark wooden panels that once adorned my parents' family room and the gaudy gold-leaf-painted coffee table that exemplified the 1970s. As I cleaned and organized the dusty frames, I grew curious about two young Native American girls who appeared in many of the photographs: sitting at my parents' dinner table or opening gifts in front of the family Christmas tree. Who were these girls, and why were they in my home?

In the fall of 2004, several years prior to my discovery in the attic, I began graduate study at the University of Nebraska where my advisor introduced me to potential Native American research topics, including the Indian Student Placement Program (ISPP) operated by the Church of Jesus Christ of Latter-day Saints. From 1947 until 2000, the Mormon Church directed this voluntary and seasonal foster care program for Native American youth. I had never heard of the program, but I had no interest in pursuing Mormon history. My limited exposure caused me to prematurely (and erroneously) deem all such scholarship as parochial and hagiographic. I did not wish to invite such criticisms into my future career and promptly put the topic out of my mind. Serendipitously, I repeatedly encountered the junction between Mormons and Native Americans over the following years, and I finally indulged my curiosity by writing a graduate seminar paper that emphasized Indian fixations in the early Mormon Church. I found the historiography deep, divided, and fascinating. A few months later, I stumbled across the old photographs of Roberta and Ellen, who lived in my parents' home only two years before my birth. They were from the Navajo and Hopi Nations, respectively, and resided with my parents as foster children.

In 1976, my parents joined the Mormon Church's Indian Student Placement Program and accepted these two Native children into their home. They hoped to provide reservation children with an opportunity to attend a suburban school and experience the amenities of white, middle-class life. Each summer the children would return to their respective reservations. After just a few months, however, unrelated financial stresses dictated my mother's return to the workplace and my parents withdrew from the program. Nevertheless, their short-lived participation proved the final and irresistible indication that I should indeed write about a program that was so close to both my scholarly training in Native American history and my Mormon cultural heritage.

Mormon missionary zeal directed at American Indians originated with the church's founding in 1830, but largely stalled at the close of the nineteenth century. The former urgency to convert Native Americans remained chiefly dormant until 1947 when Latter-day Saints living in Richfield, Utah, informally initiated a new program. These Mormons volunteered to house Navajo migrant workers' children who wished to attend local public schools. After six years of informal operation, the Mormon Church officially institutionalized the program and administered it from headquarters in Salt Lake City. The ISPP offered educational opportunities and cultural exposure to impoverished Native American youths, but it also distanced them from their indigenous roots and separated them from their families during the school months. Unbeknownst to many, this program continued until 2000, when the last student graduated from high school. In total some fifty thousand students (mostly Navajo) left their respective reservations to participate in Placement for one or more academic years.[1] Excitement about perceived success during the 1960s and 1970s led the LDS Church to launch a myriad of associated education programs and redouble its efforts to convert Native Americans culturally and spiritually. The massive ISPP remained the flagship of the Indian program.

There are many themes that may be emphasized in the history of the Placement Program, perhaps the most obvious being colonization. The Placement Program constituted an undeniable effort to transform Native people into an image largely crafted by white Mormon Americans. It not only imposed religious beliefs, but also surrounded Native youth in what French sociologist Pierre Bourdieu termed *habitus*—an inescapable cultural context through which power relations are imprinted upon bodies and consciously or unconsciously repeated back.[2] Many children who participated in the ISPP not only professed faith in the LDS Church, but also came to dress accordingly, speak the language, and in many ways internalize a foreign lifestyle that they no longer separated from themselves. This is a standard process of acculturation in social groups, but colonialism comes into play when one group imposes its culture upon another. The imbalanced power relationships created by the United States' longstanding colonization of Native Americans created a window through which Mormons could initiate and maintain their own unique program to inscribe new, Mormon identities on Native bodies.

Colonialism is a term that bears an academic history that affects its meaning and use. At the turn of the nineteenth century, Frederick Jackson Turner's nationalistic narrative identified waves of civilizing conquest that ended in 1890 with the closing of the frontier as settlement of the West by whites reached fruition. Though essentially silent on Native Americans, Mormons, and other people, Turner's foundation served as the theoretical origin of Western American history. Over time, scholars augmented Turner's narrative with foci on the environment, ethnic and gendered groups, and class struggle, but a positivist premise of progress that continued to marginalize Native Americans or cast them as flat characters and foils lingered in many works.

In 1961, the Western History Association organized as an umbrella for growing ranks of enthusiasts and scholars who addressed the region through ever-evolving methods. In 1978, The *Western Historical Quarterly* published an article by Calvin Martin, "Ethnohistory: A Better Way to Write Indian History." It pointed to history that drew on anthropological research and methods as the ideal means to resolve the apparent discord between "the Indian of anthropology and the Indian of history." Thereby scholars might finally "confront the Indian who confronted us—this time on *his* terms."[3] With an eye set to contextualizing historical actors in an ethnographic setting, a new generation of scholars employed indigenous sources as they penned biographies and tribal histories that broke free of the linear progress model that reinforced the nationalistic metanarrative evident in previous Turnerian works.

Meanwhile, the postmodern critique spurred new forms of inquiry in anthropology, sociology, literature, and history. Michel Foucault, Jacques Derrida, and others deconstructed human relationships and discourses to reveal power structures that shaped the world around us. Edward Said's *Orientalism* pointed to preconceived notions of normative and exotic that defined relations and veiled true understanding. Robert Berkhofer's *The White Man's Indian* similarly explored the images whites thrust upon Native Americans, noting that the former defined the latter in terms of inadequacy and savagery as a means of defining themselves in contrast.[4] Since then, broad scholarship has sprung from those postmodern roots.[5]

Historians fused political and ethnohistorical analysis as they examined, with increased focus on the marginalized, institutions of power designed to transform and assimilate Indians. David Wallace Adams's *Education for Extinction* set a new standard for exploring a system of colonization by examining both policy history and the experiences of Indian children within boarding schools. Beginning in 1880, the federal government directed tens of thousands of Indian youths into facilities intended to "strip away all outward signs of the children's identification with tribal life" and instill "ideas, values, and behaviors of white civilization."[6] By 1900, the Annual Report of the Commissioner of Indian Affairs reported 153 boarding schools and another 154 day schools with a combined attendance of 21,568 Indian youths.[7] Adams explored the clothes issued to children, the change of their names, cutting of hair, medical examinations, diet, punishment, and forms of resistance. His work inspired a generation of graduate students, resulting in a wave of dissertations and monographs analyzing individual boarding schools, each one exploring mechanisms of power and efforts to transform Native youth. That approach of assessing students' experiences within assimilationist education programs is also evident in this history of the ISPP.[8]

Understanding the student experience within a colonization framework begins with the recruitment of ISPP students; it leads us to consider the physical/material changes the experience wrought upon Indian bodies and the discourse it imprinted in their minds. It also focuses on student responses to the program and requires the use of oral histories to provide an alternative narrative to the policy-driven perspective preserved in institutional records. Most importantly, the lens of colonization emphasizes the agency of the marginalized; it reminds us "that there are things that have survived, that [indigenous people] do have power, that the margins are in fact the centres."[9] Exploring both subtle and manifest power structures from indigenous perspectives demands the inclusion of Native voices to articulate their unique experiences.

Over the past two decades this approach has redefined boarding school histories.[10] These works include Native voices to an unprecedented degree, but also fall into a frequent pattern of illustrating agency by way of resistance. A recent and particularly relevant example is Elise Boxer's work on the LDS Church and the ISPP.[11] She and others draw inspiration from early national decolonization texts such as Frantz Fanon's *The Wretched of the Earth* and Albert Memmi's *The Colonizer and the Colonized*.[12] The consequent approach assumes a conflict-bound binary of colonizers and the colonized and, in the spirit of empowering historical actors, focuses on resistance efforts.

While offering a valuable lens, this narrow use of colonialism does invoke certain restrictions.[13] As Edward Said indicated, preconceived notions, including reliance on a single method of analysis, can restrict vision and obviate the need to see contrary complications. It conceals complex human interactions that defy the reductionist dualism of oppressor and resistor. Long before this recent methodological trend, historian James Clifford criticized dichotomies that "do not account for complex historical processes of appropriation, compromise, subversion, masking, invention, and revival."[14] More recently, Craig Cipolla's history of the Brothertown Indians called for a more "pragmatic approach" that "serves to further eradicate the dichotomous tropes that continue to haunt the archaeology of colonialism." He hoped to draw attention to the "social pluralities of colonialism" typically born of "the admixture of the 'traditional' with the 'foreign,' and the redefinition of each in the process."[15] I echo his thoughts, and those of J. Edard Chamberlin who affirmed that "postcolonial theory certainly provides a useful way of looking at the lands, the livelihoods, and the languages of Aboriginal peoples. But it is not the only way. Other ways may complement or even contradict it. That shouldn't bother us."[16]

What is required, then, is an approach uninhibited by methodological flag waving, one that borrows from postmodern awareness of power structures, emphasizes the marginalized, draws on ethnohistory's interest in cultural context, includes Native voices and perspectives, and thereby reveals how power is exerted and colonization proceeds, but does not exclude varied forms of inquiry or the nuanced reality of historical subjects' experiences. In this book I seek to offer such an approach, all the while realizing that I am examining a subject that tends to polarize and elicit black-and-white judgments. In short, I apply the lens of colonialism to expose assimilative pressures, but also allow for diverse responses that include, but are not limited to, resistance.

This history of the Mormon Church's Indian Student Placement Program explores the institutional history as well as the experiences of those who lived between and across real cultural binaries. To do so it balances more traditional archival work with over one hundred interviews, memoirs, and correspondences, as well as biographical sketches. These sources recover voices of participants and reveal the power structures that permeated student experiences while demonstrating the agency of not only those Indian youths who resisted the program, but also those who embraced it, as well as those somewhere in between.

Such a history of the Placement Program must begin with the early doctrine and colonization efforts of the Mormon Church. Mormonism introduced a theology, tucked within the foundational text of the Latter-day Saint faith, which centered on a romanticized image of Indians and a call for their redemption, and hence, colonization. The Book of Mormon chronicles the account of a refugee family who fled Israel in 600 B.C. and who fathered rival nations descending from the eldest son, Laman, and his younger brother, Nephi. God cursed Lamanite wickedness with dark skin, setting them apart from their more industrious and God-fearing kin. To Mormons, Lamanites served as a repository for traditional western notions of savage Indians while Nephites represented a more righteous, civilized, and lighter-skinned ideal. The sacred scripture tracks the eventual destruction of Nephites at the hands of wicked Lamanites, leaving a godless, dark, and loathsome people who until recently the church identified as the primary ancestors of Native Americans.

From its 1830 inception through the twentieth century, the LDS Church instituted a variety of outreach programs intended to redeem the Lamanites through their conversion to the Mormon faith and compliance with western notions of civility. The first "Lamanite mission" departed in 1830, soon after the church's organization. After arriving in Utah, Brigham Young and other church leaders developed an extensive conversion and education program that included raising Indian children in white homes. During the nineteenth century, Latter-day Saints operated missions, demonstration farms, and informal reservations and purchased, indentured, and adopted Indian children, many from Utes who had acquired them through raids on neighboring tribes. By 1900 these programs had dissipated, although ecclesiastical leaders continued to supervise, advise, and administer to small colonies of, particularly, Southern Paiutes and Shoshones. In the middle of the twentieth century the Indian Student Placement Program emerged as the Mormon Church's last and greatest colonization effort. Mormons believed that Indians would become "white and delightsome" as they adopted Western models of dress, behavior, industry, and, most importantly, the LDS Church. In this way, Mormons intended to assimilate Native Americans, and Indian compliance played an essential role in validating Mormon theology that anticipated an eventual redemption of the Lamanites. Yet the assimilative intention of the ISPP only represents part of the story, and to emphasize the colonization process alone is to ignore and negate the agency of participants.

Native people understood the use of schools to assimilate their youth. In the late nineteenth and early twentieth centuries, private organizations and eventually the Bureau of Indian Affairs operated rigid, military-like boarding schools that sought to erase Native cultures. Their acculturating efforts took deculturing as a necessary corollary. Yet Indian students, through accommodation, avoidance, subversion, resistance, acceptance, or filtering, helped determine the long-term impact of this coercive experience on their lives. Their choices were constrained but their agency not eliminated. And to the degree this education offered access to the affluence and opportunity American society promised, some families even volunteered their children for enrollment. Like their parents who attended boarding schools a generation earlier, ISPP youths strove to bridge Indian and white worlds. Native Americans hated the harsh and impersonal boarding schools, which remained a vivid, unpleasant memory for many Indians; though practices had moderated somewhat by the mid-twentieth century, Native Americans continued to view such institutions as culturally and individually abrasive, as well as academically inferior. Many parents readily enrolled their children in Placement as a preferable alternative. They believed suburban schools held the key to a genuinely useful education and a possible road out of poverty, and they valued the idea of a nuclear family setting where children would receive individual attention. Submersion in white society offered a different type of educational experience that seemed more inviting and flexible to students in their formative adolescent years. In this context students responded differently to their varied experiences and cultural encounters. Some certainly resisted the colonizing efforts of the program, including religious conversion and culturally derived behavioral expectations of families and teachers, and frequently did so covertly for fear of expulsion from the program. Others outright withdrew. Spotty enrollment records offer little data on retention rates, but one study suggests as many as half of the students enrolled dropped out of the program for various reasons.[17] Their voices are represented in this text in the form of displeased and critical students, frustrated foster parents, and social critics; however, this book is admittedly less concerned with the stories of those who dropped out. Part of that is due to the records available—there is simply less information available about those who chose not to participate— but it is also by design.

The focus of this book is upon those who enrolled year after year, engaged with, and even embraced part or all of the foreign identity ISPP provided. What are we to make of those who internalized the message presented by the LDS Church and foster families? Some of their contemporaries called them "apples" or "coconuts" and other derogatory terms intended to indicate their abandonment of indigenous culture. Dismissal of these students' choices discredits the legitimacy of their agency and reduces their self-identification to a product of outside forces.[18] To be sure, Mormons were guilty of "aggressive benevolence," as two church biographers tactfully put it. While participation was voluntary and free of the corporal punishment common in boarding schools, the alien environments, separation from biological families, behavioral regulations, and social pressures constituted inherently coercive dimensions.[19] Such criticisms, though, do not eliminate the reality that many students derived a new identity from the program, one that merged Native heritage with Mormon beliefs.

This new Lamanite identity served as a source of strength and opportunity for many. These self-identified Lamanites complicate any simplistic binary between colonizer and victim and necessitate a broader view of cultural authenticity. They came of age in a contested ideological environment, but their experience is no less valid. Each person's story deserves to be told, including those of ISPP students who accepted and internalized a foreign ideology at the risk of weakening their claims to traditional cultural authenticity.

Clifford hashed out this issue of authenticity several decades ago. He commented, "This feeling of lost authenticity, of 'modernity' ruining some essence of source, is not a new one." He explained:

> Intervening in an interconnected world, one is always, to varying degrees, "inauthentic": caught between cultures, implicated in others. Because discourse in global power systems is elaborated vis-à-vis, a sense of difference or distinctness can never be located solely in the continuity of a culture or tradition.

He concluded, "Identity is conjunctural, not essential."[20] Nevertheless, we tend to essentialize because the human mind often prefers clarity by way of categories. Indeed, during the 1960s and 1970s, a "two worlds" theme burst into literature, art, and academic inquiry in an effort to capture the cultural shift. N. Scott Momaday's Pulitzer Prize–winning *House Made of Dawn* (1969) introduced readers to the emotional distress of such a conflict, and Native Americans transitioning between reservations and urbanity often faced a similar experience regardless of the institutional program that facilitated their relocation. It is more useful to assess individual and community identities not according to some measure of genuineness but "by the style in which they are imagined."[21] The key question is not of authenticity but rather how Placement students imagined themselves.[22]

An understanding of student agency begins first with an exploration of their constrained choices, in essence, the context of colonization. The following chapter examines a discourse used by early Mormons well before any interactions with Native Americans and how those Mormons' assumptions about Indians' Israelite heritage shaped their church's nineteenth-century policies toward the Native tribes and individuals they encountered. Chapters three and four offer institutional histories of the Navajo and Mormon efforts to education Indian children. The tribe had long endured colonizing efforts vis-à-vis educational facilities, but their longstanding attitudes of resistance changed during the mid-twentieth century. Concurrent efforts by local Mormons to redeem Indians through voluntary seasonal foster care informally laid the groundwork for the centrally planned and managed Indian Student Placement Program. Chapters five and six examine the experiences of these students, exploring the colonizing pressures they faced as well as their varied responses. The seventh chapter follows those children and other Mormon Indians into young adulthood at Brigham Young University (BYU) where they engaged with competing claims for authenticity. Church leaders promoted a new definition of self-determination that emphasized individual effort over tribal rights and absent the collective activism characterized by Red Power. The decline of the church's Lamanite programs, including the ISPP, is the focus of chapter eight. Though apparently undaunted by 1970s criticisms, the program's demise stemmed from institutional reorganizations of the correlation program, along with a fear that the program had indeed failed to fully colonize its participants. Though the church backed away from Native American–specific programs, the Lamanite trope continued to hold meaning among white and Indian Mormons.

For better and worse, the Placement Program influenced the lives of tens of thousands of Indian children during the latter half of the twentieth century. This work moves beyond a binary colonial framework to examine identity formation in the context of the organizational rise and fall of the program. For the LDS Church, the Navajo Nation, and many individuals like Roberta and Ellen who briefly lived in my parents' home, this program facilitated a transformative experience with lasting consequences.

2

REIMAGINING ISRAEL

*The Emergence of Mormon Indian Theology
and Policy in the Nineteenth Century*

We also bear testimony that the "Indians" (so called) of North and South America are a remnant of the tribes of Israel; as is now made manifest by the discovery and revelation of their ancient oracles and records. And that they are about to be gathered, civilized, and made *one nation* in this glorious land. They will also come to the knowledge of their forefathers, and the fullness of the gospel and they will embrace it, and become a righteous branch of the house of Israel.

—Proclamation of the Twelve Apostles of the Church of Jesus Christ of Latter-day Saints, 1845

The Indian Student Placement Program is not an anomaly in the history of the Latter-day Saints; rather, it was the logical result of a theological position drawn from the church's foundational document: The Book of Mormon. Following the publication of that work and the organization of the church in 1830, early Mormons conceived of a special role for Native Americans.[1]

Just as Americans have always gazed upon non-Western cultures with mistaken understandings, so too did early Mormons look upon Native Americans with a naiveté that imposed a simplistic narrative upon diverse indigenous peoples. The Book of Mormon chronicles the division of a pioneering

Israelite family who arrived at the New World six hundred years before the meridian of time. Rival nations emerged and clashed, and the wicked Lamanites prevailed. Though long fallen into apostasy, the blood of Israel in their veins gave special status to their Native American descendants. The holy scripture endowed them, as Israelites, with an exceptional (though temporarily unrecognized) ordination to gather and erect a new Jerusalem from which they would bless the earth as leaders of God's latter-day restoration.[2]

Though early Mormons readily anticipated the conversion of Lamanites to their millennialism movement, few Native Americans ever joined. Indeed, once Mormons relocated to Utah they found that competition for resources and consequent conflict more readily defined frontier Indian relations. Nevertheless, missionary and other outreach efforts continued to invite Native Americans to accept their envisioned destiny as civilized members of the Latter-day Saint church.

In recent decades historians have argued that the present-day affinity Latter-day Saints hold for Native Americans—imagined if not real—skewed the historiography of Mormon-Indian relations through most of the twentieth century.[3] In truth, once in the Utah Territory the Saints intermittently exhibited both benevolent and hostile policies towards indigenous populations. But long before skirmishes with Utes and others, early Mormons living in New York and Ohio held more optimistic views about their eventual relationship with Native Americans. This transition from optimism and inclusion toward removal and conflict requires some explanation. How and why did this religious sect that initially revered Native Americans devolve into the typical American paternalistic treatment of Indians? The answer lies in both changing historical circumstances and theological interpretations.

Between 1830 and the 1850s the Latter-day Saints increasingly interacted with Native communities who did not neatly fit into the romanticized notions held by the Mormons. The Indians they encountered largely rejected the LDS Church, and exhibited no inclination toward the Israelite gathering prophesied by the Old Testament. In response to that frustrating reality, the Latter-day Saints reinterpreted the roles of Native Americans and themselves as well. Mormons increasingly constructed their own identity as "elect" latter-day Israelites and thereby undermined the special status initially thrust upon Israelite Indians. As Mormons claimed for themselves all the rights of Israelite lineage, the vaunted status of Indians declined.

This theological displacement of Native Americans worked in tandem with historical events to lead Mormons to view themselves as gatekeepers to salvation with typical paternalistic attitudes toward Native Americans. This new attitude manifested in the benevolent assimilationist policies of the LDS Church in Utah during the mid- and late nineteenth century, as well as during the mid-twentieth century. That said, this chapter is less about Native Americans than Mormon perceptions and attitudes relating to "Lamanite" Indians. It asserts that the Latter-day Saints' emerging self-perception as latter-day Israelites, combined with the realities of close physical proximity and competition for resources, caused romanticized notions of Indians to give way to paternalistic policies of assimilation and conflict.

Early Mormon reverence for Indians as lost Israelites draws from a rich historical context that predates the publication of the Book of Mormon. Late seventeenth- and early eighteenth-century Romanticism and Primitivism movements popularized the noble savage image of Native Americans. It fused anxieties about conflict and hostility with romanticized notions of a people uncorrupted by the ills of civilization. Theorized in enlightenment arguments and popularized in American exploration narratives and fictional literature, the noble savage icon endowed Indians with a dualistic image reflecting both barbarity and complex attributes of innocence, moral courage, innate wisdom, and harmony with nature.[4]

Historians Richard Slotkin and Philip Deloria suggest that Americans internalized those romanticized views of Indians and the untamed new world to construct a uniquely American identity.[5] As part of that emergence, Euro-American fascination and mimicry of Indians occurred sporadically during the late colonial and early republic eras, most notably at the Boston Tea Party. The proliferation of the noble savage image inspired some Americans to reform their conception of Native Americans with exotic origins. Immediately following the American Revolution, one popular legend explained that a lost Welsh colony survived somewhere among the Indians and credited any appearance of Indian "civility" with European origins. Extended contact progressively pushed that imagined heritage farther and farther west to tribes lesser known to Europeans. The imposition of Israelite heritage drew even more attention and support. Immediately following the collision of eastern and western hemispheres, Europeans speculated that

America's inhabitants originated in ancient Israel. James Adair's 1775 *The History of the American Indians* and Ethan Smith's 1825 *View of the Hebrews* popularized the concept in the American mind.[6] This recasting of Indians as American Israelites is more revealing about the Euro-American crafter than their manipulated trope. By identifying Native Americans as remnants of a lost civilization, Americans displayed a psychological need to make sense of the foreign people and revitalize their own sense of self-identity.

Even before the organization of the Church of Jesus Christ of Latter-day Saints, the Book of Mormon emphasized the special role of Native Americans. Like other Americans, Mormons interpreted tribal customs and culture as evidences of Israelite heritage.[7] Apostle Orson Pratt explained that Indians' "color, features, customs, dialects, traditions" as well as ceremonies and inscriptions clearly testified of Israelite origin.[8] The dispersion of Indians upon the advance of Europeans further resonated with Isaiah's prophecies of a scattered latter-day Israel. But Israel's diaspora was not the only biblical theme to resonate with latter-day prophesy.

As lost Israelites, Native Americans enjoyed special covenant privileges reserved for the House of Israel. In 1832, the Mormon newspaper *Evening and Morning Star* explained that "Israel, the twelve tribes of Jacob, are the Elect of God," and "children of promise, the heirs of the Celestial kingdom."[9] In the Jewish and later Christian traditions, the Lord blessed Jacob (later named Israel) to birth the twelve tribes—God's covenant people. Mormons expected latter-day Israelite Indians to resume that special role in the restoration of God's church—and so Native participation was necessary. Fortunately, the Book of Mormon assured, the Lamanites "shall not deny that which you have received, but they shall build it up, and shall bring to light the true points of my doctrine."[10]

Mormons anticipated Native Americans' "gathering" to a central location—a New Jerusalem or Zion.[11] The Book of Mormon introduced the "remnant" of Joseph—a group that left Jerusalem and came to the Americas. It promised:

> The remnant of the house of Joseph shall be built upon this land; and it shall be a land of their inheritance; and they shall build up a holy city unto the Lord, like unto the Jerusalem of old; and they shall no more be confounded, until the end come when the earth shall pass

away.... And then cometh the New Jerusalem; and blessed are they
who dwell therein, for it is they whose garments are white through
the blood of the Lamb; and they are they who are numbered among
the remnant of the seed of Joseph, which were of the house of Israel.[12]

Once gathered, the Israelite Indians would build up a City of Zion, and the
American scripture explains that through this American "city of righteousness," or "New Jerusalem," the seed of Israelite Indians would bless all other
people.[13] Apostle Parley P. Pratt articulated this concept in the 1837 printing
of *A Voice of Warning*. He explained that the Indians would be gathered to a
central place "where they will finally build a New Jerusalem, a city of Zion,
with the assistance of the Gentiles." These lost Israelites seemed to hold a
sure position, as opposed to the "Gentiles" whose blessings required they
"repent of all their abominations, and embrace the same covenant, and
come into the same place of gathering" or face destruction.[14] By the mid-
1830s, however, Smith and other leaders interpreted the gathering more as
an inclusive and interethnic phenomenon; nevertheless, in the early 1830s
such an inclusive conception is not so clear.[15]

Several scholars likewise identify changes in the conception of "the
gathering." John Stott published the argument that for Mormons the gathering
to New Jerusalem was initially a Native American–centered concept which
Smith abandoned after the failure of the famous 1830–1831 Lamanite mission. David Pursuitte also identifies an early intention to place Native Americans at the center of Zion which Smith abandoned after the 1838 collapse
of Independence, Missouri. Thereafter, Pursuitte argues, Smith interpreted
the gathering as a multiethnic and multilocale phenomenon, diminishing
the need for a central City of Zion. Instead, Smith emphasized discrete communities of Euro-American Saints representing individual stakes in Zion.[16]
A third scholar, Arnold Green, also finds that Smith balanced conflicting
emphases on the blessed Israelite line as well as "universalism" (notions
of gentile inclusion through conversion). He argues that in the post-Smith
decades the inclusive concept of the elect and the gathering eclipsed the
emphasis on direct descendants—Native Americans or Jews. He also explains
that while Brigham Young and succeeding presidents emphasized lineage
as a determining factor in salvation, they identified Native Americans as
a cursed lineage because their forefathers enjoyed and then rejected the

gospel. They would be redeemed, eventually, but for the time being were only slightly better off than the Jews or descendants of Cain. All of these assessments of how lineage theology evolved conclude that in the post-Smith years it was the fresh Euro-American converts to Israel whom God had chosen in the latter days. Their assimilationist message taught that Israelites by blood (Native Americans and Jews) would need to join the Mormon Church in order to achieve their promised covenant blessings.[17] Stott, Pursuitte, and Green thus point to the centrality of Native Americans in the early vision of gathering followers to a New Jerusalem in America, and a fading of that doctrine.

To usher in the Indian-centered gathering, in September 1830 Joseph Smith called the second general conference of the church. There in Fayetteville, New York, Smith issued two significant revelations. First, the "gathering" would commence. Smith called upon believers to bring together the Lord's "elect."[18] He did not define "elect," but the second revelation gives grounds for some speculation. The prophet also called upon Oliver Cowdery, Parley P. Pratt, Peter Whitmer, and Ziba Peterson to travel to the "borders of the Lamanites," likely referring to the western edge of Missouri and present-day Kansas. Smith's instruction to the elders made that function clear. Channeling the Almighty, Joseph Smith gave insight as to the purposes of the Indian mission: "And now behold I say unto you, that it is not revealed, and no man knoweth where the city shall be built, but it shall be given hereafter. Behold I say unto you, that it shall be among the Lamanites."[19] The Lamanite missionaries accepted a responsibility to secure Indian converts so that New Jerusalem could be organized in Indian land.

This first "Lamanite mission" commenced in December of the same year. The missionaries began in New York where they encountered the Seneca and Onondaga Nations in New York. Next the Mormons visited the Wyandots in Ohio, and then they crossed the Missouri River into Indian Territory. After the missionaries met with the Shawnee and Delaware Nations the local Indian agent, Major Richard Cummins, expelled the delegation. The missionaries appealed to Superintendent William Clark in St. Louis but never received a license to override Cummins's ruling. The men returned to New York without any Indian converts.[20]

The Latter-day Saints interpreted the mission as successful despite this appearance of failure. While out west the elders obtained more knowledge about other distant tribes, specifically the Navajos, and also enjoyed encouraging courtesies from the Delawares. This is not to say that the Delawares eagerly accepted the new religion, only that Cowdery's and Pratt's reports conveyed an energy and excitement of *perceived* acceptance, restricted only by Cummins and the missionaries' expulsion.[21]

The church leadership remained enthusiastic about the prospect of Indian converts and upon organizing a settlement at Independence, Missouri, Joseph Smith directed Sidney Gilbert to set up a community store with a special mission to neighboring Indians. The July 1831 revelation instructed Gilbert to acquire an Indian trade license and develop relations with Indians so that "the gospel may be preached unto them." Furthermore, Smith also issued a July 1831 revelation stating that the Latter-day Saints soon would marry Indian women.[22] This was possibly a strategy to overcome residency obstacles, presuming Euro-American men married to Indian women enjoyed greater access to Indian communities or even land, but these developments may also reaffirm the Mormons' intent to join with the Indians.[23]

The better-known success of the Lamanite mission entails the mass conversion of Sidney Rigdon's Ohio congregations. Rigdon received a license to preach in 1820 and eagerly went about endorsing the Campbellite revolution. He regularly ministered to over half a dozen congregations in Ohio and held strong ties to groups in Mentor and Kirtland when Pratt introduced Rigdon to the Mormon faith.[24] The pastor quickly accepted Mormonism, as did many in his congregations, including such Mormon notables as Newel K. Whitney and Lyman Wight. Pratt recorded that within three weeks 127 local residents entered the waters of baptism and soon after the region's membership soared to one thousand.[25] In an instant the general membership of the church shifted from Smith's close friends and relatives in New York to hundreds of restorationists in Ohio.[26] The newly baptized Mormons only knew the gospel as preached by the Lamanite-focused missionaries and as they ascertained it from the Book of Mormon, which Cowdery defined as an account of Native Americans' "origin, and a prophecy of their final conversion to Christianity" who would then "be reinstated in the possession of their lands of which they have been despoiled by the whites."[27]

Local newspapers quickly reported an unusual behavior of the suddenly Mormon congregations. Eighteenth-century American folk Christianity already exhibited a variety of unusual practices and totems such as magical incantations and dowsing rods, which might seem outrageous to the modern reader but only minimally noteworthy to these early converts.[28] Still, records indicate that some in the converted congregation adopted Lamanite-mimicry in their services as they spoke and sang in tongues attributed to Indian nations.[29] One witness wrote:

> Their conduct grew more and more eccentric and absurd. Sometimes they imitated the grotesque antics of the wild Indian, in knocking down, scalping, and tearing out the bowels of his victim, thus anticipating the hour of their fancied mission to those lost souls of Jacob... often followed by the wonderful gift of tongues, as was supposed, in Indian dialects; which, indeed, none could understand except by direct inspiration.[30]

Sometimes these performances included symbolic and actual baptisms of congregation members in a reenactment of anticipated Indian baptisms.[31] John Corrill, a disenchanted convert, reported, "They conducted themselves in a strange manner, sometimes imitating Indians in their maneuvers, sometimes running out into the fields, getting on stumps of trees and there preaching as though surrounded by a congregation." Corrill did qualify the observation that only a portion of the congregation adopted such behavior, and that other newly baptized Mormons demonstrated no such mimicry.[32]

What are we to make of this symbolic simulation? Perhaps this is a less-than-extraordinary occurrence reflecting natural frontier tensions. Baptist frontier revivals during the 1830s exhibited outbursts of emotion, "eccentricities, and much fanaticism in this excitement."[33] Still, the curiosity of local papers may suggest the uncommon nature of this behavior, and E. D. Howe's openly antagonistic 1834 exposé of the early Mormon church also makes clear that this Indian-specific behavior was initiated only after the Campbellites' conversion and Mormon elders pronounced the gift of the Holy Ghost upon them.[34] Such behavior may have deeper meanings. As they embraced Mormon-specific ideas of the gathering, only vaguely defined church theology gave form to their longstanding advent anxieties. New Mormon frontier congregations grasped onto the charge to gather the elect and reach out to Indian Israelites in emotionally stirring rehearsals. Such behavior allowed actors to inscribe theological texts and ideologies about Indians upon themselves to bring their belief system into reality.[35] Early Mormons sought to locate themselves within an ideological realm that offered salvation with one caveat—convergence with Indians in the City of Zion.

As Mormons expanded their membership with Euro-American followers, they could not help but notice an absence of the one group they were explicitly charged to gather—Native Americans. Though entitled to a principal role in the New Jerusalem, Native Americans proved reluctant participants and even the appearance of such an allegiance contributed to the Latter-day Saints' persecution and eventual expulsion from Independence.[36] The centrality of the Book of Mormon (as a record of Israelite Indians) and Smith's emphasis on gathering the elect (if not solely then heavily emphasizing Native Americans) proved highly inconvenient. Without the elect Israelite Indians, how could the work go forward? Who would build the New Jerusalem? The Latter-day Saints needed a solution that did not overturn their foundational beliefs but which minimized the need for Native American converts. The answer, the Mormons found, was themselves.

By the mid-1830s Mormons increasingly saw themselves as the elect, equal in every way to their seemingly unresponsive Israelite Indian neighbors. Only token references to converting Native Americans exist from the mid-1830s to mid-1840s. Instead, church publications emphasized the accessibility of the House of Israel to penitent gentiles.

The March 1833 edition of the *Evening and Morning Star* declared that membership in the church represented "the new covenant" and transformed converts into "heirs of the promises of the Holy One of Israel." Soon thereafter, the June edition explained that upon joining the church "each man receives a warranty deed securing to himself and his heirs, his inheritance." In 1834 the April, May, August, and September editions repeated similar messages. Those who joined the church and participated with faith "obtained the blessing of being called his children, and had secured unto them the blessings of Abraham as well as the sure mercies of David."[37] In November 1834 another Mormon newspaper, the *Messenger and Advocate*, explained that by faith the gentile received celestial inheritance and thereby "became fellow-heirs, and fellow citizens, with the Jews."[38] Euro-American Mormons could now take upon themselves the blessings of Israel's covenant with God.

This ideological shift allowed Mormons to reprioritize; Native American conversions remained a revelatory charge, but the urgency of that responsibility faded as Euro-American Mormons took on the responsibilities once reserved for Native peoples. Still, the Latter-day Saints (or at least Smith) held to the belief that Indians would *eventually* predominate. As late as 1841, the prophet told Sac Chief Keokuk that Native people would inherit "the latter day city" (presumably the Mormons' then current residence at Nauvoo), though Keokuk's interest in annuities outweighed any designs on the town.[39]

A handful of familiar but rarely assembled historical factors accompanied this ideological shift. It is impossible to endow any one variable with exclusive causal authority, but early Mormons projected an Israel-specific identity upon themselves through five measures: (1) organization of church leadership and structure; (2) the use of Hebrew-sounding code names and identities; (3) patriarchal blessings bestowing Israelite lineage upon Euro-American members; (4) the extension of temple blessings; and (5) an infusion of non-Indian converts. All of these factors impacted Mormon self-perception and facilitated their transition from idolizing Indians as a chosen people to self-recognition as latter-day Israelites.

Though Smith chartered the Mormon Church in April 1830, several years passed before he fully formed the organizational structure. Over the first six years Smith ordained devout men to a variety of newly constructed councils and committees. In February 1831, Joseph Smith appointed Edward Partridge as the first bishop in the church, and five other men to the high priesthood only a few months later. In November a new revelation called for men to preside over each priesthood office, further expanding the priesthood. In January 1832, the general membership accepted Smith as president of the church. In February 1834 Smith organized a standing High Council in Ohio, and in July he formed another council in Missouri to oversee the church there. In February 1835 former Lamanite missionary Oliver Cowdery, along with David Whitmer and Martin Harris, was ordained an apostle, and not long afterward Joseph Smith identified others to complete the latter-day Quorum of Twelve Apostles. The apostles oversaw missionary work, and after baptism new converts fell under the authority of newly organized high councils. Smith also tidied up his authority to govern. He had long served as president of the church by a regular vote of the membership, but in the 1835 printing of the Doctrine and Covenants he reversed part of an 1829 revelation that explicitly limited his authority to translating the Book of Mormon.[40] In 1835 Smith also organized a "Council of Seventy," and by January 1836 general priesthood quorums organized to enlist dutiful males to perform religious rites and responsibilities. In March of 1836 Joseph Smith remarked to three hundred men gathered in Kirtland that he "had now completed the organization of the church."[41]

In crafting extensive governing structures staffed by Euro-Americans, the church membership increasingly associated Israel with non-Indian leaders. In January 1831 Smith recorded a revelation that the Latter-day Saints gathering in Ohio would be organized under the leadership of "certain men among them," suggesting the earliest abandonment of Native American leadership.[42] Then, in a September 1832 revelation identifying Missouri as the location of the New Jerusalem, Smith explains that those (presumably Euro-American) Latter-day Saints who are faithful, take up and fulfill priesthood responsibilities, "become the sons of Moses and of Aaron and the seed of Abraham, and the church and kingdom, and the elect of God."[43] Smith organized the various leadership structures with the only adherents he had available.[44]

Native Americans did not hold leadership positions in the church until fifteen years after its organization. Lewis Dana of the Oneida Nation received baptism in 1840 and was the first Indian admitted to any leadership quorum within the church. His 1844 arrival in Nauvoo reinvigorated optimism that the day of the Lamanite was at hand, and in 1845 the Council of Fifty admitted Dana to its ranks.[45] Smith had organized the Council of Fifty in March 1844 to look west for the Latter-day Saints' new homeland. Following Smith's death in June, Brigham Young reconvened the committee, appointed Dana, and charged him to find a new homeland with receptive Indians. The Council of Fifty dispatched Dana and other missionaries to an anticipated council of Native Americans in Indian Territory; however, the churchmen arrived at the destination two weeks after the rumored council and only found disinterested Indians. Young shared the mission's failure with the Council of Fifty in September 1845, and by January 1846 he resolved to look toward the Salt Lake Valley for the new homeland with hope that those Indians might be more receptive.[46] Thoughts that Dana might inaugurate the awaited Indian resurgence proved unlikely. Without significant Native American membership, white Mormons took upon themselves the responsibilities once imagined for Israelite Indians.

As Native Americans failed to fulfill anticipated leadership roles or even general membership, Mormon leaders sought to replace Indians through the use of code names that reflected their own imagined Israelite identity. Code names used from 1832 to 1835 served to protect leaders from financial liability during Kirtland co-op and banking experiments, but the very same code names surfaced throughout Smith's nonfinance-related revelations.[47] More important than their purpose, the form of these names stands out. Even to the untrained linguist there are obvious phonetic similarities between these code names and others found in the Old Testament. Code names like Alam, Ahashdah, Mahelalee, Olihaha, and Shederloamach strike an uncanny similarity to Old Testament names like Elam and Ulam, Ahishar, Mahalaleel, Onihah, and Shalmaneser, respectively. Smith's mimicry of Hebrew names is curious. Much like the earliest Ohio Mormons who imitated Israelite Indians, the church leadership exhibited a fascination with Israelite lineage by adopting Hebrew-sounding names. In 1836, Smith even hired Joseph Seixas to teach Hebrew to the leadership, which reflects an intent to better understand Old Testament language and culture.[48] Regardless of purpose, code names reveal an obsession with Israelite-sounding nomenclature that enabled church leaders to experience some degree of association with an Israelite heritage.

In addition to Hebrew-sounding names, the introduction of patriarchal blessings in 1833 endowed the believers with Israelite heritage.[49] In 1833, Joseph Smith ordained his father, Joseph Smith Sr., as patriarch.[50] Smith Sr. officiated as the voice of the Lord and issued blessings to family members wherein he pronounced Israelite heritage upon each. Joseph Smith Jr., for example, received "the blessings of thy fathers Abraham, Isaac and Jacob, and even the blessings of thy father Joseph, the son of Jacob."[51] In February 1834, Smith Jr. received the revelation that all church members "are children of Israel, and the Seed of Abraham."[52] That summer Smith Sr. pronounced patriarchal blessings (and Israelite lineage) upon the first Latter-day Saints outside his family. In December of 1836, the general church leadership regularly received patriarchal blessings, and by 1837 the demand for patriarchal blessings required Smith Jr. to appoint local patriarchs for growing Mormon communities. Even after the 1840 death of Smith Sr., succeeding patriarchs continued the tradition of pronouncing intimate personal blessings that reaffirmed individuals' Israelite lineage.[53]

Patriarchal blessings did not make the Mormons adoptees of Israel; rather they "revealed" an unrecognized genetic heritage. The clearest explanation of this doctrine came much later from Brigham Young. In 1855 he explained, "It is Ephraim that I have been searching for all the days of my preaching, and that is the blood which ran in my veins when I embraced the gospel. If there are any of the other tribes of Israel mixed with the Gentiles we are also searching for them." He continued, "We want the blood of Jacob, and that of his father Isaac and Abraham, which runs in the veins of people. There is a particle of it here, and another there, blessing the nations as predicted."[54] Like Puritans who understood good works as evidence of preordination, Mormons interpreted conversion and membership as evidence of some remnant blood of Israel. Once baptized, patriarchal blessings offered white converts reassurance of their Israelite lineage—they too were among the elect.

Just as patriarchal blessings relieved anxieties about salvation and extended promises of Israelite lineage, so too did sacred temple blessings. The Kirtland (and later Nauvoo) Temple facilitated a series of rites, the first of which Joseph Smith introduced in the spring of 1836. Smith led a few church leaders into the church printing house, washed them with purified water, and then took them into the schoolroom of the Kirtland Temple. After consecrating oil, Smith pronounced a special blessing upon his father. Then Joseph Smith Sr., perhaps acting as patriarch, issued special temple blessings to the other church leaders beginning with the oldest and continuing through to the youngest. The blessing pronounced on Joseph Smith Jr. charged him to lead latter-day Israel and again sealed upon him the blessings of Jacob. Others similarly received confirmation that they would fill leadership roles in Israel. After ordination to the office of elder, Wilford Woodruff recorded that on April 4, 1837, he and other church leaders received washings and anointings—a reconstruction of an ancient Israelite ceremony—and temple blessings. Woodruff received the promise that "God would bless me with all the powers of the priesthood & give me a multiplicity of blessings that kings would tremble upon their thrones at my word, that I should become a Counselor & multitudes should seek counsel at my mouth."[55] Without Indians to take the lead, Smith ordained non-Indian leaders like Woodruff to manage and lead the growing church. As the Saints completed the Kirtland and Nauvoo Temples, other men and women entered to receive sacred instruction and special blessings that confirmed their role as latter-day Israelites.

Finally, demographic changes in the church deemphasized the role of Indians. Following the 1834 conversion of Sidney Rigdon's Campbellite congregation, the church population centered in Ohio. Financial troubles struck the region in the 1830s and in 1836 the church created the Kirtland Safety Society Bank, succeeded by the Kirtland Safety Society Anti-Bank Company in 1837. The institution attracted the church members' investments and issued credit notes but after a short boom it fell into disarray. Charges of mismanagement led to controversy and mob protests and several hundred Mormons left the church. This decline in membership inspired Smith to send missionaries abroad in an attempt to offset that membership loss.[56]

Church leadership targeted Britain for the first missions outside North America. Heber C. Kimball, Orson Hyde, and Willard Richards quickly departed and enjoyed great success, baptizing some fifteen hundred converts by April of 1838.[57] One study tabulated the arrival of three hundred British converts in 1840, nine hundred in 1841, more than fifteen hundred in 1842, and more than one thousand in 1843.[58] Thousands of British converts certainly impacted the American-based Mormon population. The latent or otherwise cultural and psychological Indian fixation that historians observe in Americans of this era cannot characterize the incoming European Mormons. While likely aware of "noble savage" literature, these foreign-born Latter-day Saints brought no frontier heritage or any vestige of an Indian-European identity complex beyond their brief exposure to Mormon missionaries.

Meanwhile, extensive missionary activities within the United States similarly infused the once Campbellite-dominated church population with diverse Americans of varying backgrounds. Whether baptized in the United States or in Britain, many of the new converts had distant roots. As the Latter-day Saints gathered in Kirtland and later in Nauvoo, new members overwhelmed those early Indian-focused converts.

This population influx also contributed to a redefinition of "the gathering." As Mormon definitions of Israel changed to include Euro-Americans, so too did the meaning of the gathering. This prophetic occurrence no longer referred primarily to Indians complemented by gentile

TABLE 2.1. CHURCH POPULATION,
1830–1845

YEAR	POPULATION
1830	280
1831	680
1832	2,661
1833	3,140
1834	4,372
1835	8,835
1836	13,293
1837	16,282
1838	17,881
1839	16,460
1840	16,865
1841	19,856
1842	23,564
1843	25,980
1844	26,146
1845	30,332

Source: 2005 Church Almanac *(Salt Lake City:* Deseret Morning News, *2004), 632.*

supporters, but instead pointed to a national and international gathering of formerly unrecognized Israelite converts who then dwelt among all nations and tongues. In 1836 Smith explained,

> In speaking of the gathering, we mean to be understood as speaking of it according to the scripture, the gathering of the elect of the Lord out of every nation on earth, and bringing them to the place of the Lord of Hosts, when the city of righteousness shall be built, and where the people shall be of one heart and one mind, when the Savior comes.[59]

The church existed to gather any "Israelite" converts for the purpose of building the kingdom, and Indians were no more special than the Britons or any others.

As the Saints settled Independence, Missouri (Zion), many grew excited about the potential fulfillment of latter-day prophesy.[60] In the debut printing of the *Evening and Morning Star* (June 1832), recently ordained Bishop Edward Partridge pointed to widespread misunderstandings regarding the gathering of the elect. Partridge extended a special invitation to faithful converts to settle Zion—the gathering of Israel had begun; this is among the earliest evidences of the inclusion of Euro-Americans.[61] Indeed, an article penned by Editor W. W. Phelps explained the new periodical's very purpose was to announce the restoration of the gospel and "the gathering of the Saints."[62] In September Smith announced "that the city New Jerusalem shall be built by the gathering of the Saints," and did not specify Native Americans.[63]

A flurry of new LDS-sponsored publications were organized to spread the word of the gospel and interconnect the membership. Consistent with Phelps's declaration of purpose, however, the most quoted passages in these periodicals was modern-day 3 Nephi chapter 21, which articulates the gathering in detail.[64] It outlined specific blessings for non-Indians who "repent, and hearken unto my words, and harden not their hearts." The Book of Mormon promised:

> [They] shall come into the covenant, and be numbered among this remnant of Jacob, unto whom I have given this land for their inheritance, and they shall assist my people, the remnant of Jacob; and also, as many of the house of Israel as shall come, that they may build a city, which shall be called the New Jerusalem; and they shall assist my people that they may be gathered in, which are scattered upon all the face of the land, in unto the New Jerusalem.[65]

While this promise did exist in even the earliest printings of the Book of Mormon, its popularity emerged in the mid-1830s. Indeed, nearly all of the scripture passages quoted in the early publications directly related to the gathering, and the cooperation of Indian and non-Indian converts described served as evidence of the Lord's appointed restoration.[66]

In October 1834, Oliver Cowdery explained the joy he experienced from knowing of thousands who "embraced the same covenant" and joined in the building up of the church and gathering of the elect. His letter to the editor of the *Messenger and Advocate* was followed by others that also interpreted the gathering without reference to Indians. By the 1840s Euro-American converts settled Zion with fervent urgency, but still the discourse placed no emphasis on Indians. The anxiety that once urged the Latter-day Saints to unite with Indians simply refocused on a more generic gathering in Zion, with only peripheral hope that Indians might also attend. Missionary E. Owen Jr. conveyed this anticipation when he penned, "O brother, pray for us...that we may be worthy to receive an inheritance in the city of cities, which shall be called Zion."[67]

These factors of leadership and organization, Hebrew-sounding code names, patriarchal and temple blessings, and an infusion of European converts, are indistinguishably intertwined in the ideological transition from Indian emphasis to Euro-American emphasis. By the mid- to late 1830s Euro-American Mormons clearly saw themselves as inheritors of an ancient covenant with decreasing need for Indians. As church growth required practical solutions of Euro-American leadership and organization of Zion, the Latter-day Saints began to view the restoration of Lamanites as a long-term goal. As fellow heirs of Israel, Mormons no longer felt an urgency to convert and join with Native Americans; indeed, the believers discovered their own Israelite origins and enjoyed the hope of salvation while waiting for Indians to come to them. Still, Indians could not be forgotten entirely, and lingering interest ebbed and flowed over the following century.

During the 1840s and 1850s Mormon perception of Indians as noble Israelites shifted to a new image of degraded savage. Mormons less often revered Indians as exceptionally "elect" but instead reinterpreted Indians as physically and spiritually impoverished Israelites in need of guidance from the Latter-day Saints. Though processed through their own unique theology that imagined a glorious potential, Mormons' conceptions of Indians as culturally depraved ultimately mirrored that of other Americans.

As the Mormons built up Nauvoo, Joseph Smith welcomed various Native Americans to the city. Several chiefs visited in the summer of 1842, in April of 1843, and at other times later that year. Unlike Oliver Cowdery's 1830 Lamanite mission sermons, Smith did not plead with visiting Indians to recognize their Israelite heritage. Instead, Smith admonished Indians to trust the Mormons as friends and "advised them not to sell any more land, but to live in peace."[68] The emphasis of his interaction shifted

towards maintaining functional social relationships and regional stability. Instead of reminding Indians of their divine role, Smith tried to keep
the peace between Native Americans and the frontier settlement of Nauvoo.

Nevertheless, the church continued to perfunctorily dispatch missionaries to Indian communities. Participants remained optimistic about Indian
conversion but as before found few converts. In the early 1840s, Smith called
a dozen men to Lamanite missions. One delegation departed in 1840 and
the church sent two others to minister among the Sioux in 1842. John Butler
recorded, "We had but little success among the Indians," which was an under-
statement given their near-death encounters. In frustration they recorded that
those Indians "did [not] or could not understand the principles of the gospel."[69] Church leadership dispatched a few other missionaries to the Indians
through the 1840s and 1850s. In March 1845 Elders Phineas H. Young, Jonathan Dunham, Charles Shumway, Lewis Dana, and S. Tindale departed west
on a mission to the Lamanites, possibly in Texas.[70] In 1846 Young dispatched
Charles Shumway and Phineas Young to the Senecas back east, and issued
the two missionaries a certificate to any indigenous communities they should
encounter. It read, "We feel extremely anxious that you share in the . . . promised blessings to Israel and . . . we send . . . you these our beloved brothers . . . to
grant them your assistance that your people may be enlightened with truth."[71]
Empowered with Israelite lineage the Latter-day Saints invited Indians to join
them, but the lack of Indian converts kept the focus on Europeans.

Other missions seemed more materially motivated than spiritually
driven. In 1843 the church sent Apostle Lyman Wight to the Chippewas and
Menominees in Wisconsin with instructions to teach the gospel and harvest
timber for the building of Nauvoo and the temple in particular. In Wisconsin Wight created "a mission of those true and full-blooded Ephraimites,"
who exhibited a natural "love of the truth." Wight was pleased with his
success, and in a February 1844 letter to the First Presidency he suggested
the church also initiate missionary activities among the Southwest Indians. His proposal was initially rejected and then the June 1844 murder of
Joseph Smith strained church organization. Wight rushed to Nauvoo but felt
alienated from church leaders and determined to separate himself from the
apostles. He returned to the 150 Mormons still in Wisconsin and led them
down the Mississippi River and west into Texas in November 1845. The colony quickly transformed into an independent splinter society led by Wight

who articulated firm ambitions to convert local indigenous communities in a bold proclamation to the world. However, Wight's devotion to the ministry of Native Americans later proved a point of division between him and the main body of the church. His dedication to Native Americans was out of touch with evolving views.[72]

Soon after Smith's 1844 martyrdom, Brigham Young led the largest faction of Latter-day Saints west to rebuild the new Zion prophesied by Smith before his death. Nonspiritual motivations—in this case the seeking of a new and safe homeland—increasingly complicated Mormon-Indian interactions. In 1845 church leaders dispatched a mission to "proceed from tribe to tribe, to unite the Lamanite and find a home for the Saints." Some missionaries returned from several eastern tribes with exciting news of their kindness and plans to either relocate near the Senecas in New York or explore farther west for a homeland with the assistance of Indian guides.[73] Converting Indians quickly became peripheral to the reality of social tensions and western migration.

Church leaders did not abandon all hope of converting Indians but continued to preach the Lamanites' *eventual* recognition of their role. An 1845 "Proclamation of the Twelve Apostles," written by Apostle (and former missionary to Native Americans) Parley P. Pratt, declared the Israelite Indians "are about to be gathered, civilized and made *one nation* in this glorious land" (italics in original). Any privileged or even joint heir status granted to Native Americans in the earliest church period gave way to a more paternalistic view as Euro-American Mormons remained the dispensers of salvation to the Lamanites. The proclamation continued, "The sons and daughters of God" will instruct "the children of the forest."[74] Having assumed the identity of Israel once associated with Native Americans, Mormons asserted themselves as the gatekeepers to Indian salvation; the onus now fell to Indians to bind themselves to Mormon society, rather than the reverse. This new theological power structure placed Mormons in the position of authority, not only independent of Indians but also ultimately responsible for their salvation. This Mormon version of "the white man's burden" both empowered Mormons and redefined their relationship to Indians in terms of colonization. As self-defined covenant members of Israel, the Euro-American Mormons granted themselves both salvation and the moral authority to reach down to their downtrodden Indian brethren.

As Mormon communities moved west their close and personal encounters intensified their increasingly paternalistic attitudes toward the Indians. During their 1846–1847 winter along the Missouri River, the Latter-day Saints erected camps and frequently interacted with neighboring tribes. Because Nauvoo was densely populated and protected by a private army, Indian depredations never seriously threatened the Mormons. But immersed among the Omaha and Ponca along the Missouri, many Mormons experienced their first genuine Indian interactions. They extracted increasing quantities of timber and game from the region and local Native peoples responded by seizing livestock. Despite Young's extralegal negotiations with the Omaha and Ponca, relations deteriorated.[75]

While some Latter-day Saints thus conflicted with the locals, others felt sympathy and noted how the Sioux preyed upon weaker tribes. Many Mormons recorded the pity they reserved for the peaceful Omaha, Ponca, and Pawnee. Others observed the Indians' "backward" nature and the church's "duty to bring the Indians from their benighted situation and raise them as a branch of the House of Israel to a knowledge of the true and living God."[76]

When the Latter-day Saints arrived in Utah in 1847, any residual romanticized perception of Native Americans quickly faded as they faced the cold reality of prolonged close contact and Indian resistance to what amounted to a Mormon invasion of the Salt Lake Valley and surrounding regions. Many in the church viewed Indians as irritants—as obstacles to be civilized or removed. Settler Eliza Gibbs remembered that in the years immediately following the Mormons' arrival, there was "nothing to annoy us, except some Indians." Another, William Leany, recorded that in 1848 "we subdued the crickets, grasshoppers, and Indians" in the Salt Lake Valley. Mormons complained to one another that meddlesome Indians stole horse bridles and oxen, and continually obstructed the Latter-day Saints' conquest of the land, even requiring settlements to post local guards.[77] As the Mormons displaced indigenous communities and gobbled up their best resources, Natives increasingly confiscated Mormon horses and cattle. This competition periodically erupted in violent conflicts, beginning as early as the first months of 1849, and by the close of that year the Mormon-occupied Fort Utah recounted several engagements with local Indians. By 1850, Brigham Young initiated an extermination policy throughout the Utah Valley.[78] Historian Paul Reeve suggests that Mormons employed a new rhetorical device to justify the violent encounters. Young characterized the local inhabitants as Gadianton Robbers, a particularly vile and perhaps even irredeemable segment of Lamanites introduced in the Book of Mormon.[79] Nevertheless, the hypocrisy of dispossession was not lost on U.S. Army explorer John Gunnison who recalled the violence of 1850 and penned,

> It is a curious matter of reflection, that those whose mission it is to convert these aborigines by the sword of the spirit, should thus be obliged to destroy them—but they stoutly affirmed that these people will yet, under their instruction, fulfill the prophecy that "a nation shall be borne in a day;" and when they have completed the destined time, will listen to the truth and become "a fair and delightsome people."[80]

Despite once-romanticized notions, the reality of close contact and limited resources often led to conflict rather than cohesion between Mormons and Indians.

Minor skirmishes occasionally broke out, and some gave way to widespread conflict; between 1849 and 1851 Mormons killed almost sixty Utes and Goshutes.[81] The first occurred in February 1849 when Salt Lake officials dispatched Captain John Scott with thirty to forty men. They engaged a band of Timpanogos Utes at Battle Creek (near present-day Provo). The church offices recorded four Indians died, but over the following winter hostilities continued to rise.[82] Joel Hills Johnson, member of the recently organized provisional State of Deseret House of Representatives, noted that in the winter of 1849–1850 one engagement near Salt Lake resulted in the death of twenty-five Indians.[83] In 1850, a settlement in Sanpete also recorded conflict with Indians. "The Indians were driving off the cattle and horses and often the news would come of some man being killed."[84] Meanwhile, the Ute chief Wakara increasingly grew dissatisfied with the Mormons' usurpation of Ute lands. The outbreak of the Walker War in 1853 punctuated and reinforced the growing perception of Indians as hostile enemies. For one brutal year the Walker War forced Mormons to face a reality of resistant and hostile Indians. This and later conflicts, such as the 1856 Tintic War and the 1865 Black Hawk War, reiterated the physical reality of Indian conflict after the Mormons arrived in Utah. This resistance surely problematized perceptions of Indians as "fellow heirs" and brothers, not to mention the Latter-day Saints' role as their cultural and spiritual saviors. By the mid-1850s the Mormons' theological universe that once viewed Native Americans with unique respect and admiration devolved to a typical adversarial relationship. While Mormons always viewed Indians as Lamanites, and Lamanites as apostate Israelites, this special status was no longer the only basis for Mormon-Indian relations, nor was Indian salvation a central precept of Mormon society. Still, violence alone did not characterize Mormon-Indian relations.

Despite the hostilities spawned by close contact and competition, residual theological perceptions required some degree of continued colonization. In parallel to hostility and violence, extensive efforts to draw Israelite Indians into the fold expanded once in Utah and continued through the close of the century. Brigham Young and his followers continued to dispatch missionaries to Native populations, developed demonstration farms, sponsored Indian adoptions, and even made some effort to promote intermarriage. As early as 1849 Chief Wakara agreed to let the Mormons dispatch men to his territory to instruct the Utes' band in the construction of homes, husbandry, and religion.[85] Over the next decade Young opened a half-dozen similar missions to Indians throughout modern-day Idaho, Wyoming, and Nevada.[86] However, by 1858 all but one mission had closed as Indian interest faded.[87]

The remaining Southern Mission continued with dual purpose to convert and civilize Indians. Parley P. Pratt directed the missionaries to "save the remnants of the house of Israel" with the universal language: "kindness and sympathy." He continued, "Feed, clothe, and instruct them.... You can teach them habits of cleanliness and industry." One of these missionaries, James S. Brown, recalled his directive "to operate as peace makers among the Indians, to preach civilization to them, to try and teach them how to cultivate the soil, to instruct them in the arts and sciences if possible, and by that means prevent trouble for our frontier settlements and emigrant companies." In an 1856 conference in Cedar City, Joel Johnson received instruction to "establish a missionary station to teach the Indians to labor and to teach them the principles of civilization and establish a school to educate their children."[88] In addition to these efforts in Southern Utah, the church organized its most impressive Indian mission colony in the north along the modern Utah-Idaho border. Missionaries gathered Shoshone and other Native people to a promising agricultural experiment engineered by the church. By 1875, the Washakie colony brought seven thousand acres under cultivation and constructed a canal system, sawmill, chapel, school-house, and mission home, and erected residences for the Indian converts. However, a decade later the prosecution of polygamous leaders distracted from this and other projects.[89]

Beyond missions and demonstration farms, as early as May 1854 Apostle Orson Hyde "recommended the marrying of squaws in the most positive and strong terms and particularly the immediate taking [of] Mary, an hag-gard mummy looking one who had been here all winter." One missionary promptly took Mary on as a plural wife, as several Mormon trappers had already done with women in neighboring tribes.[90] Though Joseph Smith's 1831 revelation encouraging Lamanite missionaries to intermarry enjoyed little immediate observance, by the 1850s the practical value of intermar-riage long observed by fur trappers and made easier by the doctrine of polygamy facilitated a few intermarriages. Among the earliest occurred in 1850 between a Mormon trapper and a Shoshone woman. Indian mission-ary James S. Brown also recorded, "We were to identify our interests with theirs, even to marrying among them, if we would be permitted to take the young daughters of the chief and leading men, and have them dressed like civilized people, and educated."[91] Even in joining with the Indians, the sense of ethnic superiority predominated.

In addition to occasionally taking Indian wives, Mormons also took Indian children into their families as part of a civilizing program to redeem Indians. The earliest recorded instance occurred during the Latter-day Saints' first winter in Utah when a band of Ute traders, accustomed to the existing Spanish slave trade, offered up two children to the Mormons. The Latter-day Saints initially refused, but after the Utes executed the first and prepared to murder the second, "Charley Decker bought her and took her to our house to be washed and clothed." Similar encounters occurred over the next few years as Mormons reluctantly engaged in the Southwest Indian slave trade.[92] In 1851, President Young instructed the Latter-day Saints to "buy up the Lamanite children as fast as they could and teach them the gos-pel." He continued, "I knew the Indians would dwindle away, but let the remnant of the seed of Joseph be saved."[93] These words indicate the fallen status of Indians and Young's anticipation of their redemption. Mormons began to seek out opportunities to purchase Indian children and justified their removal from Native society by the material poverty they observed and the spiritual apostasy they suffered outside the Lord's covenant; Mormons viewed themselves as rescuing Native Americans from depravity and spiritual darkness. By 1852, the proliferation of such exchanges inspired the Utah territorial legislature to pass a law regulating the treatment of Indian children, many of whom labored in Mormon homes as indentured servants where they could learn the gospel and become "civilized." The law noted the poor status of slaves under Indian ownership, encouraged their purchase, and instituted basic regulations.[94] Sporadic Indian child adoptions continued through the close of the century.[95]

These colonization efforts demonstrate the persistence of the Israelite Indian doctrine and the church's anxiety over the need for Indians to realize that role, but more than that, these efforts illustrate the Latter-day Saints' identity as saviors and civilizers to the Indians. Mormon efforts to "teach habits of cleanliness and industry," "preach civilization," and instruction to "cultivate the soil" show that Mormons envisioned themselves as culturally superior vis-à-vis Indians. Mormons took upon themselves the "white man's burden" that similarly characterized broader Euro-American views of Native Americans. Mormon-Indian policy in Utah is characterized by missionary outreach for their Israelite brethren as well as armed conflict with those who resisted that role. Relations grew far more complicated once the Mormons moved beyond imagined Indians and actually encountered Native Americans. Over the course of the nineteenth century, Mormon efforts to convert and civilize Native Americans gradually declined until almost no such efforts existed by 1900.

Early Mormons living in New York and later in Ohio constructed a reality in which they raised up Native Americans as a romanticized "other." They envisioned a future wherein they would join Israelite Indians, but Mormons gradually dislodged Indians from that special status as they embraced their own role as Israelites. As Mormons took upon themselves the covenant of Israel, they negated Native Americans' initial significance. As the Latter-day Saints arrived in Utah, increased contact and physical proximity to Indians further complicated their relations.

Mormons faced contradictory notions of Native Americans that conflicted deeply with their physical reality. This rift commenced with the lack
of Indian converts from the first Lamanite mission but did not culminate
in an unavoidable confrontation until after the Mormons arrived in Utah.
Once Indian-revering Mormon society faced the reality of Native American
opposition, resistance, and open conflict, Mormons postponed the role of
Native Americans. Despite theology to the contrary, Mormons—like many
other Euro-American groups—simply could not transcend the intrinsically
imperialistic nature of Western society.

C. S. Lewis once spoke of the consequences of conflicting realities.
As their distinction broke down, he explained, he realized the great com-
fort he formerly experienced when the universe was neatly divided.[96] For
Mormons, the two perceptions of Native Americans—noble Israelites and
resistant savages—had to be reconciled and typical Western paternalism
offered the perfect solution. Mormons could at once view Indians as Israelites but still play the dominant role in the relationship as saviors sent to
indoctrinate and civilize their lost Israelite brethren. In this way the Latter-
day Saints' theological world could once again make perfect sense in the
otherwise chaotic reality of daily life among often noncooperative Native
Americans; for Mormons the gospel remained true.

3

TURNING TO PLACEMENT

The Navajo Nation, Helen John, and the Pursuit of Education,
1880s–1940s

The man who does not have education is one who cannot get anywhere,
like his wing is cut off and he cannot fly around. It is the man who has an
education who can get about freely like a free bird.

—Sam Gorman, Navajo Tribal Council

In the early twentieth century, the capacious Navajo reservation seemed a
plentiful wilderness to its inhabitants. Children grew up learning valuable
skills that harnessed the land's resources, from sheepherding and rug
weaving to silver working. The land provided for all their material and cultural needs. Outsiders seemed to constitute the only threat to this romanticized vision of harmony. It was the Bureau of Indian Affairs' agents and
officers who seized children to whisk them off to distant educational facilities to learn seemingly useless western knowledge. Federal Indian education
policy originated in 1819 when Congress appropriated $10,000 for a "civi-
lization fund"; however, the expansive Navajo lands allowed the tribe to
avoid much of these colonizing efforts until the turn of the century. During
the late nineteenth century, boarding and day schools penetrated the reservation but largely met with Native resistance. Animosity toward outsiders climaxed in the 1930s when the BIA also imposed wave after wave of

livestock reductions in an effort to salvage the declining range. Despite signs of eroding resources, most Navajos continued to believe that their homelands provided all that was needed if only the outside world could be kept at bay.

The 1941 attack on Pearl Harbor, and consequent war, changed Navajo attitudes. Thousands of Navajos served as combatants in World War II, and tens of thousands filled defense industry positions both on and off the reservation. Some fifteen hundred Navajos found local work at an army ordinance depot at Fort Wingate, and thousands more left the reservation to find employment in munitions factories, clinics, and other war-effort industries.

Navajo participation in World War II heightened the impact and valuation of outside influences and engendered Navajo desires for education and intercultural understanding. Ever more Navajos increasingly sought out formal education but they quickly found that reservation facilities struggled to meet the rising demands. Even as the BIA expanded both day and boarding schools, many Navajos found these institutions overcrowded and still uncomfortably foreign. Parents reluctantly sent their children to such schools, but many did so with unpleasant memories of their own hated boarding school experiences.

For some Navajos an alternative educational opportunity presented itself in Richfield, Utah. Each summer Navajo families migrated up to central Utah to work in the beet fields. A few built trusting relationships with local farmers, and ultimately a voluntary seasonal foster program emerged wherein Navajo children stayed with white host families to attend school each fall and spring. The local Mormon Church quickly took on organizational leadership to locate viable homes for the growing number of interested children. Mormon foster homes offered a variety of positive alternatives to the widely disdained boarding schools, including a better quality of education and a nurturing nuclear family environment. By 1943, the inaugural year of the unofficial Indian Student Placement Program, Navajo opinions about education were in transition and the tribe sought out a variety of educational opportunities. Placement attracted dozens and then hundreds of children each year not because of any spiritual uniqueness, but for educational opportunities. Though the BIA and Mormon advocates for Indian education did so with colonization in mind, Navajos pursued this avenue for their own advancement.

Student motivations varied, but by and large the primary reason for enrollment centered on education and intercultural exposure that seemed necessary for success in the changing world. Some also joined the Placement Program for spiritual reasons or for the anticipated leisure of middle-class wealth, but overall the program enrollment steadily climbed because Navajos aggressively pursued any and all educational opportunities during the 1940s through 1960s. This chapter traces the evolution of this social context that made the ISPP a readily accepted answer to the Navajo's self-perceived educational depravity.

Formal education first infiltrated the Navajo reservation soon after its 1868 organization, initially led by Presbyterians. U.S. president Ulysses S. Grant's so-called "peace policy" forced Native Americans onto reservations and transformed their experience there, relying largely on religious organizations to care for Indians better than their unscrupulous predecessors. Federally subsidized parochial schools, and eventually federally operated schools, eroded Navajo isolation. Education and religious ministry remained tightly bound together in the reservation's first decades, and white schoolteachers and reformers worked tirelessly to acculturate Native peoples.

In 1869, educational reformer Charity Ann Gaston organized a Presbyterian school for Navajos at Fort Defiance, Arizona. Gaston had previously served as a missionary and teacher to the Choctaws. The Department of Interior used funds guaranteed by the Navajo Treaty of 1868 to hire her away from a school in Santa Fe and open that first contract school among the Navajos. Soon after, Presbyterians founded a school for Navajos seventy-five miles to the north in Jewett. In 1890 Methodists established a mission at Fort Defiance and dominated missionary work in the region throughout that decade. In 1894 the Episcopal Church sent Eliza Thackara to organize a hospital at Fort Defiance, Arizona, and the Good Shepherd Hospital first admitted patients in 1897. At the turn of the century the Presbyterians resurged in influence and organized missions at Ganado and Tuba City.[1]

The independently governed schools shared a common curriculum including English, basic math, and often industrial training. Americans believed that with the proper assistance Indians could climb from a degraded state and advance their race. In 1877, U.S. Commissioner of Indian Affairs Lewis Henry Morgan published his ideological opus titled, *Ancient Society;*

or, Researches in the Lines of Human Progress from Savagery through Barbarism to Civilization. The text echoed the cultural evolution theory of the time and many Americans believed that through education Native Americans might be redeemed from barbarism. Mainstream America looked upon Native Americans as a people without culture, savages in need of reform. Educational facilities offered a white solution to "the Indian problem" and a rash of both private and governmental schools opened their doors in the late nineteenth century. By 1899, some twenty-four off-reservation schools operated nationwide under federal management and largely modeled on Richard Henry Pratt's Carlisle Indian School.[2]

In 1875, Lieutenant Pratt took an assignment at Fort Marion, Florida, to watch over Cheyenne, Kiowa, and Comanche prisoners of the Red River War. Though they arrived in chains, he removed their irons and placed the men in surplus military uniforms. He trained them in English and granted them access to the local St. Augustine community where they sold their wares and could make purchases using those funds which Pratt deposited in individual accounts. In 1878, the men were released but nearly two dozen agreed to relocate with Pratt to Hampton Normal and Agricultural Institute, a Virginia school that served to educate and train African Americans. The experience confirmed Pratt's belief that vocational training offered the key to Indian uplift, but he feared white racism towards blacks might inhibit the progress of his Native Americans.[3] He also noticed the difficulty in transforming grown adults, and determined to open a school exclusively for Indian children where they might be raised up with Christian values of industry. The following year he secured funding and facilities to open Carlisle Indian School in Pennsylvania.

Carlisle ironically used old cavalry barracks for a new form of conquest. Pratt's oft-recited motto, "Kill the Indian in him and save the man," dictated the school's function.[4] His program has attracted the attention of numerous historians over the past few decades. Just as at Fort Marion, military discipline regimented daily activities, from morning bells to uniform inspections, classes, and meals. Students divided their time equally between academics and trades. Pratt also pioneered an outing system whereby students spent the summer months and up to three years after graduation living with a rural white farm family.[5] Historian David Wallace Adams explained, "The ideal solution—Pratt's fantasy—was to scatter the entire population of Indian children across the nation, with some 70,000 white families each taking in one Indian child."[6] By 1882, Carlisle received large congressional appropriations and similar boarding schools emerged across the nation.[7]

Schools typically followed Pratt's model as they actively sought to separate Indian children from their heritage. One superintendent of Indian schools clearly indicated this intent to "strip" away Indian culture and "clothe him with the clean garments of civilized men."[8] Geographical distancing was necessary, as one federal agent in Arizona noted, because as soon as pupils returned home they would "drop back into their old filthy ways."[9] These schools actively expelled any indicator of Native customs. Historian Margaret Jacobs summarized their methods as "cutting hair, destroying old clothing and dressing children in new uniforms, renaming the 'inmates,' introducing the children to new foods and dining rituals, and requiring them to sleep in unfamiliar beds in large dormitories."[10] Schools enforced those policies with strict disciplinary action that included corporal punishment, dietary restrictions to bread and water, and popular ridicule. Belt lines formed for defiant students who had to run a gauntlet of peers beating them with belts; others found themselves locked in isolation in guardhouses or basements, or issued scissors and an assignment to cut the lawn on hands and knees. Students could be punished for major offenses like running away or minor infractions such as failing to properly polish their shoes.

Typical days began with reveille and early morning inspections, marches, and breakfast. Children lined up at the mess hall in silence as they waited for grace, sat and ate their meal in a twenty-minute period, and then marched out to musical accompaniment. Throughout the day they fell under the watchful eye of program administrators and older youths who often received authority to discipline younger children without sufficient oversight. This rigid program sought to stamp a new identity and culture onto the children.

The boarding school curriculum included both academics and vocational training; however, students often received outdated trade skills such as saddle making and sewing, and typically reservations lacked the equipment to practice those skills; girls also learned domestic skills that seemed equally irrelevant. By the turn of the century, Commissioner of Indian Affairs Francis Leupp (1905–1909) further shifted focus away from academics.

He believed academics needlessly detracted from training for their future careers as "lumbermen, ditchers, miners, railroad hands or what not." He continued, "If anyone can show me what advantage will come to this large body of manual workers from being able to read off the names of the mountains of Asia, or extract the cube root of 123456789, I shall be deeply grateful."[11] By Cato Sells's administration (1913–1921), a three-tiered system of instruction eliminated academic education after the first six years to allow full focus on preparation for manual work.[12]

Native American children detested the boarding schools, and their parents often longed for the former day schools that allowed their children to join them in the evening hours. Nevertheless, federal funding for boarding schools increased during the late nineteenth century, and the schools benefited from coercive legislation that forced Indian families to surrender their children to often distant educational facilities. In 1891 Congress passed an appropriations bill that empowered government officers to institute mandatory attendance policies among Native Americans, and two years later Congress strengthened that policy by granting Indian agents the power to "withhold rations, clothing and other annuities" from Indians who refused to release their children.[13]

Navajo Jim Dandy recalled that when his father was a child just after the turn of the twentieth century, his family hid the boy from government representatives. Dandy explained,

> One day a car with government officials came looking for children to be placed in school, and his family hid him in an underground pit where they stored wool. They put him in a large burlap sack used for shipping wool on wagons. Dad hid in there as the officials looked for him and other young school-aged people.[14]

His experience was not unique; many Navajos avoided boarding schools at the turn of the century.

Navajos resisted the enrollment of their children in these schools for a variety of reasons. Some feared the changes outsiders might impose on their children and deemed such foreign education unnecessary for a traditional Navajo lifestyle.[15] Others lamented the practical loss of labor because family sheep herds required the help of all members, including children. A 1924

Bureau of Indian Affairs report explained that few youth could be spared for schooling, and those who attended would likely forfeit their inheritance and condemn themselves to poverty.[16] Additionally, distant BIA boarding schools remained the only educational facilities available to many Navajos. Such schools earned terrible reputations among Indians and later among historians as dilapidated and dangerous, impersonal and at times violent, and hostile to Native language and culture. The transformative colonizing passage was surely an emotionally turbulent experience. Consequently, most Navajos resisted schools altogether, and stories of evading recruiters and government officials permeate Navajo oral traditions.

By the early twentieth century Indian aversion to boarding schools benefited from national criticisms of the schools. A variety of political pressures stemmed from the financial windfall the schools offered to local communities, but which western politicians saw as an inappropriate redirection of funds to often eastern facilities. Consequently, they portrayed boarding schools as wasteful indulgences and called for local day schools in their place. Commissioner Leupp supported this initiative, and in 1908 issued a directive prohibiting nonreservation boarding schools from recruiting at reservation agencies.[17] His successors, Robert Valentine (1909–1912) and Cato Sells (1913–1921), continued the initiative to erect local day schools.

Meanwhile, social advocacy groups pointed to the neglectful status of boarding schools. Perpetual budget cuts intensified during the 1920s and created overcrowded schools of malnourished children. The famous 1928 Meriam Report outlined a variety of problems within Indian Affairs, including education. Budget cuts reduced funding to nine cents per student each day. A Red Cross observer at Rice Boarding School in Arizona reported that the children's daily meals included bread, syrup, and coffee for breakfast, boiled potatoes and bread for lunch, and more boiled potatoes for dinner, along with only three-quarters of a cup of milk dispersed to each child daily.[18] Malnutrition led to epidemics, most commonly tuberculosis and trachoma. The report recognized that vocational training did not adequately prepare youths and also called for culturally relevant curriculum that met local community needs.[19] As funding declined, students took on greater responsibilities to operate laundries and kitchens while also tasked with facilities maintenance.

In an effort to resolve the concerns within the Meriam Report, President Herbert Hoover appointed an optimistic reformer as commissioner of

Indian affairs. In that capacity, Charles J. Rhoads turned to the author of the Meriam Report's section on education, W. Carson Ryan, and appointed him director of Indian education in 1930. But as the Great Depression unfolded, budget cuts intensified and Rhoads and Ryan could not secure funding for many of their initiatives. Undaunted, Ryan oversaw the closure of a dozen boarding schools and redirected existing funds to smaller day schools. Day schools, he argued, offered a cheap alternative that Native American parents preferred because it kept children close to home. He further realigned curriculum away from algebra, literature, and American history that once served to teach Anglo-Saxon supremacy, and promoted culturally relevant courses including Navajo rug weaving and Pueblo pottery. The election of 1932 brought fresh blood to both the presidency and subordinate positions. Franklin Roosevelt appointed activist John Collier as commissioner of Indian affairs in 1933, and Collier appointed Willard Beatty as his director of education; the two reformers continued the shift away from boarding schools and ethnocentric curriculum in favor of culturally responsive day schools. Boarding schools declined from sixty-five in 1933 to forty-nine in 1941, while Works Progress Administration funds enabled Collier to erect nearly one hundred day schools during that same time.[20]

Despite these efforts, the Navajo Nation proved a uniquely difficult challenge. Vast and sparsely populated lands proved troublesome for the day schools model, and sticky mud paths that turned into icy roads with deep ruts in the winter months further obstructed daily transportation to and from schools. In 1928, only one-third of Navajo children attended school of any sort, and enrollment only marginally climbed by 1940. Budget cuts further necessitated the closure of twenty day schools on the Navajo reservation by 1944. By then, attitudes had changed and desperate parents even volunteered to watch children overnight in day schools so that their children could enjoy an education.[21]

This unexpected change among Navajos in the years immediately preceding and following World War II requires some explanation. While many Navajos continued to avoid formal schools in the early twentieth century, tribal leaders (often themselves the products of boarding schools) increasingly advocated for educational opportunities. As early as 1925, the Tribal Council called for "higher education and better industrial training" and nine years later earmarked $2.5 million from public works funds to construct new schools.[22] Even so, most rank-and-file Navajos remained skeptical of the white men's schools.[23] Collier's efforts to preserve the Navajo grange through livestock reduction magnified those suspicions. Additionally, as World War II commenced, materials designated for school construction, repair, and transportation went to the war efforts and further dismantled the educational system on the Navajo reservation, leaving two-thirds of the children with no access to schools.[24]

Regardless of these shortcomings, Navajos increasingly engaged the outside world during the 1940s, in large measure due to World War II. Their participation in the war, as soldiers and in domestic industries, accelerated their contact with the outside world. Some 3,600 Navajos enlisted in the service; thousands of Navajo women joined the Women's Army Corps, and another 10,000 to 12,000 entered war-related industries.[25] Ever-growing border towns penetrated the reservation with radio broadcasts and a cash economy, and many Navajos sought to equip themselves and their children with the necessary skills to compete in this new reality. After the war, many of these Navajos returned to the reservation with a newfound understanding of the outside world. They saw firsthand the obstacles and barriers they faced and wanted better for their children.

Tribal leaders quickly called for new funds and schools, but severe poverty and the sheer number of children (approximately 20,000) slowed any remedy. On July 12, 1945, the Tribal Council unanimously passed a resolution that called for the construction of schools and acknowledged that "the Navajo Tribe is handicapped with poverty, poor health, limited resources, inability to speak English, and lack of training for improving our condition." These Navajo leaders believed "education like the white man's is needed to learn better farming, to learn how to improve livestock, to learn to improve health, and to learn trades," and they called on the commissioner of Indian affairs to request congressional appropriations to begin new school construction projects.[26]

The council also broke with the recent trend to construct day schools on reservations—a movement under BIA commissioner John Collier's administration that was intended to make schools less about colonization and more about linking the institutions and students to local communities. Surprisingly, Navajo leaders cared less for such cultural sensitivities and instead called on the BIA to construct boarding schools where greater cultural immersion could exist. District 18 representative Jim Hale explained,

I think we members of the Navajo Tribal Council are in complete agreement on this question of education and therefore I want to make a
motion that the Tribal Council respectfully request the Commissioner
of Indian Affairs to adopt a boarding school program and a better system of education for the Navajo people, and that the Commissioner
throw out this day school system of education.[27]

Boarding schools and dormitories remained a necessary option for Navajos because of the expansive reservation and dispersed population. Additionally, a 1947 report from Director of Navajo Schools George Boyce indicated
that the lack of fresh water necessitated fewer but larger schooling centers,
equipped with dormitories.[28] In the aforementioned council meeting, Carle
Mute further explained that the Protestant and Catholic boarding school
graduates outperformed those who attended BIA day schools.[29] Indeed, a
year after this meeting the council even entertained a resolution to recruit
the Mormon Church to build schools on the reservation. The bill recognized
the historic relationship between Navajos and Mormons, and emphasized
the latter's success in building schools elsewhere. It explained a plan to
entice the church "to establish at proper and convenient places schools
with accommodations incident thereto" in order "to supplement and complement the present schools now furnished and operated by the Government and by other churches and agencies."[30] However, the bill was tabled
and never revisited; instead, the tribe waited for a response from the federal government.

One year earlier, in May 1946, the council sent its first political envoy
to Washington, D.C., to advocate for schools, and by the time the council debated the proposed Mormon schools an increase in federal funding
reduced the need for such an alliance.[31] Tribal Chairman Chee Dodge led
the twenty-three-man delegation. When visiting Utah senator Carl Hatch,
who chaired the U.S. Senate Committee on Indian Affairs, Dodge identified
education as "our gravest need." He wanted the Navajo youth "to be educated to such an extent that when they are through with schools on the reservation they will be able to compete with the white people."[32]

The tribal representatives successfully drew the attention of three
congressional subcommittees, Secretary of Interior Julius Krug, and President Harry S Truman. On December 2, 1947, President Truman issued a

statement wherein he identified Navajo poverty, health and educational shortfalls as a national emergency.[33] This concern ultimately culminated in the passage of Public Law 80-390 on December 19, 1947, and the Navajo-Hopi Long Range Act in 1950. The former authorized $2,000,000 in immediate relief, and the latter authorized $88,570,000 for public works and earmarked $25,000,000 for education.[34] The Navajo-Hopi Long Range Act authorized unprecedented funding for the two overlapping reservations.[35] Truman's interest also helped urge the Third Supplemental Appropriations Act of 1948, which allotted another $500,000 for welfare of Indians, most of which was directed toward the two tribes. In 1953, Congress appropriated another $6,448,000 for schools on the two reservations.[36]

Over these years the tribal council approved new government-funded schools at Toadlena, Shiprock, Kayenta, Kaibeto, Tohatchi, Nazlini, Coyote Canyon, Hunters Point, Round Rock, and Fort Defiance.[37] Like federal agents and U.S. congressmen before them, in 1947 these Navajo leaders turned to compulsory education for Navajo children aged six to sixteen. In a February council meeting, District 7 representative Roger Davis romanticized the days when Indian police caught him and whipped him to coerce him to return to school, and the council followed his comments with loud applause and new legislation.[38] The council also launched a special five-year program designed to move uneducated Navajos aged twelve and above through an accelerated curriculum that focused on Anglo cultural exposure and trade skills to help Navajo succeed in the non-Indian world. In some ways it followed the Carlisle model: students lived off reservation in dorms at Sherman Institute in Riverside, California, and learned skills from cooking and cleaning to machinery, craftsmanship, and personal finance.[39] In desperation, the Navajo Nation replicated much of the widely hated boarding school model.

This anxious pursuit of Western training and facilities challenges simplistic accusations of colonization. Relations of power certainly enticed Navajo cooperation, but ultimately the tribal leaders and ordinary Navajos independently took action to adopt elements of Western culture. They had seen the material wealth of the white man, perhaps even tasted of it while employed in the wartime industries, and they wanted it for their children as well. To discount those efforts is to disregard the agency of these Navajos whose attitudes clearly changed as they demanded schools and increasingly enrolled their children during the 1940s.

Despite the tribe's and federal government's best efforts, many Navajos had no access to schools during the 1940s and much of the 1950s. A 1949 report found that over the preceding three years the number of Navajo children without access to education had only marginally declined from 15,000 to 14,000.[40] Secretary of Interior Krug's 1948 report counted only eight overcrowded boarding schools (Tuba City, Keams Canyon, Chinle, Fort Defiance, Shiprock, Toadlena, Fort Wingate, and Crowpoint) serving a few thousand Navajo children, and some fifty day schools plagued with 3,500 empty seats because Navajos lacked daily transportation to the facilities. In fact, the reservation had less than 100 miles of all-weather roads across its vast 27,000-square-mile domain. Some 1,500 Navajos attended off-reservation boarding schools, but overall the gross majority of the nation's 24,000 children had no access to schools.[41]

In this context one Navajo family became willing participants in a new educational opportunity. As a young child, Helen John and her siblings grew up on the Navajo reservation. Like other children, they hid when cars passed on distant roads for fear that Indian agents might take them away to boarding school. In just that way their Uncle Clarence disappeared one day, only to resurface five years later as a product of the Phoenix Indian Boarding School. His education there seemed to poison him against his culture, his family thought, because thereafter he did not return home to his reservation. But in the wake of federal livestock reductions in the 1930s, the John family no longer required the daily labor of all their children.[42] Their diminished herd and consequent household income could no longer support or even feed their children, and so they turned to Bureau of Indian Affairs (BIA) boarding schools for sustenance more than education. The children in the John family attended BIA schools on a rotation, one at a time, and the remainder of the family served as migrant laborers in the beet fields of southern Utah. By 1940, the Johns developed a relationship with the Avery family in Richfield and regularly worked their fields. Helen John's decision in 1947 to remain in Richfield grew out of that familiarity.

Several conflicting stories about Helen's arrangement with the Avery family continue to circulate among Mormons familiar with the Placement Program. The program's first coordinator, Golden Buchanan, recalled that the experiment was entirely Helen John's idea and that "we tried to discourage her, telling her she would be lonesome, probably discriminated against by white children, and no doubt, would be unhappy, yet she persisted."

He continued, "We were, naturally, somewhat dubious.... However, she was so sweet and sincere and determined to get ahead in the world that we allowed ourselves to be persuaded into taking her on a trial basis."[43] A popular rendition depicts her father as hesitant to release his seventeen-year-old daughter to live with *bilagaanas* [white people], but eventually caving to Helen's firm conviction to reside with friends of the trusted Avery family: the Buchanans.[44] In contrast, Helen John's account of these interactions identifies Amy Avery as a missionary who "was always asking us to come over." Avery played games with the John family girls—Helen and Ruth—and told them stories from the Book of Mormon. At Helen's request, Avery taught the Indian girls to read. Then one day, Helen recalled, Golden Buchanan arrived and suggested she could "stay in a home in Richfield and go to school." She was afraid but curious about the opportunity, and turned to her siblings for advice. Her oldest brother expressed his own regrets that he did not obtain a formal education, and contrasted his life cleaning toilets to the future she might enjoy. With that, Helen accepted Buchanan's invitation.[45] This conflicting narrative suggests more is at stake than finite details, at least for Buchanan and the Latter-day Saints who would like to minimize colonizing efforts by attributing the original plan to Helen.

Golden Buchanan lived in Richfield where he owned a lumber mill and fulfilled church responsibilities as a member of the Sevier Stake Presidency and as a special Indian coordinator.[46] He frequently interacted with Navajo migrant laborers and helped to find them work in nearby beet fields. It "irked" him when they did not receive proper treatment—insufficient food and poor tents—and so he emerged as a local Indian advocate. In the 1947 Fall Stake Conference, a then quarterly church meeting, Buchanan addressed Richfield's combined congregations regarding proper treatment of migrant workers. He chastised the Latter-day Saints who "wanted the Indians to work for them, but they didn't want to do anything for them." Only a few days later he learned about Helen.[47]

Buchanan grew excited about the potential benefits for Indians who briefly lived in Mormon foster homes and dispatched a letter to newly ordained apostle Spencer W. Kimball, who chaired the church's Indian Committee in Salt Lake City, Utah. The Indian Committee organized in the 1940s at the request of then apostle George Albert Smith, who soon after took Kimball and another newly ordained apostle, Matthew Cowley, to visit the

Navajo reservation to meet with tribal officials and other Christian sects.[48] When Smith placed Kimball at the head of the committee in 1943 he issued the instruction: "I want you to look after the Indians—they are neglected."[49] Kimball's grandfather had served as an apostle under Joseph Smith but, more importantly, his father had served first as a missionary and then as the president over Indian Territory. Young Spencer W. grew up hearing stories about the Lamanites, and his own patriarchal blessing promised he would minister to those people, though in young adulthood his mission call dispatched him to Europe. His lingering curiosity about Native Americans continued when he returned to the States and built his own family in Stafford, Arizona. He observed Indians riding on top of boxcars and lamented their poor economic and social status, but lacked a concrete solution.

Kimball could hardly contain his excitement when he learned of Buchanan's proposal for a widespread program with "dozens and hundreds and even more families" taking in Indian children. These youths would carry the same responsibilities and enjoy the same benefits as other children in the foster families. "Not only would they be trained in scholastic affairs in the schools," he continued, "they would learn to keep house, tend to a family, learn to manage a house and a farm. The boys could learn to work on the farms and learn to operate modern machinery."[50] In many ways it paralleled Pratt's outing program of several decades earlier. Buchanan further anticipated that children could also spiritually benefit if placed in the homes of local church leaders. Eventually, he hoped, they would serve missions for the church and spread the gospel among Native Americans. He concluded that the program would "cut down the time it takes to restore this people to their former blessings by a generation or two."[51] Several days later, Kimball arrived at Buchanan's home and instructed him to personally take in Helen as a foster child. Golden Buchanan's wife, Thelma, was shocked, having no prior knowledge of her husband's plan. After thinking on the request, the family invited Helen John into their home.[52]

Helen stayed with the Buchanan family for the 1947–1948 academic year. She started in the seventh grade, struggling in math but excelling in art, even winning a national contest. At the end of the school year, she joined her biological family in the fields. When school resumed in the fall of 1948, Helen returned to the Buchanan home. Her younger sister, Ruth, also remained in Richfield and quickly surpassed Helen's academic achievement. Ruth's success proved embarrassing for Helen, who then dropped out of school. As an alternative, Thelma Buchanan enrolled Helen in a local art school.[53] Helen also entered the waters of baptism sometime during those years. When the Buchanan family relocated to Gallup, New Mexico, Helen joined them and enrolled in a local beauty school there while Golden Buchanan served as the Southwest Indian Mission president. She met missionary Kenneth Woolsey Hall who she married after serving an LDS mission herself. In 1957 Elder Kimball performed the sealing/marriage ceremony in the Salt Lake Temple and the young couple moved north of Salt Lake City where Kenneth secured work on Hill Air Force Base. Helen returned to night school there and graduated in 1979 from South High School, and all four of her daughters graduated from Brigham Young University.[54]

Helen John's experience well represents the educational void that existed on the Navajo Reservation, the earnest desires of Indians to secure education, and the opportunity this created for Mormons. In this context, the Placement Program blossomed. In the fall of 1948, not only did Ruth join Helen, but also their cousin Regina Acothley and several other children: Pattie Lane, Carol Begay, Johnny Kiabitony, and Rex Singer.[55] Still others joined the next year.[56] Golden Buchanan recounted that he carefully informed Indian parents about the program articulating the value of Western education and intercultural exposure the experience offered. He promised white foster parents would nurture and teach the children in a way unmatched by boarding schools. He then placed Indian and Mormon parents in contact with one another to work out the details of their arrangements.[57]

Participation swelled as a dozen new Indian children joined each year from 1948 to 1953.[58] Buchanan continued to coordinate placements, but Native families increasingly organized their own transportation and foster homes.[59] Navajo enrollees as well as zealous Mormon traders and missionaries in the Southwest Indian Mission helped find and enroll new students.[60] Traders often took active roles as they initiated informal and independent placements beyond Buchanan's oversight. He welcomed the efforts as fulfillment of latter-day prophesies, and he and other Mormons eagerly recruited any and all Navajos whom they encountered, regardless of their religious affiliation.

Buchanan and others often solicited Navajos who were not Mormon because few Navajos shared the faith and he hoped participation could lead to their conversion, and possibly their parents' as well. Buchanan boasted that the placement of non-Mormon youths served as key to converting many more. After only a few years of operation he recounted, "We have now brought into the church approximately 75 new members by their living in our homes, but we have [also] opened the doors of 75 homes to the missionaries, and the homes of countless friends and relatives on the reservation."[61] Such efforts did not always succeed. Navajo Ben Tsosie, for example, penned a letter in response to an invitation that he send his children on Placement. He replied that he had no affiliation with the LDS Church, and no interest in sending his children off to Mormon homes.[62] Still, most of the dozens of students recruited each year had no affiliation to the church and their parents made no such objection. Buchanan optimistically explained that if officially adopted by the church, this "outing program" could serve thousands of Indian children over the next couple years. Buchanan boldly wrote:

> We could develop leadership that would, in time, completely dominate the affairs of the Indian people from a religious and economic point of view. Our elders then would have no difficulty entering homes on the reservation and our proselytizing would go forward on an intensified scale.[63]

Through this program, Buchanan argued that the church might achieve its longstanding charge to redeem Native Americans through both spiritual and socioeconomic advancement.

Just as Mormon theological motivations inspired outreach to Indians, a shortage of educational facilities on the Navajo reservation drove many parents to pursue educational alternatives. Longtime program caseworker Dale Shumway aptly explained that "the goals of the Navajos and the goals of the church came aligned after World War II."[64] Over the following decades, Navajos turned to the program for a variety of reasons, but education remained central for nearly all applicants.

Navajos understood that public schools in towns bordering the reservation enjoyed better facilities and teachers; they also thought English emersion would further enable their children to succeed in the outside world.[65] Many such parents found that LDS Placement offered an avenue to access these "better" off-reservation schools. Former Placement student Rhonda

Lee commented, "My mom always said that the school systems were a lot better and I could learn how to speak English a lot better."[66] As late as 1971, BIA Schools Services representative Nancy Evans commented, "There is no education available on the reservation that is competitive with that provided through Placement homes. Public schools are much better in Salt Lake City, for instance, than here."[67] Indeed, an early 1970s study found that 85 percent of the parents of placement students felt the program offered a better education than BIA schools or other public schools neighboring the reservation.[68] Several years later the church funded the Wasatch Research Opinion Report which concluded that 90 percent of parents and children listed a "better education" as their first or second reason for considering participation.[69] One ISPP child's mother commented to a *Saturday Evening Post* reporter, "It was hard letting my boy go...but it is the best thing for him, and that is what I want."[70]

While Indian parents did not always fully understand the consequences of enrollment in the Placement Program, many anticipated inevitable cultural implications. Some instructed their children to take the white man's education but not his religion. Others anticipated deeper changes in their children; many parents had spent time at boarding schools and knew that life abroad could change them.[71] Still, they hoped their children could take the best of both worlds and succeed in the strange new future that approached. Some even encouraged their children to adopt new ideas from their foster home. Former Placement student Rose Denette Sohsy recalled, "My dad would tell us that the traditional way of life was going to eventually phase out. He [would] say, 'I want you sitting in nice offices, where it's air conditioned in the summer and warm in the winter and be receiving a paycheck for it.'"[72]

Beyond education and a cross-cultural experience, many Indians hoped white foster families would provide a more nurturing and supportive environment than cold, impersonal boarding schools operated by the BIA. Indian parents fought their own demons in the turn-of-the-century boarding schools and even at mid-century these facilities gave cause for alarm. Students related stories of dilapidated structures, stolen clothing, bullies, and failed academic achievement. Navajo (and eventual Placement Program participant) Harry James recalled that in 1947, at age six, he began attending a Catholic boarding school in Houck, Arizona. He said, "I used to get beat up almost every noontime."[73] Navajo Jim Dandy recalled of Tuba City Boarding School in the 1950s, "I walked around nervous because somebody was always looking. I had to watch my step in whatever I did." Youth placed in charge took aggressive measures. Dandy explained:

> They forced you to do things, twisted your ears, hit you in the head with their pocketknife, or kicked you for no reason, and you had to live with that. They were the worst ones because they did not care what they did and would beat you up. There was nobody to back the younger children; so when you told on them, you got punished worse.[74]

In 1950, Lewis Singer enrolled at the BIA's Tuba City Boarding School and recalled similar experiences. He said that "students who misbehaved got whippings, stood at attention, scrubbed walls, or re-cleaned the bathrooms."[75] Navajo Ronald Singer spent three years at Tuba City Boarding School and remembered that the institution "was kind of a prison environment." He remembered that his mother "got tired of it too" and she "put me on placement the first chance she got."[76] Donald Mose commented that his "mother was never quite pleased with the education system on the reservation." He continued, "When the LDS program came along, it sounded very good to her. She decided to send my brother and me."[77] While pursuit of education encouraged many to join the Placement Program, a hatred of the boarding schools also directed quite a few into Mormon homes.

In addition to a perception of better schools, socioeconomics provided another incentive for participation. The pursuit of education certainly promised long-term gain, but for others the Placement Program also provided an immediate solution to poverty. In his 1948 report to President Truman, Secretary of Interior Julius Krug noted that the average Navajo family made less than $400 each year, perpetuating widespread malnutrition.[78] Even thirty years later one Navajo official looked back on the program and commented that students who enrolled often came from economically depressed families. He said, "They're all families who are just barely subsisting on salary. It's not uncommon for a family with eight or nine kids to have to live on one minimum-wage salary or even less."[79] Placement student Maybell Begay recalled her impoverished childhood on the Navajo Reservation during the late 1950s. She said, "In those lonely

days, we would survive by taking turns eating from a jar of peanut but-
ter or a box of raisins. When normal food wasn't around, we would often
dig up sego-lily bulbs or eat the edible parts of the prickly-pear cactus."[80]
Placement recruiters probably also benefited from unrelated BIA relocation brochures and pamphlets that promised a better life in urban environments.[81] Financially struggling parents and children saw placement
as a positive alternative to reservation poverty.

Escaping poverty constituted only part of the equation. Others sought
placement because it seemed to promise otherwise unattainable middle-
class leisure. DuWaine Boon recounted that among other incentives, "I was
also captivated by the stories my older cousins told about living with a rich
Mormon family and receiving Christmas presents."[82] Former ISPP student
Mabel Yazzie recalled, "The only thing I knew about placement was that
when my cousin came back from her placement home she had nice clothes
and pretty patent-leather shoes."[83] Indeed, many students came to expect
such amenities. Rhonda Lee explained that many students "always want a
rich family. If they don't get that, they really get mad about it."[84]

Spirituality also provided a motivation for some students and parents,
particularly after the program was well established and recruited more
from families already converted to the Mormon faith. In fact, one survey
found that 53 percent of parents and 67 percent of students listed "spiritual growth" as their first or second reason for participation in the ISPP.[85]
Eventually, about two-thirds of the students came from homes where
either one or both parents were members of the church; however, over 90
percent said they felt no pressure from church leaders to enroll their children.[86] Navajo politician Walter Atene explained that he sent his children
on placement for several reasons, including education and cultural exposure, but "number one is they become active in church."[87] Placement was
not merely an educational alternative; some anticipated a spiritual journey of self-discovery.

Many also enrolled their children in Placement to escape negative influences, often within their own families. Reservation poverty and economic
distress perpetuated a variety of social ills, including pervasive use of alcohol. Laura Brown recalled, "I remember a lot of drinking on my dad's part
and physical abuse because of that. Later on, my mother told us that when
she heard of the Placement Program, she saw a way out for her children."[88]

Through a translator, another mother explained her reasoning. "My husband is—he's drinking a lot. He didn't think about those kids."[89] One student explained that his mother worked long hours and could not be home to watch over the children. In her absence she "worried that we would all start running around and drinking," and consequently enrolled her children in the Placement Program.[90]

The seemingly wholesome middle-class image of Mormon families also proved attractive to such students and parents who bought into the integrationist message and wanted their children to value and function within a mainstream nuclear family. Rosie Tsosie-Bingham's parents put her on placement as an alternative to the impersonal and military-style boarding schools. Rosie's parents liked the family structure that the ISPP offered, as well as the opportunity to visit their daughter.[91] In the aftermath of her parents' deaths, Geraldine Goenett sent her siblings to placement. She explained, "Every child needs a mother and father. They need examples, models from parents. I know without a doubt my brothers and sisters are loved where they are. I know they are happy. Though it was hard to part with my family, I know that this was the right decision."[92]

A variety of conflated factors ultimately drew students into the ISPP. Generally speaking, most Indians saw it as an avenue to something better for their children. Whether escaping negative influences or reaching for what they perceived as something "better," enrollment benefited from Indian perceptions of depravity on the reservation. A study conducted by the church in the late 1970s and early 1980s identified similar factors.

Of course, this only accounts for the motivations of half of the participants. Just as Indians made a conscious choice, so too did good-intentioned white Mormons who opened their homes without financial compensation. They believed in Book of Mormon prophesies that Lamanites would someday "blossom as the rose," and the Placement Program seemed the obvious medium for that change. These Mormons supposed that if Indians could only internalize the gospel messages, they could rise up out of poverty and perceived social backwardness to become industrious Americans. As word of the new program spread among traders and Mormon residents living on or near Indian reservations in the Southwest, many eagerly opened their homes and invited others to do likewise. With ambitions of redeeming Lamanites, hundreds of Mormons took action and opened their homes to

TABLE 3.1. REASONS FOR ENROLLING IN PLACEMENT

Education-related	44%
Church-related	19%
Gain new experience, or learn independence	5%
Learn Anglo ways, get along with whites, improve English	5%
Have better life, better living conditions, better care, financial opportunities	5%
Leave bad environment, avoid trouble, avoid learning bad habits	4%
Other family members previously participated and encouraged	4%
Get away from problems at home	3%
Peer influence	3%
Encouragement from LDS Church representative	2%
Other reasons	5%
Total	99%

Source: Bruce A. Chadwick, Stan L. Albrecht, and Howard M. Bahr, "Evaluation of an Indian Student Placement Program," Social Casework 17, no. 9 (November 1986): 522.

Indian youth. For some this program represented a prophetic refocusing upon Lamanites that once captured the hearts of early Mormons.

While these Latter-day Saints acted out of theologically charged white guilt and paternalism characteristic of broader American policy towards Indians, in many ways the Mormons shared common interests with the Native Americans they hoped to assist. From the 1950s through 1970s, the Navajo Nation and the LDS Church shared a unified goal to provide education and transform Native Americans into similar visions of educated and economically independent people capable of controlling their own destinies. Though the Indian Student Placement Program represented a recommitment to a long-forgotten spiritual imperative—to bring Lamanites into the fold—for most Indians the ISPP appeared simply as an exceptional educational opportunity.

During the 1940s and 1950s, Navajos longed for any educational edge to elevate the status of their people. Agnes Holm, granddaughter of Chairman

Chee Dodge, remembered that until World War II, "you couldn't fill Navajo schools, partly because you couldn't see what good school would do. It didn't lead to any kind of worthwhile work at all." However, "during World War II, a lot of people went into the services, but even more people worked off-reservation and saw that, for better or worse, you were at a real disadvantage without an education."[93] The confluence of interests created an environment where Navajos and Mormons worked together as willing participants in the Indian Student Placement Program. Certainly Mormon colonization was at play, but so too was Navajo self-interest. Though Native American youths and parents did not fully understand the complete program (that is discussed in succeeding chapters), those that chose to participate did so because it appeared to offer the best chance at an education. Navajos desperately sought schools and Mormons obliged them as a means of fulfilling their own prophetic expectations. Like Pratt and others before them, they opened an outing program as a means to transform and redeem Native Americans from perceived cultural deficiencies that only Western culture could rectify.

4

THE INSTITUTIONAL RISE OF THE INDIAN STUDENT PLACEMENT PROGRAM

1947–1972

I see the Indians becoming educated through government programs, other church programs and our own program.... I fully expect that within the next few years there will be a great increase in the acceptance by the Indians of the programs and of education and that the pyramiding benefits will bring increasing growth and development to the Indians each year better than the year before.

—Spencer W. Kimball, 1963

As Navajos and other Indian youths sought some sort of educational alternative to insufficient boarding schools, the LDS Church and Apostle Spencer W. Kimball in particular promoted the Placement Program as a viable path to education and self-improvement.[1] This "outing program" (so called because it took Indian children out and placed them in white homes) soon gained official church recognition and evolved into a massive bureaucratic organization monitoring thousands of students each year. Despite an impromptu and informal origin in 1947, recruitment efforts intensified as missionaries canvassed reservations and offered enticing visions of middle-class leisure.

Church officials made conscious efforts to smooth relations with Navajo authorities and the Bureau of Indian Affairs, and worked to professionalize the program with trained social workers and standardized regulations. By the 1971–1972 school year the ISPP enrollment approached five thousand students. As the program spilled over from state to state and drew children from across the United States and even Canada, the church launched other Indian-specific efforts from Indian Seminary to Brigham Young University programs. By the 1970s it appeared the "Day of the Lamanite" had finally arrived, and the Indian Student Placement Program served as the crown jewel of the church's Lamanite program.

Spencer W. Kimball emerged as the leading advocate and architect of the Placement Program. During the late 1940s and early 1950s, the program relied on social networking through the church but did not officially exist as a formal program. Kimball used his apostolic mantle and the reverence Latter-day Saints held for his position to encourage their participation and to court the approval of other church leaders.[2] He carefully plotted the program's growth and used the church's Indian committee to administer the program well before its formal recognition as an institution within the church. In June 1948, Kimball created a new calling, "coordinator of Indian Affairs for the church," and appointed Golden Buchanan to that position.[3] With this responsibility Buchanan could move the informal outing program forward with implicit church approval even though the apostles and First Presidency (the president of the church and his two counselors) knew little about the program.[4]

In August 1949, Kimball informed LDS Church president George Albert Smith about the unofficial outing program. Kimball explained that the program operated at the "urgent request of Indians on the reservation" and that the children enjoyed a positive experience. They attended excellent schools, participated in church, and "almost all of them have joined the church and are very happy in their associations in this area."[5] The First Presidency approved and directed Kimball to continue without formal recognition. Kimball instructed Buchanan, "We can't give you any money for it or any traveling expense. We can't do one thing for you, but the Brethren are watching it.... They don't want you to stop, but they can't tell you to go forward."[6] Nevertheless, the apostle directed southern Utah's stake

presidents to lend their implicit support by hosting in children as examples to the general membership.[7]

At this time, Kimball and Buchanan also gathered several new administrative supporters. Miles Jensen, a migrant labor recruiter for the Gunnison
Sugar Company, accepted an invitation from Buchanan to foster an Indian
child. Jensen also volunteered his business trucks to transport placement
students to and from the reservation.[8] Meanwhile, Kimball recruited the
support of the LDS Church's General Relief Society president, Belle Spafford.[9] The General Relief Society operated much of the church's welfare
and outreach programs, and already possessed a license from the state of
Utah for general foster child placement services. In 1949, Spafford volunteered her agency to serve as an umbrella that could legitimize the Indian
placements and prevent legal obstacles.[10] Spafford moved forward with the
approval of the Presiding Bishopric, who oversaw the General Relief Society and reported to the First Presidency.[11]

Despite the General Relief Society's involvement, during the early 1950s
the program remained unofficial and lacked any standards, policies, or central administration. Buchanan and Jensen continued to promote the program, but others acted independently to solicit, transport, and house Indian
children. The program advanced in this decentralized, quasi-approved,
and legally questionable manner without any comprehensive regulations.
Indian parents sometimes withdrew students mid-year; foster parents can-
celled arrangements without notice; miscommunications between those on
and off the reservation perpetuated confusion. Despite all of this, enrollment rose each year.[12]

The informal program gained further church endorsement in 1951 when
Elder Kimball called Buchanan to serve as the president of the recently
organized Southwest Indian Mission, located squarely on the Navajo and
Hopi Reservations. Once there he could advance Indian recruitment efforts
while Jensen transported the children and assisted in their housing arrangements. Buchanan explained:

> Sometimes we would just put them on busses and call the people at
> the other end to tell them they were coming. They would meet the
> bus and report to us that the children had arrived safely. When it
> was time for them to return home in the spring they would call the

mission office to tell us they were putting them on the bus and we would be there to meet the bus and take the children to their homes.[13]

Most importantly, Buchanan's new calling offered him the mission's resources: dozens of full-time proselytizing elders who took on a significant role in locating and recruiting potential converts. Jensen recalled, "At the time most of the children who were coming were non-LDS. Immediately they began to study the gospel and became acquainted with the church."[14] The outing program and the search for Indian converts remained fused thereafter.

Buchanan's prestigious calling as mission president, along with the clear support of an apostle, certainly helped Jensen locate new foster homes. Still, the men knew not to press this appearance of church support too far. Kimball instructed Jensen, "We have to be very careful. I can't write any letters to you that someone would interpret as me giving you church authorization to do something."[15] Nevertheless, the clear advocacy of an apostle and the Southwest Indian Mission president gave the impression of church endorsement, and the program grew steadily. Though the decentralized and independent nature of the early program makes it difficult to accurately reconstruct participation figures, Buchanan later estimated that enrollment steadily rose by a dozen or more students each year until it reached sixty-eight students in the 1953–1954 academic year.[16]

The seasonal trafficking of poor, malnourished, and often ill Navajo youths caught the attention of Jensen's wife, Celia, who determined that students needed closer medical attention. She resolved to transform her home into a sanitation and medical way station for the many children in transit. As a registered nurse, she quickly assumed the role of chief medical advisor. Using tin tubs and her own bath she washed the children, checked for lice, and issued an examination before sending the children off to their respective foster homes.[17]

As the informal program assumed some notion of standardization, Kimball continued to play a dominant role in persuading local church authorities to support the program. In 1948, Kimball authored a massive, two-part article in the church-printed magazine *Improvement Era*. Kimball outlined Navajo history, criticized the federal government for its failure to educate Navajos, and called for the expansion of schools.[18] In the second part, which appeared two months later, he outlined the socioeconomic distress on the reservation in graphic detail with sensational language. Kimball wrote, "The Navajo today shivers in the cold; he dies prematurely with diseases because of malnutrition and because of lack of sanitation; his standard of living is far below that of European peoples who we seek to assist; he is without many of the necessities of life."[19] He pointed to the absence of running water, baths, toilets, and stoves, and identified the prevalence of tuberculosis and other diseases in a context of overcrowded and undersupplied medical facilities. He portrayed their homes as little more than dungeon-like caverns made so by the unfortunate poverty on the Navajo Reservation.[20] Just a year later, Kimball's General Conference remarks to the church membership again addressed the Navajos and instructed Latter-day Saints to help Indians as the Good Samaritan treated the injured man on the road.[21]

Kimball also worked to slowly convince church leaders who opposed his plan and made it difficult to obtain official recognition. Kimball instructed the Indian Committee to actively seek out any articles or other stories that illustrated Navajo depravity. Each week Kimball took the best human-interest stories and presented them to the Quorum of the Twelve Apostles to soften opposition to the informal placement program. Week after week the church authorities responded, "We're not ready, we're not ready."[22]

Despite the resistance of several unnamed apostles, Kimball received encouragement from President George Albert Smith until his death in 1951, as well as his successor, David O. McKay.[23] Miles Jensen recalled the instructions he received from President Smith and Elder Kimball. They said:

> We want you to go to this stake conference and we want you to have these cute little Indian girls on the front row and we want you to go to the stake president and get these kids into their homes. We want you to have the kids give the talks and the prayers and all of this type thing so that the Brethren, as they come to stake conference...will start to be exposed to what is going on and see these kids, and one by one they would become a little indoctrinated.[24]

In those years traveling authorities frequently presided at stake conferences and Kimball hoped to win their support and that of the general membership with such displays. However, this also brought about some conflict in the early 1950s when Jensen followed similar orders at the North Sanpete Stake conference. Visiting apostle Mark E. Petersen presided at that conference and in the afternoon session he took the pulpit. He said, "I've been hearing about the Indian program of the church. People have been asking me, 'What should we do? Where will we get this help? How should we do this?'" He answered, "Publicly now," as he slapped the pulpit, "I want you to know that there is no Indian program. The people involved better clean their doorsteps."[25]

Jensen sat on the front row with half a dozen students and the stake leadership whom he had coaxed into supporting the program. Jensen recalled that "of course, this really flushed me down in this stake." He reported back to Elder Kimball who issued the reassurance that he would handle the conflict.[26] Even after the program's official approval in 1953, Kimball continued to run interference for Jensen and others as needed to protect the project.[27] Regardless of occasional resistance, the program continued to increase enrollment and to expand geographically. By the fall of 1951, placements occurred in Southern California, Idaho, Oregon, and Utah, often without the knowledge of Buchanan, Jensen, or Kimball.

In 1954, Kimball's efforts finally paid off when the First Presidency officially sanctioned the program.[28] The church hierarchy typically remains quiet about how decisions are made in the upper echelons, but the repercussions are readily visible. The institutionalization of the Indian Student Placement Program (ISPP) ushered in new levels of organization and structure, policies, and procedures. It also required leaders rein in independent placements under the new organization's direction. The Indian Committee assumed administrative governance and erected an organized structure to perpetuate the then official Placement Program.

Kimball called Miles Jensen into his office to convey the exciting news on August 1, 1954. Kimball then announced that in the morning he would leave the country for a six-week church tour in Europe and told Jensen to use the apostle's desk to organize the new program.[29] Jensen immediately sold his business and took up the new full-time, salaried responsibilities of managing the program. Before leaving, Kimball gave two directions to Jensen. First, the First Presidency wanted seventy-five students enrolled before school started in two weeks. Second, in Kimball's absence another apostle already attending a chapel dedication in Cedar City, Utah, would serve as Jensen's contact and coordinator as the men recruited local LDS Church leaders and Native American students. Jensen remembered that he almost cried when Kimball identified that apostle as Elder Mark E. Petersen, the same who had undercut his efforts in North Sanpete.[30]

From the very beginning, Petersen determined that the ISPP would be a "correlated program." Correlation was an organizational trend in the church hierarchy throughout the twentieth century, and particularly during the 1950s and 1960s, which called for priesthood leaders to oversee all programs. Nothing should operate outside priesthood oversight. Petersen concluded that each stake would assign a high councilman over the Placement Program participants within their boundaries. Jensen and Petersen then set about calling every stake president along Highway 89 in Arizona and Utah to recruit foster families.[31]

A week and a half later, the First Presidency circulated a letter to stake presidents in southern Utah inviting their participation in the new program. It explained that Sevier, South Sevier, North Sevier, Gunnison, South Sanpete, North Sanpete, and Moroni Stakes could participate and laid out the expectations of the program. Students should be treated as "a welcome member of the household to enjoy the spiritual and cultural atmosphere of the home, and to be given such schooling in the public schools as may be afforded to him." They were not to be treated "as a mere guest, nor a servant." The letter also warned that volunteer host parents would accept obligations to finance their student's "food, clothing, transportation, and other incidental expenses."[32]

The First Presidency also stipulated that every participant would be baptized members of the church. Jensen looked at the last requirement with shock; two-thirds of the students slated for the year were not LDS. He asked Petersen, "What about these kids that aren't baptized?" Petersen replied, "What are you there for? Get them baptized." Mormon youth are routinely baptized at eight years of age, and so it seemed a simple enough task. Dozens of anxious Indian children quickly entered the waters of baptism in order to continue in the suddenly official program. However, this simple and well-intended policy had serious consequences.[33] With Golden Buchanan serving as Southwest Indian Mission president and church expectations restricting enrollment to baptized members of the church, missionaries quickly transformed the program into a proselytizing tool. It remained such for the next two decades.

The First Presidency's instruction that all students would be baptized members of the church, and the direct oversight by one of the Twelve Apostles, also set in motion another pattern: a tiered and at times distanced bureaucracy. While Jensen and later caseworkers and administrators oversaw the program's routine logistics, the often disconnected church hierarchy determined policy. Upon returning from Europe, Kimball once again took lead of the Indian Student Placement Program and remained actively engaged in every detail. As long as Kimball served as the apostle over the program, it grew and enjoyed unyielding support from the church.

During those first couple years of formal operation, Kimball maintained an open-door policy and Relief Society president Belle Spafford correlated with him as needed, usually several times a week. As enrollment increased and placements expanded geographically, Kimball wanted to pool resources. He gradually organized weekly meetings which co-opted and regularized the pre-existing Indian Committee's sporadic meetings. In practice, the ISPP dominated the Indian Committee meetings during the 1950s and 1960s. During those years, a variety of church leaders, legal and medical advisors, and governmental representatives met sporadically with the committee as they outlined and revised the operations of the ISPP. The primary committee members included Kimball, Spafford, and Jensen as well as other General Authorities who rotated through committee responsibilities, including Antoine R. Ivins, Mark E. Petersen, Ted Tuttle, and S. Dilworth Young. The committee often invited visitors for various discussions. Intermountain seminary teacher Boyd K. Packer attended a few early meetings, as did medical professional Robert F. Hansen of the United States Department of Health, Education and Welfare. In April 1954, Utah state director of the Bureau of Services for Children John Farr Larson attended one such meeting to emphasize the importance of the Relief Society's licensure.[34] Two months later attorney T. Quentin Cannon joined the meeting to offer legal counsel to that end.[35] Each week a variety of ranking church leaders and unofficial advisors met to define policies and procedures for the program.[36]

This early series of Indian Committee meetings yielded several new conclusions. Though Jensen would remain a caseworker despite his lack of formal training, all future employees needed academic and professional preparation in social services. The church punctuated that policy in 1954 when it hired Margaret Keller to serve as the Relief Society Social Services director, which oversaw the Placement Program and other licensed social work. Keller personifies the transition to trained professionals. Though not LDS at the time, she had earned a B.S. degree from Brigham Young University in 1933, and after working for the Federal Relief Administration she completed graduate studies at the University of Southern California and the University of Chicago, the premier child development and social services university of the era. Once installed as director she fiercely advocated for the ISPP.[37]

The committee also determined to restrict enrollment to school-aged children, ages six to eighteen years, and expanded Celia Jensen's informal cleaning and medical waypoint into a full-fledged reception center for all children. The Indian participants received a thorough cleaning, medical evaluations, and standardized instructions about ISPP policy. With such a plan, the committee also determined to cease the independent and unreliable private transportation and opted to rent buses that would gather up students at semiurban centers on the reservation and bring them into the Richfield Reception Center under Jensen's direction beginning in the fall of 1955. That year, fifty to sixty Indian children traveled all through the night and arrived at the Reception Center at the Richfield Stake Center.[38]

The typical reception center experience began at six a.m. Children exited their buses, received name tags, and filed into the large cultural hall where the local Relief Society women waited with cereal, eggs, bacon, and fruit.[39] After breakfast adult volunteers moved the children through a systematic process beginning with a bath. Church Welfare provided the food and most of the supplies, and the American Linen Supply Company donated hundreds of towels. The children then lined up for the medical clinic, staffed primarily by volunteers, medical students, and several doctors and nurses on loan from the United States Health Service. Students received a chest x-ray as well as eye, skin, ear, and dental examinations.[40] Doctors conducted complete physicals and searched for tuberculosis, venereal diseases, or other illnesses that might endanger host family members. The medical check-ups concluded with a series of needle-jabbing immunizations and the nurturing efforts of Mormon women assigned to guide the children back to the large room where lunch awaited them.[41]

For the children, the remainder of the afternoon centered on food and games as foster parents arrived and received training of their own. Foster parents drove in from all over Utah where Kimball, Jensen, or other program leaders issued words of advice and appreciation. By 1959, Brigham Young University produced a movie on Indian lifeways to help these participants understand their foster child's cultural transition. Caseworkers then called parents and individual children into small rooms where they made introductions and sent the family on its way.[42] The reception center embodied the newly centralized and procedurally standardized oversight of the ISPP.

With all the essential apparatuses and policies in place, the Indian Student Placement Program emerged fully functional by 1955. Nevertheless, several obstacles revealed deep tension between notions of unrestricted growth and quality control. These included reining in unofficial placements, assessing the sincerity of conversion for approved placements, and appeasing tribal and government officials who grew uneasy with the program.

Unofficial Indian placements in Mormon homes in the Southwest and elsewhere threatened the credibility of the program and ultimately risked the Relief Society's state license to manage child placements. This issue came to a head in 1956 and the Indian Committee ultimately resolved to discourage all Indian foster placements except those originating in the Southwest Indian Mission and passing through the Richfield Reception Center. In 1955, LDS Church President David O. McKay sent a letter to stake and mission presidents with Native populations near or within their borders discouraging independent placements.[43] The committee simultaneously worked to attract foster parents as far north as Salt Lake City in order to meet the needs of all Indian children who sought placement. This expansion, and others thereafter, necessitated growing ranks of caseworkers who monitored the children during the school year.[44]

Meanwhile on the reservation, missionaries continued to use Placement as a proselytizing tool, which ultimately led to conflicts with tribal and federal authorities. During the 1950s the church experienced sensational domestic and foreign growth, in part due to a myriad of proselytizing tactics that centered on hosting recreational activities for teens and children. Baseball leagues, beach trips, and other activities attracted youth, many of whom accepted baptism without any understanding of its spiritual relevance. Mormon historian D. Michael Quinn popularized the term "baseball baptisms" which articulates this phenomenon as it occurred in Great Britain. During the 1950s, LDS missionaries and mission presidents striving to meet quotas often used such activities to attract youth, secured parental permission, and concealed baptism as merely a meaningless act of initiation. This policy continued in Great Britain until 1963, when negative publicity drew condemnation from then president of the Quorum of the Twelve Joseph Fielding Smith.[45]

Similar activities occurred on the Navajo Reservation. One former Placement student recounted the circumstances of her baptism.

> We were going to school in Kaibito, the boarding school. This one particular Sunday—at the boarding school they have all different denominations that you can go to whichever one you want to. At the time you know, I wasn't going to any of them. And I had a friend of mine I guess went to the LDS, they had the missionaries come over and teach the classes. And that particular Sunday, I went with him to his classroom. And then I guess—I don't know how it happened, but I got on the bus for a "field trip," they called it a field trip. I think it was a week later we all got on the bus—hauled us to Tuba City and the, you know, "field trip." Of course I wanted to go on the field trip, so I signed my name on. And then when we got there, stopped at the chapel, only then I didn't know that was a chapel. And you know, they gave us little white gowns, put it on, and lined up, people were getting dumped in the water. I had no idea what it was. So I got baptized then. And then probably I think it was a year or two later that my parents sent me up for Placement program.[46]

Navajo Anna Begay recalled her baptism occurred in a similarly superficial way. She was invited to attend a basketball game, and then to play for the local LDS branch team. She said, "This is when I learned what tricky people Mormons are!" After a month of playing basketball the branch president explained that baptism was required in order to continue playing basketball. She said, "Willing to do almost anything to keep playing basketball, I quickly took the missionary lessons for a couple of weeks and was baptized on April 26, 1969, so I could continue to play in the regional playoff."[47] Lumbee Edward Clark recalled that his baptism occurred among about seven hundred other Indians aged eight to fourteen. He said, "Most were baptized without the permission of their parents. It was called 'kiddy dip.' The day I was baptized, I did not know when I left home with the missionaries that

I would be baptized when I returned." He continued, "In my naiveté I did not realize that I was joining any church."[48]

Missionaries in the Southwest Indian Mission, under pressure to ever increase baptisms and Placement enrollees, fooled children into baptism by way of youth-centered activities. The mission hosted basketball tournaments and missionaries led campouts and other activities to attract Indian teens and children. The Southwest Indian Mission's March 1978 historical report recounts a basketball tournament among its proselytizing tools, which combined with open house–format dinner parties helped to recruit ISPP students.[49] Some missionaries even cast Placement as an all-expense-paid journey into middle-class leisure. One Navajo official recalled when missionaries approached his son, who later said, "They told me we'd have lots of fun. We'd play volleyball and football, and I could have my own room if I go on Placement." He pleaded with his father to no avail.[50] In 1967 Erdman Jake learned about Placement through recreational activities hosted by LDS missionaries. The Mormon elders "initiated a sports activity that involved children in the neighborhood or whatever area they worked to be involved in that." He continued, "Then eventually you went to church, the services they offered and then they told us about the Placement Program."[51] The allure of the ISPP combined with overly zealous missionaries meant that many students enrolled who were not genuinely converted to the gospel. Rather than enroll Mormon Indians, in the early decades the program seemed to recruit almost entirely non-Mormon Indians. Navajo Jimmy Benally, a former Placement student and eventual missionary in the Southwest Indian Mission, recalled that the program worked as a proselytizing tool. He said, "I would say ninety percent of the kids were baptized to go on Placement rather than baptized into the church. I learned that on my mission." He continued, "They weren't converted to the church. They just went to get to school."[52] Caseworker Rex Ashdown substantiated Benally's recollection of children baptized solely to participate in Placement. He said Miles Jensen pressured missionaries "very heavily to use recruitment of the children as a conversion tool, as much as possible." Jensen instructed, "We'll take the child up and this will convert them to the gospel." The caseworker recounted the experience of a thirteen-year-old boy who was placed in Utah. On his first Sunday in that home the foster father prepared to take him to the weekly priesthood meeting. The boy responded, "What's that?"

and continued, "We go to Mass at home." Ashdown recounted, "The boy was in fact Catholic. How he got selected I'm not sure. The elders down there were doing the selecting. We were not."[53]

Still, some missionaries tried to impress the significance of enrollment upon potential enrollees and their families. Teddy Redhouse, a former Placement student and Southwest Indian Mission alumnus, recalled the typical discussion he issued to potential ISPP student parents. He said, "He'll be nine months in another home, and will they be willing to support him when he comes home and wants to take part in church? 'Oh, yes,' they say. And when he gets twelve he'll get the Aaronic priesthood, will you support him in that? 'Well, yes.'" He continued, "There's lots of things he won't do, and when he turns nineteen he'll go on a mission for the church for TWO years, are you prepared to support him financially in that? Each time their answer is a little more hesitant." Then he hit them with the biggest deterrent: "When it comes time for their son to get married, he'll get married in the temple and unless you're active members you can't be there to see it." Suddenly, he observed, "they're not so sure."[54] To be certain, missionaries varied in their thoroughness of student and parent preparation, and enrollees ranged from those who had already converted both spiritually and culturally to the LDS Church, to those who had never before heard of Mormons, though there were more of the latter in the early decades of the ISPP.

The zeal of missionaries and their role as program recruiters drew the criticism of some Indians and the Bureau of Indian Affairs (BIA). Following the recruitment of students in the fall of 1956, Hualapai Indians in Peach Springs, Arizona, filed complaints with the BIA offices in Phoenix about Mormons holding mass baptisms as a prerequisite to enroll in the Placement Program. BIA representatives also expressed frustrations that the program unnecessarily undermined family bonds.[55]

The Indian Committee soon confirmed three mass baptisms in the summers of 1954, 1955, and 1956 which initiated a total of sixty-six children. Each baptism preceded enrollment in the ISPP, which casts more doubt on the sincerity of the children's conversions to Mormon theology. Indeed, twenty-six of the baptized youths came from non-Mormon families. While these only accounted for a fraction of the program's total youth, it drew unwanted negative attention and proved disturbing to Kimball and the committee.[56] Elder Petersen expressed a preference that the program should only enroll the children of baptized parents and that caseworkers should personally establish that fact when they visit the reservation.[57] In the following months, Kimball and others likewise wanted the program to focus on Indian children already raised in Mormon Indian homes. However, Kimball's conflicting ambitions to expand the program's total enrollment made such restrictions impractical until a generation later.

Back in Indian country, BIA representatives and Native community members continued to voice concerns. In one instance, as caseworker Glen VanWagenen led a busload of children past the Lower Colorado Agency, a Native woman blocked the road, stopped the bus, and demanded to see VanWagenen's permits to remove children from the reservation. When VanWagenen called Miles Jensen to ask for advice, Jensen instructed him, "Tell her to go jump in the Colorado River. We're licensed." Jensen recalled that whatever VanWagenen's response, it "created a tremendous amount of hostilities."[58]

The BIA forwarded her complaint to Arizona Department of Public Welfare commissioner Fred Hildreth in Phoenix, who passed it along to John Farr Larson, the Utah director of Child Services (and frequent attendee at the Indian Committee meetings). Larson warned Kimball about the potential for BIA obstruction, particularly if such confrontational engagements continued. In response, the committee dispatched Relief Society president Belle Spafford and Miles Jensen to Phoenix to resolve the conflict. The two laid out the program for Hildreth as well as other interested professionals, such as John Farr Larson, Sam Bellson (representative from the Navajo tribe), and other unnamed government agency representatives (possibly from the BIA). Even though many of the attendees initially opposed the program, some softened their opinions. At the meeting's end Commissioner Hildreth replied, "Well, this has been very interesting. How can we get the program in Arizona?"[59] Others seemed less impressed. Some expressed concerns that the program used poorly qualified caseworkers and unnecessarily removed children from their natural homes. They believed that in doing so it drove a geographic and cultural wedge between parents and children and that the program imposed a foreign culture on children which caused parental and societal estrangement.[60]

To combat lingering criticisms and threats of governmental intervention, the Indian Committee met in December 1956 and developed a three-pronged response. First, they would secure as much information as possible regarding the baptisms of Indian youth on the reservation in previous years. Second, the committee planned to organize meetings with social service representatives to dispel any misunderstandings. Third, committee members would appeal to Utah senator Arthur Watkins, best known for his leadership in federal termination policy, and to enlist the support of Mildred Arnold, director of the Division of Social Services at the Children's Bureau in Washington, D.C.[61] Jensen also remembered that it was about this time that Kimball instructed him to seek "the pulse of the people." To do so, Jensen began to collect letters of support from Native Americans. Jensen recalled that one woman wrote, "Well, if those Mormons up there are crazy enough to pay for it, what's wrong with that?"[62]

The most noted strategy to build consensus and support for the program centers on a formal meeting hosted in Kanab, a small town in southern Utah. The Indian Committee assigned Larson to organize the meeting between Indian and child welfare bureaucrats from Arizona and Utah.[63] The meeting commenced on March 19, 1957, and drew the attendance of a variety of church and governmental representatives.[64]

Discussion largely centered on a presentation made by Relief Society Social Services director Margaret Keller. She traced the origins of the Relief Society as a welfare agency licensed by Utah for child placement and other services, and then outlined the parameters of the Indian Student Placement Program. They included parental approval, social worker evaluations of children, and evaluation of foster homes. She explained that the program placed each Indian enrollee in a family with cautious attention to family size, age of the child in relation to others in the family, and interests of the child. She discussed the benefits Indian children enjoyed through placement, such as better education, medical support, and leadership development. Keller also expressed sensitivity to estrangement issues between children and their Native American parents, and reassured listeners that frequent letters help to bridge that potential rift. Additionally, loving foster parents worked diligently to help children adjust and feel comfortable in their new environment, she explained.[65] Dr. Robert Hansen followed Keller and praised the program's medical benefits, largely stemming from the reception center.[66]

The presenters then opened the floor to comments and questions. Navajo representative Samuel Billison expressed concern at the recruitment of six-year-old participants, but otherwise valued the program as an excellent opportunity for both education and cross-cultural exposure, particularly for children in remote parts of the reservation.[67] His only other concern was that the church should better communicate which youth are participating in the program and leaving the reservation.

BIA welfare supervisor Bea Erickson questioned the impact of the program on children: how did they adjust to the cultural changes and how did their college and work experiences in adulthood differ from other Navajos? Billison reassured attendees that his own education, although not as an ISPP student, moved him off the reservation for some time and offered valuable intercultural skills and he suspected a similar benefit awaited these placement children. The comments closed with Commissioner Hildreth's endorsement of the Placement Program.[68]

Other presentations met with similarly positive responses after minor discussions. Relief Society president Belle Spafford addressed concerns about motivations for students and Mormons, and criticisms that the program served as a missionary tool. She explained that the prerequisite of baptism for participants aged eight and above (the age at which Mormons baptized their own children) was not intended to encourage convert baptisms but rather to restrict participation to Indians who already claimed membership in the church. Mormons served as foster parents, she explained, to help raise up Indian children in an environment where they could reach their potential as educated leaders. Several attendees commented about that misunderstanding, but ultimately indicated support for the program. In general, Larson remembered, "I felt there was a more cooperative spirit than a year ago" and that "there was little voiced opposition."[69]

Most of the attendees viewed the ISPP as a new approach to resolving the ever vexing "Indian problem." Indeed, the Placement Program reflected the attitude of the era. Only a few years earlier in 1954, House Concurrent Resolution 108 initiated the dissolution of tribal entities and the forced integration of Native Americans, led largely by Utah senator Arthur Watkins.[70] In this atmosphere of termination and national integration, the Placement Program proved appealing to both government bureaucrats and many Native Americans, including those representing the Navajo tribe. Once isolated reservations increasingly engaged outside markets and economies and the ISPP offered a means through which Indians could obtain education and succeed in the encroaching Anglo environment.

The Kanab conference was not merely a superficial public relations stunt. While Mormons representing the church and government agencies outnumbered Indians and non-Mormons, church leaders took criticisms seriously and worked to resolve concerns. In response to Billison's concerns, the Indian Committee determined to submit an annual list of enrolled students to the tribe and also initiated an aggressive strategy to befriend tribal leaders.[71] Additionally, the committee recognized the need to better track the success of the program to use as evidence should future concerns arise. Future reports assessed students' medical status, educational accomplishments, cultural adaptation, and even happiness. In following years caseworkers took more copious notes on the children, in terms of both needs and accomplishments.[72]

The committee also expanded and intensified the clinic at the reception center to better serve Indian youths and tracked its success in identifying malnutrition, disease, and emotional stresses. Following the 1957 processing and placement of children, Dr. Hansen declared the clinic a success. He explained:

> At the clinic the children coming into the program for the first time are easily spotted—they are usually thin, malnutritioned and backward.... [I]n checking present health records with those of two or three years ago there is a great deal more physical health in those children who have been here one or more years. They have better looking teeth and have gained an average of 12 pounds and grown an average of one inch and emotionally are able to open up and communicate with others. The physical difference is quite significant.[73]

Bolstered by his comments, the committee determined to maintain and even improve the system in the following years. In 1958, the reception center moved from Richfield to Provo where the BYU director of student health assumed leadership of the medical clinic and the program could better take advantage of extensive church facilities, volunteers, and material resources. Hansen continued to offer support until 1961, but additional supplies and staff were drawn from the Primary Children's Hospital, the Utah Department of Health's Crippled Children Services, and the Intermountain Boarding School which provided free dental services.[74] Following that relocation, the Indian Committee also expanded the foster parent orientation from an informal greeting to a more thorough two-hour training touching on medical, cultural, and spiritual needs unique to the Indian children.[75]

The most significant consequence of the Kanab meeting related to age requirements. In an Indian Committee meeting in March 1958, President Spafford suggested moving the admission requirement to eight years old in order to eliminate the enrollment of as yet unbaptized children. With such a policy, no critics could have grounds to argue the program forced itself on non-Mormon youth, she explained. However, this also meant enrolling children who began schooling on the reservation and in inferior boarding schools and would likely begin their placement experience with an academic disadvantage to their classmates off the reservation. Spafford reiterated that six-year-olds "learn the language faster, are better adjusted in the homes, and keep pace with other students as they all begin in the same school standard." Kimball weighed in and pointed to Mr. Billison's Kanab conference comments about leaving the reservation for school and suggesting that he would understand the dilemma facing the ISPP, regardless of the committee's final decision. After some discussion Kimball concluded that the age of six would remain, at least for a few months as committee members considered the options. He hoped to meet with Navajo tribal chairman Paul Jones to discuss the matter. He concluded that "for the present, we can give special preference to the older children and not make a special effort to get six year olds." Two months later placement officials met again with Navajo representatives, including Billison and a Mr. Natoni. The Navajo spokesmen again expressed preference that only children eight years and above be permitted to participate in Placement. The following month the Indian Committee acquiesced to that request and generally limited enrollment to children aged eight or older who already received LDS baptism. They did allow for some exceptions, however. The committee believed that they needed to look at the individual circumstances of each child and make a decision based on "(1) Liquor in the home, (2) Poor or no schools available ... (3) Highly underprivileged, (4) Gross immorality, and (5) Peyote." The psychoactive plant constituted a central sacrament in the Native American church, which grew in popularity on the Navajo Reservation during the mid-twentieth century, despite the resistance of the Tribal Council who viewed the practice as corrosive to Navajo traditions. Navajo leadership and the LDS Church then shared similar objectives in curbing peyote use, alcohol abuse, poverty, and insufficient access to education. The Indian Committee determined that enrollment of any children under the age of eight would require an additional report citing one or more of the aforementioned threats as grounds for the child's inclusion.

Several weeks later the committee reaffirmed the new age requirement, but the ease of making exceptions proved problematic when far too many underage children who did not meet the committee's rules for exception enrolled in the following year. In September of that year, Kimball worried that so many enrolled children under eight years risked tribal and governmental interference. He complained, "We ought to be able to control our own program without getting told from other people what 'we can' or 'we can't' [do]." He concluded that "before anything like this happens again another year we had better lock the door and not bring any under eight unless they have our counsel and approval." This effectively raised the age to eight years and the committee hoped the policy would help calm some fears about cultural stress placed on young children taken from the reservation.[76] To further remedy such concerns, the committee also resolved to require that all students return home to the reservation each summer. The use of the program as a missionary tool constituted the final and most difficult issue to resolve. How could the program restrict enrollment to church members without encouraging its use as a missionary tool?[77] This final question would plague the growing program for the next several decades.

Following the Kanab meeting the steady growth of the program required more and more clinically trained caseworkers. In theory they visited reservations to interview prospective students and their parents, and then worked closely with those youth throughout the school year. This increasingly clinical context diminished the role of overeager missionaries and reduced the likelihood that the program would function as a missionary tool. In reality, however, missionaries often located and prepared potential enrollees for caseworkers to interview during their seasonal reservation recruiting excursions. Even with the elevated minimum age for enrollment after 1958, participation steadily rose from 68 in the 1954–1955 academic year to 365 in 1959–1960.[78] Kimball particularly pushed for its expansion, and frequently shared a vision of the future where thousands of Native Americans secured solid education and passed through the halls of Brigham Young University on their way to serving missions and assuming powerful leadership roles in an unmatched revitalization of Indian country.[79] Jensen recalled the apostle would frequently say, "Well, they're qualified. Let's take all who are qualified."[80] Kimball seemed to believe that anybody who expressed interest, and whose parents did not resist, was "qualified."

On the other end of the spectrum, the Indian Committee understood the need to methodically develop the Placement Program in a controlled environment to protect it from and organize a response to any criticisms. John Farr Larson, an informal but frequent committee member, expressed such concern about "uncontrolled growth" in 1958. Kimball replied, "We have thousands and thousands of people yet who need it, but we are being so fenced in by the technicalities and red tape that it will take years and years the way we are going." Elder Petersen offered some compromise and suggested that a couple of caseworkers could be added each year.[81] Other committee members similarly endorsed expansion at the rate of a caseworker or two each year, and that model won out.

The Indian Committee sought to employ a new wave of young men who were not only passionately connected to the church's work with Native Americans but also professionally trained in social work. During the late 1950s several new employees joined the Relief Society staff. In August 1957, the program hired Clarence Bishop to replace Rex Ashdown. Like many who followed, Bishop formerly served as a missionary in the Southwest Indian Mission and held strong convictions that the Lamanites constituted a special group that would rise up to latter-day glory. By the turn of the decade the Relief Society's ISPP staff included six caseworkers, one secretary, and a half-time administrative assistant, as well as legal and psychiatric consultants, all of whom eagerly anticipated a Lamanite resurgence and interpreted the ISPP as a means to that end.[82]

As the program grew, the committee remained concerned about unofficial placements independently coordinated by well-meaning Mormons but outside the protection of the formal program. Several such placements occurred in California and elsewhere during the late 1950s and early 1960s. Also, word of several more mass baptisms by overeager missionaries caused alarm among the committee members who worried about alienating their indigenous support base. This practice irritated Kimball who feared such behavior might endanger the program.[83] It was obvious that stronger central control was necessary to ensure the long-term viability of the ISPP.

With these and other initiatives, the program crossed several thresholds toward a more centrally organized structure during the late 1950s and early 1960s. It created the first manual of instruction that clearly outlined program expectations. In 1959, the program secured a tax exemption for foster parents hosting Indian children.[84] In January 1960, the ISPP initiated the first systematic and comprehensive canvassing of the Navajo Reservation to heighten awareness, evaluate parental motivations and child preparation, and ultimately increase enrollment. Again in 1961 and each year thereafter, caseworkers traveled throughout the reservation several times a year to visit current and potential students and their parents.[85] In 1964, the Relief Society organized the Placement Program as an independent organization and promoted caseworker Clare Bishop as the program's first director.[86] The growing bureaucracy paralleled increasing enrollments as the program attracted more Navajos and other Indians each year.

To boost enrollment the ISPP administrators reached out to Navajos through personal caseworker visits, but also by mass advertising at the Navajo Fair, full-time missionary proselytizing, and personal correspondence and visits with Navajo leaders.[87] Overtures by church leaders to Navajo officials received mixed responses. These efforts minimally began during the administration of Chairman Sam Ahkeah, but accelerated with great success under Chairman Paul Jones. Ahkeah served as Navajo chairman from 1946 until 1955. He joined Chee Dodge in the 1946 delegation that appealed to Washington, D.C., for greater educational opportunities and continued to advocate programs to that end, even leading the 1953 campaign for the Navajo Tribal Scholarship Program to fund post-secondary training and education. The ISPP emerged and remained fairly small during his tenure, and the greater point of interaction between Ahkeah and the LDS Church centered on the chairman's resistance to the church's efforts to secure land for chapels and to grant missionaries freedom to proselytize on the reservation. Southwest Indian Mission president Golden Buchanan (1951–1955) and other church leaders consciously worked to develop a relationship between the church and Navajo leaders. Apostles Spencer W. Kimball and Matthew Cowley joined President George Albert Smith in a visit to Window Rock in October 1945. The churchmen intended to speak at a meeting of Christian churches hosted by the tribal council and meet independently with tribal leaders, but the Navajo leadership refused to see them privately on that occasion. Smith and the apostles joined the conference and listened for several days as others voiced concerns about recent Mormon expansion into the reservation, among other topics. One participant suggested restricting Mormons from the reservation altogether. When granted the floor, Smith expressed the church's intent to "bless your people" but did not likely change many opinions at that conference or among Navajo leaders during Ahkeah's chairmanship.[88]

As Paul Jones succeeded Ahkeah in 1955, the ISPP gained enough momentum and enrollment to attract the chairman's attention. Jones enjoyed some formal education as a youth, and as a young adult completed high school. He also served in the European front during World War II and pursued business school training before returning to the reservation where he served as an interpreter and assistant to the tribal council. During his two terms as chairman he presided over the modernization of the tribe, in terms of resource management, infrastructure, education, and securing sovereign authority. Aided by tribal counsel Norman Littell, Jones rejuvenated economic and infrastructural development on the Navajo Reservation, erecting chapter houses, relief programs, and extensive public works projects. The two valued education as the conduit to a stronger Navajo Nation, and in Jones's 1955 inaugural address he explained, "We must be educated in order to be absorbed with the rest of the people of the United States.... Those of you who have been educated must tell your people of the benefits of education ... [because] it is the greatest hope that we have for our Navajo people." His 1959 inaugural address also highlighted education. He said, "We must extend help to the extent possible to those pioneering their way in the white man's world in the various states of the United States." In 1959 he asserted Navajo nationalism and development, calling for outside investment, better roads, community centers, work relief programs, and above all education as tools to pull the Navajo Nation into the twentieth century in terms of technology and industry. He envisioned "a Divine providence" and "the unfolding of unlimited opportunities for every young Navajo in search of education and advancement."[89] His goals neatly aligned with those of Kimball and other advocates of the ISPP.

Soon after Jones's inauguration, Relief Society Placement Program coordinator Margaret Keller arranged a private meeting in Window Rock and later reported the chairman was "warm and accepting."[90] Keller continued to reach out to Jones, attracting him and other tribal leaders to various functions. Jones committed to visit the reception center in the fall of 1958. The Indian Committee anxiously planned a luncheon and special performances for his visit; however, he withdrew and sent Sam Billison who continued to offer his approval. At the reception center Billison expressed particular appreciation for the program's effort to integrate Navajo children into the dominant white culture, though he remained concerned about the enrollment of young children, independent placements, and the legal adoptions carried out by white Mormons that occurred independent of the ISPP. Despite his concerns, the Indian Committee felt that Billison "is a very good friend of the program.... His attitude toward us is one of very great support, and believes he feels this is one of the best things that has happened to the Navajo people."[91]

To ensure they had the chairman's support, or at least toleration, the Placement Program administrators launched a letter-writing campaign. Dozens of letters from foster parents and Navajos arrived expressing their appreciation to Jones for permitting the program to operate, and recounted students' scholastic success, community relationships, and familial affection. Foster parents sent in letters continually expressing their love for the Navajo children they watched over, the healthy and successful nature of the children's experiences, and their appreciation to Jones for permitting them the opportunity. The Fox family was just one to participate in this campaign. In describing the Navajo boy living in their home, they wrote,

> When John first came to our home it was quite some time before he mingled freely with the neighborhood children. Now he is one of them and they all look forward to the day when he comes back in the fall.... His teachers have always reported him to be a fine boy. He is average in his class work, but always excels in the arts. We do extra "tutoring" in the home to help him in reading, arithmetic (times-tables, combinations, etc.). He is one of us in all ways. He has participated in programs in our church too. He has had one year in piano lessons and is studying again. Should he desire to learn an instrument later, that will be O.K. with us, but since he voluntarily wanted to play piano, we gave him lessons.[92]

Orville Gunther also wrote Jones about the Navajo girl that his family fostered. He focused on the benefits the girl received from her Mormon foster family. He wrote, "We have given her eye care, medical care, dental care, clothing; in short, everything just as we do for our own." He expressed his genuine love for the girl and noted that she had matured into a beautiful and intelligent girl who graduated junior high at the top of her class and earned a spot on the high school honor roll. But more than that, "She has learned to play the piano, to speak in public, to dance, and sing. She dresses well, and takes good care of her physical and moral self." Gunther even pledged to pay for her college, assuming her biological parents consented.[93] The campaign also included a few notes from natural parents who similarly attested to the success of the program. Hazel Lincoln wrote, "I hope that someday we will be able to see our own children, who are now getting their education through the Church of Jesus Christ of Latter-day Saints program, sit in many offices from which they will help their own people."[94]

The letter campaign caught Jones's attention, and he did attend the reception center in the fall of 1959, and then visited foster homes and previewed the program's Navajo Fair display. Jones concluded, "As far as we are concerned this program is excellent."[95] He explained that he preferred the nuclear families provided by Mormons to boarding school dormitories, and expressed his gratitude for the volunteers who took in children. His comments offered the explicit tribal approval that the Indian Committee had long sought. Keller recalled several other positive experiences with the chairman, and concluded that Jones was "very impressed" with the program.[96] Program administrators resolved that they would win tribal approval by exposing Indian leaders directly to the program and to those touched by it.

In 1963 Raymond Nakai assumed leadership of the Navajo tribe, and Indian Committee members again worried about the new chairman's support. Nakai shared his predecessor's value for education and the technological modernization of the reservation but also placed great emphasis on Navajo economic, political, and social sovereignty. In his 1963 inaugural address Nakai warned, "I will seek advice from our non-Indian consultants, but not take orders from them."[97] This was by no means a direct reference to the LDS Church; nevertheless, the Indian Committee worried about how the chairman might interpret the ISPP and cautiously monitored his and other Navajo leaders' attitudes.[98]

Nakai soon accepted invitations to visit placement students at a banquet held in his honor in April 1965.[99] Several months later he returned to Salt Lake with half a dozen other tribal officials.[100] They took note of welfare and educational facilities, and met with the BYU director of Indian Affairs as well as the university's Indian club, and watched a BYU Film Studio production that highlighted education as a means for Indians to achieve their potential. Church leaders felt positive about the tribe's feelings toward Mormons and the ISPP after the visit, and recalled that one member of Nakai's entourage commented, "If I were a boy, I'd want to take part in this program."[101] During the 1960s, the Indian Committee effectively neutralized government and tribal obstacles through an aggressive public relations campaign. Despite difficulties perpetuated by the church's entanglement of religion into outreach efforts, government bureaucrats, tribal officials, and the LDS Church all shared similar goals of self-empowerment through education. Navajo families and tribal leaders generally supported, or at least opted not to obstruct, the Placement Program.

The church continued to clear the path for its efforts on the Navajo Reservation but some resistance lingered. In July 1969, newly promoted ISPP executive director Clare Bishop reported from his recent visit to Window Rock where he met with several tribal and local church leaders, some of which overlapped. He learned that Councilman Frankie Howard and several community members opposed the Placement Program and moved the issue onto the tribal agenda. Bishop worked with tribal councilman John Brown, a Mormon who volunteered in the Southwest Indian Mission presidency, to prepare a response should the council take up discussion on the ISPP. The item never did surface and the ISPP continued without any Navajo tribal resistance. The church continued to reach out to the succeeding tribal chairman with success. In 1971, recently elected chairman Peter MacDonald attended an annual Lamanite youth conference in Salt Lake City where he spoke to attendees and even employed LDS language to refer to himself as a Lamanite.[102]

Without any serious tribal or governmental opposition, the Placement Program grew from several hundred students in the early 1960s to several thousand by the close of the decade. The ISPP expanded foster homes into Arizona and then other states and even Canada. Arizona opened in 1962 at the request of six stake presidents. With the support of Arizona State Public Welfare commissioner Fen Hildreth, the Relief Society extended its Utah licensures into Arizona under the premise of a semiautonomous nonprofit corporation called the Arizona Relief Society Social Services which followed the direction of a local board of directors (the six stake presidents) and an agency director who oversaw multiple caseworkers.[103] In reality, Kimball and the ISPP director (then Clare Bishop) closely managed the program from church headquarters in Salt Lake City.[104] Under their direction, Arizona's enrollment climbed steadily towards its climax in 1970.[105]

The success of Arizona encouraged Kimball to expand the Placement Program. As early as the fall of 1963 he directed the Calgary Stake presidency to solicit interest from local Indians. Kimball then invited Canadian stake presidents to Salt Lake City where he unveiled a plan to expand the ISSP into their cities using the same model as Arizona.[106] By August 1964 three voluntary social workers placed seven Native students from the Blood Reserve (Alberta), Carry-the-Kettle Reserve (Saskatchewan), and Vancouver Island (British Columbia) in Canadian Mormon foster homes. Also, as in Arizona, the program operated its own reception center and the agency grew steadily as it added new students and caseworkers each year.[107] In August of 1965, thirty-one busloads of Indian children arrived at reception centers in Arizona, Utah, Idaho, and Canada.[108]

Emboldened by these successes, Bishop unveiled an aggressive plan in November 1965 to radically expand the program over the next five years. According to the plan, in the fall of 1966 the ISPP would open two new Utah caseloads of approximately seventy-five students each: two in Utah, one in Arizona, three in Idaho (requiring an agency there), and one in Canada. The following year he intended to open one agency in Florida and another in Colorado. In 1968 the Los Angeles, California agency would open with four caseloads, and Oregon would follow the following year with two caseloads. Finally, in 1970, the program would open in Washington and Nevada, with two caseloads in the former and one in the latter.[109] Though not exactly as Bishop planned, the program continued its rapid expansion over the next few years. From 1967 through 1978, additional agencies opened in Oklahoma, Georgia, and Washington. Meanwhile existing agencies continued to add new caseloads each year.[110] Total enrollment soared through the close of the decade.

As the program expanded both geographically and in sheer enrollment, Bishop provided a valuable role in unifying the program as a whole.

TABLE 4.1. EXPANDING ENROLLMENT BY REGION, 1960–1971

SCHOOL YEAR	UTAH	ARIZONA	CANADA	IDAHO	TOTAL
1960–1961	418	-	-	-	418
1961–1962	423	-	-	-	423
1962–1963	460	54	-	-	514
1963–1964	498	72	-	-	570
1964–1965	809	162	7	-	978
1965–1966	978	221	48	103	1,350
1966–1967	1,000	293	93	183	1,569
1967–1968*	-	-	-	-	2,147
1968–1969*	-	-	-	-	3,132
1969–1970*	-	-	-	-	4,467
1970–1971*	-	-	-	-	4,997

*There is no record for the enrollment of each individual state during these years
Source: Indian Placement Program Files, 1970, Church Archives; Bishop, "Indian Placement," 95.

He created uniform enrollment standards and expectations, circulated forms, tracked student evaluations, and trained staff. He developed the program's first brochure in the spring of 1964 and printed a hundred thousand copies for circulation at Indian fairs and on various reservation trips and at public relations presentations.[111] During the 1960s the ISPP evolved from a local and informal program to an increasingly complex interstate bureaucracy with tiers of administrators, staff, and scores of caseworkers. Bishop's passion for Indians, and the unfailing support of Kimball, served to unify an otherwise segmented system.

In addition to changing the structure of the program, rapid expansion also drastically altered enrollment standards. Interested students had always outnumbered potential foster homes, but that discrepancy diminished during the 1960s. In the early part of the decade the ISPP rejected over half of its applicants, and generally accepted the strongest students who already demonstrated leadership qualities and religious devotion.[112] As the program opened in new states, a growing number of Indian children could enroll who otherwise might have been waitlisted for lack of sufficient foster homes in earlier years. Dale Tingey, president of the Southwest Indian Mission from 1969–1971, recalled that by his tenure the missionaries actively recruited "dysfunctional" families. "If it's a good family we didn't want to disrupt that," Tingey explained.[113] Longtime caseworker Dale Shumway estimated that by 1970 about one-quarter to one-third of the total enrolled students came from "troubled homes." Missionaries and caseworkers looked at young Navajos and other Indians struggling in poverty, a situation often accompanied by alcoholism and abuse, and focused on students they thought needed the Placement Program in order to succeed in life. Caseworkers gave little thought to the problems some youths brought to their foster families. Shumway lamented, "We were naïve about that in the beginning."[114] Caseworkers and missionaries eagerly enrolled as many as they could house and sometimes more.

The rapidly rising ISPP enrollment sent a clear signal to the Indian Committee and the church hierarchy; not only did the program appear a success, but its larger mission of redeeming the Lamanites appeared equally triumphant. The ISPP and other Indian programs operated by the church seemed to coalesce into one awe-inspiring system of recruitment and empowerment of Indians through spiritual and secular education. The church commenced an Indian Seminary program in 1949 at Intermountain Indian School in Brigham City, Utah. It offered religious instruction to Indians there and by 1971 serviced seventeen thousand Indian youths at boarding schools nationwide.[115] The church already offered seminary to all Mormon high school children, and Brigham City instructor Boyd K. Packer worried that a great many Indian children at boarding schools missed out on this opportunity to receive spiritual instruction. The church rapidly expanded the program to include hundreds of full-time missionaries across dozens of reservations. Missionaries visited parent homes and shared nonreligious instruction about communication, home life, and happiness, and offered to continue that instruction with their children at boarding schools. As Indian parents registered their children, the missionaries' Indian seminary classes grew. The lessons continued much as promised to their parents, but they also emphasized leadership, identity, and the divine role of the Lamanite.[116] Like the early ISPP, Indian Seminary relied on missionaries to recruit and teach many of the classes. Most participants were not LDS when they enrolled; however, the class worked as a missionary tool and many received baptism soon after classes began. A memo circulated in the Southwest Indian Mission explained, "Sign-ups ARE as good as baptisms, for in virtually all of the cases, un-baptized children usually are baptized in their first year of instruction, when they are of age." The memo explained how to sign up children so that the BIA would permit their participation in the program.[117]

Many graduates of Indian Seminary and the Placement Program later enrolled at Brigham Young University where yet another program operated to further instruct Native Americans from across the country. Indians nationwide also gathered in dozens of branches and wards.[118] Catawba Indians in South Carolina trace their earliest converts to the 1880s, and in 1952 the church dedicated a new chapel there and instituted Indian seminary classes. Indian baptisms during the 1950s and later paved the way for a flurry of branch organizations nationwide in the 1960s, including on: the Shoshone Duckwater Reservation in Nevada; Paiute Moapa Reservation in southeast Nevada; Umatilla Reservation in Pendleton, Oregon; Muckelshoot Reservation near Auburn, Washington; Lummi/Marrieta Reservation near Bellingham, Washington; and the Quillayute Reservation in Washington. Additionally, during this era the church initiated worship services at several boarding schools, including Haskell (Lawrence, Kansas), Chilocco (Chilocco, Oklahoma), Fort Sill (Lawton, Oklahoma), Riverside (Andarko, Oklahoma), and Cheyenne-Arapaho Indian School (Concho, Oklahoma). Again, the Navajo Reservation proved a particularly fertile recruiting ground. Church leaders organized the Central Navajo Branch in 1957, and over the next ten years additional branches operated in Polacca, Window Rock, Chinle, Ganado, Tuba City, Kayenta, Lukachukai/Round Rock, and Pinon. By the end of the decade still others opened in Sawmill, Many Farms, Perea, Crow Point, Toadlena, and Sheep Springs.[119] By 1965, the church boasted 141 Lamanite wards and branches, 437 Indian seminaries, and 150 outreach programs to Native communities via BYU research projects.[120] The excitement of all this apparent success is captured in the ISPP's 1968 theme, "The Day of the Lamanite Is Now."[121]

In addition to rapid growth among Native Americans, LDS Church programs and membership exploded abroad among others with indigenous ancestry. The church opened the work in South America in 1851, but maintained a limited presence until 1924 when Germans in Buenos Aires requested missionaries. Still, nonwhite membership in Central and South America remained almost nonexistent until the mid-twentieth century. The Pacific Isles demonstrated only slightly better growth. In 1962, scattered wards and branches united into Samoa's first stake, and six years later Tonga organized its first stake. By 1968 the church's Pacific Islands and Latin American Religious Education Program directed schools in Samoa, Tonga, New Zealand, and Tahiti, as well as in Mexico and Chile. By 1970 the church operated fifty-eight primary schools and another seven secondary schools for Lamanites.[122]

For many, the 1960s success among Pacific Islanders and Latin American peoples, as well as Indians, made the expansion of the Lamanite trope a logical reinterpretation. Some always interpreted Pacific Islanders and Latin Americans as Lamanites, but it is evident that during this era of international growth the church made efforts to solidify a broader definition of the term. The church's 1968 Lamanite Handbook overtly explained, "The Lamanite population of Latin America constitutes a sizable percentage of the total population of many countries," and went on to offer exact population percentages for Bolivia, Ecuador, and other countries to the south. In 1971 Kimball commented, "Lamanite includes all Indians and Indian mixtures, such as the Polynesians, the Guatemalans, the Peruvians, as well as the Sioux, the Apache, the Mohawk, the Navajo, and others." A 1972 *Ensign* article titled "What Is a Lamanite?" clarified the definition for the larger church population. Sociologist Armand Mauss argues that the 1950s and 1960s is the very point of transition during which "Old Lamanites," meaning Native Americans, were absorbed into a broader "New Lamanites" conception that included Native Americans, Latin Americans, and Polynesians. Mauss credits both the international growth and 1940s archaeological discoveries in South and Central America as the impetus for a broader definition. The Lamanite theme of the December 1975 *Ensign* clarified any lingering confusion as author after author employed a larger definition of Lamanite as they discussed the history and prophetic future of that people. For Kimball and the LDS members associated with Indian work, there seemed to be a flurry of energy concerning the Lamanite peoples.[123]

An *Ensign* article in 1971 reveals that Latin Americans did not always embrace the Lamanite term. Chilean Jamie Villalobos commented, "In my country we think of ourselves as Chilean members of the church and not as

Lamanite or non-Lamanite members. Our self-image has a national base, rather than an ethnic foundation; we do not think of ourselves as a benighted people." Marta Valdez from Peru agreed, but thought the message applied to the more rural "Indians" of Peru (and not the general population); Mexican and Guatemalan students more readily accepted Lamanite identity; Argentine and Uruguayan members also identified Lamanite with Indians but, the article explained, "we hardly ever see an Indian in the main part of Argentina and in Uruguay." The article's author, and ISPP administrator, Harold Brown concluded,

> Emphasis on the "chosen people" heritage of the Lamanites is fruitful where national leaders have been inspired to help dignify the Indian heritage, where tribal groups have retained a sense of ethnic dignity on their own part, and where Lamanites have had an opportunity to understand and respond to the message of the Book of Mormon; but where ethnic difference have hardened into class distinctions, the Lamanite question has to be handled with sensitivity on both sides.

Brown went on to clump "Indian and mestizo peoples (the mestizo being of both Gentile and Lamanite origins)" as "Lamanites."[124] By 1971, the church counted approximately 250,000 total Lamanites with 30,000 in Central America and 100,000 in the Pacific Isles. Twenty percent of the Tongan islands converted and attended in the three stakes organized there; another three stakes existed in Samoa; three more in Mexico City, as well as others in Guatemala, Peru, and New Zealand.[125]

The elaborate and interconnected Indian program advanced toward its enrollment peak in the early 1970s. Missionary success among Latin American and Pacific Island Lamanites experienced even greater success. To Kimball and other Mormons, it seemed the church was fulfilling the longstanding mandate to save the Lamanites. By 1971, some five hundred full-time missionaries worked among Indian peoples and 152 Indian branches and wards served some thirty-five thousand Indian members. The Placement Program fostered five thousand students, and Indian Seminary boasted fifteen thousand students.[126]

The dramatic growth of the LDS Church among Native Americans, Latin Americans, and Pacific Islanders seemed to reaffirm the theological message of the church. In a 1972 address to the Native American students at Brigham Young University, Kimball related the rapid growth of the church as a whole to Daniel's Old Testament prophesy of an unstoppable stone rolling forth. He echoed Brigham Young's comments about the readiness of the blood of Israel when Kimball observed that Lamanite people accept the gospel more readily than the non-Lamanites of Europe. To him, their conversion testified to their prophetic role. He concluded: "This is the day of the Lamanite, and they are receiving the gospel with great eagerness."[127] This notion of accepting a former identity allowed Mormons to overlook the obvious colonizing nature of the programs. The growth of the church among Native Americans, via the Southwest Indian Mission, Indian Seminary, and the Placement Program all seemed to reinforce the notion that, indeed, the Lamanites' day of redemption had arrived. During the 1960s the Placement Program's centralized control engaged government and tribal critics, and expanded to reach across new states and into Canada. The program itself seemed much as Daniel's boulder, rolling forward unimpeded.

Kimball surely took pleasure in the progress of the Indian Program, and of the Placement Program in particular. From its 1954 adoption as a formal church program, the ISPP steadily expanded its geographical presence and student enrollment. Thousands of Indian youths entered Mormon homes each year and attended public schools. The ISPP's growth is directly connected to its incorporation as an official church program. This maneuver brought licensure and standardization from the social-services-oriented Relief Society. A bureaucratic system emerged with professional caseworkers at the bottom who reported through a chain of agency directors, state boards of directors, and a program supervisor; at the head, the Indian Committee balanced growth with oversight. This administrative system oversaw growth and effectively dealt with outside threats to the program's continuation. As an officially sanctioned program, it coordinated efforts to combat resistance and expanded both its geographical scope and student enrollment.

From 1947 to 1953, the Placement Program evolved from an informal and unofficial process into a well-organized church institution. It constantly expanded and attracted students for a variety of reasons, though largely as a means to acquire education. Missionaries assumed roles as recruiters, and as the church extended official recognition the ISPP developed a centralized structure and standardized management under Kimball and the Indian Committee. Kimball intimately directed the program during these early decades and encouraged its constant growth. Despite some concerns from Native people and BIA officials, under Kimball's leadership the ISPP continued to grow until it emerged as the flagship institution within the church's expanding Indian programs.

By the 1960s, the ISPP had become the bellwether of the church's Indian policy. En route to this status the ISPP faced several challenges which began almost immediately after its incorporation into the LDS Church. As the Indian Committee formed a structured organization to manage the ISPP and to handle the complaints against it, program officials met with tribal and government representatives to resolve concerns and expand the program. As a consequence of growth and central planning, the ISPP evolved over the first two decades of official operation from a local and informal program to a systematic, bureaucratized, and legally recognized international program with rapidly expanding participation. By the 1971–1972 school year, enrollments approached five thousand. At this same time, other LDS efforts to assist Indians likewise reached their full stride. The day of the Lamanite, many concluded, had finally arrived.

5

THE PLACEMENT EXPERIENCE

Entering Mormon Homes and Communities

I remember that first night I woke up ... and I walked outside to the sound of lawnmowers and airplanes and that was really weird for me. But I think one of the first things I noticed was that everything was kind of green. The grass was green, the hillside was green. I kind of thought it was paradise-ish. ... And the streets, paved streets, sidewalks, kids playing outside, there were motorcycles, boats I saw. ... I just sat there and said, "Wow; this is totally different from the reservation."

—Orlando Tsosie, Navajo, 1999

Spencer W. Kimball captured the Latter-day Saints' impetus to share the gospel with Indians in 1957 when he counseled a fellow Mormon with the simple words, "We have a definite responsibility to the Lamanites." Kimball explained that Christ's second coming simply could not occur until Mormons fulfilled that obligation.[1] This predisposition to reach out to that population allowed the Indian Student Placement Program to rapidly expand into white Mormon homes. As the ISPP grew in both enrollment and geographic scope, it touched the lives of thousands of people, both Native students and white church members. Students enrolled on their reservation and then traveled by night to volunteer-staffed reception centers where program officials processed the youth. Administrators assigned each child to a Mormon foster family and ushered them into a new world of experiences. Strange sounds and smells, new technology, and rigid schedules stood out to many youth as they assessed the peculiar new environment. Students also took note of what seemed an overly dense population and consequent lack of privacy and freedom in the new world. For the most part, foster parents treated children with kindness but ultimately expected them to adjust to a white, middle-class American society.

Children participated in a variety of activities intended to instill middle-class virtues of hard work and self-reliance, both of which Indians seemed to utterly lack in the eyes of Mormons who sought to redeem a fallen people. As with their own biological children, Mormon foster parents assigned Indian children household chores, encouraged them to excel in school and participate in extracurricular activities such as clubs and athletics, and also expected regular church attendance on Sunday and throughout the week, as well as midweek youth activities. Indian youth participated in Boy Scouts, performed secular and spiritual service projects, and completed structured self-advancement activities to earn religious awards and advancement. Academic achievement only constituted part of the program driven by Mormons' self-perceived responsibility to save these Lamanites. By the close of the school year, Indian foster children experienced far more than they or their biological parents anticipated.

Each fall Indians entered a new cultural terrain that began with awkward moments which for some persisted all year. Some foster families found the stress of another child difficult, regardless of race, and foster siblings played out rivalries that are typical to most families. Schoolchildren identified Indians as "others," and responses varied from full inclusion to outright rejection. More often than not, Indian children seemed to fit in; however, they remained keenly aware of the cultural differences they saw.

Student experiences clearly illustrate the intense colonizing pressures of acculturation that weighed on Indian youth in foster homes. These children gathered at departure points on the reservation, rode buses through the night to reception centers, and found themselves assigned to new foreign families. The youth were exposed to a variety of mainstream American values and practices, as well as Mormon theological notions of redemption through self-discipline. As former placement students look back on those experiences they draw a variety of conclusions, ranging from a sense of cultural loss to one of empowerment. Many embrace the "two worlds" discourse common among Native people who left traditional homes for boarding schools or other nontraditional experiences. Ultimately, the Placement Program provided these children the educational and cross-cultural experience it promised but did so with far deeper impact than expected.

Upon learning about the Placement Program and determining to enroll, each student followed a fairly standardized admission process that remained constant over the course of the program. Those who were not already baptized members of the LDS Church obtained that ordinance from missionaries, who also provided much of the clerical support for enrollees. Missionaries and caseworkers usually visited the home of applicants and spoke with the children's parents. During such visits, church representatives informed parents that their children would be placed in a distant home and available only through letters, phone calls, and occasional visits cleared in advance through the foster family. This voluntary abdication of parental responsibilities may seem startling, but such was common for Navajos among whom boarding schools had long familiarized the concept of child removal.[2]

Caseworkers toured the reservations each June and July. They assessed the social and spiritual capacity of prospective students as well as the interest level of Indian children and their biological parents. As a rule, participation required the approval of both the child and parent, though one often weighed on the other to acquiesce if both were not initially in agreement.[3] Caseworkers also met with local bishops and branch presidents (usually white men drawn from local traders, government officials, or towns just off the reservation) to gather information on applicants and identify additional potential students.[4]

The 1968 ISPP *Natural Parent Guide* outlined the program expectations, and it is likely that caseworkers took copies of it during their summer visits to the reservations. It clearly explained that "the object of the Program is to make possible for Latter-day Saint Indian children educational, spiritual, social and cultural opportunities." The manual stated that eligible children must be eight years old, in good physical health, demonstrate average or better academic ability, foster a desire to participate, and be "comparatively free from emotional disturbances." It also explained that while on Placement, students would share in family responsibilities and abide by church standards, both during the school year and when living on the reservation during the summer months. Caseworkers discouraged long-distance phone calls and family visits during the first year because "it increases homesickness for young children." Nevertheless, students were encouraged to maintain regular communication with natural parents through "letters, pictures, cards, or other communication."[5] Once caseworkers fully disclosed the program and secured parental signatures releasing youth, they took photographs of the children and submitted the application to offices in Salt Lake City.[6]

After a few weeks, students and parents received notification of acceptance, and they began to prepare for their stay in a foreign land with new and different people. Navajo parents often solicited a medicine man to offer a blessingway so that students could enjoy protection and balanced health while submerged in the foreign world.[7] On the day of departure, families gathered in central locations such as chapels and shopping centers where charter buses transported children off the reservation. Excitement and hope combined with tears of love and sadness as parents tenderly bade farewell to their children. Lenora Tsosie, Navajo, joined Placement in 1980, as she began high school. She recalled the difficulty of that departure:

> And then it finally hit. I remember giving my natural parents a big hug and not wanting to let them go. To my surprise, my parents were emotionally strong, very supportive, and offered me words of encouragement. While I was still hugging my mother, I looked around the Griswold's parking lot and saw the other students' mothers and grandmothers emotionally crying until I saw my classmates... shaking their natural parents' hands, saying their goodbyes to them, and got into the Greyhound bus.[8]

Former participant George Lee remembered a similar experience several decades earlier, "Many Indian families had gathered together to see their children off to Utah. I thought I was coming to a funeral. The parents, especially the mothers, were weeping and trying to find a way to say good-bye as their beloved children boarded the bus."[9]

Chaperones and bus drivers loaded luggage in the undercarriage, and one by one each child stepped onto the bus. Each carried a small bag and sometimes a pillow.[10] Chaperones checked off names as students entered and then conducted a final count once the doors closed. Some students remember the departure as a time of excitement. They opened windows on the bus and waved to their families. Children who did not go on placement ran behind the bus cheering their siblings.[11]

Others remember a more somber experience. These strove to hold back tears of sadness and fear as the buses pressed on through the night. One recalled, "I cried every time when I got in my seat, and, thankfully, all the lights were off, so I just sat there."[12] In his autobiography George Lee vividly recalled the sounds of students crying as the bus departed:

> As the engine wound into a roar, all outside seemed silent. The waving people, parked pickup trucks, and buckboards slid past the window where I sat. I gripped the seat as my body braced itself.... There was no turning back now. Through the unspeakable darkness of the August evening, the bus drive from Shiprock to Cortez proceeded more like a funeral dirge than anything else. The sobbing children and their sniffling noses made a fog inside the bus. The windows were clouded up. All the whimpering produced more of the same. It seemed that the sobs echoed by a circular route according to seat pattern. With each unintentional outburst, a surge of emotion filled the person either in the seat ahead or behind, depending on who was charged and ready. The sobbing movement was similar to an oval-shaped course set with upended dominoes. All it took was one to fall and one to keep up the momentum.[13]

Students typically fell asleep as the buses drove through the night. One can only speculate on the dreams they had as they left the world they knew behind and anticipated a strange new life.

In the morning students awoke to daylight streaming through the windows. Chatter and excitement gradually dominated the bus. The students, most of whom had made the trip before, typically played card games like Crazy Eights, Old Maid, and Speed. Some listened to music on eight-track tapes, while others walked up and down the aisle to socialize with different groups. Younger children played with crossword puzzles, mazes, Hang Man, Tic Tac Toe, coloring books, and other activities. Lenora Tsosie recalled that the bus driver and chauffeurs gave children quite a bit of freedom.[14] Still, some students remained more withdrawn, and sometimes the older youths

comforted younger children. The children all shared stories and expectations as they made new acquaintances. The bus provided a transitioning
time as students prepared to enter the nonreservation world. Within this
colonizing environment students found their own ways to cope with and
prepare for the dramatic cultural shift ahead.

Beginning about six in the morning, buses arrived in waves at LDS
chapels that Placement officials and local members converted into temporary reception centers. George Lee recalled that when he was on the Placement Program, the bus stopped in a Utah church parking lot and men in
white dress shirts busily unloaded the luggage. The energy, industry, and
precision with which those men promptly emptied the undercarriage and
laid out the luggage reminded Lee of a colony of ants. One man, Miles Jensen, welcomed the group. He told the children not to fear the doctors who
would examine them and promised everyone a hot breakfast. He concluded,
"Don't worry about what to do; we've got plenty of nice people here to show
you."[15] The children then departed the bus and lined up to enter the building.

As students walked into the church, volunteers greeted them at a small
table full of name tags. Then, the new arrivals entered the large cultural hall
where white Mormon women served them breakfast. The smell of hot food
and the general warmth of the fervent volunteers seemed to calm many of
the students. Children sat down at tables and shared in eggs, toast, cereal,
and milk.[16]

Following breakfast, however, students had to face the medical clinic.
Volunteers divided boys and girls into separate parts of the building. They
picked through children's hair for lice, bathed and shampooed them, and
brushed each child's teeth. Sometimes volunteers also dispensed haircuts.
One student traumatically recalled that "we had to be bathed and printed,
so to speak.... I felt like I was being tagged and printed and branded and
it wasn't a good experience. And they looked through your hair."[17] Lee also
remembered the anxiety of these medical exams:

> The rumor of shots traveled rapidly among the children. We grew
> very silent as we watched the first few victims leave to be fixed up by
> some Anglo doctor.... Once out in the hall, we were seated in folding
> chairs by a small room. And there we sat for what seemed like eter-
> nity. I listened for any wails of torment to warn of needlework in
> progress. When I didn't hear anything, it was almost worse than the

wails would have been....My mind fidgeted as I sat upon the hard seat of the folding chair next to Roger. My eyes followed everything, but my head never moved. Up and down the hall, volunteers were busily doing something—just what I did not know.[18]

A volunteer nurse approached the boys and invited them in to a doctor whose friendly demeanor surprised the youths.

Medical volunteers conducted x-rays and inspected the children's hearts, eyes, skin, ears, and teeth. Many children cried when nurses poked and prodded, took blood samples, and administered immunizations. The medical staff documented the status and health of the children and recommended appropriate action, which varied from parental monitoring to at times hospitalizations.[19]

Though terrifying to some of the children, these evaluations ultimately proved a success by medical standards. Dr. Robert Hansen provided oversight during the program's earliest years. In 1957, he reported widespread malnutrition, and the clinic discovered that 136 of the 289 total students required immediate dental care. Eleven possibly suffered from heart disease; two had untreated ear infections; two suffered severe hernias; five had scoliosis; and eight possibly required surgery for genital gland problems. The Children's Primary Hospital in Salt Lake City took in those who needed further attention, and all cases were resolved as a result of the clinic.[20] In later years as more Navajos enjoyed access to medical services, it is likely that the clinic did not find as many undiagnosed and serious medical conditions but no records exist that record that change.

After the medical evaluations, students returned to the cultural hall for lunch and activities designed to keep their attention as caseworkers singled out individual students and paired them with their respective foster families.[21] Just as students went through their own orientation, foster parents simultaneously gathered in large meetings where caseworkers and program directors introduced the program, explained the divine role of Indians, and provided a series of pep talks and training sessions.[22]

At one such orientation in Phoenix, Arizona, ISPP director Clarence Bishop complimented parents for their dedication and warned that the job would be difficult. He instructed them to invest time in teaching, disciplining, and nurturing their foster children. He also stressed that the program's function went beyond baby-sitting and discouraged passive parenting.

He explained that the ISPP existed to provide education and instill leadership qualities.[23] Parents should treat foster children as their own and help them to become successful leaders of tomorrow. Bishop reminded parents of the resources available to help them in this task, including caseworkers, medical staff, a program psychiatrist, priesthood leaders, and Sunday school teachers.

Bishop concluded with an explanation about what parents might expect from students and outlined a typical "cycle of adjustment." He called the first four to six weeks "the honeymoon," during which all participants expressed great consideration for each other. Thereafter, Bishop explained that the children and parents likely would begin to test each other's limits, which would often lead to disciplinary action on behalf of the parents. However, he assured the families that this usually was followed by a "leveling off" that lasted until the end of the school year. Bishop closed by sharing his conviction about the truthfulness of the gospel, the inspired direction of the LDS Church Indian Committee, and the program itself, noting that "this program is a product of divine revelation."[24]

After the orientation meeting, caseworkers directed parents into small rooms throughout the church and matched them with children who nervously waited in the cultural hall. As students gradually vacated the large room, those remaining grew increasingly anxious. One student remembered that as they called students' names, the youth "left the room and you never came back!" She continued:

> I was nine years old, sitting there. I didn't know anybody but my aunt and now that she left she didn't come back, and it was just really scared [sic] and I was about to cry and I'm looking around to see if I knew anybody else, and you know I didn't know anyone! And finally they called my name. And I went out into the room where my foster parents were and I met them and they were really nice.[25]

Lee also commented that "many just sat there, refusing to move until those whose names had not been called persuaded them to go. Others cried uncontrollably."[26]

One by one, caseworkers introduced students to the foster parents in private rooms. For those returning to familiar families the stress was markedly lower, but they too had been through this first introduction process.

Even still, some returning children received assignments with new families because their previous foster home withdrew from the program or requested a different child. Ronald Singer, Navajo, remembered the experience of meeting his foster parents:

> They called my name, and I went forward. There was this big tall guy. He was the father. I got introduced to him and then the rest of the family. As soon as I was introduced, I turned and ran into the restroom because I was so scared. I knew that was where I wanted to be and that's where I should be. On the other hand I was really scared. Then I came back out, and they motioned me over. The caseworker took me to a little room. The mother and father were there, and they talked to me. I talked to them and signed some papers. The older boy of theirs and I went and got my suitcase. Off we went.[27]

Such was the start of these new and different relationships. Caseworkers made the introductions and sent the new families on their way.

Foster parents and Placement caseworkers tried to smooth the children's transition into their white foster homes. Placement officials also tried to place Indian children with families that would best resemble their home environment or interests. Caseworkers worked to pair girls with homes that had girls, and boys with families of boys, and tried to match child and foster family interests. Director Clare Bishop explained, "If they liked horses we would try to put them in the country."[28] Still, the shock of a new family and immersion in a new culture initially spawned discomfort for most. Many children remembered that their foster families tried to soften the chaotic mixture of homesickness and outright fear that accompanied Placement; more than one stopped for ice cream during the drive home.

As students arrived at their foster homes and engaged in the new world around them, they noticed significant differences between life on the reservation and that embraced by their foster family and mainstream American society. On first look they quickly observed exterior contrasts like the geographic terrain and appearance of the people. Rose Denette Sohsy recalled:

> We were on the freeways, and I just remember seeing all these bridges that crossed over, under. And seeing it, it was like, how do you people know which way they're going? How can you tell? And I felt like I

was entering another world...where people seem to be hurrying everywhere.[29]

Another girl commented on the difference between herself and her hosts. She said that "they all had freckles, and I didn't have freckles. My hair was pure black and it was below my bottom.... [T]hey all had light brown hair."[30] Another foster daughter made similar observations, and her new mother took measures to resolve the disparity. Unaware of Navajo adoration of long hair, the well-intended foster mother took the child to a salon and had the waist-long hair cut and permed.[31] Still, physical appearances only represented the first of many cultural differences that stood out to students. Others included technology; the abundance and use of food; privacy and personal space; the emphasis on numbers, schedules, and the rigidity they promoted; and generally the texture of a place so different from their own.

Technological innovations rarely seen on the reservation made an impression on many children, especially those with limited urban or boarding school experiences. George Lee related the kitchen to a visit to Disneyland. He said, "All the appliances—stove, refrigerator, toaster, and electric mixer—were new and strange. As we turned from room to room I was overwhelmed at the hugeness of all I saw. Furniture was everywhere."[32] He was even more enamored by the television—a new technology for most Placement students. One foster parent shared the following story about their student's encounter with Western technology:

> Light switches were a positive delight to David. He would flip them several times when entering or leaving a room, smiling at either their magic or with the hope that he could catch them asleep. He actually bolted from his chair the first time he heard the telephone ring at suppertime.... David said not a word but fixed the phone to his ear and with rapt attention would have left it there had not the dial tone alerted us that the monologue was over.[33]

Additionally, the flowing water, electricity, and household appliances engendered a degree of sanitation unfamiliar to many of the children. In the early years, many came from Navajo hogans on the reservation where a clean home simply meant that large debris was removed from the dirt floor.

These new technologies caused a complete redefinition of the word clean, as they came to use washing machines, vacuums, and showers.

The use of food constituted another oddity regularly identified by students. More than anything the quantity available astonished students. Former student Maybell Begay, Navajo, later recalled:

> A strange thing I noticed about the Cox family right off was how much and how often they would eat. It was different to see a family eat three big meals every day. Where did they get all that food? Don't get me wrong; I loved it. But at first I thought it wouldn't last, and I was tempted to take some food and put it in my bedroom drawer, but my foster brother David, who was always helpful, told me not to.[34]

In addition to the unexpected quantity, students noticed the behavior surrounding food also differed from home. George Lee commented that his foster family seemed insistent on speaking to each other at the dinner table. Another student scoffed at the gluttonous monthly meal that followed the LDS practice of fasting on the first Sunday of each month.[35]

Another cultural difference Indian students experienced stemmed from changes in the land. These students found the urban geography noticeably different and absent the familiar and iconic land formations. Distinct topographical structures on the reservations served to ground their identity and deeply impacted their worldview as young children. Anthropologist Keith Basso has argued that constructions of place have far-reaching cultural ramifications that range from wisdom and morality to tact and discourse.[36] Navajos typically believed that "the whole land is sacred," which means the terrain and the land play an important role in their culture. Particular topographical formations communicate stories and lessons that instill heritage and behavioral norms.[37] For example, the stories surrounding the Navajos' Spider Rock, an 1,800-foot rock spire in Arizona, enable a geological formation to reach beyond the physical and into the cultural. It evokes the legends of Spider Woman, the sacred origins of Navajo weaving, and the generous hand of that deity in the crafting of society. The absence of these important, grounding formations in this new environment did not simply remove interesting topography, but distanced cultural markers that once anchored identity.

Beyond the absence of geocultural markers, foster communities also restricted students' privacy and space. On the reservation many Navajo children herded sheep and chased horses across the expansive range, surveying the terrain with little parental monitoring from sunrise to sunset. Foster homes and communities offered far less freedom. George Lee remembered:

> There were new territorial restrictions. Back home we had all kinds of space in which to roam, play, and herd sheep. All of a sudden, I found myself in a home with houses on all sides. There was not much space, and I felt crowded in. My new home was fenced. I had to get used to a small play area.[38]

Ironically, while urbanity served to constrict students' mobility, many enjoyed access to larger personal space, such as a bedroom of their own. This new space was very different and often seemed empty to children accustomed to the close physical proximity that characterized the small family homes on the reservation. In the early weeks, many homesick students retreated into those lonely places to escape the foreign culture that surrounded them.[39]

Heightened parental and community monitoring also emerged as a point of frustration for some students. Crowded spaces led to more watchful eyes, many with high expectations of a genuine Indian undergoing spiritual and social redemption. Students frequently voiced concerns that they had lost their independence. A former student commented, "You couldn't do anything without going out the door and telling your foster parents."[40] Another explained, "In the Mormon home, it was more structured. You know, you went out, you came back at a certain time, you had curfews, you know, you had to tell where you were going."[41] Many later reported the environment and parenting as "strict."[42] In Logan Utah, Navajo Rosie Charley also observed that her foster parents asserted tighter control than her natural parents. She said, "Whenever I wanted to go anywhere with a friend I had to go through the ordeal of questioning, such as, 'Where are you going?,' 'Who are you going with?,' 'What are you going to be doing?,' and 'When will you be home?' It wasn't worth going through!"[43]

In addition to crowded spaces and watchful eyes, students also had to adjust to an unfamiliar rigidity affixed to time and a strange veneration of appointments and schedules, just as their boarding school counterparts. One youth explained:

> One of my biggest adjustments was getting used to time schedules. The Indian way of life really did not have much structure. We were not used to planning, meetings, and appointments, and time was not broken into minutes and hours, eight hours a day, or forty-hour weeks. We lived by the sun: when it was up, we were up. Also, we were concerned about surviving today and not worried about setting goals for the next day or the future. What we would find to eat each day was of primary concern. Now I had to learn to live by a schedule.[44]

Others voiced similar concerns over their hosts' fixation on schedules and numeric exactness. When foster parents asked Maybell Begay her birth date and grade, she thought, "Why do you whites have this big thing about numbers, and why do you have to be so exact with everything?"[45] Latricia Charley commented, "It was very different because my [foster] family was very structured and organized, everything was planned in advance."[46] In time, students grew accustomed to scheduled meals and meetings.

Upon arriving at their various foster locations, which ranged from urban communities to rural farms, students saw and felt the foreignness of the terrain and new cultural directives. One former student explained:

> The first thing I noticed was the smell. Everything smelled different. I mean, I miss the cedar of the reservation, the sage and the rain and the smell of my grandfather doing his ceremonies and so forth. And in the white man's world, it was—everything was—it smelled like plastic. It smelled like metal.[47]

Another commented that the sounds and smells of fresh-cut grass and motor vehicles startled him on that first morning in suburbia.[48] Even when Latricia Charley entered Placement in 1991, well after much of the western world had penetrated the Navajo Reservation, she still noticed significant differences between the reservation and the city. She identified the odd sensation of traveling on pavement.[49] Sidewalks constricted and directed foot traffic and inherently valued particular destinations. The precise cultural ramifications of the physical environment are speculative at best; however, students certainly recognized the new environment as different. These sounds, smells, and sights reinforced a different set of culturally specific values based on Western ideals that jolted Indian children from their past and besieged their senses with a new reality. A new and unfamiliar land— its appearance and feel and smells—facilitated a physical and cultural separation from the geographically informed reservation cultures and prepared students to create new cultural associations in the strange new world.

If Anglo-American society seemed awkward, the unique characteristics of the Mormon subculture surely raised an eyebrow. Mormon foster homes constituted an environment that blended mainstream Western society with uniquely LDS attitudes, particularly in relation to American Indians. The Book of Mormon traces the collapse of the righteous Nephite nation at the hands of the wicked Lamanites—"a dark and loathsome, and a filthy people, full of idleness and all manner of abominations."[50] It conflates religious, social, economic, and biological characteristics within a polarized paradigm of righteous and evil, industrious and idle, white and dark.[51] Indian Committee executive secretary Dean Larsen explained that "so began the nation of Lamanites, children of folly and iniquity." He continued, "While the Nephites were industrious and skilled in all manner of building, commerce, and learning, the Lamanites 'did become an idle people, full of mischief and subtlety, and did seek in the wilderness for beasts of prey.'"[52] Until 2009 the introduction of the Book of Mormon clearly identified modern Native Americans as the "principle" descendants of those corrupt and fallen civilizations. Consequently, Mormons historically interpreted Native cultures and practices as invalid—an apostate residue of a formerly genuine God-inspired society.[53]

In this theologically defined reality, skin color took on great significance as an indicator of righteousness. Wicked Lamanites exhibited the "curse" wherein "the Lord did cause a skin of blackness to come upon them."[54] The Book of Mormon further explains that "skins of the Lamanites were dark, according to the mark which was set upon their fathers...because of their transgression and their rebellion."[55] During the late twentieth century the church downplayed the overt link between skin tone and righteousness.[56] Nevertheless, Rose Denette Sohsy, Navajo, recounted, "They used to call us Lamanites. But because we didn't listen to God, we were cursed then. We came out with dark skins and black hair."[57]

Regardless of this abysmal status, Mormons believed that Lamanites could overcome this stigma through industrious and moral behavior. The Book of Mormon offers several examples where "scales of darkness" fell from the penitent wicked.[58] Many Latter-day Saints believed the transition from dark and sinful to white and pure occurred in gradations that paralleled perceived degrees of Western civility, and that Lamanites could become as spiritually, culturally, and biologically white as their Nephite kin. Like other Americans who attributed indicators of "civilization" to a lost Welsh colony or other mysterious European origins, early Mormons also associated industry, sedentary dwelling, and lighter skin tones among the Pueblo Indians as a sign of royal Israelite lineage.[59] Mormons continued to associate skin color with culture and righteousness into the late twentieth century. They believed that proper behavior could lead to physical transformations of skin tone, and many expected such of their American Indian foster children. In 1979, a science professor at Brigham Young University voiced his frustrations about that popular folk belief in an interview with the *Los Angeles Times*, "It's a problem we ignore and have very little occasion to address."[60] Soon after, the church edited the oft-cited passages in the Book of Mormon that anticipated their restoration to a "white and delightsome" people; thereafter it read "pure and delightsome."[61] The 1978 repeal of priesthood restrictions on African American Mormons also served to erode the association between skin tone and morality. Nevertheless, such ideas certainly affected the preconceptions, interactions, and relationships between the white foster families and the Native children.

When Placement students began to join white families and adhere to Mormon practices, many Latter-day Saints anticipated biological changes to occur as well. Relief Society president Belle Spafford remarked, "After a few years, [they] look as if they were more white than Indian."[62] At the 1960 General Conference of the LDS Church, Spencer W. Kimball explained that "the children in the home Placement Program in Utah are often lighter than their brothers and sisters in the hogans on the reservations," and he showed photographs to verify his observation.[63] Kimball also related the following story:

At one meeting a father and mother and their sixteen-year-old daughter were present, the little member girl—sixteen—sitting between the dark father and mother, and it was evident she was several shades lighter than her parents—on the same reservation, in the same hogan, subject to the same sun and wind and weather. There was the doctor in a Utah city who for two years had an Indian boy in his home who stated that he was some shades lighter than the younger brother just coming into the program from the reservation. These young members of the church are changing to whiteness and to delightsomeness.[64]

Skin tone thus indicated imagined degrees of spiritual and cultural evolution; dark skin suggested a work in progress. At least one former student confided that it always bothered him that Mormons expected his skin would turn white.[65]

In addition to associating skin tone with morality and civilization, the Book of Mormon also prophetically anticipates the last days when the Lamanites would return to Christ's true church—the LDS Church—and become redeemed. Just as in the eighteenth century, nineteenth-century Mormons believed redemption involved the adoption of Western culture. In a 1978 interview, Kimball reiterated this perception of Western culture as a redemptive mechanism:

> When you go down on the reservation and see these hundreds of thousands of Indians living in the dirt and without culture or refinement of any kind, you can hardly believe it. Then you see these [Placement] boys and girls playing the flute, the piano. All these things bring about a normal culture.[66]

Just as the church provided spiritual scaffolding whereby sinners might self-correct, LDS families anxiously provided cultural support whereby the uncivilized Indians could pattern their life on Western civility. Foster parents took upon themselves the responsibility to raise up and develop Lamanite youths so that the Native children could recognize their prophetic purpose. One student commented, "People had a lot of hopes that I would be what they wanted me to be. They wanted me to be their—the way I see it, kind of like their savior, to be an example to them."[67] Mr. and Mrs. Bud Gulleckson of Calgary shared this very motivation that drew them to become foster parents:

The Indian Placement Program of the Church of Jesus Christ of Latter-day Saints is truly inspired. By taking these sweet, unspoiled children into our homes, we are able to change their way of life and to teach them cleanliness, nutrition and good health rules, in addition to the principles of the gospel. It is our hope that they will grow up to be leaders among their people.... Given the opportunity, our Lamanite brethren will live up to their proud heritage and fulfill the prophecy that they will be gathered unto Israel.[68]

Foster parents imagined a pure, perhaps even equal child of God, faulted only by cultural shortcomings and spiritual ignorance. Another foster parent shared her motivations with her former Placement child, but only years after he graduated and left the home. The former student remembered his foster mother's words:

Don't you realize that we brought you into our home so that you could learn a better way of life? And don't you know that we brought you into our home so that you could learn the gospel? And don't you know that these are the things that you are supposed to teach your people? We taught you this, and now it's up to you to teach your people.[69]

By taking in foster Indian children, Mormon families also could help fulfill their own doctrinal expectations regarding the latter-day resurgence of Native Americans. Instilling Western culture and Mormon theology constituted the first step in that direction. The ISPP and students themselves became powerful symbols to validate the Mormon worldview.

Because Mormons so closely bound rearing Indians with theological expectations, the ISPP recruited the most devout Latter-day Saints to serve as foster parents. Indeed, the program leaders actively sought the participation of ecclesiastic leaders whose previous church service clearly indicated strong support for the church and its doctrines, as well as professionals and other icons of productive Western society. Kimball affirmed, "There are stake presidents, bishops, mayors, editors, doctors, farmers—the finest people in the communities of Utah and the world."[70] Program policies stipulated that parental applicants had to be active in the church; observe the Word of Wisdom prohibiting alcohol, tobacco, and other chemicals; demonstrate a stable marriage; maintain good health; and possess a "desire to assist an Indian child."[71] In 1978, an LDS Church press office official characterized the Placement participants as "card-carrying Mormons, nonsmoking, nondrinking and churchgoing."[72]

Caseworkers located potential parents through local bishops and conducted a home study to secure legal foster care candidacy in the eyes of the state. One extensive survey found that foster parents most often joined the program in response to a request from a church leader. The second leading motivation identified by parents was "a love for Lamanites."[73] Caseworkers regularly sought out new foster parents during the 1950s, 1960s, and 1970s because the program grew so rapidly and so many parents quit after their foster child graduated, or sooner.[74] In 1963, Clarence Bishop reported that one-third of foster parents simply dropped out, and that number likely escalated in later years as rising enrollment drew in a wider segment of youths, many of whom clashed with foster families.[75]

In many ways these Mormon foster families seemed like many other mid- and late-twentieth-century American nuclear family households. Married couples argued over common issues (e.g., time, money, children, sex) and exhibited comparable quality of life. Still, some variations separated Mormons from other Americans. One survey conducted in the late twentieth century indicated that Mormons experienced slightly less daily contact with their children but proved more likely to hug and praise children and to share family meals and prayers.[76] Mormon households practiced traditional gender roles more than other families, and women less often worked outside the home. Mormons placed greater value on education than the American norm, and Mormon men more often held professional positions. Mormons also emphasized self-control (following rules, controlling tempers, behaving responsibly) more than the national norm, and demonstrated more conservative sexual behavior prior to marriage.[77]

Perhaps the greatest point of division between Mormons and mainstream Americans could be found in the ritualistic progression that began at a young age. Historian Jan Shipps argued that twentieth-century Mormons, in comparison to the national norm or even to nineteenth-century Mormons, held greater fixation on rituals of advancement which bound individuals to the LDS community and the culture. Shipps explains that Latter-day Saints are actually made through the formula "Conversion to the LDS gospel + fitting into LDS religio-ethnic community = Latter-day

Saint." She cites a series of rites through which Mormon children pass that progressively link them to the Latter-day Saint culture, including baptism at eight years; initiation in the Aaronic priesthood (for boys) at age twelve and the MIA youth program (boys and girls); elevation within the Aaronic priesthood at fourteen years and sixteen years; scouting activities for boys; endowments at temple beginning at age eighteen or nineteen; mission at young adulthood; temple marriage typically from age twenty-one to twenty-five; and priesthood callings extended throughout adulthood.[78] Placement youth arrived in such homes which simply expected Indian youth to follow the same trajectory. These children certainly observed their foster siblings' progress through various ordinances, offices, and callings, and Indian children usually participated in these cultural rites as well.

These steps only constitute one way in which foster students engaged a system of acculturation much larger than their immediate family. Students and foster families also met with caseworkers in varying frequencies, depending on parent availability and caseworker vigilance. Some met monthly, others hardly at all. During meetings caseworkers offered parents training and instruction on how to assist the children.[79] Additionally, the *Foster Parent Guide* provided a quick reference. It outlined adjustment cycles and repeatedly instructed parents to make the students feel comfortable, loved, and wanted, while also directing parents to "remember that his natural parents are important to him. Do not try to take their place." It continued:

> Anything that would divide his loyalties is a potential source of trouble. Criticizing his parents or making light of his background will only frustrate him and confuse his feelings toward you, himself, and his natural family.[80]

This sort of instruction played out in two particularly noticeable relationships: first, in the student's conflicted loyalties to parents; and, second, in the student's struggle between the two cultures.

Foster parents typically treated children with kindness and love, but students felt awkward about their status as members of the family. Erdman Jake commented, "You knew you were not part of their family, yeah, you were part of the family as a member for the family, but you weren't blood."[81] Another girl remembered the pain of her exclusion from a family photograph. She said, "I remember being hurt, real hurt."[82] However, many others always felt as though they were "part of the family." Julius Ray Chavez commented, "I belong to that family. They say that I'm just one of them."[83] Another commented, "They would always introduce me as one of their daughters."[84]

Some students overtly resisted family integration. One girl remembered, "I refused to say Dad and said, 'Forget it.... Nobody can replace my mom and dad. I don't care what you do.'"[85] Students understandably felt mixed about the whole situation. Most parents simply invited foster children to call them "Mom" and "Dad" and hoped the child might gradually adopt the terms. Meanwhile, the foster parents also followed ISPP policy and encouraged contact with biological parents at home. One former student explained, "My family told me my real family is back home and that I should love and respect them. It was a little patronizing, but they meant it."[86]

Foster parents sometimes welcomed natural parents into their homes for short visits, particularly for holidays, graduation, or other points of celebration.[87] Additionally, foster parents encouraged their children to write home to the reservation, and they sent photographs to chronicle the child's development.[88] In the late 1950s, the program launched the *Thunderbird* newsletter to share student accomplishments among fellow students and with their parents. In truth, the periodical remained largely inaccessible to many Native parents who could not read English and only glimpsed the magazine when visiting caseworkers shared a copy.[89] The dynamics of two very different families surely created some awkward moments, just as in any foster care system, but children and parents worked to find a common understanding.

Most foster parents did not attempt to forcefully impose cultural or religious assimilation onto foster children by wiping out all Native language and culture with harsh punishments used in boarding schools and other institutions of assimilation; rather, foster parents thoroughly exposed youth to white, Mormon culture while still encouraging Native language and those tribal customs that did not overtly clash with LDS teachings. As a result, many participants continued to express and value elements of their native culture, and even earned recognition for their proficiency among other Native Americans. Navajo Nora Begay, who spent eight years in Placement and later went on to win the 1971 Miss Indian America pageant, testified,

"My foster parents were patient, kind and willing to have me take my own time in learning new concepts and a different way of life. They also were interested in learning about me and my ways."[90]

Caseworker Dale Shumway explained that neither culture was universally superior, but that both offered valuable elements from which students could choose. The strength of white culture, he asserted, was "being organized and planning ahead and goal setting and those kinds of things." He also identified negative side effects of materialism and selfishness, and pointed to Navajo cultural values of cooperation and humility as preferable traits. Unfortunately, he concluded, not all foster parents shared his pluralistic valuation. Shumway explained:

> You have to say white culture and Indian culture—they both have their positives and their negatives. But I think not everybody understood that. Some foster parents thought that white culture was superior but there are beautiful things in Indian culture too. But that was one of the things some people were always wrestling with.... The students I worked with, I think they understood this.[91]

Some foster parents surely pushed students to assimilate, but a great many also shared Shumway's philosophy and the program overtly directed foster parents to help children strengthen their bond with their biological family and community. One foster parent explained:

> We have no desire now for David to take on all of our non-Indian ways, and we don't want his cultural heritage to be extinguished. We would rather help him to share in life's opportunities, shouldering those responsibilities that could help him to become a better person among his own people or in our own frenetic world.[92]

Church leaders hoped the children would select those attributes Shumway venerated—organization and industry—and then return to their reservations as leaders armed with the best attributes of both worlds and capable of bridging the two cultures. Even still, pressures to adopt Western values certainly outweighed efforts to retain indigenous heritage.

As part of this effort to instill industry, foster parents followed program instructions to assign household chores to Indian children. Children placed in urban environments shared duties with siblings, such as dishwashing and childcare.[93] Those placed in rural homes also took on family responsibilities, though there seemed to be far more chores to go around. In such homes, students milked cows, fed horses and chickens, and harvested hay and other crops.[94] Julius Chavez recalled that "there was planting to do, sprinkler changes to do, taking care of the sheep, horses, and chickens, gathering eggs, milking cows, and taking care of the milk."[95] Some children interpreted such assignments as exploitation. One former participant commented, "I was feeling like I was more like a maid than anything else."[96] She and others felt as though parents habitually instructed their behavior in all things.[97] However, most accepted the chores as a regular part of family life in their new home. Another explained, "It was very natural, they equaled out the chores."[98] Though white society seemed more constricting, Mormon parents hardly singled out foster children any more than their own. One former Placement child explained, "When I was being disciplined, I thought I was getting picked on, but then I realized that other members, my brothers, sisters and family, had the same disciplinary action also."[99]

Even leisure time proved tightly controlled as parents worked to mold Indian children into assimilated Americans through participation in "traditional" American activities. A great many parents signed up their foster daughters for piano lessons, which seemed to Mormons as the epitome of proper Western culture.[100] One recalled, "I didn't have much free agency about taking piano lessons, which at first, was about as much fun as studying my times tables." [101] Some children took swimming lessons, and many played on organized athletic teams—track, wrestling, football, and basketball, which was a popular sport on the Navajo reservation.[102] Frankie Gilmore, Navajo, explained, "I loved sports, and I participated in track, where I ran the mile, in football, where I played quarterback and safety, but my best sport was wrestling, in which I qualified for the state meet."[103] Others adopted their foster parents' interests in "high culture." Ella Bedonie, Navajo, recalled that her foster parents spent considerable amounts of time and money to take her to see performances like *West Side Story*, *Funny Girl*, and *Fiddler on the Roof*.[104] Still, students also enjoyed less-structured actives, such as talking on the phone, climbing trees, or riding horses on the farm.[105]

In addition to structured leisure activities, students also experienced parental involvement in their studies. Foster mothers frequently took on roles as tutors and teachers to help Indian students catch up with white classmates of their same age. Caseworker Dale Shumway explained that he generally recruited foster parents who would provide academic support to their children because the typical enrollee was three to four years behind and not accustomed to rigorous studying.[106] In a letter to Navajo chairman Paul Jones, the Fox family wrote about the support they offered their Placement child: "We do extra 'tutoring' in the home to help him in reading, arithmetic (times-tables, combinations, etc.)."[107] One foster father reported:

> Whenever I came home from work and saw a multiplicity of objects on the table—oranges, carrots, toothpicks, or beans—I knew that it was arithmetic time for David. But alas, that tangible bridge into the abstract world of arithmetic was difficult to cross. Countless cardboards were divided fractionally. Clocks with movable hands were provided. Dominoes were used to make a game of it. When my wife's aspiration became too intense at his lack of progress, I took compassion on her and tried my hand at a simple problem in addition.[108]

Foster parents invested significant time to prepare students for academic and professional success in mainstream American society. This individualized attention made Placement a far better educational experience than boarding schools.

As parents worked closely with their foster students, their attitudes about the Indians evolved from a simplistic, theologically focused form of sympathy and outreach to sincere love and concern for students whom they came to view as their own children. Though the relationship originated from evangelical responsibility, Mormon parents' benevolent sympathies developed into genuine love for their foster children.[109] When children returned to the reservation each summer, many foster parents released them with a sadness comparable to Native parents nine months earlier. Janice Kapp Perry recalled the surreal feelings on the morning that her foster child would leave: "At that moment I realized how much I considered myself to be Wayne's mother." She continued, "How can I let him go? As I sat by his bed, looking at him for a few extra seconds before awakening him, I felt numb."[110]

While some white foster siblings shared similar loving devotion to their Indian brothers and sisters, many did not. Rivalries and competition for parental attention frequently perpetuated conflict between foster and natural children. Maybell Begay remembered, "I think it was hard for my older foster sister Kalin to have Vernon and me sharing and competing for the attention, love, and affection of her parents."[111] Erdman Jake similarly explained:

> They had one young man who was almost the same age as I was and we seemed to be constantly in competition with each other, fighting with each other. That could be another reason why I chose not to go back because I didn't want to continue to live in that kind of circumstances.[112]

Another student remembered her strained relationship with foster siblings. She said, "I think it was a threat to her to know that I was in the family."[113] Others also remembered similar sibling tensions.[114] An early 1980s internal report found that while parents often bonded with Indian children, white siblings more often found the foster relationships difficult.[115]

However, not all participants expressed difficulties in their sibling relations. Some Placement students did not experience any sibling relations because their foster parents did not have other children or had grown children who had already left the home. Others with siblings also managed to get along, and some even grew to love each other. One Placement child wrote:

> I like my foster brothers and my two little foster sisters. My oldest foster brother, I really like him. He gives me everything like stereo tapes and pictures and things like that. I really like him but he left on his mission three weeks ago, and he really wants me to keep up with my art. He was happy that I went out for track. He told me to keep up with my work. When he left on his mission, I knew that he is a good brother. I have never seen a boy like that.[116]

Much as children in any family, Placement Program siblings had their share of conflict and love, though perhaps a little more the former than the latter.

The foster family constituted only the first social circle with which Indian children interacted. Public schools also proved a highly structured experience for Placement students, but more importantly they immersed students in Western culture via sports teams, gymnasiums and auditoriums, junk food, interracial friendships, and new clubs and social activities. Integrations with other students, teachers, and educational institutions reinforced the correctness of the Western culture in which students temporarily resided.[117] As they internalized this structured culture of production and consumption, many must have wondered why their reservation homes had comparatively so little material wealth. School experiences certainly validated Western society and likely led students to question their reservation culture.

Schoolteachers often recognized the unique needs of Placement students who, when first entering the program, were years behind in reading, math, and science.[118] Some teachers exhibited discriminatory feelings and questioned the Indian children's ability to perform academically like white students.[119] Native tendencies to avoid competition and self-assertion only contributed to such misconceptions. More often, however, teachers made an extra effort to help Placement students succeed in the classroom. When Frankie Gilmore finished sixth grade at Kayenta Boarding School, he only read at a third-grade reading level. He joined Placement and later recalled the special tutoring he received: "My English teacher, Mrs. Henry, used to work with me a half hour after school every night to help me catch up to my grade level."[120] Many also offered encouraging words. Roy Talk recalled that one teacher counseled him by saying that "we've never yet had a Native American as president of the United States. Roy, you could very well grow up to be the first one."[121]

Foster parents also engaged teachers and school administrators to advocate for their Indian students. One foster mother remembered that she withdrew her Navajo son from the classroom of an unsupportive teacher.[122] Julius Chavez, Navajo, similarly explained that many years after Placement his foster mother explained how she fought school administrators to keep him mainstreamed in regular classes.[123] Ultimately, many students embraced the support they received and competitively engaged their classmates in the schoolroom and in other activities.

Indian Placement students usually found their classmates welcomed them with minimal hesitance. Celina Jake, Navajo, enrolled in Placement at age thirteen and lived in a foster home in Salt Lake City. She attended Highland High School in the late 1980s and was certainly aware of social cliques, but "never felt like I was a different race." She said, "I never experienced any type of discrimination."[124] Another commented, "All of the kids were real nice and they were really friendly towards me and I made lots of friends."[125]

Some students did observe minimal prejudices. Orlando Tsosie, Navajo, went on Placement in 1980 and lived with a family in Bountiful, Utah. He generally got along with other students, but remembered, "In elementary school there were times when people said some things, but it was just that, they said things and [I'm] sure I said some things back. But overall, I was accepted very well."[126] Still, a few observed more troubling discrimination. Emery Bowman, Navajo, went on Placement in the early 1970s. He mostly socialized with white students and officers on the school council, but remembered that on one occasion other children called him "dirty Indian," "savage," and "squaw."[127] Perhaps facing similar attitudes, Julius Chavez took action. He explained, "The first day, I remember beating up three kids because I was Indian. I was pushed through two doors. . . . Of course, I had to fight to let them know that they can't get over me."[128]

Surprisingly, some Placement students found that they enjoyed a special status as Indians. Jim Dandy explained:

> To my social and ethnic amazement, they really accepted me! In speaking the truth, I was a novelty since I was the first Indian student to attend that high school and I was smiley and friendly. I was treated like a king! The students and faculty cared about me. Some of my peers offered to carry my books. The teachers encouraged me and gave me extra help.[129]

Donald Mose Jr., Navajo, similarly commented, "I was always treated special because I was an Indian. The children my age at that time thought it was unique to have an Indian, a real Indian, out on the playgrounds with them."[130] This wonderment and admiration of Indianness, misunderstood as it was, empowered Placement students to not only retain but also promote their indigenous identity in the classroom and on the playground. Ronald Singer enjoyed the uniqueness his Indianness offered. He said, "It never bothered me because I was kind of like a novelty. I was accepted. I never felt discriminated against. I felt just like one of the people there." He remembered, "I had friends that were Mexicans. I had friends that were white."[131] Some Placement students used this stereotype-based adoration to gain popularity. A *Saturday Evening Post* reporter observed:

> During my stay in Utah I made a point of asking as many people as I could about possible discrimination in the classroom and on the playground. I found none. As a matter of fact, most Indian students are popular with their schoolmates. They become student-body presidents, football and basketball captains, editors of school newspapers.[132]

In time, students grew to know and view each other as individuals more than as ethnic stereotypes, and Placement students developed a variety of friendships. Some preferred whites to other Indians; some invested their energies in Native friends; but most made little effort to maintain racially determined friendships.[133] One former student explained, "I never made any distinction between them, even here and always have—no prejudice that I noticed!"[134] Still, a few ISPP students felt out of place with both groups of children.[135]

Placement students participated in social activities with their (typically white) schoolmates. They joined school clubs, attended dances, and competed in sports.[136] Some initially resisted the competitive nature of athletics, but many ultimately participated. George Lee recalled the decision to join an art contest and how it represented a cultural leap:

> I knew there would be winners and losers. And, I did not want to win if it meant that my friends would lose. Being sensitive, I really didn't want to enter the contest because I didn't want to hurt anyone's feelings....And to be singled out went against the grain of my Navajo cultural upbringing. Yes, it was important to have recognition, but only equal to that of my friends, whom I admired and respected....I received a lot of publicity over winning the contest. My picture and poster, along with those of the other winners, appeared in the local newspaper. My beautiful mother diligently cut out and pasted them in a scrapbook....We had a lot of visits, phone calls, and letters. I was not sure how to handle all this. Nothing like it had ever happened to me.[137]

One overachieving Placement student fondly recalled the activities in which she participated. She said:

> I quickly adjusted to the school and participated in junior varsity and varsity athletics throughout my high school years. Delta High always took state in wrestling respectively. I was on the volleyball and track and field teams. I was involved in various school clubs known as The Triangle, the Delta High newspaper, partook in leadership activities relating to The Club of Many Feathers, a Native American club, The Future Business Leaders of America, abbreviated term for FBLA, and Future Homemakers of America.[138]

During her senior year, she participated on the school council and served as the vice president of the Native American club. A great many Placement students engaged their new social environment through activity in school clubs and sports teams. Roy Montclair explained, "I played wide receiver and defensive back on the football team, and I was the point guard on the basketball team. My best friend was the other starting guard and the football quarterback."[139] Quite a few Placement students also engaged with other schoolmates through social clubs, often an Indian club in areas with high Native enrollment or school music groups like glee and band.[140] The 1973 *Indian Student Guide* boasted that Placement students "take part in school activities such as sports, drama, clubs, debate, and serve on committees in school."[141]

Not all students eagerly participated in student government and school sports. Indeed, most children new to the Placement Program initially found the entire experience overwhelming, and nearly every child experienced intense homesickness at the outset which often lasted weeks or longer. For some, this attitude transitioned into passive resistance or even outright delinquency.

Homesickness heavily impacted students during the first weeks of Placement, and during the first year it could last for weeks or even months.[142] Ella Bedonie remembered, "I was lonesome for my family. I remember crying sometimes."[143] Homesick students turned inward, sometimes through crying, but also through withdrawn silence and daydreaming. Loretta Chino commented that she "often found myself wishing I could ride a horse or herd sheep."[144] Foster parents tried to help students adjust but earned mixed results. Tommy Holtsoi said:

> I remember them trying everything they could to try and get me over the lonely feeling. They even brought my cousin to stay with me, and they had a swimming pool in the back yard.... And course they got me in the pool and I just went over to a corner and just stayed there. I wouldn't come out of my corner.[145]

Bedonie also recalled that "they would try to take me places to get me out of that."[146]

Pervasive homesickness constituted one of the largest obstacles for program administrators. An early 1980s comprehensive study of the ISPP found that homesickness accounted for the bulk of the student-request drop-outs, which it estimated at 40 percent over the preceding decades.[147] Vanta Quintero recalled, "I cried for two weeks until my parents came and took me back home." She explained, "My foster parents were so good to me and tried everything to make me feel welcome, but after two miserable weeks, my own parents came all the way from Ft. Apache (over 600 miles) and took me back."[148] Roberta Bennally reported that her homesickness carried all the way through December, and when her parents visited for Christmas, she went home with them.[149]

Many resented the structured nature of their new lives and often complained about it to other students. One study collected an assortment of quotes from disgruntled Placement students.[150] Even students who remained in the program, graduated, and attended BYU frequently voiced complaints about the ISPP. They pointed to the aforementioned rigorous routine, arbitrary structure and rules, segmented time into rigid schedules, and what they perceived as unequal standards with families that pitted natural and foster children against each other. Overall, their criticisms were less about forced cultural erosion and more about imposed structure, expectations, and accountability.[151]

A few students even took a more active role in defiance. No official statistics quantify the rate of occurrence, though longtime caseworker Dale Shumway estimated only five percent of students he worked with ever acted out in troubling ways. He recalled one who tried to burn down the school, but the most commonly observed delinquency involved fighting, alcohol and tobacco use, and intentional underachievement.[152] Former foster mother Kay Cox recalled an incident when her Navajo foster son attended a dance in Salt Lake City with two other Placement students. When he came home at four a.m., the family car smelled of beer. She said:

> The caseworker called and said the other two boys were dead drunk and their parents were most upset. At first Virgil denied it, then confessed. He had drunk part of one can and then thrown the rest out, but Bill had downed twenty-three cans of beer. Steve had done almost as well.[153]

Kay Cox remembered that another student she fostered chewed tobacco regularly and that her efforts to discourage the habit failed.[154] The aforementioned *Saturday Evening Post* reporter bumped into a Placement student in Ogden, Utah, trying to buy whisky and cigarettes at a local grocery store. When asked how she felt about the program, the student replied, "I hate it!...I'm not coming back next year!"[155]

Delinquency was met with a variety of punitive measures, ranging from reprimands to expulsion from the program but nothing approaching the methods used at boarding schools. The 1973 *Student Guide* outlined a tiered approach to discipline beginning with "verbal probation" and the loss of some privileges before progressing to written probation and finally expulsion for those who refused to follow the rules.[156] The early 1980s report found that deviant behavior only caused foster parents to send home about eight percent of students.[157] More often caseworkers committed the children to improve and then transferred them to another family for a fresh start.[158] This policy contributed to a high turnover rate among foster families, and a great many "burned out" and withdrew from participation. This also meant that most students, deviant or not, lived in multiple families.[159]

Even those who grew discontent knew that the ISPP required some degree of obedience if they wished to continue in the program. From the program's earliest stages, Kimball suggested that noncompliant children "be told that unless he changes and cooperates, he will have to go home, and perhaps that might motivate him to behave better."[160] In 1959, the Indian Committee determined that "the ability to get along" and "their ability to conform" should serve as primary determinants when selecting students to return each year.[161]

Perhaps because of the program's voluntary nature, most children seemed to accept or even embrace their situation. Many Placement students interpreted the experience as an opportunity to learn and grow. George Lee remembered:

> I decided to do my best to be a good example and to leave a good impression on my new family. Being quite sensitive to the feelings of others, I did not want to hurt them in any way, and I did my best to do whatever they asked.[162]

Lee took extra initiative to "always be one step ahead of my foster parents. I made up my mind during that first year in the Harker home that I would never have to be reminded to do such chores as making my bed or picking up my clothes."[163]

Other youths seemed equally appreciative of the experience. In a letter to the Indian Committee, Larry Tracy expressed his thanks. He said, "I would like to thank you for starting this student Placement Program and for making it what it is now." He continued, "I have been in the program for ten years and I have liked every minute of it."[164] His were among many comments collected for a gift to the committee in 1964.[165] The Placement Newsletter similarly carried regular statements of gratitude made possible by the support of parents and the larger Indian program. As these gestures demonstrate, quite a few students valued and appreciated the ISPP and their foster parents.

As students cooperated with the program, they increasingly resembled their white foster environments in appearance and behavior. Still, this was just the beginning of the transformation. Certainly the ISPP existed to provide educational and cultural exposure and opportunities, but it also had a much deeper-reaching intention. The program strove not simply to assimilate Native Americans, but to make them into a hybrid that included Indian cultural trappings and Western emphasis on productivity and leadership, through which they became redeemed Lamanites.

At the end of each school year, ISPP students returned home to parents who often assumed their children would behave and think much as when they departed. However, the Placement experience fundamentally changed those who internalized white Western cultural values and Mormon theology. These students made critical choices about their own place in society as they determined how their newly appropriated Western culture and values fit into an Indian environment. Some abandoned one culture and embraced the other; others avoided the conflict entirely by maintaining each separately and flip-flopping between them based on their current cultural environment. Still others asserted one identity over the other regardless of societal context. For Indians who embraced Mormon theology, the Lamanite identity provided one such bridge to reconcile the two worlds.

Native Americans engaged in the Placement Program as well as in boarding school and other urbanization efforts often employed a "two worlds" model to interpret their experiences and frame their identity, much as their peers who attended boarding schools and joined federal urban relocation programs. In a 1997 study examining the self-perceptions of former Placement students, the author recognized three self-identified groups: Mormons, Indians, and those trapped in between.[166] More recently, historian Philip Deloria articulated four notions of identity that stemmed from the conceptual bifurcation of experience into two distinct realms: gradual or immediate affiliation with one or the other; alienation from both; proficiency in both, separately; and syncretism of the two into a singular functional worldview and identity.[167]

The remarks of former Placement students similarly reflect the "two worlds" discourse and the four consequent perspectives. Many felt entrenched in one culture or the other. One Native American Mormon reiterated the argument that no one can really remain loyal to both white Mormon and Native cultures, at least not for long. She explained, "Many of my Indian brothers and sisters have given up their cultures to become Mormon—to be acceptable to their Anglo Mormon brothers and sisters. How long do they last?" She continued:

Some feel they must choose between being Mormon and being Indian....I remember my grandmother, the first Indian member of the Relief Society in the Uintah Basin. After years of faithful service, she went back to the traditional ways. For her, the gap got wider and wider until she had to choose.[168]

Though no statistics testify to the demographics, quite a few ISPP students withdrew back to their respective Native culture after the Placement experience.

While some quickly returned to reservation life, others embraced Mormon culture. George Lee commented, "My parents were a little concerned that I was becoming too much of a *Gaamalii* (Mormon) instead of being a Navajo. I was even called *Gaamalii* by my family for a while."[169] After graduation from high school (and, by extension, the ISPP), George Lee moved to Utah where he continued his education among Mormon peers and progressed in the church leadership.

Other former Placement students felt incomplete and alienated from both the white Mormon lifestyle and their respective Native culture. It is difficult to imagine ISPP students' sense of returning home to a place that no longer seemed familiar. Their feelings are perhaps best conveyed in the words of Navajo student Irene Stewart who was not on Placement but similarly left her homeland for educational purposes. She said:

> Once having left hogan life, and having gotten used to living where there are hygienic facilities, it is very hard to live again in the old hogan way of life. A Navajo boy or girl wants a suitable home, a chance to live the life he has been taught, and an opportunity to find suitable work to support himself and later his family.... When I had left the Navajo country years before, I felt heartbreak; now I was disappointed in it. I could not make up my mind to stay on the reservation. Hogan life—once a great pleasure to me, and in later years so satisfying—was not for me.[170]

Some ISPP students felt a sense of awkwardness in both the white and reservation environments. Years after opening his home to Helen John and then building up the Placement Program as the Southwest Indian Mission president, Golden Buchanan looked back on the ISPP with similar concerns about such alienation:

My fear is that we neither make fish nor fowl out of them. They're neither white nor Indian, and we take them out of their own culture and their old way of thought. Then we don't give them enough of ours that they're happy, that they can make a living and that they can adjust. Then they become outcasts. They can't go back to their old way because they've enough of the new way in them that some of the old way is repulsive and not good. They don't have enough of the new way to fit in completely. Therefore, they're in no man's land in between, a people who have lost their way...some way, somehow, we've got to help them bridge the gap and we're not doing an entirely good job.[171]

This liminal status threatened to undermine functionality and identity in either world.

Still others deemed themselves equally proficient in both societies. Former Placement student Mabel Yazzie, Navajo, commented, "I am adapted to both cultures. I feel equally comfortable in them."[172] Ella Bedonie explained:

I acted the way I would act being around my family, taking part in everything; that was a natural part of me. And then when I went back [on Placement], I made that transition back to the white world. I had to work hard at it....I didn't really have a problem going back and forth in those worlds.[173]

For such "bicultural" students and graduates, the essential strategy was the separation of both worlds, intellectually and, if possible, physically as well. Another student explained:

When I go back on the Placement program, I have to think, "Oh, yea, okay, I'm back in this world now, and now I have to do what I'm supposed to do here, and not have this other mind that's on the reservation." And like I get up in the morning, take a bath, whatever, do errands, do my homework, and all this stuff, and when I go back to the reservation, I cook, I clean the house for my parents, or I babysit. But here [in Utah] I don't do that, because I'm always too busy doing something else."[174]

She explained that in Utah "you dress nicely, you know, glamorous and all this stuff. Makeup and stuff. You know, clean clothes every day. But then at home when I go it's kind of uncomfortable to do that because—it's like showing off."[175] Those who embraced biculturalism cautiously avoided conflict of the two cultures. They participated in all that either environment offered and engaged each by their respective values. Rose Denette Sohsy commented that "my family always had a beauty-way ceremony for each of us. It was to bless our minds and make us strong so that we wouldn't have any problems with learning. When we used to go back [on Placement], they would ask us, 'Did you have any ceremonies?' And I would have to say, 'No.' So I felt like I was violating both; I wasn't being true to my culture, and I wasn't being honest with the other culture."[176] These self-described bicultural students felt they could draw resources from both sides and worked diligently to maintain functionality in both.[177]

Finally, many students embraced the fourth tactic: syncretism. They found a way to blend the different cultures into one worldview. Syncretism is not necessarily an equally weighted negotiation, and the final product is a unique creation that allows individuals to interface with the former two systems.[178] One anthropologist defined syncretism as "the integration (and consequent secondary elaboration) of selected aspects of two or more historically distinct traditions."[179] Syncretism "may be tacit, passive or technically unconscious, and the objective result may yet be the systematic incorporation of the foreign element into the Native culture"; two cultures are blended together, but not always equally.[180]

Many Placement students found ways to synchronize their Native and Mormon cultures. Orlando Tsosie commented:

> I can still go to the ceremonies as long as I don't do some of the things they do, sure, but they can coexist. The doctrines themselves are not that far apart. If you really study the symbolism of some of the theology of some of the Navajo religion, the creation story for example, they really co-tangle.[181]

Such efforts inherently included a religious synthesis of sorts but also a bit of selective editing and purging from each culture. Students needed to know where Mormonism and Native American society could overlap in positive ways, and where to draw lines that they could not cross. Mormon Indians had at their disposal a unique tool for that complicated negotiation.

Mormon theology offered a ready-made device for synchronization: the Lamanite identity. For some Placement youth, the notion of a Lamanite offered a prefabricated narrative that bound both cultures together. To be a Lamanite was to embrace both cultures as one, according to some students. By accepting the Lamanite trope students could purge some "teachings of their fathers" that scored low on that Mormon theological spectrum of civility, and by doing so students could interpret themselves as progressing. Customs that did not clash with Mormon theology could still be retained as quaint and nonthreatening variations of a generalized Lamanite "culture." Church leaders rarely identified specific elements to purge, and so such decisions fell to individuals. Disturbing as it may sound, this system empowered Mormon Indians to pick and choose from each culture while claiming membership in both.

The Lamanite ideal thus proved both racially and theologically charged. It drew white Mormons to participate in the Placement program so they could "civilize" their Indian brothers, but it also offered some Indian participants a flexible term that they could—to some extent—bend to permit them access and functionality in both white and Native cultures. In binding traditional and Mormon lifeways, the Lamanite ideal certainly privileged the latter but nevertheless offered tolerance and even encouraged more superficial Native practices that did not overtly conflict with Mormon theological teachings. The ISPP was a vehicle of colonization that eroded Native customs but also provided a means of navigating two worlds that many Indians eagerly sought to traverse.

Characterizations of the program as simply assimilationist are correct but also incomplete because that interpretation does not allow space for the cultural tolerance and even encouragement that did exist, limited and constrained as it was. Indian youth who enrolled in Placement never faced restrictions on their language or on many customs that boarding schools sought to purge. Though smoking tobacco, consuming alcohol, and participating in premarital sexual relations were all forbidden by LDS theology, each student accepted those rules as terms of their participation. The more subtle transformation that parents and children did not expect stands out as a greater concern. In taking children from their biological families and placing them in a different cultural context, the program instilled different values and goals and to some degree disassociated the children from their cultural roots. The ISPP also consciously worked to instill Western notions of productivity and leadership, and encouraged children to obtain the necessary training to return home and transform that environment. In this way the program most certainly was an institutional system of colonization and many rejected it as such by withdrawing or disobeying program objectives. Their resistance is given more attention in the following chapter, along with those who embraced the theology. Regardless of student responses, the ISPP constituted a gross change of environment that exposed Indians to much more than academic education.

6

THE PLACEMENT EXPERIENCE

Becoming a Lamanite

This program is not a welfare program; it is a leadership program designed to motivate individuals and give them an opportunity to learn.

—Clare Bishop, 1963

Enrollment in the Indian Student Placement Program exposed Native youth to more than schools and white society; it introduced and sought to entrench a new Native identity. It portrayed Native Americans not simply as degraded Indians, but rather as the lost remnant of Israel endowed with special, albeit underrecognized, potential. Spencer W. Kimball explained, "It is not a name of derision or embarrassment, but one of which to be very proud." He continued, "You had a rugged history with many tribulations, but you have a brilliant future. You are a chosen people; your destiny is in the hands of yourselves, your friends and of God."[1] The Book of Mormon clearly taught that these chosen people had once accomplished great feats and wonders and were destined to again rise as eminent leaders of the LDS Church and world. This empowering message served as a central ideological tenant of the Placement Program, and it helped students transition from their reservation cultures into white Mormon society with greater confidence. Indeed, the program offered far more than an education or even cross-cultural exposure to middle-class white American values; it provided an identity to formidable young children.

The use of the Lamanite title in a positive context requires some explanation. For over a hundred years, Mormons equated Lamanites with Native Americans and viewed their culture as the apostate residue of a lost branch of Israel. The Book of Mormon's description of Lamanites as wicked apostates aligned neatly with nineteenth-century perceptions of Native American savagery. Competition for resources in the Salt Lake Valley reinforced those negative perceptions, but during the mid-twentieth century increasing numbers of Native American youths converted to the church and adopted its doctrine and the cultural trappings of middle-class white America; to Mormon onlookers these Lamanites appeared on their way to achieving the anticipated day of restoration. This not only allowed white Mormons to accept Indians among them, but it also provided Native Americans a flexible self-perception that enabled them to integrate and function within the two separate cultural worlds. Certainly some Indians rejected the identity, but those who accepted it deemed "Lamanite" an ennobling term.

This newly improved Lamanite identity fostered pride in a proficiency in both Native and Western cultures, much as the Nephites personified in the Book of Mormon. Self-described Lamanites embraced white Mormon values of industry, education, leadership, and self-advancement, and in so doing they took upon themselves a whiteness of sorts. At the same time, they could take pride in traditional language, history, arts, and other elements of their indigenous culture that did not openly conflict with Mormon theology. By the 1970s church leaders promoted that identity among indigenous inhabitants of South America and even the Pacific Isles, and developed smaller educational programs there as well.

The Placement Program served as the primary mechanism to recruit and train such Lamanites. The ISPP proved highly effective in gathering Indian children into white homes; it instilled Western cultural notions and charged youth to disseminate those values into their Native communities whereby they might begin a larger transformation of Indian country. Such a policy certainly constitutes colonialism; however, many youth and their parents openly sought similar goals of education and cultural exposure, though participants did not fully understand the transformation that would occur.

The Indian Student Placement Program initiated a series of colonizing pressures designed to transform Native youth into self-driven and self-identified Lamanites. Placement students received direction from their foster families, their larger ward or congregation, and program officials who organized activities that ranged from social dances to leadership conferences. They also served in leadership capacities spreading Lamanite theology to their peers. Much of this training served to prepare students for a time when they would leave the foster home and return to the reservation to spread their values.

As Placement students left foster homes each summer and returned to the reservation, and even after graduating from the program, many felt some degree of estrangement. Placement youth had changed during the school year, and while some boasted greater confidence, others felt out of place as they encountered linguistic and cultural rifts. Likewise, their Native communities received them with mixed responses. Meanwhile the church launched a series of summer programs to help Native youth fortify their values and identity as Lamanites.

During the school years and summer months, the church operated an aggressive colonization program to guide Native American youth to redefine themselves as upwardly mobile Indians. The ISPP impressed upon Indian participants the notion that a Lamanite identity and heritage was an indigenous model for rigorous self-development, education, and leadership in the LDS Church and Native community. That unique program, and student experiences therein, is the focus of this chapter. Challenges to Lamanite authenticity by traditionalists and modern activists eventually followed, and many Native youth rejected it altogether. Even still, thousands embraced the Lamanite as an ideological source of strength that borrowed from both cultures. These students defined their own identity within contested spaces as they individually integrated cultural elements to craft what they believed was a superior and more authentic model for Indianness.

In 1972, Elder Spencer W. Kimball addressed upwardly mobile Indian students enrolled at Brigham Young University, many of whom formerly participated in the Placement Program. He interpreted their enrollment as the fulfillment of LDS prophesies anticipating the restoration of the Lamanites. He said, "The Lamanites all over this world are seeming to remember something they knew before." He continued, "The day of the Lamanite is surely here, and we are God's instruments in helping to bring to pass the prophecies of renewed vitality, acceptance of the gospel, and resumption to a favored place as a part of God's chosen people."[2]

After a year or two in the Placement Program, enrollees certainly understood the role of Lamanites in the Latter-day Saint worldview; however, the degree to which they accepted or understood the gospel prior to enrollment varied greatly. Some students learned Mormon theology from a young age and were raised by devoutly LDS Indian parents; others learned gospel principles from missionaries and local primary meetings that mingled activities and spiritual lessons. Still others knew nothing of the LDS Church prior to their application to the program. Many in that last group simply interpreted baptism and conversion as hoops to jump through prior to enrollment. For such students, the ISPP proved the first meaningful instruction to their identity as a Lamanite. Indeed, the program inscribed this theological sense of self upon the youths through a series of measures designed to both instill identity and train them for their prophetic role as community and church leaders.

Scholars and laymen have discussed and defined the Lamanite identity in detail.[3] What requires more attention here is the mid- and late twentieth-century re-creation of the Lamanite ideal and its imposition upon Placement students. As Indian foster students adopted the trappings of white culture, the Lamanite ideal thrust upon them promised to transform students from what the church believed to be the degraded, even "cursed," savage Lamanite into a powerful leader. Some, including Kimball, believed that ISPP students could overcome the apostate "traditions of their fathers" and fulfill their prophetic destiny. With this in mind, some Native Americans viewed the term Lamanite as disparaging. Quite often, however, Native American Mormons enjoyed the special status "Lamanite" offered them within the larger LDS culture. That title entitled the bearer to a prophetic resurgence of sorts. Cultural resurgence movements fueled by foreign and traditional elements have long inspired Native people located in compromised and colonized positions.

To this end, foster parents, program representatives, and church members generally offered words intended to encourage Indian youths. They told them that with hard work they could overcome the sins of their forbearers and achieve their divine potential. One Navajo commented that "on placement they were always telling us we were so special."[4] In an autobiographical portrait of her childhood on the Navajo reservation, Ella Bedonie remarked, "There's a scripture in the Book of Mormon that they always brought out, and it says that in the Latter Days the Lamanites will blossom as a rose, that they're the ones who are going to save the country, and stuff like that."[5] Dan Smith, Navajo, related how the Lamanite theology bolstered his self-esteem. He explained, "When I began my placement experience, I had low self-esteem, and I thought Indians were at the bottom of the barrel, in last place, compared to others." After joining the program and immersing himself in the theologically charged environment, he recounted, "I began to believe in myself and that I had a purpose in life." He continued, "Through the gospel plan I learned of my true identity as a loved and respected child of a loving Father in Heaven. I began to feel good about myself and happy that I was born an Indian."[6] The prophetic potential outlined for Lamanites proved a motivating force for change and for acceptance of the theologically based identity.

The Book of Mormon intertwined a historical account of the past with prophetic promises of the future, which appealed to many students. George Lee articulated the significance of the book in teaching him the love and destiny God reserved for American Indians:

> Words cannot describe the sweetness, the warmth, and the tremendous impressions that the Spirit made upon me when I realized that God loved my people—the Indian people; that God loved me as an Indian; and that we had a great future and a great destiny. After these experiences, I spent many happy days almost walking on air, knowing that God looked favorably upon my people and that they had a glorious, beautiful future ahead of them, even though they were then plagued with poverty, illiteracy, alcoholism, and other problems.[7]

In creating this narrative, the Book of Mormon and the accompanying theology promised Indians eventual triumph over their depressed socioeconomic condition. The Placement Program and other outreach efforts served as a means to instill Western values and self-confidence and the individual accomplishments to achieve these aspirations. Crafting identity as a Lamanite provided a powerful motivating force. Former Placement student Teddy Redhouse further articulated that the "premise of the placement program . . . [was] to help them gain this identity through: one, teach that an Indian is a child of God; two, identify a deeper meaning than the traditional ideas, through the Book of Mormon; and three, develop a feeling of self-worth.[8] By embracing the Lamanite ideal, students could become socially valuable within the Mormon society in which they temporarily resided. Those who embraced the message found that it provided a source of strength as they pursued the Western notions of success.[9]

Becoming a good Lamanite required that Indians not only embrace the LDS gospel but also illustrate a Protestant work ethic to demonstrate that internalization.[10] Mormons have long been a Christian sect that emphasized works and the pursuit of perfection. The church's birth during America's Second Great Awakening, along with other millennialist, adventist, and perfectionist sects, speaks volumes about Mormons' cultural emphasis on behavior as a physical manifestation of spiritual maturity. That anxious dutifulness continues in the church today.

In addressing Lamanites, the church generated a myriad of manuals to instruct Indians in the proper standards of Mormon life, often with little understanding of or concern for Native lifeways.[11] One such manual clearly outlined the expectations of a good Lamanite. It asked Indian readers, "are you an eagle" or a chicken and provided checklists to accomplish as evidence of eagle status. "Are you a positive influence among your friends? Are you doing your best in school? Are you developing and sharing your talents with others?" It continued, "Are you helping other people to succeed in life? Are you active in promoting education for our Indian youth? Are you supportive of positive programs for youth leadership? Are you on the honor roll of your school? Are you doing well in athletics?" It also instructed students to visualize their goals and included almost comical images to convey the two tropes. A sloppy and downward-looking Indian with ruffled hair included the caption, "I don't want to be anything. I quit." A juxtaposed image of an assured and upward-looking Indian, with hair parted and dress shirt, included the caption, "I will become something. I will try." Alongside similar images the manual asked readers which appeared happier and directed readers to look into a mirror and find the face of a happier, self-driven Indian. A section titled, "Let's Talk About Being Indian" reinforced these values as authentic aspects of true Indian culture—not some foreign imposition.[12]

Mormon theology provided Navajos and other Native people a new explanation of their origins and history. Former Placement student Tommy Holtstoi explained that he never believed in the Navajo explanation of origins or the land bridge theory. He questioned, "But then where did we come from?" He found the Book of Mormon narrative a more palatable explanation: "Here's the record, and it spells it out where we came from. We're Jews! Well, son of a gun! Jews!"[13] Former student Floyd Nelson similarly explained, "I've come to understand who I am, as a Native American, through the Book of Mormon." He continued, "The Book of Mormon teaches us that the Native Americans will rise up in power again. They will become a people who will finally figure out who their god is."[14]

Many drew strength from Mormon theology that incorporated aspects of "tradition" within a larger historical narrative. Placement Program director Clare Bishop explained that the role of the foster parent was to teach the child "so that he doesn't lose his identity as the child of another culture. We don't want to make white children out of them, we want to build the Indian concept."[15] In 1965, Spencer W. Kimball explained such synthesis to BYU Indian students, most of whom had participated in the Placement Program. He said:

> Any beautiful ideas not in conflict may be incorporated into the Program. But rather than over-emphasize the Indian ways, we are going to emphasize the Lord's ways. We do it in the Lord's way.... Now, then, as proud as they are to be Indians, they are not Indians first. They are Latter-day Saints.[16]

A Lamanite could embrace cultural traditions such as language, arts, or even history, but had to jettison Native spirituality as they adopted the Christian faith. Indeed, the Placement Program encouraged students to explore any cultural roots that did not challenge the LDS Church's doctrine or undermine the Indian Program's emphasis on self-improvement.

Many foster parents even encouraged their Indian students to learn about their Native cultures, particularly the elements that offered no clear challenge to LDS theology, such as history, language, and visual and performing arts. George Lee explained, "Glen and Joan often encouraged me to bear with pride my cultural heritage. They wanted me to take pride in being an Indian, in being a Navajo, and to do everything I could to set a good example for my people."[17] Many Placement students shared their tribal histories and cultural practices with white schoolmates and community members via classes and public speaking engagements.[18] One former student recalled how emersion in white society forced her to ask questions about her Native culture, and that she initially struggled to articulate even basic concepts that she had never before presented.[19] With practice and encouragement, such students became local experts on tribal language, dress, and activities, and their confidence grew with each presentation. Cultural presentations imprinted elements of indigenous culture upon these youth.

In such light, the Placement Program and the LDS Church provided what Mormons interpreted as greater cultural awareness that gave the Indian students a better understanding of their true identity. Kent Begay, Navajo, remembered how foster parents and other Latter-day Saints reinforced his heritage, as outlined in the Book of Mormon. He said, "I was told they were a proud people. The prophet Moroni, a Lamanite, was considered a hero and that all Native Americans should be proud of who they are [and] where they come from."[20]

As foster families helped Indian children understand their Lamanite heritage, they blended aspects of Native cultures into a singular construct derived from the Book of Mormon and LDS theology. Though Mormonism worked to purge cultural practices that clashed with LDS theology, it also promoted other various traditional practices that could be appropriated into the pan-Indian Lamanite heritage, such as weaving, silver working, dancing, and language skills.[21] As an intertribal notion, the Lamanite served as the new foundation for Indian identity upon which nonconflicting tribal traditions could be attached as variations of the authentic core culture. Caroline Sue Tsosie, Navajo, explained that Navajos, Apaches, and even South American Natives "are just one big family" with a shared Lamanite heritage.[22]

These Lamanite-appropriate activities reaffirmed the Native elements of the trope, and students who subordinated these practices within a larger context of LDS Church–approved behaviors thus disciplined and transformed themselves to a white Mormon standard. As early as 1959, Spencer W. Kimball recognized this ability to reform Indians into good industrious Lamanites as the strength of the program. In this way the ISPP could prove far more effective than the longstanding colonization institutions of reservations and boarding schools. Through Placement, Kimball explained, "they are not institutionalized but individualized."[23] Through family centered activities foster parents and children experienced close one-on-one contact and instruction. Indian students participated in family time, church meetings, and youth activities that encouraged self-development and reinforced the Lamanite identity. Together, these experiences worked to shape young Native American youth.

Placement students joined foster families in a variety of recreational bonding activities. Maybell Begay recalled the Cox family joined together "in frequent and varied outdoor activities, which always featured lots of food and fun." She recalled clubbing fish in Utah Lake, family basketball and football games, camping in Zion's Narrows and Havasupai, swimming in a reservoir near her foster home, and tubing down snowy hills with her foster siblings.[24] Others strengthened parent-child relations while gardening or working on other projects intended to illustrate the fruits of labor.[25]

Mormon families also gathered weekly for Family Home Evening (FHE) to play games and share spiritual messages, and in the process they grew closer together in their shared goal of gospel conversion and adherence. They read scriptures as parents taught children gospel principles like faith, service, and obedience. Recreational activities and treats often followed the religious instruction, and the entire weekly affair served to socially and emotionally bind families together around the teachings of the church.[26] Calvin Yazzie, Navajo, explained, "I greatly cherish the closeness, love, and warmth that we experienced through our family home evenings." He recounted that those activities afforded an opportunity to grow closer together with family.[27]

For families fostering Indian Placement students, a discussion of Lamanites was inevitable and probably periodic. Beverly Foster, Navajo, articulated how her foster home helped her to understand her identity and thereby empowered her. During weekly FHE they explained that the Book of Mormon chronicled her Indian history, and that by embracing that knowledge and the accompanying prophesies Indians could achieve great accomplishments. It is difficult to underestimate the suggestive influence of Mormon foster families on their Placement children as they located their own identity. She explained:

> I am a Lamanite (Indian) with great blessings promised me if I will
> learn about and live the teachings of the Church of Jesus Christ. I am
> an American with the freedom to be educated and the opportunity to

learn to work. I have an obligation to become a leader and help my people to lift themselves up to assume the responsibility of their heritage. Who am I? I am a child of God.[28]

Others similarly attributed FHE and family time as foundational in their understanding and belief in the church.[29] DuWaine Boon recalled that his foster family taught him three principles: first, to "be diligent in attending my church meetings"; second, "to be diligent in my daily reading of the scriptures"; and third, "to be diligent in saying my prayers."[30] Another former student commented that his foster mom "put that drive in me."[31]

Weekly FHE often included reading from church magazines and discussing the content together. The *Indian Liahona* magazine reminded Indians of their divine potential and carried inspiring stories about Placement students and poems submitted by other students in the program.[32] A 1964 issue included Spencer W. Kimball's 1959 General Conference remarks that outlined the glorious origins and collapse, and prophesied the rise of Native Americans who accepted the church's teachings. He instructed Indians to be proud of their Lamanite heritage that gave birth to a wonderful civilization of technological innovation and spiritual wisdom. Despite the collapse of their civilization and wayward drifting into centuries of apostasy, modern Lamanites could reclaim their destiny as they obtained education and took leadership roles in building their communities. He said:

> Tomorrow you will be highly trained, laying out highways, constructing bridges, developing cities, building temples, and joining in inspired leadership of the church of your Redeemer and Lord.... You will arise from your bed of affliction and from your condition of deprivation if you will accept fully the Lord, Jesus Christ, and his total program. You will rise to former heights in culture and education, influence and power. You will blossom as the rose upon the mountains.... These promises can be fulfilled and come to you through one channel only; the path of righteousness and faith, else all these are but empty promises, unfulfilled dreams. I bear witness that this is the truth.[33]

Kimball imbues Indians with a sense of their Israelite origin, but more than that, he tells a moving saga of a great civilization with impressive spiritual strength and achievements that had fallen into disarray. The time is at hand for their revival, Kimball explains, and he calls upon Indians to take up that charge to restore the mythical greatness. The tone and content of the passage, and much of the Book of Mormon, reads like an epic written by C. S. Lewis or J. R. R. Tolkien. It evokes a grand struggle between good and evil with a special quest assigned to all Indians. Such readings likely proved powerful motivators for impressionable children immersed in Mormon theology. It promised that despite the reservation to which they would eventually return, they, too, could achieve the wealth and social status of their host families.

Many students wrote in to the *Liahona* with passionate stories of their own personal triumphs. Indian children shared their thoughts and hopes in letters to the magazine. In 1971, the *Liahona* published the following poem from a young Native American. It appropriates the structure of "If," Rudyard Kipling's famous work, in order to assess the qualities she associated with being a Lamanite.

> If you can be an Indian and a leader too
> The Lord will keep the promise that he once made to you
> If you can be as wise and brave as Indians were before
> If you can strive to be humble and understand more....
> If you can love your people no matter what their tribe
> If on your very heart Gospel truths you can inscribe....
> If you believe the sacred prophecies of old and do all the work big
>   or small
> If you can treasure promises made only to you yet share the Gospel
>   with all
> If you can preserve your culture but not let it stray from its place
> If you can accept any challenge with a happy smile on your face....
> If you can be an Indian and a Leader too
> The Lord will pour his blessing down in abundance upon you.[34]

This poem, likely written for the routine contests hosted for Placement students, outlines the assignment for Indian youth: leadership; bravery; humility; intertribal love; gospel adherence; perseverance; and a positive attitude. All these, the author contends, can be accomplished while preserving Native culture, which must not "stray from its place." In essence, one can adopt these LDS tenants and still be a true Indian, and in so doing the Lord will "pour his blessing down in abundance upon you." These types of messages, published and circulated among Indian children, reinforced the charge for students to reach their potential as defined by Mormon theology.

During family activities, whether recreational or overtly spiritual, all participants understood the Native Americans as Lamanites and directly or indirectly reinforced that sense of identity for Indian foster children. Erdman Jake, Navajo, entered Placement in 1967 at eleven years of age. He dropped out of the program for four years before returning in 1971. Jake resisted the imposition of a spiritually and culturally apostate identity that he initially associated with Lamanites. However, through family contact he gradually grew to accept the Lamanite identity as a representation of his potential. He said:

> My foster father just took me aside and had me read the title page of the Book of Mormon, which for me was a real turning point in my life in my perspective in seeing and not being offended that the Lamanites were a dark and loathsome people, that they were a chosen people, that they were here for a purpose.[35]

Emery Bowman, Navajo, recalled that his foster father "taught me a lot of things about where the Lamanites came from. He used to say I was special, too." His foster mother also would say, "We're not going to try to make you believe it. We want you to understand it for yourself" as she gently encouraged him to read the Book of Mormon.[36] Loretta Chino, Navajo, similarly explained that her foster dad took her aside and spoke with her "about good things that would happen to me if I trusted in the Lord." She recalled he often told her she was "a special person" and that "I must never forget who I am and where I came from and where I want to be someday."[37] Other students likewise commented about their foster parents' subtle but constant reinforcement of the Lamanite trope and their potential to succeed.[38]

Beyond the foster family, each Indian child inherited a ward family that worked to help that child understand a divine role. Rhonda J. Lee, Navajo, recalled, "I was accepted by everyone.... I knew everybody in the ward. They all thought highly of me."[39] Ward activities reached well beyond Sunday meetings. Wards typically organize talent shows, dances, holiday parties, and service outreach. The 1973 *Student Guide* clearly outlined the expectation that Indian students would "attend and take part in all Latter-day Saint Church activities available to you such as priesthood meetings, Sunday school, sacrament meetings, M.I.A. [Mutual Improvement Association], primary, and seminary."[40] Such activities quickly filled up children's (and parents') schedules. Carole Sue Tsosie, Navajo, remembered that she never attended powwows or other Indian activities because she was simply too busy with the regular youth activities organized by the church.[41]

All active Mormon children under twelve years of age attended sacrament meeting with their ward each Sunday, but also attended midweek primary activities where volunteers shared stories and lessons designed to reinforce gospel principles, strong character, and gendered roles that included scouting for boys and homemaking and motherhood for girls.[42] During the 1970s, these meetings collapsed into a new three-hour Sunday block schedule, though older children continued to attend midweek gatherings in addition to Sunday worship services.

Youth aged twelve to eighteen attended midweek Mutual Improvement Association meetings designed to cultivate talents, build leadership, instill moral values, and progress toward achievement goals.[43] Ronald Singer, Navajo, remembered making goals and deciding to serve a full-time mission when he was only a twelve-year-old boy.[44] Caseworker Dorothy Clark served in the Los Angeles area where she instructed Sunday school and MIA leaders to work closely with Indian children and help them fit in with other students. She said, "The big job is to help them have testimonies of the true Gospel and to reject false religious ideas be they those of other churches or of the Indian religions."[45] Additionally, teenage boys received the Aaronic Priesthood and began officiating small duties for the church, which ranged from preparing and passing the weekly sacrament to collecting fast offerings and assisting older men in home visits.

Additionally, all active LDS youth enrolled in daily seminary classes before attending school or during school release time in densely Mormon areas. Lenora Tsosie, Navajo, remembered how she and the other students raced to find passages in those daily classes where children learned the gospel and church history through scriptures marked for memorization.[46] Alvin Watchman recalled, "One day the teacher challenged us to find out if the Book of Mormon was true." He took that challenge, and "one day I knelt down and started praying about the Book of Mormon and its truthfulness.

God answered my prayers!"[47] Personal prayer served to reaffirm that which had become normal for the children.

The LDS Church's youth curriculum divided boys and girls into separate programs that emphasized personal development. Young men participated in the Boy Scouts of America while young women pursued achievement or "honor" badges and awards.[48] Foster mother Kay Cox outlined the young women's program during the 1970s and explained her foster daughter's determination to complete the work. She wrote:

> Each achievement completed earned an "honor badge," and each girl was expected to earn twelve badges each year but might do as many as she chose from the one hundred possible areas. The badge work included a written report of one to three hundred words. One to three words would be an accomplishment for Eva, but she had an uncanny desire to try. She would write for hours in beautiful microscopic handwriting without making one complete sentence or even a coherent thought.[49]

Meanwhile, boys completed merit badges and advanced in scout ranks. As they advanced toward becoming an Eagle Scout, each boy developed skills and served in leadership capacities.

In 1964, David Talayumptewa, Pueblo, became the first Placement student to earn the rank of Eagle Scout. He said, "I wanted to be an Eagle Scout because it is the first big achievement in my life and it is a real challenge." He attributed his success to supportive foster parents and a sibling who had already achieved the rank.[50] Two months later the program boasted its second Eagle Scout and others followed.[51]

Youth activities throughout the church emphasized personal development, public speaking, and leadership roles. Many students filled local youth leadership offices among their peers at church, and the most outgoing Placement students occasionally took on extra responsibilities as leaders within the ISPP. Each caseworker monitored several districts containing dozens of students, and every district required student leaders to organize activities.[52] Some caseworkers even enlisted students as informal caseworker assistants who worked closely with other Placement students to ensure their proper adjustment from the reservation to white Mormon society. Placement student Emery Bowman recalled visiting other students, along with their caseworker, in order to assist in assessing and resolving frequent concerns.[53] Another student similarly remembered that "my caseworker put me kinda like in an assistant caseworker and I worked with the kids in my district." She helped to listen and counsel other students who struggled to get along with their foster families or otherwise adapt to the new environment.[54] In this way students took on roles that entrenched their own spiritual and cultural conversion as they assisted others in the transition. Student recruitment also increased caseworkers' outreach and better enabled them to connect with each student.

Caseworkers visited students and foster parents each month to resolve any concerns and ensure smooth operation in white society.[55] They checked on students' academic progress and social adjustments in school and within the foster family. Caseworkers helped students and parents with any problems (such as fighting and alcohol or tobacco use) while giving encouragement. They also developed student leadership by assisting the youth who planned upcoming events for the district. Caseworker Dale Shumway explained the obstacles he faced while engendering leadership qualities by relating the story of a Navajo woman who once said to him, "Goals are for you white people. We don't have any goals because nothing works out any good anyhow." Such comments demonstrate feelings of futility on the reservation and a common Navajo notion that the future is driven by "faith, fate, and luck." Shumway worked to instill Spencer W. Kimball's oft-quoted motto, "If it is to be it is up to me."[56] As caseworkers met with Indian students, they tried to work through these and other cultural barriers. They dutifully tracked social behavior and filled out standardized monthly progress reports that assessed spiritual development, foster home adjustment, school progress, social adjustment, and communications between the foster and natural homes.[57]

Students' audible and public professions of faith before their white congregation offered the best indicators that they understood and internalized the cultural expectations. Mormon youth spoke to their respective ward each year or so, and every month a testimony meeting opened the floor to youth and adults who wished to share their feelings about the gospel. Placement students often participated and in so doing grew more comfortable with public speaking as they reaffirmed their faith in the church. Caseworkers also solicited their students for additional presentations at firesides and other events to stir up support and foster volunteers for the program.[58] As students spoke before peers and adults, they confirmed their belief in the gospel and the divine inspiration guiding the Placement Program. In 1960, Betty Redhouse issued one such talk. She said:

> I would like to tell you today about the difference the church has made in my life.... Without the knowledge of the gospel I would still believe that old medicine man could heal and I could still believe the superstitions. Through the church I have got my light and truth. The light and truth which some day I might put into use among my people. This light and truth which has made a difference in my life. Perhaps I can tell you about the Navajo reservation my grandma lives on, a place where there is no light or truth, where the people have jealousy and discouragement that leads to drinking, the superstitions that turn their faces to the medicine man. All this makes me want to seek harder and try to gain more.[59]

As students stood before others and testified of their conversion and trust in the gospel, they reaffirmed to themselves that which their cultural environment already assumed—that they were indeed Lamanites who needed to break free from an apostate Indian culture to restore a more glorious and correct culture.

In addition to regular ward activities and caseworker visits, Placement students also participated in meetings and socials exclusive to the program's youth. These activities grew out of 1950s-era fears about interracial socialization, dating, and marriage. Golden Buchanan and Spencer Kimball separately commented that anxieties about miscegenation constituted one of the greatest obstacles to the program's approval by the church in 1954, and those fears continued over the next several decades.[60] Indeed, Mormon theology embraced a caste system of sorts that rationalized American racial fears, wherein the righteous covenant people should not mix with the apostate gentiles, often indicated by darker skin.[61] Kimball perpetuated this segregation in some of his speeches, though he relied more on cultural cleavages as sources of conflict rather than a racial or biological hierarchy.[62] His comments offered revelatory approval for concerns held by many Mormons and other Americans of the era. Indeed, foster parents and community members did not always feel comfortable when Native American boys sought to date their white daughters.[63] By the 1970s and 1980s, however, such concerns subsided significantly, and interracial dating increased with less alarm.[64]

To help alleviate those early concerns, the Indian Committee determined to organize socials where Placement students might come together across geographic distances to develop relationships through dances and other "wholesome" recreation.[65] Initially this took the form of annual Christmas parties, which began in 1954 and continued for many years. At the annual party, students gathered for games and activities, including a visit from Santa Claus. They encountered more than the European folk tradition of St. Nick, including the other rituals surrounding the holiday, such as caroling, gift exchanges, and seasonal treats. The Christmas parties also served as a consolation to children upset that the ISPP initially did not allow them to return home for the Christmas season. Though intended simply as a fun activity, this and other parties also reinforced Western notions of appropriate social exercises and behavior.

That first 1954 social occurred when a Placement student took the initiative to host a party with other local ISPP children. Miles Jensen served as the caseworker over the girl, and thought the activity could provide an excellent tool to build relationships between Placement students. He was excited about the party's potential to bring together ISPP students who likely felt isolated and alone in the strange new culture. He recounted:

> At the party they saw others like them who were able to be very happy with the same program. They learned that other students had problems as well as themselves. They saw others were happy and enjoying the things that were happening to them. They were able to see how neat and clean the other children were and they felt a desire to be the same way.[66]

Jensen further explained that the party proceeded with "mixer games" and was pleased that "everyone had a chance to get acquainted." Many students even began corresponding with each other thereafter.[67]

In January 1959, Spencer W. Kimball instructed caseworkers to gather Indian children more regularly "so they will be more inclined to socialize with and marry within their own race and not inter-marry with the white people."[68] Beginning that year caseworker Clare Bishop organized regular "Indian-only" socials in his districts.[69] Again in February and March of 1960, Kimball directed caseworkers to increase the frequency with which they hosted socials for Indians as a means to remedy interracial dating.[70] By June 1961, Bishop reported to the Indian Committee that each district participated with another in a social every other month, in addition to the annual Christmas party.[71] The 1973 *Student Guide* stipulated that students would "take part in and help plan the district activities of the Indian Student Placement Program."[72]

The type of activity varied from month to month and from district to district. Some caseworkers proved less conscientious about organizing get-togethers while others reliably gathered the children each month. A typical calendar of activities might call for a welcome-back social in September, bowling or skating in October and November, and a Christmas social in December. January might include a spiritual fireside, followed by a basketball tournament in February, district conferences in March, regional or church-wide conferences in April, and an end-of-year social in May.[73] Former students recall various activities, including trips to theme parks and theatrical presentations.[74] In December 1969, a group of Placement students gathered to perform "From the Eagle's Bend," an LDS pageant originally performed by BYU students that employed lip synchronization and pantomime to narrate the afterlife of a Native American soldier who died in Vietnam and learned the gospel in the spirit world.[75] Some developed strong connections through these gatherings. One former student explained that through such activities she bonded with other Placement students. After meeting other local Placement students at ISPP activities, she said that "we pretty much hung out together."[76]

Despite these efforts, monthly gatherings proved far less able to bind students than day-to-day interactions with their classmates and neighborhood friends. Aneta Whaley, Navajo, remembered several infrequent parties each year. Consequently, she recounted, "I think I had a closer relationship with girls that were from my neighborhood. They weren't Navajos; they were Bilagaana [white] girls. I think I was closer to them than I was to the Navajo kids."[77] Erdman Jake similarly remembered another medium for social interaction that the ISPP facilitated. Basketball is particularly popular among Navajos, and the Placement Program hosted tournaments that were sure to bring students together. Jake recalled that those tournaments were among the few Placement-sponsored activities that he participated in, and that it successfully acquainted him with other youths.[78] Navajo Stephanie Chiquito remembered periodic ISPP activities and how the geographic distance strained those loose associations. She said:

> We would have [activities] once maybe every semester. I tried to get to know the other kids. I tried to have a good relationship with them. It was kind of hard in a way because we all had our different families and different things we did. We tried to get together a little.... We had youth conferences every year. In our agency we got together and we talked about placement every month. It was nice.[79]

The ISPP efforts to gather students seemed to provide a large, but usually secondary, network of friends.

The activities that participants most clearly remember are the annual district, regional, and church-wide Lamanite conferences. Caseworker Glen VanWagenen remembered that the conferences emerged out of the smaller group meetings and a desire to promote youth leadership. He and then director Clare Bishop determined that the Indian youth required additional opportunities because their poor communication skills and cultural differences made it less likely that their respective wards would give them such prospects. VanWagenen explained, "We felt it would be important to have an Indian experience for them where they could lead out and which hopefully would carry over to the reservation."[80] Individual districts organized two and sometimes three days' worth of activities modeled in part on preexisting youth conferences hosted for the general youth membership of the church. Local Placement Program conferences included group discussions, a banquet, a dance, general sessions with spiritual- and leadership-focused presentations, talent contests, a testimony meeting, and awards.[81] These gatherings proved to be fantastic social extravaganzas as well as intense training sessions, and rapidly gained popularity as the climactic focal point of each year on Placement.

The Southwest Indian Mission hosted its own Indian Youth Conference at Window Rock in June 1962. Between 1,200 and 1,500 youth attended the two-day conference and participated in the activities, which included modern and traditional dances, performances, games, speeches, talent contests, and awards such as the most "ideal boy" and "ideal girl" who embodied the characteristics of Mormon spirituality and white leadership.[82] Following suit, the Placement Program hosted its own massive interdistrict youth conference in April 1963.[83]

Over 120 Native youths attended the ISPP's first youth conference in 1963. Its stated objectives were to foster "meaningful social inter-action," "provide an opportunity for the students whereby they may prepare, perform, and discuss educational goals," and "provide an opportunity for the students to feel part of a large group of students."[84] The conference program included prayers, musical numbers, guest speakers, and a presentation of quivers to special guests from the church hierarchy as well as newly elected Navajo chairman Raymond Nakai. For the remainder of the day, students participated in a talent show, athletic activities, a social dance, and an award ceremony.[85] Each year thereafter similar conferences gathered Latter-day Saint Indian youths for socialization, leadership training, and spiritual motivation.

At the 1963 conference, participants elected a fourteen member student planning committee to organize the 1964 conference.[86] In the program newsletter, the committee announced the conference theme which indicated their acceptance and internalization of the Book of Mormon and the prophetic future of Lamanites: "Our History Foretells Our Future." The committee organized two planning meetings during the school year and determined to host a conference for Indian youth aged fifteen years and above. It would include a banquet, dance, testimony meeting, and sightseeing tour of Salt Lake City, as well as three separate youth competitions: powwow, athletics, and one that encompassed "speech, essay, and talent, including fashions, arts and crafts."[87] The conference began on a Thursday with fry bread and chili, and nearly 200 student participants registered that day. Speech contests and talent shows occurred on Friday, and Apostle LeGrand Richards offered remarks during a banquet, which concluded with awards and a dance. Saturday featured separate boys' and girls' basketball tournaments and an afternoon testimony meeting where adolescent Placement students shared their conviction in the truthfulness of the gospel and inspiration of church leaders and the ISPP.[88] In 1965, students chose "Eternal Life— My Responsibility" as the program theme to emphasize their agency, and secured Navajo chairman Raymond Nakai to deliver the banquet address for the conference.[89] Similar conferences continued over the next thirty years, each emphasizing student education, leadership, and religious devotion. As students took an active role in planning and executing the conferences, they not only reflected the colonizing message but internalized it as their own.

In June 1965, the Indian Committee recognized the increasing significance of the conferences. They determined to move future gatherings to Brigham Young University where they might dovetail with the university's annual Indian Week celebrations and where college-aged Indians might serve as leaders and examples to formative adolescents in the Placement Program. Additionally, Apostle Boyd K. Packer instructed ISPP executive director Clare Bishop to plan for regional conferences in other areas as the program expanded into Arizona, Idaho, and Canada. Last, the committee explored the function of the conferences. Kimball echoed the value in marital matchmaking. General Relief Society president Belle Spafford suggested it might motivate students to strive for admission to BYU's growing Indian program. The Indian Committee unanimously agreed on the value of the conferences in reforming Indian youth.[90]

The 1966 ISPP youth conference featured much of the same activities. A winning poem by Ida Lee explored the multiple sources of identity that she saw within herself and the primacy of one over the others. She wrote:

> *At school they call me Indian,*
> *At church I'm Lamanite,*
> *Great Grandpa says that we are the people*
> *I think they all are right.*
> *By whatever name he seeks me,*
> *It will matter not at all*
> *For I am my Heavenly Father's child,*
> *And I'll answer to His call.*[91]

Lee's poem illustrated that ISPP students were well aware of the different labels that could be affixed to them, but that the important factor was not so much the titles as the core sense of self which remained resilient and unaffected by the labels. For Lee and others, that central sense of self was defined along spiritual lines derived from LDS theology. Their comments reveal the synthesis of identities comfortably housed within the LDS theological worldview and the primacy and encompassing nature of her religious identity. The 1967 conference included a new high of three hundred youths and featured the theme "Let Our Light So Shine Before Our People."[92]

In 1968 and subsequent years, the Placement Program sponsored conferences expanded to include all Lamanite youths of twelve years and older, and Placement students could only attend if they won a speech, essay, talent, or handicraft contest in their district or regional conferences, or if they otherwise served in leadership capacities. Maybell Begay, Navajo, remembered, "In order to qualify for youth conferences we either had to write an essay or give a speech on the theme of the conference, and we were judged."[93] The four hundred Indian adolescents gathered in late April where they embraced the student selected theme for the year: "The Day of the Lamanite Is Now."[94] Elder A. Theodore Tuttle of the Indian Committee spoke to the youths, stating, "Now is the time to fulfill your destiny—your people have waited long years for the type of leadership gathered in this room."[95] In May 1969, nearly five hundred Indian youths attended the first official church-wide Indian Youth Conference; each prepared to share their talent, essay, or handicraft.[96] By 1970, regional conferences were held across the United States and Canada, in places like Richfield, Ogden, and Tooele, Utah; Gallup and Albuquerque, New Mexico; Phoenix and Tuba City, Arizona; Idaho Falls, Idaho; Seattle, Washington; Lethbridge, Alberta, Canada; Rapid City, South Dakota; Oklahoma City, Oklahoma; and Charlotte, North Carolina. These conferences funneled the best performers and leaders into Provo for the annual church-wide conference.[97]

The Lamanite conferences gathered the LDS Church's brightest, most outgoing and obedient Indian youth and provided them with unique training and access to church and secular leaders. In April 1971, Navajo chairman Peter MacDonald attended the conference as a special guest and mingled with the students. Spencer W. Kimball addressed the eighteen hundred youth gathered under the theme "A Lamanite: Who Am I?"[98] Kimball taught that the Indian attendees were the descendants of the great prophets of Israel, including Joseph, Jacob, Abraham, and Isaac. He explained, "Be proud of him and know that you are of royal blood; with your royal blood you can achieve, rising to the top."[99] Chairman MacDonald also offered encouraging remarks to the youth. He even referred to himself as a Lamanite and charged the students to continue preparing for the great service they would provide to their people.[100] Former youth conference president

George Lee returned as a motivational speaker who exemplified the purpose of the program. Having recently completed a graduate degree from Utah State University, Lee addressed that conference and issued bold expectations: "This will be your responsibility in the years to come, to be in positions that will help you further the blossoming of the Lamanites."[101] By encouraging students to obtain education and facilitating public presentations and leadership opportunities, the Lamanite conferences offered the instruction and training to help participants fulfill their prophetic charge. As leaders in the church and in their reservation communities, they could help "redeem" American Indians.

Awards issued at the conferences reinforced obedience to and internalization of the LDS Church Indian Program and student leadership within the church. In addition to regular awards for speeches, poetry, handicrafts and other talents, and academic success (measured by a minimum 2.8 GPA), the 1971 conference issued awards linked to spiritual accomplishments. Students received recognition for following church standards, attending meetings and seminary, identifying and explaining LDS Church Indian programs, memorizing scriptures, presenting talks on the destiny of Lamanites, holding "significant" leadership roles, completing genealogical work, and serving as class officers at school.[102]

Testimony meetings also constituted a standard aspect of the conferences. Students voluntarily stood and testified to their peers about their belief in the church and its programs and their divine role as Lamanites. Some fifty students spoke at the 1971 conference. One commented, "Isn't it great to be part of something like the Lamanite movement of the Church of Jesus Christ of Latter-day Saints?" Another said:

> I want you to know I have a burning testimony of the truthfulness of this gospel and regardless of what anyone says or tells you, please remember that this church is true and don't let anyone kid you. By golly, you are in the driver's seat and you are in control and you can do with your life what you want to![103]

His comments seem to fuse the gospel and its characterization of Indians with notions of self-control, agency, and upward mobility. The Lamanite trope gave youths confidence that they could succeed and reinforced their faith and commitment to the program. The testimony meetings contributed to the program's holistic goal of reframing student identity along notions of value and self-driven accomplishment. As one student said, "They made you feel that you were worth something."[104]

As students attended Lamanite conferences and district meetings, worked with caseworkers, their ward, and foster families, they certainly felt pressure to internalize the LDS gospel and reach for its expectations. The Indian program established a specific trajectory that began in youth while on Placement.[105] Quite a few students culturally and theologically converted to the church and served full-time missions. Thousands enrolled in BYU's Indian programs or at other colleges, and many married in Mormon temples.[106]

Indians enrolled in the ISPP found that it promised them hope and self-confidence as well as training to achieve success in school in preparation for a professional career. One student said, "Now I think, 'I can do as well as the next person.' This came from Placement."[107] Placement students who followed the program and re-enrolled each year tended to earn higher grades than their Indian classmates back home.[108] They also reported more positive self-image.[109] They believed they were qualified for a bright, new future filled with opportunities.

While many embraced the program's message and the Lamanite identity, others did not. In his study of ethnic identity in the LDS Church, sociologist Armand Mauss identified several common responses to the Lamanite trope. A great many embrace "the positive and ennobling aspects of it, as a basis for full assimilation into the modern Anglo-Mormon way of life."[110] They look beyond the potentially disturbing ramifications of Mormon race theory and the negative associations of dark skin. Others never internalize or fully understand the ramifications of the identity. For them, it serves no function in their lives beyond the material and educational resources offered by membership in the LDS Church. Still others "try in various ways to straddle and embrace both identities, Lamanite and tribal, to enjoy the social benefits of each."[111]

Certainly in the case of Placement, a fourth common response emerges: outright rejection. Briefly enrolled as a Placement student, Lacee Harris stated her resistance to the identity along historical and theological terms. She said, "Lamanite! I am not a Lamanite. They are a wicked people. I am not a wicked person."[112] Harris resented the displacement of her Ute culture with the generalized and superficial Lamanite identity. She continued, "My people were good, deeply spiritual, in tune with the rhythms of the earth and with their own needs. How could I be descended from a wicked people?" Leslie Ellis similarly said, "First of all, I'm not a 'Lamanite.'" She continued:

> I didn't like the term when I HAD to go to church....I never really agreed with the way the LDS teachings were/are....The LDS Church is just trying to do what the government has been trying to do since the beginning of time. The LDS Church is trying to get rid of the Indians, and make them like them....Indians that I went to church with are no longer affiliated with the church anymore either.[113]

Ellis interpreted the use of Lamanite as a mechanism to assimilate Indians into white Mormon society, and equated it with longstanding governmental assimilation efforts. For Ellis and others, the negative elements of the Lamanite heritage proved too inconsistent with the cultural heritage associated with their tribal identity. Likewise, former Placement student Behe Reck expressed concerns about Mormon theology's conflation of skin tone and morality, and he resisted the Placement Program's efforts to convert him to such perspectives. He wrote:

> The thing I remember the most about Mormons is that they told me that my people were "cursed." That god had cursed Indians and that's why they were black. Or rather, their favorite phrase was "dark and loathsome" while the white people were "light and delightsome." And that Mormons were put here to save the "dark and loathsome" Indians from their heathen ways. I was in the "placement program" from 1962–1965, between the ages of 8 and 12. They tried to brainwash me of my Indianness and Indian ways, and they succeeded for a while...but I eventually regained my humanity slowly but surely. It was a long process.[114]

As the words of these students demonstrate, some on the Placement Program found that the ideological meanings associated with the Lamanite were simply too negative to overlook.

Those who rejected the Lamanite ideal often joined the church and ISPP merely as a means to access education and were not prepared for the conforming pressures Placement issued. Many never read or believed the teachings of the Book of Mormon, or even of Christianity. They lacked the foundation necessary to justify adherence to the strict and structured Mormon lifestyle. One foster parent wrote to Elder George P. Lee, the former Placement student who then served as a church-wide leader in the Quorum of Seventy, to express his dissatisfaction with the behavior of Placement students whom he supposed lacked that foundational testimony. The foster parent wrote:

> Thursday October 21st you spoke to all the placement students in Orem and as you spoke Beulah seemed to make light of things you said, was not particularly interested in listening to your remarks about Christ or a need for a testimony yet was not against it either.... Beulah said she didn't want to be Mormon. She was peyote church and elders told her join the church so she could go on placement.[115]

Such students often quit the program, and afterwards many of them bore feelings of resentment.[116] For them, the reservation proved a much-needed retreat from which they were unlikely to return. For most, that traditional landscape remained free from the expectations of white Mormon society and the watchful monitoring of foster parents and caseworkers who imposed racially offensive ideology.

Following the 1954 regularization of the ISPP under the Relief Society and Indian Committee, administrators mandated that all children would return home each summer. This policy grew out of the Indian Committee's intent that Native parents maintain bonds with their children, but also that children might return home and serve as examples for their Indian families.[117]

Program officers regularly shared this charge with students to encourage their good behavior over the summer. Navajo Rose Denete Sohsy explained, "They would tell us, 'Now it's your job to go home and to teach your family about the church and to help them understand it, so they can'—they didn't say 'so they can be saved'; 'so they can blossom like the rose, too.'"[118] Ernestine Cody, Navajo, similarly explained, "When we go back from the white man's home to our own people, we should try to set an example of what we have learned in these past years. Then our people will want to join the church and learn of modern ways."[119]

Indian children almost never remained in foster care during the summer months. When addressing a congressional subcommittee, the LDS Church attorney explained as much. Under only the rarest of circumstances, and at the admonition of the biological parents, students might remain in foster care over the summer. He explained, "It is a very, very rare exception, and about the only case I know of is where at home there was a serious illness in the natural parents."[120] Lynn Lee, president of the Mexican Hat Branch on the Navajo Reservation, confirmed the regular application of the policy. He said, "I have about twenty-five young people in the program each year, and am not aware of a single one who has remained in the foster home during the summer." He continued, "I, personally, have never been aware of any placement student who has not returned home for the summer."[121] With extremely few exceptions foster parents bid farewell to their children each summer.

Much as their departure from the reservations, Indian students met at designated chapels and meeting places where buses gathered to take them home. The Student Guide instructed them to leave winter coats, boots, and good school clothes (generally purchased by the foster families) and prohibited students from taking any animals or large items like wagons or bicycles.[122] Nevertheless, Clare Bishop recalled, they typically departed with larger suitcases than those with which they arrived.[123] George Lee recalled, "I was going home taller, heavier, and with a suitcase full of nice clothes."[124]

Just as nine months earlier, the departure proved emotional for many. Carletta Yellowjohn, Shoshone, remembered how difficult it was for her foster mother who could not bear to join her at the appointed gathering place. Yellowjohn said, "She kissed me goodbye and didn't want to go because it broke her heart. My foster father and my foster sister Denise took me over. We all met at the bus stop. Then we said our goodbyes, and that was it."[125] One foster mother remembered the scene of Indian youths loading onto the buses, and the sadness that followed her foster son's departure:

> The huge buses waited, as did many little groups of people; each
> family together and each one alone, trying to think of bright things

to say. It was useless. The buses pulled out to cries of "Be good!" "Be careful!" "See you soon!" "Write!" Then silence.... We drove home. No one spoke, because no one trusted his voice. We all went straight to bed. As I stopped to tuck David in, suddenly he looked up through tears, and, with his voice breaking, cried out, "Oh, Mom, what will I do without Virgil?"

She concluded, "So, the night he left us, we cried ourselves to sleep as Virgil had cried the night he came to us."[126]

As the bus worked its way toward the reservations, the students recognized the country from which they came. Kent Begay recalled a sense of belonging, "of knowing who you are and knowing where you come from. Once you hit Chinle, Arizona, the sight of Canyon de Chelly—home. This is where I come from."[127] The buses dropped children off at various centers where they met their parents. George Lee remembered the children scattering into buckboard wagons and pickup truck beds, but also the strong feelings of joy and sadness. On one such occasion he embraced his long-missed biological mother and the two cried together as they hugged. He remembered, "The pounding of her heart told me how much she had missed me."[128] As families reunited and departed for their homes, they updated each other on their experiences. Another former student remembered, "I wanted to share with them what I had learned, to share with them things that I learned in school. It would be something new to my family. I wanted to see how my family had grown when I was absent."[129] Emery Bowman fondly recalled the closeness his family felt after the long separation. He said, "We were all away from each other nine months of the year, and when we got back, it was just a huge reunion. We were all happy through the summer. We didn't get tired of each other."[130]

When students returned to the reservation each year, they were confronted by a variety of reminders that they were again in a different cultural environment. On a purely physical level, they noticed distinct differences. In the early decades, Navajos returned to hogans with dirt floors, kerosene lanterns, and small reservoirs of hand-carried water. They saw their family herds and remembered the sense of openness presented by the land.[131] These emblems served to remind them of their Native cultures and lifeways.

Children resumed former duties working alongside their families. Ella Bedonie wove wool, butchered sheep, and hauled water.[132] Others resumed family migratory work on nearby or even distant farms. George Lee remembered:

> After a week or so, I was back into the normal swing of things—living, thinking, and behaving as a Navajo. Before I realized it, I was completely immersed in the activities of my family, which included herding sheep every day or going out looking for the horses so water and wood could be hauled. A family tradition was to attend the Ute Bear Dances; these were held in Towaoc, Colorado. At other times we went together to squaw dances, rodeos, or Navajo sings.[133]

Though the students had spent the last nine months learning and committing to the exclusivity of the Mormon faith, many fulfilled cultural expectations as Navajos during the summer months and engaged in rites of passage such as the women's Kinaaldá puberty ceremony, or in other Blessingways and Enemyways, or even in the peyote rituals of the Native American church.

Placement students' participation in the Mormon Church typically declined or disappeared altogether during the summer, despite the program's policy demanding their weekly attendance at their local reservation congregations. Some simply did not want to attend. For many the summer offered a break from the strict rules of Mormon society, and the short summer proved insufficient to build social bonds with reservation wards and branches. "It was always fun to come home," said Omaha tribal member Edwardo Zondaja. "It was kind of like a vacation in more than one sense. We were able to sleep in on Sunday although we'd get knocks on the doors from some home teachers." He continued, "We used to go to church every now and then."[134] One former student commented, "I didn't like church really when I was at home, I didn't like going to church."[135]

One missionary in the Southwest Indian Mission reported with horror that a great many students seeped back into Native lifestyles or at least failed to live according to Mormon expectations. He recorded that of the twenty-four recent students living in the area he ministered, only two lived the LDS Church standards. Most said that the church leaders expect "too much from them." He continued:

One twelve-year-old girl, who came off the program early because of problems with her foster parents, has become involved in some serious difficulty. My companion and I found her in the hills one morning where she had stayed all night with a young man who had just signed up to go for next year. Another person spent two weeks living with some fellow, and then decided to get married. Another girl spent two weeks in jail because she stayed [out] all night, and wouldn't mind her mother.... One young man, who was a Priest and was one of our sharpest boys, spent the weekend in jail with two other members that had been on the program a year ago. Two other young men have never been to church since they got home and now are chain-smokers and drinkers.[136]

Such behavior caused great alarm among devout Mormons who resided on reservations and feared Placement failed to make substantive changes to its participants.

A disappointed bishop in Tuba City explained that many Placement students simply treated their summer on the reservation as a vacation from Mormon rules and structure. They disregarded values espoused while on Placement and did not even attend church. He concluded, "The kids never caught the vision of what we were trying to do. I would say a large percentage of the kids that went on placement didn't catch the vision of what was in store for them."[137] Indeed, quite a few—maybe even a majority—of students chose not to attend church and other Mormon activities during the summer months. This intentional absence speaks volumes about their ability to play Mormon, as they developed skills and spoke the language, but still retained much of themselves while in foster care.

Other Indian youths tried to attend church but found themselves distantly removed from any chapel and without transportation—the same problem that had long haunted the reservation and inhibited the growth of local schools. George Lee remembered walking and hitchhiking for twenty miles only to arrive at the chapel just as the meetings concluded. On his second attempt he caught only the final thirty minutes of the meeting and then, unable to hitch a ride home, he ran the distance.[138] Those experiences demonstrate not only his conviction, but the lack of parental support that Lee and other students frequently faced. One woman recalled, "I always tried to ask my parents to take me to church but they said, 'No, we don't have enough money' or something. 'It's too far.'" She remembered, "I felt kind of uncomfortable asking them to take me to church."[139] Even those who lived near a chapel found that responsibilities, traveling for work, and family visits made regular church attendance difficult. One former student explained, "I'd attend, if I was there, but [not] if I was at my grandma's.... Besides, my grandparents and my aunts and uncles, they're not members."[140]

Clearly an emerging cultural rift created some degree of awkwardness; however, more often than not, students readjusted to their reservation environments. George Lee explained:

> Even though I never was ashamed of being an Indian, somehow because of the delightful experiences I had during my first year on placement, I more or less forgot who I was. I never did totally reject my Indian ways, but it took a return home that summer, and each following summer, to help me realize I was Indian with a Navajo family and home. Once I came to this realization, I simply made up my mind that when I was back home on the reservation, I was going to adjust quickly to life at home and to act accordingly. I tried hard not to dwell on the beautiful experiences I had been through while staying with my foster family, and I made up my mind simply to live the way my natural family did and to accept my family as they were.[141]

Students generally adjusted back to reservation life with few problems.

Upon their return to the reservation, Placement students usually fit in well with other Indians. In part this may be due to the reality that many Navajo families lived in geographically isolated homes that only sporadically interacted with a larger community. A 1979 internal report found that 84 percent of parents and 81 percent of tribal leaders thought children returning from Placement got along "well" or "very well" with friends who had remained on the reservation, and only 12 percent of parents and 15 percent of leaders believed that the returning students had a hard time with these relationships. Students themselves revealed slightly less positive but comparable results. When asked if they experienced difficulty "getting along" with friends who did not go on Placement, only 7 percent of current students and 14 percent of discontinued students said there was "a

TABLE 6.1. PERCEPTIONS OF PLACEMENT STUDENTS

SURVEY QUESTION: Are children returning from Placement considered outsiders by members of the tribe?

	% OF TRIBAL LEADERS	% OF CURRENT STUDENTS	% OF DISCONTINUED STUDENTS
Definitely yes	3	5	7
Probably yes	16	12	15
Probably no	25	14	20
Definitely no	49	63	53
Don't know/No response	7	6	5

Source: Wasatch Research Opinion Report, 1979, pp. 101–2, Church Archives.

great deal" of difficulty, and 22 percent of current students and 16 percent of discontinued students noticed "some" difficulty. Just over half of both groups described the degree of estrangement as "not much at all." Equally interesting are the respondents answer to, "Are children returning from Placement considered outsiders by members of the tribe?" The gross majority indicated "no" in one form or another. The survey indicated that only a few students, parents, or tribal leaders noticed any trouble as Placement students returned to the reservations each summer. In truth, of course, during those summer months many continuing students had little opportunity to interact with peers beyond their own, often isolated families.

Nevertheless, some former students expressed discomfort regarding their return to the reservation. Some felt unsettled by the lack of electricity and indoor plumbing, dirt floors, and former responsibilities like herding sheep.[142] Ella Bedonie remembered that some students came home and refused to sit on the floor to eat. They insisted on washing their hands frequently, rejected dietary norms, and were generally dissatisfied with the conditions of their families' homes.[143] Native parents surely found such behavior agitating. Loretta Chino recalled that her mother "would comment about 'them' changing me from my upbringing. At one point, she was not going to let me finish the program."[144] Only with great effort was she able to convince her mother to permit further enrollment.

Some of those who quit Placement and returned to schools on the reservation did find points of contention between the two cultural environments. These former ISPP students believed other Indians viewed them as
religiously and culturally self-righteous because they embraced white culture's emphasis on speaking up and standing out.[145] One former student
explained, "They didn't see me as Indian sometimes, they only saw me as a
non-Indian person." He attributed this rift to his increasingly outgoing communication skills. He continued, "I guess my way of communicating probably
to teachers or to people was more aggressive, more outgoing. . . . Sometimes
Indians at home are more submissive and quiet and they don't speak out
loud."[146] The newly instilled assertive culture stood out in the more reserved
Native cultures. One LDS social worker openly admitted, "They sometimes
get teased by other kids for being on the program."[147] Some faced more
than mere teasing. George Lee related how gangs of boys accosted him at
squaw dances. He remembered, "One night I ran many miles, all the way
home, in the middle of the night, to escape their wrath." He concluded, "I
was rejected more by my own people than by the Anglos up in Utah."[148]

Such conflicts stemmed from the adoption of some white cultural trappings and the apparent rejection of Native ways. For some, their very Indianness was questioned by others and even by themselves. One Navajo
woman explained what she perceived as the exclusivity of Indianness.
She said that "any true Navajo will never be anything but a Navajo," and
though they "may join other churches" it was simply a tactic to appear "a
little more acceptable to other people." She concluded, "The true Navajo
will never be anything religiously [other] than what he was born with."[149]
This comment reveals a very real challenge for Placement students or any
others who might attempt to equally manage the demands of two cultures
that, at times, seemed mutually exclusive. For some Navajos, any attempt
to blend the two represented a betrayal of Native ways. Cultural cleavages
were inherent to the program, but by returning children to the reservations
each year, the ISPP administrators hoped to minimize such rifts and maintain some biculturalism.

Though the Placement Program released children to their reservation
homes during the summers, the church did not cease all efforts to maintain the cultural and theological inroads made during the school year. The
ISPP issued very specific expectations of summer behavior for students

who wished to re-enroll in the fall. The 1968 *Natural Parent Guide* outlined expectations for Placement students while on the reservation each summer. It required that they and their families attend church regularly.[150] The 1973 *Student Guide* further stated that Placement students would "maintain church standards while they are home in the summer. This includes things such as attending church, keeping the Word of Wisdom, and helping out in ward branches."[151] It also stated that students should "help your family and friends become better members of the church."[152] Rose Denette Sohsy recalled that "before we left every year to come home, they would tell us, 'Make sure you go to church. Don't go to any ceremonies, like squaw dances. Don't have any ceremonies.'"[153]

A variety of mechanisms reached out to Indian youths while on summer break. Caseworkers made visits to Indian youths and their families, and some foster families even took family vacations to visit Indian children and re-establish bonds during the months apart. A few foster families even helped those children avoid their reservation home life through employment and/or enrollment in summer programs. Most important, the local wards and branches, as well as the Southwest Indian Mission, orchestrated expansive programs to draw Indian youth out to church functions that reinforced school year instruction.

Caseworker visits constituted the only genuine ISPP monitoring of youth during the summer months. While orienting new enrollees, the caseworkers also met with continuing students and their local church leaders to verify their activity in regular meetings.[154] The *Student Guide* warned students to anticipate these visits and instructed, "You and your family should be there to meet with him."[155] Fulltime missionaries assigned to the Southwest and Northwest Indian Missions directed caseworkers through backcountry roads and located hogans and other homes without postal addresses.

Less common, foster parents who paid visits to the reservation often put themselves and others in an awkward position. The program required students to write their foster family each month, but many students did not follow the summertime instructions, and writing letters likely seemed an out-of-place experience for a child again living in a remote and mostly non-literate environment.[156] When foster parents did arrive at children's homes, the visit often surprised the natural family and created an uncomfortable experience. George Lee's biography recounts one such interaction and the sense of shame he felt because of his natural family's reservation lifestyle. He recounted the embarrassment he felt when his foster parents drove up to his hogan. He questioned, "What would they think of me after seeing where I lived? Maybe they would not want me back, or maybe they would say something bad."[157] One foster mother also remembered such an experience as her biological children exited the Volkswagen bus in front of her former foster student's hogan. She recounted:

> He stood in the ankle-deep dirt, desolate. Tears dropped and formed balls of dust at his feet. I tried to put my arms around him, but this was not Utah, and others were watching. Under his breath he demanded, "What did you come for?" I could feel his chagrin, though I had no answer.... [H]is family was having a hard time economically, and he felt defensive.... We were confused. Here was the same boy who six weeks ago called us Mom and Dad and threw his arms around us. Now he seemed to hate us. We were to learn later that this is a common reaction. Having two sets of parents is fine if they are far apart in time or space. But the two sets of parents together, and a child's loyalty is overly burdened.... Hesitant, he finally led us to one room in the cluster of huts. There on the bed lay his sick mother with her sick baby. Her husband was drunk and was sleeping beside her. Another bed and one small table filled the rest of the room. The only sign of food was a half-filled baby bottle on the window ledge. There was no stove, no cupboard, no water, no food, no soda pop, no "Tucky Fried Chicken"; but make no mistake—it was home to this small boy, and he loved it better than any other.[158]

She concluded, "We returned home feeling our vacation was a failure."[159] The arrival of foster parents forced a collision of two worlds otherwise neatly divided by many students. With both sets of parents present it was difficult for Indian youth to switch back and forth between cultural norms, and quite simply, white folks did not belong on the reservation. They were out of place from the beginning, and though students could express affection and excitement about Western culture while on Placement there was an entirely different standard on the reservation. While there, students largely adhered to local cultural norms. Still, a few issues, such as alcohol consumption or some religious activities, created a conflict for some students.

In an effort to avoid such divided loyalties and emotions, a few older students evaded the normal summer reservation experience altogether. They avoided any social gatherings during the summer, or even feigned to have lost their Navajo language in order to withdraw socially.[160] Some secured employment away from their parents' home or even off the reservation. When Maeta Holiday returned to the reservation after her first summer on Placement, she "panicked" and called her foster parents who quickly found her a summer job working for the National Park Service at Pipe Springs. She performed farm work and gave tours there in an effort to avoid the reservation home she once knew.[161] Teddy Redhouse found employment at a trading post on the Navajo reservation where he could put his arithmetic skills and outgoing personality to use.[162] Another Navajo, DuWaine Boone, recalled he found work digging lines for sprinklers in southern Utah.[163] These experiences also may be indicative of the program's success in instilling a productivity oriented mindset.

A variety of summer programs also enabled a few youth to technically leave their foster home while also avoiding their Indian home. An extreme case is represented by one Navajo girl who hardly returned to the reservation at all during her high school years. She said, "I was always going to school in the summertime, doing something, or traveling."[164] Between her sophomore and junior years she traveled to Germany and, upon returning, enrolled in a summer program at a nearby university. Then, during her last summer break she enrolled in the "Upward Bound" program at the University of Utah.[165] Another remembered the tears she spilled when her foster mother explained that her attendance at summer cheer camp depended upon her natural mother's approval.[166]

Foster parents often financed such summer leaves. They wanted to provide their foster children the same opportunities afforded their own children, and some probably did not mind that it replaced some portion of the students' time on the reservation. One foster sibling offered insight into that mindset. She said:

Why displace a child from his natural environment and bring him into a totally new and improved environment for nine months out of the year, have him acclimate and adjust, only to have every inch of progress made during the school year wiped out during the summer months. In both cases our foster brother and sister were from very deprived backgrounds: drunken parents, incest, dishonesty, etc.[167]

While such dysfunctionality was not universal, it was very common among the families of enrolled students, and it certainly reinforced negative perceptions of reservation life. Such notions surely lingered in the minds of many who supported alternative summer experiences, including church leaders who organized youth missions to occupy the students' entire summer break. Hundreds of Indian teens aged sixteen years and older lived with full-time missionaries on the reservation or elsewhere; they served as a third member of the regular two-person mission teams. They, too, proselytized for sixty or more hours a week and shared boarding in an apartment or spare room.[168] One student commented, "I got off and went back on youth mission again, all summer long I was on a youth mission."[169]

In the summer of 1970, the church's social services department initiated a new leadership program on reservations in Idaho, Montana, North Dakota, and South Dakota. The week-long program offered Indian children ages eight to sixteen "an opportunity to have fun and at the same time develop leadership skills through participation in activities such as athletics, arts and crafts, dance, song, campouts, cooking, nature lore, storytelling, and a myriad of other activities." The program existed to fill the "void for the placement students."[170]

The majority of students, however, did return to their families each summer where their local congregations reached out to provide constant reminders of their obligations as baptized members of the church. Ward and branch activities oscillated between and blended spiritual and purely social activities. The Chinle Branch organized a Mormon pageant titled "Go My Son" in June 1969.[171] Students performed and sang to a theatrical personification of the Lamanite identity. It narrated the pursuit of education and consequent cultural uplift of Native youth. In the process, Indian youth shed many of their tribal customs and appearances for roles in Western society, though they retained some selected dances and other outward appearances of Indianness. The following summer that branch hosted a youth conference with two thousand teens in attendance.[172] In the summer of 1969, the Sawmill Branch hosted a variety of summer activities for youth, including a basketball tournament, youth powwow, softball tournament, and a Placement student social with over seventy students in attendance. At the party the branch leaders showed films and organized a talent show where some ISPP students contributed musical performances.[173]

Throughout the summer months, local wards and branches also worked to attract Placement students to regular worship services and youth activities. Missionaries often drove to distant areas to give children rides, but often had to persuade them to attend.[174] Midweek Mutual Improvement Association activities also reached out to Placement teens.[175] One student recalled that those fun activities drew in youth who otherwise remained disinterested. Her "rowdy cousins" did not care for the more serious Sunday meetings and "only wanted to go to Mutual for the fun of it." She boasted that her own faith had greater depth. She said, "I on the other hand learned the meaning of going to Mutual and its purpose so I was more of a loner at these functions." She also volunteered her musical talents to lead children in song and played the piano for church functions.[176]

Beyond local ward and branch activities, the church hosted other programs designed to draw in Indian youth and maintain the values and ideas instilled during Placement. Beginning in 1960, the LDS Church's Department of Education organized new youth-centered programs on different reservations. In 1964, the programs expanded to the Yakima in Washington, the Nez Perce in Idaho, the Lumbee in North Carolina, and the Navajo Reservation in Arizona, New Mexico, and Utah. Activities included sports, such as volleyball, softball, tetherball, croquet, tennis, horseshoes, and swimming, as well as movies and dances. In 1964 the youth of the Chinle and Window Rock areas participated in a father-and-son outing, a girls camp, an all-sports day, arts and crafts, and a special summer party for Placement students. Those near Tuba City participated in a boys and girls' chorus, talent shows, arts and crafts, sports, firesides, and "cultural programs" that taught the Mormon interpretation of the true Indian, or Lamanite, history. Missionaries and local church members helped to transport hundreds of Indian teens, sometimes using the seminary buses, and local youth committees organized to direct the festivities.[177]

The mission also organized its own youth outreach programs. Conferences similar to those held at the close of the Placement year provided an equivalent spiritual and cultural thrust for Native American teens. The mission experimented with this idea in 1961 and in 1962 launched a much larger "second annual Southwest Indian Mission Conference."[178] These conferences continued each year with few alterations, though the 1969 conference also included a "horseless rodeo" that attracted youth with "calf roping, bull dogging, cowhide surfing, wild steer racing, wild goat tying, and pig catching contests."[179] In the summer of 1970, Many Farms hosted the conference for twelve hundred Indian teens which included a horseless rodeo again. Apostle LeGrand Richards addressed those youth. He echoed the function of the conferences and larger Indian program when he said, "We want to help you develop a love for the Lord and for the church" and "We want to make you leaders."[180] The mission also added a Hawaiian luau to the festivities (indicative of the expanding notion of Lamanites) and, as usual, the entire event ended with a testimony meeting.[181]

The Southwest Indian Mission also organized other activities. Sports proved particularly useful in attracting new converts as well as retaining foster students. The mission took advantage of the popularity of basketball and planned a highly successful tournament in March of 1964, and by 1966 it moved the games to the summer months when Placement students could participate alongside other Indians.[182] In July 1969, the mission presented *From the Eagle's Bend* pageant at the Toyei Boarding School and heavily encouraged Placement students to participate.[183]

Placement expectations and close monitoring by caseworkers and foster parents as well as activities hosted by local wards and branches, the Southwest Indian Mission, and other groups provided a variety of ways to maintain the Placement Program's initiative. Students who wished to return to Native family life certainly could; however, those who wished to avoid it found ample opportunities. In this context of relatively free choice, wherein most opted to abstain, the preference of some to continue participating in the church's Indian program indicates some degree of voluntary allegiance independent of colonizing pressures by caseworkers and local leaders.

Whether during the summer months on the reservation or during the regular school year, the entire Mormon Indian program, and specifically the Placement Program, combined to instill a new notion of Indianness that stemmed from a model of self-driven Western achievement. In this way, the program was far more than lodging and access to public schools. The program taught youth that a "good" Indian—a Lamanite—should pursue education and take a leadership role. The trope also offered assurance that such a personal transformation was indeed possible. Family members and local church acquaintances and teachers reinforced that message, and students took on the role as they assumed leadership responsibilities within the ISPP and participated in Lamanite conferences.

This new self-perception dismissed former notions of Indianness as a merely degenerate vestige of a once industrious and Christian-centered civilization that could be restored through adherence to the restored Mormon gospel. In 1978, Don Hunsaker, president of the Arizona Holbrook Mission that succeeded the Southwest Indian Mission, commented that "the church is interested in preserving the true Navajo culture.... We are interested in restoring their religion to its original state."[184] Clare Bishop also justified the use of this cultural white-wash as a restoration of origins that displaced modern Indian apostasy from their Christian origins articulated in the Book of Mormon. In challenging the significance of modern reservation cultures, he replied, "What culture? The culture of alcoholism and drugs? The culture of poverty, joblessness, and despair? They need to have those traditions changed. Besides, according to the Book of Mormon, Lamanites changed long ago from one culture to another."[185] Elsewhere Bishop also stated:

> What is culture, and when is it good and when is it bad? And what's sacred about it? My grandmother came from Denmark. She gave up her complete culture to come to America and be a member of the church. Is that wrong? Is that bad? Which culture did these children give up? Did they give up their original culture, where they had the Gospel of Jesus Christ in their life, or did they give up another culture that they came to when they left the Gospel of Jesus Christ?[186]

His comments certainly reflect a belief in the superiority of Western culture and a confidence in the history contained in the Book of Mormon which chronicled an apostasy and prophesied restoration. Equally interesting, however, Bishop questions the very notion of culture itself as sacred.

Culture is indeed fluid and ever changing. The common conception of culture suggests a homogeneity that rarely exists because various aspects of all cultures shift over time. Navajos are well known for their frequent and thorough integration of non-Navajo ideas and practices, ranging from the eighteenth-century incorporation of Pueblo clan names and nineteenth-century pastoral sheep-herding to the 2011 crowning of a black Navajo woman as Miss Navajo Nation. Navajos and others hold no reluctance to incorporate foreign ideas and concepts. What makes the Lamanite trope so offensive should be less the foreign nature but more the uneven relationship of power whereby Mormons instituted a theology that discarded so many traditions and rewrote history and identity.

The ISPP offered a new identity that reached well beyond the education and cultural exposure students and biological parents anticipated. By way of family and ward activities, youth leadership training, and related programs, along with summertime initiatives, Mormons worked to instill the Lamanite identity. While some students rejected it, others embraced this self-perception as an empowering tool for themselves, and adopted it as their true Indian identity. Regardless of the system of colonization they experienced, what are we to make of Native Americans who claim ownership of this term and define themselves by it? Though artificial in the eyes of those outside Mormondom, the identity became a real source of direction and strength for many Indian youths, and their struggle to define and assert that notion is the focus of the following chapter. Regardless of colonized origins, which some rejected, the Lamanite remained a real and even ennobling concept for many Native American youth who participated in the ISPP.

7

RIVAL IDEOLOGIES
AND RIVAL INDIANS

Self-Determination in the 1960s and 1970s

...but then I found the church and another identity—Lamanite. A Tewawina, an Indian, a Lamanite. Who Am I? Lamanite is the name I love most....As a Lamanite I am who I make myself to be, and because I live in two worlds, my struggle for identity became harder.

—Pershilie Tewawina, Tewa, 1971

As student participants in the Placement Program graduated into adulthood, and in many cases attended Brigham Young University, in some ways their lives paralleled the excitement that permeated the Navajo Reservation and Indian country as a whole during the 1970s. Over the previous two decades Navajos rapidly expanded their access to education facilities, enrolling in BIA, contract, and public schools in unprecedented fashion. The tribe invested heavily not only in schools but in broader infrastructure and programs intended to gird up their youth. Much as LDS aspirations for Lamanites entering adulthood, Navajo tribal leaders hoped their youth would lead Navajoland into a new age of socioeconomic success built on infusions of Western knowledge and technology but tempered by Navajo control over education and tribal resources. An intense anxiety and optimism over this new, educated generation of Navajos poured across the reservation with the anticipation of a bright new future for the tribe. For many, however, such dramatic changes also ushered in fears of cultural loss.

The consequent struggle to define Indianness on the Navajo Reservation represented a much larger national debate. Red Power activists asserted ethnic pride and called on Indians to adopt new notions of Indianness. They protested colonizing efforts, from the BIA to the Mormon Indian programs. Self-identified Lamanites competed with Red Power activists, each asserting their own values and ideals. Meanwhile, at Brigham Young University, Mormon Indians disputed among themselves and school administrators as they determined the permissible limits of indigenous culture within the Lamanite identity.

In debating among themselves and others, these Mormon Indians demonstrated sincere commitment to their respective interpretations of the Lamanite identity. Theirs was no simple example of cultural code-switching under watchful eyes of colonizers, but rather a genuine debate over their identity that centered squarely on the appropriate blend of two cultures. More often than not, Mormon Indians endorsed the church's preference for quiet, individualized efforts, and not the high-profile and confrontational tactics employed by Red Power activists. Still, others felt torn between the two ideologies in their shared goal of Indian uplift.

As these rival ideologies competed for adherents, national support for self-determination culminated in legislative victories for Native communities. The loss of Native American children to white homes, through adoption or otherwise, emerged as a major concern of the era. The impending legislation that promised to protect tribal interests also threatened the Indian Student Placement Program, the key recruiting ground for Lamanites. In response, LDS leaders protested in congressional hearings and reaffirmed an ideology that focused more on individual development and advancement than communal rights. As Red Power leaders and national legislators called for indigenous self-determination, the LDS Church sought to redefine the term to reflect the personal liberties of individual Indians while downplaying notions of collective activism. Eventually, the church secured an exception in the Indian Child Welfare Act, but the debate over cultural authority and authenticity remained unresolved.

Red Power activists, Mormon Lamanites, and reservation-bound Navajos constituted three groups coming of age in the 1970s. Each sought to usher in a new era for their people and questioned the authenticity of the others. They each identified as the true Indian model destined to lead their peers. Despite common goals of Indian empowerment, these competing notions created a tumultuous sociopolitical environment far different than that which gave birth to the ISPP.

This complex and changing sociopolitical environment, much of which existed independent of the ISPP, eventually contributed to the program's closure. However, the focus of this chapter is not that dissolution but rather the changing Navajo and national sociopolitical landscape, and contested notions of Indianness therein. During the 1970s, self-proclaimed Lamanites and non-Mormon Indian activists shared a hopeful optimism for the future of their kin, but they often differed in the ends to elevate the status of Native Americans. Claims about authenticity, however, overshadowed commonalities and also obscured the varied adaptation of Indianism endorsed by Mormon Indians as they worked out for themselves the limits of the Lamanite identity.

In 1953, only half of school-aged children living on the Navajo Reservation attended school, leaving fourteen thousand without access to formal education; however, enrollment rose over the following decades through a grassroots movement and from efforts stemming from the Tribal Council, Bureau of Indian Affairs, and U.S. Congress.[1] At the local level, some Navajos campaigned to persuade many parents that schools indeed offered legitimate value to their children. They addressed hesitant Navajos who had endured early twentieth-century boarding schools which generally taught outdated vocational skills that served little value on or off the reservation. The *Navajo Times* frequently warned about job market competition and characterized formal classroom education as the key to a bright future. One journalist passed clear judgment on those who withheld their children from school: "These are the people who retard the education of the new generation."[2] Navajo parents increasingly recognized that the changing world around them required different knowledge and abilities than they could offer their children. At significant personal and economic sacrifice, parents sent their children to boarding schools throughout the Southwest.

Just as parents accepted the need to formally educate their children, Navajo tribal policies similarly sought to extend educational opportunities. Director of Navajo Education Hildegard Thompson pioneered the reinterpretation of Public Laws 815 and 874, both passed in 1950.[3] Though initially drafted to fund educational facilities for children living on nontaxable military bases, Thompson argued that the legislation could also fund Indian children living on federal reservations. With such support, the Navajos remodeled and expanded dilapidated boarding schools. In 1954, the tribe also initiated the Navajo Emergency Education Program (NEEP). NEEP consciously overcrowded institutions, introduced new temporary facilities, and heightened the use of off-reservation schools to educate as many children as possible. In just the first year it rapidly expanded education to an additional eight thousand Navajos. The tribe also launched a border-town dormitory program to build dorms in communities just off the reservation and enroll students in nearby public schools. By 1960, all but four thousand Navajo youths attended a school of some sort.[4]

The Bureau of Indian Affairs also expanded educational facilities on and off the Navajo Reservation to make space for increasingly interested Navajos.[5] Distant schools lowered age restrictions and took in ever younger children, which caused mixed feelings among Navajos. In 1960, Navajo chairman Paul Jones finally issued a statement of opposition to the extraction of preteen children from Navajo homes; however, others continued to support such policies as their best chance to extend educational opportunities to their children.[6]

In a 1961 press conference, newly elected U.S. president John F. Kennedy announced his intentions to combat Indian education deficiencies. Secretary of Interior and former Arizona congressman Stewart L. Udall organized a task force to study this issue and concluded that Indian education facilities remained too few, overcrowded, and even structurally unsafe.[7] An additional study in 1965 examined the Navajo border-town dormitory program and found that the swift rise in student enrollment was impressive but untenable given the rapidly growing youth population, declining facilities, and insufficient resources. Instead, local schools on the reservation offered the only long-term solution to the education of "rank and file" Navajos.[8]

As Navajos sought to educate the generation of tomorrow, the hopes of a nation rested upon those children, and Navajo students felt that weight upon their shoulders. This expectation permeated the first annual Navajo Youth Conference at Shiprock, New Mexico, in 1960. Teachers and school administrators organized panels and discussions centered on citizenship, leadership training, and juvenile delinquency. At the second annual conference, Chairman Paul Jones spoke of the "Diploma Age" and promised youth, "Through these teachers you will make up what you miss by being away from home."[9] Each year these conferences gathered to advocate a new world where Navajo youth took upon themselves the responsibilities of transforming the Navajo Nation. In 1961, chief legal counsel Norman M. Littell, himself a longstanding advocate of technological and industrial modernization, promised that "there are great events about to take place on the Navajo Reservation, and with hard work, you can be a part of those things, and the growth of the Navajos."[10] In public speech competitions across the reservation, Navajo youths stood up to claim their place as leaders as the tribe moved boldly from traditional lifeways to, as one student put it, "a jet age."[11]

This heightened emphasis on youth thus extended beyond education to a greater hope of leadership and citizenry, and ultimately set Navajo youth apart as a distinct cross-segment of society that demanded certain attentions. A 1960 letter to parents of off-reservation pupils warned that as they return home they will have certain expectations of social interaction and may not readily embrace their former lifestyle: "[T]hey may become restless if they have nothing to do."[12] Concerns about insufficient recreational facilities and the risk of "Navajo youths who are idle...wandering on streets or even hanging around local bars where trouble develops" found resolution in a variety of mediums.[13] Navajo communities developed several youth programs in the 1960s: scouting, athletics, and summer camps. Girl Scouts and Boy Scouts of America gained sudden popularity, and several schools organized units during the 1950s and 1960s.[14] Youth sports leagues also organized to provide constructive recreation for potentially idle youth. By 1960, the Babe Ruth League on the Navajo Reservation included fourteen teams, and seven years later another league organized in the Window Rock–Fort Defiance area that grew to include some three thousand players over the next decade.[15] The tribe invested in regional youth programs and facilities, such as community centers in Gallup and Todilto Park, and completed the Tribal Youth Center in 1960 to facilitate "worthwhile outlets for the leisure time."[16] This emphasis on youth programs continued through the 1960s and 1970s and climaxed in Chairman Peter McDonald's organization of the Office of Youth Affairs in 1979. That organization managed tens of thousands of dollars for wilderness trips and recreation facilities, public parks and youth development programs, and worked to coordinate all Navajo Nation programs related to youth. Incidentally, former BYU student Malcolm Curley served as the first director of the Navajo Office of Youth Affairs.[17]

Much as the Lamanite program, Navajo tribal emphasis on Western education and employment illustrates a societal effort to transform Navajo teens into a foreign model of productivity and industry; sheep herding no longer sufficed. In 1961, the Tuba City Community Center conducted interviews of youth engaged in a summer employment program. One boy reported, "I'm putting my education into practical use," and, embracing the duties increasingly ascribed to youth, he continued that "jobs like these give us opportunities to assume responsibilities."[18] The Peace Corps, formed that same year, inserted both recruiters and projects into the Navajo reservation, and, with the assistance of BIA promotion in schools, many Indian youth took advantage to "search out for themselves the new opportunities afforded by the changing times."[19] The tribe received funding from President Lyndon Johnson's Great Society programs and created the Office of Navajo Economic Opportunity, which offered vocational training for thousands of teenaged Navajos.[20] When the Youth Conservation Corps opened similar work experiences on the reservation several years later, hundreds of Navajos enlisted to build fences, transplant fish, and tag bears.[21] By way of work and a wage economy, the outside world increasingly crept into the Navajo Reservation, and Navajo youth and young adults operated at the center of the transition.

In addition to overt emphasis on Navajo youth, the reservation also experienced dramatic socioeconomic changes during this time. Transportation, commercialization, and technological modernization and conveniences increasingly penetrated Navajoland. Prior to 1950, few paved roads existed and only three highways (Highways 89, 66, and 666) traversed the Navajo Reservation, primarily skirting the edges and circumventing the majority of it.[22] Consequently, most of the reservation's population and markets remained isolated through the mid-twentieth century. The 1950 Long Range Navajo-Hopi Rehabilitation Act led to the construction of Highway 264, which connected Highways 666 and 89 and linked Ganado to Tuba City. The bill also funded a short stretch of road to connect Window Rock to Fort Defiance. As the federal government funded road construction in the mid-1950s, an oil boom on the reservation also made reliable transportation necessary for outsiders who sought those resources. By 1961, nearly 300 miles of new bridges and highways and over 350 miles of gravel roads crisscrossed the Navajo Nation.[23]

The expanse of roads and highways served to export resources and open new markets. In the early 1970s one Navajo elder recalled, "Today we are aware of the changes that have taken place. We have grocery stores filled with food; clothing markets full of clothes, and other shops equipped with whatever we wish to purchase."[24] Expanding advertisement space in the *Navajo Times* in the 1960s reflected the explosion of Navajo production and consumption of art, automobiles, household appliances, and credit cards.[25] By the 1970s, shopping centers and strip malls also emerged. In 1979 the Economic Development Administration funded its first development project on the reservation—a shopping center at Window Rock—and the tribe considered similar plans for centers at Tuba City, Chinle, and Kayenta. In 1985 construction began on a massive $3.5 million shopping center in Shiprock.[26] The rise of a wage labor economy and cash-only stores edged out longtime traders who relied on the historic barter system and their exclusive role as marketplace intermediaries between Navajos and outsiders. Pervasive consumerism increased and modern appliances changed home and family life.[27] Perhaps one of the most obvious examples of this cultural transition was the division of the Miss Navajo title, which exemplified the very definition of Navajo-ness, into the "traditional queen" and "modern queen," the latter evaluated for her "graphic demonstration of the progress of Navajo womanhood."[28] This socioeconomic transformation infused confidence and eager anticipation. Sanguine expectations rested firmly on a new generation trusted to open the gates to a hopeful future. In many ways, this transformation mirrored the energy and goals of those who participated in the ISPP and larger LDS Church Indian program.

Despite the optimism, some Navajos resented these societal changes. In the preface to his 1977 collection of Navajo autobiographical sketches, historian Broderick H. Johnson observes that "elders feel that undesirable traits may have been acquired through contact with the dominant society and through television, modern literature, and generally low quality of the cinema, the nation-wide deterioration of family life." They blamed such influences for "the growing lack of respect for parental guidance, as well as basic culture and their close family, outfit and clan relationships."[29] Some negatively interpreted the transformations as a type of "cultural loss" and identified encroaching Western values as corrosive intruders. These Navajos issued complaints about declining proficiency in the Navajo language, religious defection, defiant children, and sexual promiscuity.[30] Many Navajos employed the familiar "two worlds" discourse to explain the cultural conflicts and transitions they observed. Deescheeny Nez Tracy explained:

> A big problem is that our children are taught the Anglo culture, and then, when they return home some are uncomfortable. They do not want to live in primitive dwelling places. They are unhappy; and some leave their homes or do not want to go there after school is out. They are accustomed to soft beds, clean clothes, plenty of water, electricity, etc.[31]

These rifts revealed a perceived division in the culture as Anglo ways eroded tradition. Many perceived two distinct cultures in conflict and believed that each was exclusive of the other. Navajos could be Indian, or they could be white, and any adaptations indicative of the latter constituted an assault on *true* Indianness.

Some Navajos even vilified what they viewed as the agents of change, particularly educational institutions and other icons of Western culture. A 1971 *Akwesasne Notes* article titled "Genocide in Navajo Land" pointed to the BIA boarding schools as a system designed to isolate students and whitewash indigenous cultures and further indicted the tribal council as "a primary mystifier of the essential 'tool' in the colonial exploitation of its people." The article chastised the "complicit" Window Rock (Arizona) *Navajo Times* for its promotion of Brigham Young University and advertisements for missionaries.[32] A 1979 *Navajo Times* article commented, "The popular culture of America has weakened the religious truths of our environment."[33] A particularly dramatic rendition of this concern is captured in a comic printed in *Diné Baa-Hani*, a more radical Navajo paper. In the comic, the character SuperNavajo observes the disturbing transformation of Navajo youths into almost completely assimilated "white" Indians who have lost their cultural origins. The BIA, in particular, constituted a lightning rod for controversy as local communities demanded a greater voice in their children's education. Planned overcrowding that began with NEEP, underfunded curriculums and facilities, and the historic characterization of BIA teachers as the least qualified in America only intensified Navajo criticisms. Growing student activism and parental concerns climaxed in the early 1970s as local communities took control of day school governing boards.

Lukachukai Demonstration School was the first BIA-operated school to transition to community control. In 1966, it reopened as Rough Rock Demonstration School. Navajo tribal chairman Raymond Nakai anticipated the transition in 1965 when he charged the school to "develop programs which will make the community and parents a vital force in Navajo education."[34] This exorcism of colonizing authorities would allow Navajos to dictate the pace that properly balanced Western and Native ideals. In the following years, Navajo communities seized managerial oversight of their local schools. They replaced whites on school boards and in school administration positions across the reservation. In 1970 Ramah Navajo High School also opened its doors with a community-driven objective to retain the best elements of Navajo traditions to meld them with the best of the Anglo world.[35] Tribal members constituted three-quarters of the staff and all of the school board.[36] Perhaps the boldest statement of local empowerment is found in the curriculum, which included a class that one teacher informally titled "How not to get ripped-off at the trading post."[37] By 1971, Navajo enrollment in public schools surpassed BIA school enrollment.[38] In 1972 Bordego Pass Day School reorganized as a community-controlled school, and later that year Rock Point likewise converted to a contract school.[39] By the mid-1970s, public high schools opened at Shiprock, Chinle, Kayenta, Crowpoint, Tuba City, Ganado, Window Rock/Fort Defiance, and Tohatchi.[40]

As communities seized control of local schools, those institutions also grew into community centers and attracted the involvement of more Navajo parents. Paul Blatchford, counselor for Public School Board in Tuba City, commented, "There is more concern these days about the schools, and many Navajos are participating at board meetings. . . . [T]he parents now are involved in choosing the subjects to be taught in public schools."[41] Roughly 150 miles to the east, community members in Fort Defiance similarly gained self-governance of educational institutions. One Navajo elder explained, "We have a Parents Advisory Council here at Fort Defiance, and

I am a member. We promote educational needs and educational programs for the students." [42] School boards worked to blend the input of community members into the traditional curriculum.

As local communities strove to influence local institutions, Congress extended complementary assistance through a variety of measures designed to tie funding to community oversight. The tribe drew support from the 1964 Economic Opportunity Act (PL 88-210), the Higher Education Facilities Act (PL 88-204), and, most importantly, the Elementary and Secondary Education Act (PL 89-10). In 1972 Congress passed the Indian Education Act (PL 92-318), which provided funding and pledged per capita payments to contract schools, further encouraging educational systems independent of the BIA. Parts B and C of the bill also offered funds for bilingual and culturally relevant curriculum. The 1975 Indian Self-Determination and Education Assistance Act (PL 93-638) further empowered tribes to contract with the BIA for independent schooling facilities and empowered Indian majorities through school boards and site-based governing committees. With its passage, existing districts in Chinle, Ganado, Kayenta, Puerco, Tuba City, Window Rock, and Monument Valley secured the fiscal stability to move forward. The Title XI Education Amendments Act (PL 95-561), passed in 1978, constituted the climactic self-determination legislative work of this era. It demanded a new finance formula to make Indian education more equitable in relation to non-Indians and made such funds contingent upon parental inclusion. It also restructured Indian education so that teachers and staff answered directly to schools, not the BIA. All of this 1970s-era legislation ensured that funding better enabled individual communities to establish schools independent of the BIA or other government direction. By the mid-1970s, local communities guided most reservation day schools through parental advisory councils composed of three to seven members.

Newly empowered communities redesigned curriculum to emphasize bicultural education. Parents and teachers tried to provide students with Western training but also included more traditional Navajo teachings such as language proficiency and home production like silver working and weaving. Rough Rock School Board president John Dick explained that "education, both Anglo and traditional, must go side by side. Our children need to learn both."[43] Reservation-dwelling Navajos faced a challenging balancing act similar to Lamanites. Through this educational transformation, Navajo parents and youth learned to stand up for community control not only of education, but the degree of acculturation of their children. Local communities secured the power to determine to what extent schools introduced Western ideas and how they treated Navajo lifeways. Additionally, the proliferation of schools gave parents several options; they could exercise parental prerogatives to determine their child's attendance at any of many school options: BIA schools, contract schools, boarding schools, or public day schools.

The success of seizing their own educational facilities and curriculum proved empowering for Native groups and contributed to a concurrent and much larger nationalistic activism known as Red Power. In the early 1960s, as droves of young Indians became first-generation college students, popular dancer-turned-student-activist Clyde Warrior rallied hundreds to a radical banner. He served as voice for a new generation frustrated with senior Indians' soft resistance and deference to whites. Warrior cofounded the National Indian Youth Council (NIYC) in 1964. The title of the organization's newsletter, *Americans Before Columbus*, illustrates the aggressive tone they preferred. NIYC and other groups organized confrontational "fish-ins" wherein Native Americans asserted historic land claims and treaty rights, often accompanied by Hollywood stars like Marlon Brando to attract additional cameras.

Sometimes deemed "militant" for their confrontational tone, these types of protests increasingly defined American Indian activism. In 1968, activist Lehman Brightman organized San Francisco Indians to form United Native Americans (UNA), and the following year he founded the first American Indian Studies program at the University of California. In the same year, an intertribal coalition of activist Indians orchestrated a series of occupations at Alcatraz Island. Their third and final demonstration there gained nationwide media attention and soon other organizations replicated the model. In 1972, the newly founded American Indian Movement (AIM) organized the Trail of Broken Treaties and caravanned across the nation to Washington, D.C., where activists occupied BIA offices to demand adequate housing and living standards. The following year some two hundred AIM protestors staged Wounded Knee II, a violent two-and-a-half-month stand-off with the FBI that ended in empty promises to investigate corrupt local governance.

Like other movements associated with the New Left, these organizations pioneered a new notion of identity that centered on ethnic pride and a forceful assertion of overlooked rights. They had little tolerance for the slow-moving efforts of prior generations that had ineffectively resisted federal termination policies. In truth, the longstanding National Council of American Indians, founded in 1944, had won significant victories in the court room and through other efforts, but their failure to outright challenge the system of colonization tasted of collaboration to this younger generation. Lehman Brightman openly scorned "Uncle Tomahawks" who he believed accepted the status quo because they failed to accept this new Indian activism. Clyde Warrior further asserted this new activist model by caricaturizing all other Natives as one of five types of Indians that varied from useless drunks to sell-out phonies. He called for a new activist model, grounded in true indigenous tradition, as the only authentic Indian.[44]

These Red Power activists insisted on immediate Native control over Native lands, institutions, and people. They asserted "self-determination" and it became a buzz word of the era. Six months into his presidency, Richard Nixon surprisingly endorsed the term as he pledged to construct a new federal Indian policy that turned back old termination policies. Nixon promised an era of "self-determination," which he defined as Indian "autonomy without threatening his sense of community." The president continued:

> We must assure the Indian that he can assume control of his own life without being separated involuntarily from the tribal group. And we must make it clear that Indians can become independent of Federal control without being cut off from Federal concern and Federal support.[45]

Nixon fused old termination policy with self-empowering notions of sovereignty, and as such the term "self-determination" enjoyed broad appeal during the 1970s.

Despite broad endorsement for self-determination, Indian "militancy" enjoyed far less support. The movement shared obvious commonalities with the better known Black Power nationalism that spawned visceral opposition among conservatives. Even on reservations many Indians questioned the authenticity of largely city-raised Natives employing New Left protest tactics. For all its pomp, groups like AIM, UNA, and NIYC remained a small fraction of the larger Indian population. Nevertheless, their efforts expanded the dialogue as more and more Native Americans criticized colonizing institutions.

As Indians increasingly challenged federal intrusion into Indian lives, so too did they target private institutions, and particularly the LDS Church. Though initially caught off-guard, the church briefly tried to negotiate along their shared interest in uplifting Native Americans. However, it did not take long to reveal an impossible divide between the two ideologies. Time and time again, protests forced conversations that demanded a response from the church, leaving self-proclaimed Lamanites to awkwardly navigate a course through the ideological rift.

The earliest Indian demonstrations targeting the Mormon Church occurred in the early 1970s as AIM activists marched on Temple Square in Salt Lake City. On one such occasion the church and protestors turned to University of Utah graduate student and Pascua Yaqui Tribe member Eddie Brown to negotiate. Twenty years later Brown rose to Assistant Secretary of the Interior for Indian Affairs (a position formerly titled the Commissioner of Indian Affairs). At the time of AIM's protest, Brown served as an active local Mormon leader and as the acting director of the University of Utah Indian Studies program. Representatives from the church and AIM all met at Temple Square. Discussion there devolved into a debate over who was doing more to help Indians. Negotiations stalled, and Brown discovered the difficulty in mediating between the groups. His refusal to endorse either side left him isolated; in fact, Brown recalled that at the end of the night nobody would even give him a ride home.[46]

Activists organized several other demonstrations at LDS Church headquarters in the early 1970s. The 1972 Trail of Broken Treaties March to Washington, D.C., organized stops in seventy-five cities, including Salt Lake City.[47] The demonstration in D.C. demanded the reinstatement of $50 million cut from the BIA budget; however, when in Salt Lake City, they asked the Mormon Church for $1 million to help fund the march and other programs. Vernon Bellecourt gathered supporters, mostly University of Utah students from the Uintah and Ouray reservations, and the demonstrators arrived at Temple Square during the bi-annual General Conference of the church where security prohibited them from entering the grounds.[48] Bellecourt addressed his "divinely inspired" request to LDS Church president Harold B. Lee, but the prophet refused to see him.[49] Utah AIM coordinator

David Hill explained, "We too have had a vision, and you have to recognize the validity of our vision."[50]

In 1973, AIM protested at Temple Square during the General Conference and once more asked for $1 million to help Indians.[51] As before, church leaders locked the gates and marshaled police to keep the peace. Hill presented the monetary request on behalf of "our Indian brothers who are dwelling in poverty, sickness, hunger and who are in dire need of assistance."[52] This time the church immediately issued a press release stating that it "is already doing far more each year with its Indian self-help programs than the million dollar self-help request made by David Hill, the Utah Coordinator of American Indian Movement." The release outlined the many services offered by the church and estimated costs.[53]

David Hill led some fifty Indians to protest during General Conference in 1974, joined again by Bellecourt but also George Redstone and out-of-state activists Mad Bear Anderson, Crow Dog, Rolling Thunder, and South Wing.[54] The church countered with a press release stating that it spent $3.3 million on Indian programs and that ISPP foster parents spent another $3.5 million out of their own pockets to house Indian children.[55] The protestors demanded to speak with recently ordained LDS Church president Spencer W. Kimball, and Bellecourt issued seven challenges to the church, all of which centered on the creation of an internal Indian-dominated review board to manage the church's social outreach expenditures. National chairman of AIM John Trudell acknowledged the church's expenditures on Indian programs, but faulted its white administration with alternative motivations to convert Native peoples.[56] Bellecourt also condemned existing LDS Indian policy as "acts of cultural and religious genocide" that contributed to high alcoholism, suicide, and drop-out rates among Indian youths, which was a clear reference to the ISPP and Indian seminary programs.[57] Redstone added that the ISPP "brainwashed" students and left them in a "cultural limbo." Hill added, "We've searched the prophecies for reasons for the Mormons to help, and they've searched them to find reasons not to help."[58] The church agreed to meet with the activists on the following Monday and selected two Mormon Navajo representatives who had long supported the church's Indian policies: then Ganado College president George P. Lee and Kayenta School District guidance counselor Lewis J. Singer. However, the demonstrators requested a postponement, and the meeting never occurred.[59] A week after the protest, AIM issued a statement titled "Declaration to the Mormon Church [and] Spencer W. Kimball." Again invoking indigenous revelatory authority, the AIM document stated:

> The Great Spirit has spoken to our hearts and minds. Because of insensitivity to our religion and traditions. . . . Because of your racist attitude regarding our skin color. Because of your divisive practices, of pitting Indian against Indian. Because of your attempts at cultural and religious genocide. Because Native Americans have approached you . . . to resolve these matters and you have turned them away. You are hereby ordered to recall all your missionaries from the reservations and the areas where Native Americans frequent.[60]

The document was signed by David Hill (state director of Utah AIM), John Trudell (national chairman of AIM), Vernon Bellecourt (national state director of AIM), and George Redstone (assistant state director of Utah AIM). Their proclamation well reflects the intensity of conflict between the activists and the church's Lamanite program.

During the 1970s, the hostility between Red Power activists and the LDS Church often centered on accusations of colonization. Both the LDS Church and Red Power activists accused the other of imposing a false narrative upon Indian bodies, one which was destructive to their true identity. They each asserted their own as the true model of Indianness and denounced the other as inauthentic. One Navajo Placement student noted the rival claims to Indian authenticity when she questioned:

> What is being Indian? There are no rules and regulations. I just think that if you know it within your heart (that you are Indian) that's all you need to be. People don't need to tell you, you are Indian. I just think a lot of groups, such as AIM, just don't have an understanding, I really don't. Maybe they are afraid that they will take away our identity but who are they to say that they are the teachers for the Indian group?[61]

Just as AIM interpreted the Lamanite as a false white creation, self-identified Lamanites challenged activists' validity as cultural vanguards of Indianness. Former Placement student Teddy Redhouse recounted an incident at the annual Navajo Fair when "radical Indians" challenged his authenticity because, as a full-time missionary, he cut his hair short and wore a suit. "Why don't you go back to Utah!" they charged, as they called Redhouse an "apple," a challenge to authenticity charging an Indian of a thoroughly white core below a thin red skin. Redhouse replied in Navajo, but quickly learned the two aggressive Indians did not speak their own Native language, and he likewise discounted their Indianness. If they did not know the language, he assumed, they surely did not know the culture and could not be *true* Navajos.[62] Such incidents are particularly demonstrative of the conflicting claims to authenticity expressed by both Lamanites and activists.

Despite the seemingly united façade presented by Mormon Indians and the LDS Church as they contested Red Power activists, much of that activist ideology did in fact penetrate Mormon Indians' discussions about the definition of a Lamanite. Church leaders expected that at their premiere education institution, Brigham Young University, years of instruction would crystalize into a fully evolved Lamanite in tune with theological and cultural directives. While a mostly correct assumption, during the 1970s the campus also witnessed several debates among Indian students; some Native students questioned authority and challenged colonialism as others embraced the Indian program as a divinely inspired restoration of the true Indian ideal. Much as the incursion of Western ideology on the Navajo reservation stimulated tumultuous debate about Indianness, so too did Mormon Indians work out their own notions of a Lamanite during the 1970s.

Indian enrollment at BYU dated back several decades earlier. While the Placement Program served as the cradle of Lamanite identity, the Indian program at Brigham Young University drew in many of those students and entrenched that ideology. Indian graduates of BYU often reflected the conservative social and political views shared by most white Mormons, including an emphasis on education and working within the system rather than open challenges to authority that called for tribal and cultural sovereignty. Beginning in 1951, the university consciously developed an expansive Indian Program by actively recruiting students from the ISPP and Indian seminaries. The director of BYU Indian Education commented, "For the most part, we don't recruit in many schools across the nation, but draw our students from the church Indian Placement Program, Lamanite youth conferences and seminaries."[63] By 1970, BYU's program was fully formed with over five hundred American Indian students supported by special academic courses, community outreach and research, and social programs to assist in their adjustment to college life. According to one source, by 1980 BYU spent more on Indian scholarships than all other universities combined and boasted an Indian graduation rate of more than twice the national average.[64] Between 1966 and 1974, BYU awarded 98 Associate of Arts degrees, 114 Bachelor degrees, and 10 Master degrees to Native American students.[65]

Brigham Young University emphasized individualized pursuit of education and success as a central element of the Lamanite identity. Indian students gathered for various activities, such as Indian Week, which the Tribe of Many Feathers (an Indian club) hosted each year. Indian students also read and contributed to the *Eagle's Eye*, a student paper produced by BYU Indians for the purpose of developing technical and artistic abilities in journalism, art, and photography. It also offered leadership opportunities and provided a sense of community for Indian students across campus.

The most notable emblem of Native Americans at BYU was the Lamanite Generation, a traveling Indian dance troupe that presented the LDS Church's theological message of a latter-day Indian restoration through education. The Lamanite Generation organized in 1971 and since has traveled throughout Indian country and around the world spreading its message. A 1976 show at the Navajo Nation Fair Grounds stirred up some controversy as some observers deemed their message to be assimilationist propaganda.[66] That response may go some distance in explaining how little some Navajos felt they shared in common with the Lamanites, despite their many obvious parallels. The group's signature song "Go My Son" narrates the story told by "an Indian war chief" to his people. "He told them that education is the ladder to success and happiness. 'Go, my son, and climb the ladder ...'" Written by Navajo Arlene Nofchissey Williams and Ute Carnes Burson, the song embellishes the quote long ascribed to nineteenth-century Navajo headman Chief Manuelito: "Education is the ladder to success for my people, tell my grandchildren to climb the ladder."[67] In this way, Lamanites fused and justified their theologically driven identity with Native oral tradition.

In addition to advocating individualized commitment to education, BYU also sought to limit indigenous influences. University and church officials consciously constrained appropriate Indian behavior by restricting some expressions of indigenous cultures. This struggle to define the boundaries of appropriate Indianness erupted in 1966 when BYU director of Indian Affairs Paul Felt prohibited previously acceptable Native American–style dances during the annual Indian Week festivities. Felt expressed "distressing concern with regard to many of the traditional Indian customs," and particularly the Native dances which "left something to be spiritually desired."[68] When some students resisted his requests, he invoked an outright prohibition of Indian dances for the 1966 Indian Week and called for a variety and talent show in their stead.[69] Students appealed to BYU president Ernest Wilkinson, launched an "orderly" protest, and in an unusually confrontational move they resolved to retain the dances, regardless of Felt's directive.[70] Felt finally acquiesced; however, he determined thereafter to make greater efforts to emphasize "the spiritually damaging aspects of their apostate Indian culture, and a vital awareness and commitment to the gospel."[71]

The conflict between would-be traditionalists and administrators pushing for assimilation continued to cause tensions. Indeed, Felt had inserted a wedge that grew over time and divided the school's Indian population according to their devotion to cultural practices. By 1969, John Rainer, a graduate student at BYU and a former ISPP student and Southwest Indian missionary, echoed that assimilationist position. He issued complaints that Indian cultures, particularly traditional dances, served to undermine and even recapture the Lamanite Indian who had been emancipated by education. In a BYU Lamanite student correlation meeting, he explained:

> I'd just like to add that I feel with others on this campus that the Lamanite student is being shackled by the old identity and is being held down. When a so-called Indian student comes here, who knows nothing of his dances and so on, he feels that he has to learn these dances to identify as an Indian on this campus. [72]

Rainer expressed concern that the Tribe of Many Feathers president urged such traditions and even accused some Indian classmates of not being true Indians because they rejected "the old image of the feather, the rattle, the medicine man, the backwardness, the darkness." Rainer countered:

We're not that anymore. We're Lamanites. We're people who know who we are from the Book of Mormon, the people who have had the darkness lifted from our eyes. We're a people who know that we have come back home to that church which was originally our ancestors' upon this land. [73]

He concluded, "That is what a Lamanite is to us." He went on to explain that an Indian "is a mistaken identity which some individual students are trying to shackle the other students with on this campus by making them learn these old dances, learn these old traditions, which are not the true identity of the Lamanite."[74] Rainer was not alone in his position, and church authorities made a similar opinion known in visits and private council.[75]

More interesting than the unsurprising efforts at continued colonization is the division among Native Americans as they individually sought to determine the legitimacy of "traditional dances" and popular Indian culture as it related to being a Lamanite. This division among self-proclaimed Lamanites well illustrates the spectrum of definitions adopted by Indian adherents as it blurred the lines between colonizer and colonizee. What are we to make of those, like Rainer, who accepted the church's definition of Lamanite and promoted that identity to others? And what of those who accepted part, but not all, of that message? This debate raises difficult questions about authenticity. What exactly is a genuine Indian, and who enjoys the right to determine that answer?

For Rainer and others, a Lamanite was an Indian who fully internalized the LDS gospel message and embraced Western culture. That person was an integrated Indian or at least capable of operating outside Native cultures. Pueblo John R. Maestas, then serving as BYU's Indian Education Department chairman, echoed this position at the keynote address for BYU's 1976 Indian Week activities. He explained, "The time has come in our lives when we can no longer take the position that there is either a white man's world or the Indian's world and that the two shall never meet. We realize that all cultures have blended and we now look at a world community."[76] In 1985, George Lee shared his understanding of this concept with BYU Indian students: "You need to be able to transcend both cultures, so that you can function well in both."[77]

Though clearly based on a Eurocentric notion of stepping free from Indian cultures, this model also provided Native Americans in transition with a functional framework to access the benefits of Western society. It encouraged individual drive and accomplishments as a means to uplift Native Americans one person at a time and thus fulfill latter-day prophesy. John Maestas explained:

> If you need a cause, gee, look at your brothers and sisters and your mom and dad. There are several people who need you back home. If you have the moxie, come on to school, let's help get you through, let's get you a good job where you'll be in a position to really help.[78]

He echoed Paul Felt's words from a decade earlier. Felt explained:

> Our program, our efforts, should be such that we create a situation where these people help themselves. It should be the underlying theme of every effort—in our homes, in a class, or in any organization—that we provide a climate whereby we do help and assist, and in effect carry them upon our shoulders and in our arms; but let them, haltingly if need be, do the work.[79]

Through such reasoning, Apostle Mark E. Peterson could earnestly assert, "The [BYU] Indian Education Department believes in self-determination."[80] Such a claim might seem unfounded to others who equated self determination with tribal and broader Indian cultural sovereignty. However, the church did support individual agency and autonomous personal development through its ISPP and BYU's Indian programs, and redefined self-determination in those terms.

This individualized conception of self-determination justified an aversion to collective activism while promoting the uplift it advocated for, only on an individualized level. This meant that rival ideologies of the era shared some commonalities in their goals, even if they utterly differed in methods; even still, the differences impeded any cooperation. Omaha Stanley Snake assumed the presidency of the National Indian Youth Council in 1972 while attending BYU and avidly defended both positions.[81] "Since being a member of this organization," Snake recalled, "I have had to answer questions about the Mormon Church. And at the same time I have had to answer to the Mormons as to why I am a member of NIYC which some consider to be militant." He viewed himself as a "buffer between the Mormon Church and certain segments of the Red Power movement."[82]

More often, self-defined Lamanites and LDS Church publications opposed activist protests and encouraged Indians to look inward to self-development. The BYU-published *Eagle's Eye* magazine exemplified this attitude, which stood in contrast to other Indian-authored newspapers. It actively abstained from national news and politics and instead featured the skills and accomplishments of individual Lamanites.[83] Still, more overt statements of distaste for national Indian movements appeared elsewhere. In 1971, another church magazine warned that activists like Lehman Brightman (United Native Americans) and Dennis Banks (American Indian Movement) were "bitter" and represented a "militant" wing that "thrives on emotionalism" rather than constructive cooperation.[84] Only a month earlier Brightman and Banks had coordinated the efforts to "invade" Mount Rushmore and cover it with a massive flag which read, "Sioux Indian Power."[85] The church and its adherents typically frowned on these confrontational media tactics.

The conservative disposition of the Mormon hierarchy naturally biased them to oppose not only Red Power but the entire antiauthoritarian youth protest movement of the late 1960s and early 1970s. An article in the LDS Church's *New Era* called attention to "an army of protesting Brigham Young University students" who demonstrated their "day of violent protest" by organizing into work groups that performed landscaping work in a portion of Santaquin, Utah. The article contrasted it with more hostile outbursts of the era, noting, "They violently protested against those who riot—and they actively demonstrated that students can change things within the system."[86]

Because of the Mormon cultural and political opposition to the 1960s student movements, it is of little surprise that few self-defined Lamanites participated in the Red Power movement and that many Mormons and Indian activists saw the two as rival forces. This perception of polarity is well captured in an unusually candid 1973 *Eagle's Eye* article titled "Militancy and the Church." It read:

> When one analyzes the power of militancy compared to the power of the gospel, it becomes apparent that there is a great deal of difference. Militancy in comparison to the gospel is like a pea-shooter, in

its overall effectiveness. The gospel is infinitely more powerful and, though it is a slow process sometimes, it brings about permanent changes. Militancy, on the other hand, tries to bring about changes rapidly, sometimes by threatening people and trying to intimidate them to get what they want, but they are only temporary changes and offer no lasting benefits.[87]

The article explained that no cause justifies the use of force, "no matter how noble or right those purposes may be," and without overtly stating it, the article made a comparison to a gospel principle understood by Latter-day Saints. Mormons believe in a pre-earthly existence where Jesus Christ and Satan presented conflicting plans for life on earth, and that Satan planned to ensure righteousness by force. In an unspoken comparison, the *Eagle Eye* likened Indian "militancy" to Satanism because "militancy...involves the use of force in accomplishing its purposes."[88] BYU coordinator of Indian Student Services Royce Flandro explained that former Placement students at the university were "unburdened by the suspicion and distrust which is often associated with the non-placement reservation student."[89] His comments reflect his own biases, but also the sense of opposition between the rival ideologies that permeated both students and administration.

Apostle Boyd K. Packer addressed Indians at BYU's Indian Week in 1979 and offered a more overt statement linking good LDS spirituality to abstinence from political activism. He said, "Now there are many voices to listen to and there are militant and strident voices, activist voices that will tell you your needs are not being met." He continued by explaining that "the voice that you should listen to is that still voice, that small voice from elsewhere in the scriptures.[90] In this way, Packer linked activism with the rejection of the Lord's guiding influence. "Militant" agendas reflected the tension and hostility that Satan promoted and had no place among genuinely converted Mormon Indians.

Regardless of reluctance among Mormon Indians, Red Power activism failed to win the support of many American Indians. It typically appealed to young urban Indians but often struggled to gain adherents among reservation Natives and the older generation. Navajos seemed disproportionately underrepresented in AIM demonstrations, perhaps content in their own revitalization, and those who converted to Mormonism usually proved even less supportive of the high-profile and confrontational tactics employed by

Red Power.[91] Navajo Nora Mae Begay, a former ISPP student who went on to win the Miss Indian BYU and Miss Indian America, publicly rejected Red Power activism. She commented, "The militant movements are disgracing to the Indian heritage."[92] John Maestas recalled an occasion when AIM cofounder Dennis Banks spoke at BYU and that "some of our girls took him on the minute he disagreed with them."[93] On another occasion Vernon Bellecourt represented AIM on a visit to Utah. Maestas recounted that "we got into a pretty heated discussion.... We're not enemies, we're certainly not on very friendly terms, and that's because we don't agree with what he's doing."[94] A BYU Indian Services and Research manual explained "real Indian Power is..." and listed a barrage of self-accomplishments like earning good grades, obtaining graduate education, or operating a business.[95] In some ways, the rift is reminiscent of nineteenth- and twentieth-century ideological rifts that existed within African American civil rights movements wherein moderates who preferred to work quietly balanced more confrontational voices. Indeed, white and Indian Mormons tended to prefer self-development and working within the system over participation in any national Indian advocacy groups. In 1972, the American Indian Commission on Alcoholism relocated away from Salt Lake City for that very reason, citing a "brush off" and absence of local support from Mormons.[96]

Whether grounded in historical reality or not, both Lamanites and Red Power activists generally perceived an ideological division. They polarized discussions about improving the lives of American Indians and tried to force individuals to choose sides. When Victor Selam, an Indian from Oregon, arrived at BYU he found the conservative attitudes stifling. His efforts to challenge the dress code with long hair failed; his Indian Week panel discussion was censored when he advocated Red Power; and he was soon after expelled from the university and warned not to return.[97] When Selam spoke out about his frustrations, he accused not only the university but also the Mormon Indians who embraced that ideology. He invoked the charge of inauthenticity as he labeled Indians at BYU as "apples."[98] Perhaps his analysis drew from a recently published interview with Lehman Brightman, published in the radical student paper *Dine' Baa-Hani*, titled, "Apples Control Schools."[99]

As Red Power activists and Mormon Lamanites contended with each other, they exemplified a nationwide indigenous eagerness to empower Native people. Individual communities continued to lobby for greater control over local schools, clinics, and natural resources. Historians have only recently begun to step back and view this larger tapestry of ideologies and efforts to preserve land, rights, and culture that culminated in a wave of self-determination legislation.[100] For many, cultural sovereignty began with the identity imprinted on Native children. These concerns culminated in the Indian Child Welfare Act of 1978. The debates that encircled that legislation further consolidated ideological rivalries and the definition of self-determination in particular.

During the 1960s, some 25 percent of all Native American children lived in foster homes, adoptive homes, or government boarding schools, and according to a 1969 study, 85 percent of Native American children removed by social services were placed in non-Indian homes.[101] American Indians were keenly aware of the absence of their children but historically lacked the voice and power to demand change.

A second and more egregious form of child removal centered on adoption by white families, and many of those even occurred under the banner of the Bureau of Indian Affairs. The BIA's assimilation-minded agenda led the agency to fund the Indian Adoption Program (IAP) operated by the Child Welfare League of America. The IAP began in 1958 and reflected the termination policies of that era as it placed Indian children for adoption in white homes, mostly in the East. The BIA contracted with states to remove children without ever demonstrating just cause in any court. Over the tenure of the program, which ended in 1967, the IAP adopted out almost four hundred Indian children into white families.[102]

BIA-empowered state social workers with IAP credentials, as well as representatives from other adoption agencies, frequently served as intermediaries and exploited cultural misunderstandings to justify removing children. The aforementioned 1969 report explained that "99 percent of the cases were argued on such vague grounds as 'neglect' and 'social deprivation' and on allegations of the emotional damage the children were subjected to by living with their parents."[103] Lakota activist and author Mary Crow Dog explained:

> Many Indian children are placed in foster homes. This happens even in cases where parents or grandparents are willing and able to take care of them, but where the social workers say their homes are substandard, or where there are outhouses instead of flush toilets, or

where the family is simply "too poor." A flush toilet to a white social worker is more important than a good grandmother. So the kids are given to wasicun [white] strangers to be "acculturated in a sanitary environment." We are losing the coming generation that way.[104]

Less-advanced technology amounted to abuse and sociological damage in the minds of social workers and would-be parents who used these excuses to remove Indian children from their biological families and reservation. In 1972, the Child Welfare League published a longitudinal study of ninety-seven IAP families and concluded that most adoptive placement of Native children resulted in adequately or excellently adjusted children, which only reinforced the practice.[105]

By the 1970s, growing concerns and resistance to this practice garnered headlines both inside and outside Indian country. At the request of the Devil's Lake Sioux Reservation tribal chairman, the Association on American Indian Affairs (AAIA) began a lengthy investigation of child removal practices and recommendations for new policy.[106] Meanwhile, a flurry of articles in indigenous news sources, such as *Akwesasne Notes* and *Wassaja*, raised alarm over the high rate of removal of children from Native homes and the "psychologically disastrous" consequences.[107] One author claimed Indian children suffered removal from their family at a rate of ten to twenty times that of non-Indians.[108] These articles typically conflated permanent adoption and ISPP seasonal foster care, and the activist newsletter *Warpath* directly accused the LDS Placement Program of cultural genocide. An article titled "Mormons Steal Indian Children" boldly declared, "There is a gigantic network of baby stealing ring [sic] in the United States....This baby racket is sponsored by the Morman [sic] Church."[109]

Child care professionals and clinicians also voiced their concerns over Indian child removal, permanent or temporary. In 1971, disenchanted Mormon Dorothy Schimmelpfennig issued one of the first clinical denunciations of the church's Placement Program.[110] She deplored the cultural insensitivity of the ISPP and charged it with causing psychological disorders, including a "frantic" and "schizophrenic" sense of identity.[111] In 1972, the National Indian Education Association also issued a statement condemning the LDS Placement Program. Their conference resolution announced that "the LDS program tends to assimilate and destroy the Indian child's sense of relationship to his people."[112] In 1975, the American Academy of Child Psychology passed a resolution identifying two troubling trends: the removal of Indian children from natural homes and their placement in white homes. The resolution particularly identified Mormons as part of the problem.[113] Medical professionals also voiced concern about all forms of Indian child removal, and in 1977 several published *The Destruction of American Indian Families* to discuss the psychological trauma.[114]

Concerns about the welfare of Indian children led newly elected South Dakota senator James Abourezk to launch a series of hearings and other investigations during the mid-1970s. Soon after Abourezk entered office in 1973, he publicly expressed disdain for those who "convince these mothers and fathers that they have no choice but to give up their children, despite a lack of evidence of neglect." In an Indian Affairs subcommittee hearing he explained his intent to stop "abusive child removal practices which are destroying Indian families."[115] Witnesses attested to the inappropriate removal of Indian children by various agencies and made it clear that the problem often stemmed from conflicting cultural notions of good parenting. Though the ISPP initially was not mentioned by name or even through inference, soon after the hearings the Interstate Compact Administration (ICA) received notification that the LDS Placement Program operated without standard ICA oversight. This agency monitored foster and other child placements across state boundaries to ensure they received adequate resources and accommodations. Foster programs routinely reported the names, ages, and addresses of foster children to the ICA, but the fiscally independent nature of the ISPP and status as a voluntary educational program exempted it from such obligations.[116]

In 1976, the ICA instructed its South Dakota director, Robert E. Leach, to conduct a study of the Indian Student Placement Program. Leach sent questionnaires to fifty participating Indian families and concluded the program operated with the full awareness and support of Indian parents. This climate survey, conducted without LDS Church involvement, conclusively found that Indian parents voluntarily enrolled their students because they simply thought it was the best academic option; it found no evidence of coercion, and parents believed the program reinforced their native identity. Ninety-three percent of respondents said that they felt no pressure to surrender their children; 93 percent indicated they thought their child would receive a better education than in his own community; and 70 percent even said they felt their child's foster family helped him understand and identify with his Indian heritage. Leach reported that he "had no sense from any of those respondents that they were not satisfied with the program as it was being administered presently by the LDS Church."[117] Nevertheless, the ICA requested that the church regularly submit standard foster child information to the administration, including notification of the removal of any child from a reservation and plans to make relocation adjustments if needed.[118] Such reporting quickly emerged as a point of debate during the ensuing Indian Child Welfare hearings.

Concurrent to that study, the American Indian Policy Review Commission's Task Force IV brought additional attention to the status of Indian children, and in 1976 Senator Abourezk asked the Association on American Indian Affairs to prepare an Indian child welfare bill.[119] The legislation built on and codified recent court rulings that recognized the sovereignty of tribal courts in child welfare proceedings and moved smoothly to the Subcommittee on Indian Affairs as S. 1214, "The Indian Child Welfare Act," on April 1, 1977.[120] However, the bill then stalled during August hearings.

The LDS Church expressed concerns that the imprecise language in the ICWA legislation, designed to denounce unauthorized child removal, also might inhibit Native parents' rights to place their children in the ISPP. In preparation for the contest, Placement caseworkers gathered hundreds of student and biological parent letters of support. Some letters attested to the program's educational value; others expressed gratitude for its character building and cross-cultural exposure. Additionally, the church submitted a separate petition signed by 274 biological parents of then current Placement students. It articulated the academic and cultural values of the program and concluded with the plea, "Don't take our parental rights away from us. We want to be the ones to decide what is best for our children without having the government intervene."[121] These Indian parents, as informed by LDS representatives, did not interpret the ICWA as legislation to strengthen their families, communities, and tribes, but rather as an attack on their individual rights as parents. These documents foreshadowed the testimony from LDS Church representatives who demanded "parental self determination."[122] This emphasis on individual rights resonated with tribal termination-era legislation of 1953, Public Law 280 and Concurrent House Resolution 108, which likewise asserted the rights of individual Indians over tribal authority, but clashed with emerging 1970s notions of protecting Native Americans by way of empowering tribal entities.

On August 4, 1977, the Senate subcommittee on Indian Affairs heard testimony on the Indian Child Welfare Act. Representatives from various tribes and sympathetic organizations articulated their concerns about the frequent removal of Indian children. Bobby George, acting director of the Navajo Office of Resource Security, expressed the tribe's opposition to adoption by non-Navajos and emphasized the centrality of tribal courts in making any such decisions. His spoken testimony offered no direct or indirect critique of the ISPP; however, the written statement he submitted did make a vague reference to concerns about religious organizations. He applauded the educational and other assistance from some religious groups but noted that other activities unnecessarily "disrupted family relationships and separated children from their families under circumstances that were not in the best interests of their parents."

On a superficial glance George's comments may appear critical of the ISPP which operated the largest religious child removal program and centered its efforts on the Navajo reservation. However, George's comments centered on permanent adoption, not foster care and not the ISPP. In expressing this concern George also clarified that the tribe had largely resolved the problem twenty years earlier by use of tribal courts to approve any such adoptions. This was a reference to Navajo Tribal Council Resolutions CN-60-56 and CN-63-60, which passed in 1956 and 1960, respectively. The former required approval of an advisory council prior to removing children for any purpose other than education, and the latter established the tribal courts as the final adjudicators. Additionally, the U.S. Supreme Court upheld the exclusive jurisdiction of tribal courts relating to adoption proceedings in 1976 when the Northern Cheyenne successfully held off a Montana state court's adoption.[123]

The 1960 Navajo resolution further called on the tribal chairman to identify and exclude missionaries and others who disregarded the policy.[124] This, of course, did not impede the ISPP which enjoyed the education exemption written into those two resolutions (and likely as a result of heretofore mentioned efforts to win tribal support). In this context, George may have issued a subtle and veiled stab at the ISPP but it is far more likely he was altogether referring to the broader issues of Indian adoption which, he wrote, the tribe had largely resolved by 1977. If anything, the conspicuous absence of the ISPP from George's testimony may indicate divided tribal attitudes and an intentional effort not to deride or endorse that program. Even still, George undoubtedly shared the concerns of other tribal representatives regarding adoption and unsanctioned removal of Indian children from their respective reservations.[125]

In a sea of supporting testimony, the nearly sole voice of opposition came from two representatives of the Church of Jesus Christ of Latter-day Saints: LDS Social Services commissioner Harold C. Brown and Elder George P. Lee of the Quorum of the Seventy.[126] Senator Abourezk's response to the LDS representatives reveals much about the pressures the LDS Church brought to the legislation. Abourezk greeted the representatives:

> I guess this group here pretty much has your congressional delegation whipped into line. [Congressman] Gun [McKay] has been over personally to see me about this question; he came over to introduce you. Senator [Orrin] Hatch called me this morning and berated me over the telephone that, if I didn't treat you with great deference as witnesses this morning, he was going to do something nasty to me. So, I just want you to know that your congressional delegation is in full support of your objectives.[127]

Abourezk was well aware of the pressures exerted by the church and later made clear statements about the threat that the church represented to the bill.

Church officials also hoped George Lee's testimony would carry greater weight because he graduated from the ISPP and exemplified its positive elements. Born in 1943 to a typically impoverished Navajo family, Lee attended Shiprock Boarding School. His mother asked a local trader to help her fill out the BIA paperwork, and when the category of religion needed completion she permitted the trader to mark in his own faith: Mormon. Two years later Mormon traders recruited Lee for the Placement Program, and he spent the next seven years with the Harker family in Orem, Utah. Lee excelled in academics and extracurricular activities and went on to earn a Bachelor of Arts degree from BYU in 1968 and a Master of Arts from Utah State in 1970. He finished his PhD in educational leadership from BYU in 1975 while serving as the president of the College of Ganado, then a satellite campus of the Navajo Nation's Diné College. In July 1975, the church called him to serve as mission president of the Arizona Holbrook Mission, formerly the Southwest Indian Mission. His brief presidency ended in October of that same year when he was tapped by LDS Church president Spencer W. Kimball to serve in the First Quorum of the Seventy, a leadership position directly below the twelve apostles and prophet/president. It was the highest position ever held by a Native American in the LDS Church.[128] Lee represented the church's ideal Lamanite who could speak not only on behalf of the church but of this new generation of Lamanites who had fused two worlds.

Lee's testimony centered on legal and cultural implications of the ISPP. He challenged criticisms that the ISPP undermined Native heritage. He said, "Some critics have said that this program takes away the Indian child's Indianness or culture. But I find that it is not so, if anything, it enhanced who I am and what my responsibilities are to myself, to my family, to my tribe, to my country." Senator Abourezk cut Lee's testimony short and indicated that the submitted statement would suffice. Lee's written testimony included a bold affirmation of the ISPP's positive impact. He wrote:

> Placement did not rob me of my culture, as a few critics seem to fear. Instead, I gained a true perspective of myself—a true sense of identity. I learned that I could be proud of my heritage and rise above the problems that have kept my people from progressing.... Through placement, the uncertainty of the past was replaced with purpose, direction, and spiritual strength. I gained a tremendous desire and determination to succeed.[129]

Lee's support of the Lamanite identity, with its historical narrative and prophetic destiny, offered him and hundreds of others a strong sense of value and purpose. Though unwittingly recruited, Lee and many others had come to embrace the Lamanite ideology and program as not only a functional bridge between two worlds but also an identity that inspired success.

The other element of Lee's comments expressed concern that the bill created "a lot of policies and red tape, courts, procedures" that would make it difficult to operate the program, and likely eliminate this opportunity despite parent interest. During his testimony, he presented letter excerpts from tribal leaders who clamored for parent "self-determination." These leaders demanded that Congress cease any efforts to terminate the ISPP and preserve parental rights to send children to the school of their choice. This argument clearly sought to appropriate the concept of self-determination, which had guided federal policy since Nixon's use of the term in an address to Congress in 1970.

LDS Social Services commissioner Harold Brown's testimony outlined another way in which the proposed bill undermined American Indian sovereignty. He detailed Lee's critique about requirements that the ISPP report child enrollments to tribal offices. This would be difficult, he explained, given the disorganized nature of some smaller tribes, but also because such reports would violate the privacy of enrolled children. An uproar of skepticism from the audience interrupted Brown's comments until Chairman Abourezk called the room back into order. Brown concluded that parents who supported their child's involvement in the program could withdraw them at any time if that support changed. Because of this voluntary nature, he argued, additional monitoring was unnecessary; furthermore, it might potentially inhibit the ISPP's ability to service interested Indians, effectually undermining parental freedom to enroll their children in the program.

In each of their testimonies, Brown and Lee invoked individual self-determination to challenge the ICWA. The church representatives championed their version of self-determination as they argued that the bill required excessive reporting and disempowered parental prerogatives to place their children. Brown's unread statement explains that while "the intent of the bill is not to destroy the self-determination of Indian families, it would seriously limit or impede their choice in being able to voluntarily place their children for educational, spiritual or other opportunities." Lee's written but unread testimony also emphasized that the program operated at the invitation of American Indian parents and functioned as a voluntary system. Because the program operated at the request of Indians, they believed it was a positive symbol for Indian empowerment. Lee pleaded, "One of the rights that Indian families value most is self-determination.... We encourage you to preserve our right to self-determination through amending Senate bill 1214."[130] The ISPP empowered Indians to exercise self-determination, the church men asserted, by interpreting that concept as the preservation of personal—not tribal—autonomy. In this way, it paired the term with 1950s-era termination legislation that similarly claimed to liberate individual Indians from tribal constraints.

The church again sent representation to Congress for the Indian Child Welfare Act hearings in March 1978. Robert W. Barker of the LDS Church–retained law firm Wilkinson, Cragun and Barker, conveyed general support for the bill, but also expressed the need for an amendment that protected Indian parental rights and required tribes to file a request in order to receive information about children taken off their respective reservations. Barker reiterated Brown's comments, noting that it was simply too difficult to know the tribal affiliation of the thousands of children enrolled each year, but that if tribes identified themselves and requested information about their foster residence that the church would cooperate. He explained that, in fact, the program already followed this principle. The church typically sent the information to tribes for some 70 percent of the enrolled students, a policy that dated back to Navajo concerns voiced at the 1957 Kanab meeting.[131]

The church's efforts to amend the ICWA stirred up plenty of controversy and showed that many American Indians did not support the LDS program. During the February 9, 1978, hearings, several Indian advocates and tribal representatives voiced opposition to the ISPP and concern for the forthcoming amendment. Puyallup Tribe Social Services coordinator Faye LaPointe commented, "The Puyallup Tribe wholeheartedly opposed the LDS program and encourages this committee to discourage the efforts of the Mormon Church in their practices of genocide on our people." She took particular issue with the guise of education to conceal the assimilative program.[132] With utmost disgust, administrative assistant to the Tacoma Urban Indian Center Elizabeth Cagey expressed concern about the church's influence on forthcoming amendments to the bill. She pointed to an LDS Church–authored amendment submitted by Utah congressman McKay.[133]

Despite the church's strong opposition, the Indian Child Welfare Act passed in the House on July 21, 1978, and was signed into law on November 8, 1978.[134] The bill essentially recognized the sovereign authority of tribal entities in child custody affairs and pledged government grants to build Indian family development programs.[135] However, the bill was not as comprehensive as some had hoped. Section 4(1), which stipulated that the ICWA applies only to foster care where "the parent or Indian custodian cannot have the child returned on demand," exempted the voluntary ISPP. Outside the halls of Congress, Senator Abourezk shared his frustrations about the church's influence. He said, "We exempted it on purpose and out of necessity. There would have been one hell of a political fight if we hadn't."[136] The "Mormon exemption," as critics came to term the changes in the bill, attracted even more criticism of the Lamanite program.

In the wake of the ICWA exemption, a wave of antagonistic articles surfaced in American Indian and mainstream newspapers. Attacks came from many sides: reservation and mainstream newspapers, medical professionals, and academics. Martin Topper stood among the most vocal clinically trained critics. In a 1979 scholarly journal article, he charged that the ISPP caused trauma that left students unprepared to function in either white or Indian society. It perpetuated a "disjunction" that drove them to alcoholism and hysteria.[137] Topper made similar accusations in a variety of newspaper articles that reached a wider audience of readers.[138] Journalist Beth Wood emerged as the most vocal opponent of the ISPP. She published critical assessments of the program in Native newspapers *Akwesasne Notes*, *Wassaja*, and the *Navajo Times*, and charged the ISPP with unnecessarily splitting up families, causing psychological trauma, and leading to high suicide rates. While no child ever committed suicide while enrolled in the program, there is no record to track the life of graduates thereafter.

Other authors took aim at the ISPP in a variety of print mediums. They charged the program with cultural genocide, questioned its legality, and asserted slave-like labor conditions.[139] In 1979, one aptly titled article, "The Kids Go Out Navaho, Come Back Donny and Marie," characterized the Placement Program as a cultural whitewash. It cited a disenchanted white Mormon university professor who laid out the sinister purposes of the program as twofold: first, to use free manual labor and, second, to turn Indians into whites. The article quoted another critic who recalled "several families would work their Indians raw; if any of the children complained or caused any trouble they would be shipped back to the reservation to be replaced by a new group....I knew a dozen or so families who did it."[140] These extreme claims are unsubstantiated anywhere. In truth, caseworker oversight made such claims highly unlikely.

Although the church generally abstained from the debate, George P. Lee independently issued a response in a 1980 article published in *Wassaja*. Complaining that journalists misrepresented the program, Lee said that it genuinely served and supported American Indian families at their request. He argued that the ISPP did not damage Native family bonds and even strengthened tribal identity and culture. "The children retain a strong relationship with their families and Indian culture," he explained, "and this relationship is encouraged and fostered by the church." He also asserted that "the Mormon exception" to the ICWA came not from LDS Church lobby efforts, but from concerned American Indians.[141]

Criticisms lingered on in decreasing frequency and often conflated anxiety about permanent adoption in a larger criticism of the LDS Church. For example, in 1981 the men's magazine *Penthouse* published an article that issued one such criticism of the program.[142] Additional articles appeared in *Wassaja, Akwesasne Notes,* and *Indian Country Today,* as well as more mainstream papers including the *Washington Post* and *New York Times.*[143] Several Navajo-Mormon adoption disputes occurred in 1982–1984 and in 1988, which contributed to the negative attention and likely added to the conflation of the ISPP with permanent adoptions facilitated by the LDS Church's social services.[144]

The debate over the ICWA, from inception to post-passage criticisms, reveals an important game of illusions. On the surface the church appeared undaunted in its intent to continue with the ISPP and broader Lamanite program. The redefinition of self-determination to emphasize parental rights and personal liberties neatly reflected the conservative Mormon culture that sought to colonize Native Americans. As George P. Lee and others championed that position, the church appeared unaffected by the changing social climate. However, Indians at BYU were not quite as united as that image indicates. They questioned authorities and debated among themselves. As Indian students challenged notions of colonization and adopted other elements, they caught the eye of church authorities, some of whom would come to question the Indian program's success.

Divided attitudes among Lamanites stemmed from several stimuli. On one hand, Mormon Indians had their cultural and biological roots on the reservation; on the other, a colonizing program for many included foster homes and oversight at Brigham Young University. The rise of Red Power activism in the 1970s offered yet another competing voice, from which Mormon Indians usually distanced themselves as they carved out their own identity. While Red Power activists and the LDS Church frequently clashed, the two shared more in common than either might like to admit. Both emerged from depressed socioeconomic conditions and each asserted an ideological vision that promised a better future built upon some reinterpretation of their true identity. Like the boarding school experience before it, the flight from reservations exposed Indians to new environments and ideas and promoted intertribal networks and philosophies. Even still, the cultural and ideological rift between Lamanites and Red Power activists proved significant as each accused the other of colonization while asserting their own narrative.

Meanwhile, Navajos on the reservation experienced their own exciting transition. Chairman Paul Jones, Raymond Nakai, and chief legal counsel Norman M. Littell consciously advocated Western models of infrastructure and markets through work projects, social programs, and education; they led the reservation to increasingly resemble the outside world. Navajo leaders implicitly revered Western education as much as Lamanites and both accused each other of cultural apostasy. In this way, Lamanites awkwardly allied and conflicted with other Indians but ultimately the debates over authenticity overshadowed commonalities.

The Indian Child Welfare Act constituted the last major conflict between Mormon ideology and others, and the last effort to defend Lamanite programs that would soon face dissolution. Despite the LDS Church's vehement defense of the ISPP and Lamanite program, the national atmosphere had become permeated with conflict and controversy. The proliferation of local day schools on the Navajo Reservation and dissenting voices at BYU signaled an inevitable revision of policy. This dramatic transformation of Indian country and Native receptiveness to the LDS Church did not immediately or unilaterally collapse the ISPP, but it did create a new and less-inviting context that undermined the program and eventually led church leaders to reassess the value of the ISPP and the progress of Mormon Indians altogether.

8

DECLINE OF THE PLACEMENT PROGRAM

1972–2000

The Lord has said, "Where much is given much is expected." And of you much will be expected. I want to speak to you in such a way that you will not sit cross-legged on a blanket in the foothills waiting for Ephraim [white Mormons] and his brethren to come and to be presided over and to be led.... If it sounds like I'm scolding you just a little it will be because I am.... It pains me to see the possibility of it begin wasted.

—Apostle Boyd K. Packer, address to Lamanites at BYU, 1979

The Placement Program maintained a seemingly impenetrable façade as church leaders stalwartly ignored the negative publicity that arose in the 1960s and 1970s; however, below that calm surface internal divisions emerged and deepened during those years that ultimately contributed to the program's decline in the mid-1980s. More importantly, church leaders increasingly supported a bureaucratic reform agenda to purge superfluous programs and correlate those that remained under a singular line of priesthood authority. As this correlation movement gained momentum it eventually clashed with the ISPP and other Indian programs. Meanwhile, the exceptional international growth of the church infused it with millions of nonwhite people from abroad whose economic depravity matched or exceeded Native Americans. In tandem with that observation, Apostle

Boyd K. Packer expressed concern about the failure of Native Americans to live up to expectations and the disproportionate energies invested in special programs for them. As when the Latter-day Saints arrived in Utah, the reality of Indian reluctance dislodged prophetic expectations. Church leaders reinterpreted Lamanite-specific programs that once facilitated integration as metaphorical crutches that merely fostered ethnic individuality; correlation provided the organizational rationale to terminate such programs.

When Indian programs advocate Spencer W. Kimball fell ill in the early 1980s, his peers systematically dismantled the Indian programs he had spent his life building. Opposition to Indian programs emerged from the correlation-minded leaders who sought to terminate special programs and standardize LDS Church structures. Internal reports, initiated in response to popular criticisms of the ISPP, faulted the program and justified its reduction, particularly in light of expanding educational opportunities on the reservations. The emerging perception of the church's overextended domestic programs and underachieving Lamanites proved equally significant. Finally, a Utah lawsuit demanding tuition reimbursement for out-of-state students entering Utah offered the necessary justification to terminate the Placement Program once the last student graduated in 2000. These reports, successive internal reorganizations, and efforts to correlate all programs under a single priesthood line of authority contributed to the decline and eventual termination of the LDS Indian programs, including the Placement Program.

Spencer W. Kimball's oft-quoted praises of Lamanites, as well as the expansive Indian programs he created, generally suggest that he viewed all American Indians as a distinct people with unique needs that stemmed not from biology but rather socioeconomic depravity. He believed that in time, and given proper support, Native Americans would adapt and integrate into mainstream America. In a private letter to another Latter-day Saint in 1962, Kimball explained, "It is my feeling that the destiny of the Indian will eventually bring him into an integrated association in communities with the white men.... I firmly believe that tomorrow there will be no reservations." He concluded, "I believe that integration into our economy and community life is essential and I look forward to the day."[1] Kimball looked forward to the day when all Native peoples, Indian or otherwise, would be brought up to the same socioeconomic status that white America enjoyed.

As an extension of that vision, the Indian Committee's role progressively expanded over the 1960s to provide outreach to Native Americans and other Lamanite peoples, particularly in Latin America and the Pacific Islands. Indeed, the committee took charge of the integration of all nonwhite peoples as it orchestrated humanitarian aid, chapel construction, and educational programs. In 1963, the committee absorbed the foreign language committee, and by 1968 the church renamed it the Lamanite Committee. Then in 1970, the committee's title and responsibilities expanded yet again to reflect the populations it sought to service: it became the Committee for Lamanites and Other Cultures. This conceptual amalgamation of nonwhites into a singular other constituted a racial binary that issued clear roles that hearken back to the mid-nineteenth century: white Mormons as reformers and nonwhite Mormons as reformees. Though motivated by an assimilationist agenda, the church's overtures offered technology, training, and access to higher education which many American Indians valued as they sought new solutions to generations of poverty and social turmoil.

As LDS Church membership grew abroad, members of the Quorum of Twelve Apostles determined that integration needed to move at a brisker pace. They maneuvered to terminate "special programs" for particular ethnicities in order to rapidly erode ethnic distinction and mainstream those members more quickly. Kimball fought to retain the programs, preferring a slower integration, but he faced stark opposition in the highest councils of the LDS Church. Kimball's journal is typically silent in regard to any debates or controversy among the apostles, but in an entry from February 3, 1966, he did voice his frustration about what he viewed as the premature termination of foreign-language-speaking branches and the dissolution of Spanish-speaking missions within the United States. He recalled the committee seemed to support immediate integration, but Kimball "vigorously protested" until the president tabled the decision until the next week.[2] Kimball makes no reference to the meeting that followed; however, a year later in 1967 the church eliminated the Spanish American Mission. Thereafter, Spanish speakers fell under the purview of their respective missions, primarily the Texas and Western States Missions.[3] These changes suggest that termination and rapid integration efforts trumped Kimball's similar but more gradual efforts and institutional scaffolding.

The erosion of ethnic-specific programs continued in the early 1970s. In 1972, the Southwest Indian Mission followed the course of the Spanish

American Mission. The church renamed it the Arizona Holbrook Mission and assigned it discrete geographical boundaries that included the Navajo Reservation and neighboring white communities. The new mission surrendered all Indian populations beyond those limited boundaries to other geographically delineated missions throughout the West. Upstanding (largely white) Mormons in adjacent off-reservation communities increasingly fulfilled leadership positions in reservation congregations that white full-time missionaries once occupied. Indian communities could also be splintered and individually made into appendages of neighboring non-Indian communities that worked to assimilate and train Natives for eventual self-management modeled on a white Utah standard. The termination of the Indian-specific mission sent a powerful message that foreshadowed future changes within the church.

Former BYU director of Indian Affairs Paul Felt, an unabashedly proassimilation BYU administrator, went on to serve as the Southwest Indian Mission president during this reorganization and introduced the termination of the Indian-specific duties a year and a half earlier. As it came to fruition, he suggested that the change offered "a sound final solution to the problems incident to proselyting and integration among the Indian peoples."[4] Indians would no longer receive visits from missionaries trained in Indian culture and customs, but from missionaries who worked regularly with Indians and whites and prepared all potential converts using the same standard.

As the Indian mission gave way to a more assimilationist model, the church dissolved the Lamanite branch at BYU and distributed a circular letter to many stakes indicating that the needs of ethnic groups should be met through their integration, not through special programs.[5] These deepcutting changes, along with others, constitute a curious shift in policy. Why did a church devoted to extensive Indian uplift programs in the 1940s through 1960s suddenly terminate those policies in the 1970s?[6]

Much of the decline of the church's Indian programs may be attributed to Apostle Boyd K. Packer. Before receiving the apostolic call in 1970, Packer worked closely with local Indians and tribal representatives on and off the Navajo Reservation and he even developed the church's Indian Seminary program. In 1962, Kimball appointed Packer to the Indian Committee where he continued to advocate for Native peoples. Upon receiving a call to the apostleship, many expected Packer to continue Kimball's legacy of Indian outreach through the next generation. He did eventually succeed Kimball as the church's ad-hoc authority on Indian affairs; however, Packer envisioned himself more broadly as an apostle to the church as a whole. As a young apostle he was mentored not only by Kimball but also by Harold B. Lee, a dominant personality who opposed "special programs" that he believed derailed and cluttered the organizational leadership of the growing church. These two influences deeply impacted Packer, and over time he increasingly adopted Lee's views.

While serving as an assistant to the Quorum of Twelve Apostles and then during his own time as an apostle, Packer learned about the needs of church members well beyond American reservations. In 1964, he toured the church missions in South America. In his journal Packer recorded how a poverty-stricken boy deeply touched his heart:

> He was perhaps six or seven years old. His only clothing was a tattered shirt which almost reached his knees. He was dirty and undernourished, with all the characteristics of a street orphan.... My heart wept for him.... He came to me, and I picked him up to hold in my arms... I felt that I had an entire people in my arms.... A voice from the dust, perhaps from the dust of those small feet, already rough, whispered to me that this was a child of the covenant, of the lineage of the prophets.[7]

Packer's Indian Committee assignments took him to similarly impoverished people in the Southwest Indian Mission, the Northwest Indian Mission, and among Native American populations in the East, but he also found himself ministering among non-Lamanites. In 1969, he joined Apostle Marion G. Romney to tour Western European missions in Holland, Belgium, Luxembourg, Switzerland, and France. Later that year he returned to South America to dedicate chapels. The church grew increasingly international in the early twentieth century, and by the time of Packer's ordination to the apostleship, he had a worldview of the church that simply was not shared by prior generations of leaders.[8]

Packer's keen awareness of the church's foreign growth gave the correlation movement a particular reasonability. This policy advocated for the simplification and reduction of church organizations through the abolishment of redundancies created by its rapid growth. The movement simultaneously reinforced central administration of priesthood leaders to the ever more dispersed membership. Mild efforts at correlation began in 1908, but the trend did not really gain momentum until the early 1960s under the charge of Apostle (and eventual president) Harold B. Lee.[9] Lee long anticipated correlation but initially lacked the seniority to impose the restructuring he believed necessary until he rose in rank and recruited the support of younger apostles, including Gordon B. Hinkley, Thomas S. Monson, Boyd K. Packer, and Neal A. Maxwell.[10]

Lee characterized the movement as a divinely inspired response to church growth. Among the accomplishments of correlation, Lee organized the world into regions and later into areas, each with local authorities. This eventually led to the creation of an intermediary priesthood bureaucracy called the Quorum of the Seventy which correlated between the apostles and local stake presidents around the world. Under this plan, every Latter-day Saint received guidance from local priesthood leaders who fell under another in a "pipeline of authority," as one scholar termed it.[11] This ultimately bound each family unit with the Quorum of the Twelve Apostles and the First Presidency of the LDS Church. Every household, regardless of location or ethnicity, could receive standardized instruction from Salt Lake City. In this way, the church centralized governance and administration to induct expanding membership into an autocratic structure by standardizing the instruction and behavior of each member to a central ideal model.

The movement also took measures to either purge or fully incorporate untamed and semi-independent programs that serviced particular groups. Its advocates feared that institutions like the Placement Program, or even the Relief Society (to which all LDS women belonged), created redundancies in costs and risked conflicting efforts. Correlation, therefore, installed priesthood oversight that dovetailed into the emerging all-inclusive authority pyramid.[12] Through such efforts correlation ensured central governance and orthodoxy at all levels of the church.

As an assistant to the apostles, Packer received an assignment to draw up a report for the LDS Church's Education Committee, which evolved into the Priesthood Correlation Committee as it undertook some of his recommendations. Packer argued the church was disorganized and consequently mismanaged its finances as it carried out often redundant programs. Too many Mormons, he worried, wasted energies completing tasks for programs that ultimately proved inefficient and sometimes even conflicting.[13] He later commented, "When we overemphasize programs at the expense of principles, we are in danger of losing the inspiration."[14]

In 1960, the First Presidency directed the Committee of General Authorities to re-examine the function of its auxiliary programs like the Relief Society, Mutual Improvement Association for youth, and Primary for children. By 1964, Lee chaired the Priesthood Correlation Committee with other apostles in supportive roles. The committee instituted screening committees composed of apostles and members of the Quorum of Seventy who evaluated and standardized teaching manuals, finances, and chapel construction. It also professionalized the welfare system and placed it all under the Presiding Bishopric by way of the Relief Society, but all of those administrative and ecclesiastical heads would then report to the Welfare Committee chaired by a rotating member of the Quorum of Twelve Apostles.[15] By 1972, the movement reached a climax as it placed all organizations, curricula, and periodicals under the direct guidance of priesthood lines leading to committees controlled by the apostles.

Initial assumptions that Packer would be a friend to the Indian programs proved inconsistent with his correlation agenda. Packer said, "I do not want nor wish to be known as an apostle to the Lamanites as President Kimball was. . . . I am not an apostle to the Indians but to the whole church."[16] This does not mean that Packer held no sympathies for American Indians— he certainly did—but he also saw the needs of many other Latter-day Saints throughout the world, and he wished to give them equal attention. As early as 1965, he expressed reservations about special admission standards for Indians at BYU. Kimball refuted him, but less than a year later BYU issued new rules on admissions and required Native Americans to meet the same entrance standards as all other students.[17]

Correlation's victory over BYU admissions standards and Packer's support of this shift in policy signaled many changes to come. Beginning in 1969, the ISPP and other Indian programs fell subject to a series of reorganizations that moved them out of the hands of Spencer W. Kimball and the Indian Committee and into more standardized lines of authority consistent with priesthood correlation; the Placement Program drifted from Kimball's control. This began when correlation-minded apostles took advantage of Kimball's absence from a scheduled meeting and voted to move the

program from his oversight in the Lamanite Committee into a newly organized administration to oversee all church social services. Kimball's son,
who later authored a biography of his father, wrote that the "Indian Affairs
Committee still had some responsibilities, but the heart of its activities had
been cut out and transferred."[18] As the Lamanite Committee's significance
dwindled, Kimball found it more difficult to cross lines of authority to support Indian programs that no longer fell under his personal stewardship.[19]

In October 1969, the First Presidency organized the Unified Social Services under the direction of Elder Marvin J. Ashton of the Quorum of the
Seventy.[20] As managing director, Ashton provided the priesthood oversight
for the hired professionals. These "executive assistants" each managed a
branch of the social services and reported to Ashton, who then reported
to the Welfare Committee, which was composed of several apostles, the
Presiding Bishopric, and Relief Society presidency.[21] The new Unified
Social Services would oversee foster care and adoption services, as well as
the formerly independent ISPP. Local agency directors oversaw all of those
programs in their area and reported to their Unified Social Services state
boards, who continued to take their direction from Salt Lake City. Former
ISPP director Clare Bishop retained oversight of the Placement Program in
LDS Church headquarters, as part of a four-man committee that oversaw
each welfare program and reported to managing director Ashton. However, Bishop lost the direct access to apostles that he once enjoyed. Rather
than reporting directly to Kimball, his recommendations passed through
a chain of priesthood leaders who did not always share his strong conviction about the ISPP's value.[22]

Contemporary to this restricting an internal report indicated a need for
closer oversight of loosely managed Indian Programs to a priesthood line
of authority.[23] Consistent with that analysis, in 1971 the First Presidency
instructed Unified Social Services to coordinate all church programs for
Lamanites and other cultures under the direction of priesthood leaders who
oversaw the Welfare Committee.[24] A 1971 *Church News* article explained
that the Unified Social Services would take on "all facets of the Lamanite
church program" formerly coordinated by the Committee for Lamanites and
Other Cultures.[25] Just as the committee lost oversight of the ISPP in 1969,
by 1971 all Indian programs shifted away from Kimball's purview to a separate priesthood line of authority.

This bureaucratization marginalized Bishop and segmented case-workers as it distanced them from any policy determining body. As a consequence of rapid growth, Bishop recalled that the program became "quite fragmented" as some agencies' directors neglected the ISPP and left their caseworkers to act without instruction.[26] The change troubled many of the caseworkers. Bishop said, "There was some resistance.... We saw ourselves as an educational program and not as a welfare program or a social service program."[27] In essence, the restructuring demystified the ISPP as a unique and inspired program and relegated it to a common welfare service. By the 1970s, the ISPP amounted to just one of many social services.

In 1974 the church again reorganized its social services, this time creating LDS Social Services. The new entity retained the old administrative subservience to the Presiding Bishopric and Welfare Committee but assumed legal independence to protect the church from any lawsuits stemming from social work.[28] Then managing director Robert L. Simpson determined that the Unified Social Services four-member committee was an inefficient system of management, so the Presiding Bishopric purged the executive assistants to the director and left only the managing director (and renamed the position "commissioner"). Simpson reassigned Clare Bishop, formerly the executive assistant over the ISPP, as the director of a local agency in Utah, further distancing him from any group that determined policy. A few months later the church removed him from Social Services altogether when he received a call to serve as a mission president in the South Dakota Rapid Cities Mission, which had already abandoned its unique focus on Indians for broader proselytizing among all people. One can only speculate as to the motivations behind and the origin of these transfers. Meanwhile, another executive assistant, Victor Brown Jr., assumed the new commissioner role. Like Ashton and Simpson before him, Brown had no particular commitment to Lamanites and the Indian programs. Still, he did call to his aid several long-time ISPP caseworkers, including Glen VanWagenen and William "Dale" Bush, who assisted with the ISPP's management.[29]

Commissioner Victor Brown Jr. reported directly to the Welfare Committee, formerly chaired by the presiding bishop, a position coincidentally occupied by Brown's father, Victor Brown Sr.[30] In theory, Brown Sr. explained, the Presiding Bishopric operated directly under the prophet; however, he said that apostles typically maneuvered themselves in between by way of ever-proliferating committees that empowered apostles as chairmen; this created another level of bureaucracy and endowed the apostles with greater authority as gatekeepers to the prophet and First Presidency. The ISPP-focused executive assistant reported to the Social Services commissioner, who reported to the General Relief Society, who reported to the Presiding Bishopric, who then took direction from the apostles who chaired the Welfare Committee. This meant that a great deal of policy decisions occurred without the oversight of the First Presidency or the commissioner, and certainly without the involvement of caseworkers who actually carried out the program. Apostles with varied experiences and perspectives often issued directives that drastically impacted the Social Services systems. Depending on the vigor of a given apostle, the Presiding Bishopric alternated between assisting in policy making to, more often, policy administering.[31] By the mid-1970s, Indian Placement's strongest advocates—relegated to caseworkers and agency directors—seemed farther than ever from the councils of policy making.

Presiding bishop Victor Brown Sr. recalled that the apostles often expressed "strong differing opinions" that made his administrative role difficult because policies "flip-flopped" according to who served on the Welfare Committee. At times the messages came to phase out the Indian Placement Program, only to be counteracted by directives to expand enrollment. Brown lamented, "We make drastic changes. We go out and then come back and then go out and come back." He characterized the apostles as dominant personalities with often conflicting feelings. Brown, who enjoyed a successful corporate career of his own, concluded, "I don't know how it could function in an orderly fashion with the present mode of operation that they have."[32] This element of dysfunction stemmed from the increasing authority seized by the apostles, and was evident as early as May 1967 when the First Presidency gathered for a private meeting. Then prophet and president David O. McKay recounted that his first counselor, "President [Hugh B.] Brown stated that it seemed evident that the First Presidency is losing its grip on the activities that are going forward, and that more and more we are being regulated and ruled by committees. . . . He felt that the First Presidency is taking rather a second place to the committees in these matters."[33]

Beginning in the mid-1970s, apostles sent several policy changes to the office of Victor Brown Jr. and his successor, Harold Brown (no relation). As

TABLE 8.1. STUDENT ENROLLMENT AND
PERCENT CHANGE, 1969–1979

YEAR	ENROLLMENT	% CHANGE
1969–1970	4,467	+44.6%
1970–1971	4,997	+11.9%
1971–1972	4,730	-5.3%
1972–1973	3,833	-19.0%
1973–1974	2,917	-23.9%
1974–1975	2,350	-19.4%
1975–1976	2,293	-2.4%
1976–1977	2,697	+17.6%
1977–1978	2,563	-5.0%
1978–1979	2,500	-2.5%

Source: Indian Placement Program Records, 1978, Church Archives.

commissioner, Victor Brown operated under the notion that the ISPP was to be phased out. With that intention he made little effort to expand the program. Enrollment had peaked in 1971 just before his tenure and steadily declined under his administration until stabilizing under Harold Brown.[34]

Locating the origin of the instruction to phase out the ISPP is particularly difficult given the conflicting directions to the Presiding Bishopric and the closed-lip nature of the church hierarchy. However, Clare Bishop recalled a distinct feeling of opposition to the ISPP from the church hierarchy just as Harold B. Lee assumed the mantle of prophet and president in 1972. Bishop recalled, "I felt a feeling that maybe we ought not to have the Placement Program to the extent that it had developed, if we should have it at all."[35] The program's declining enrollment likely originated in the highest councils and it certainly engendered a feeling of abandonment among the caseworkers. Dropping enrollment carried an unspoken message that the once dynamic program now seemed "uninspired."[36]

Among the most significant factors in the declining enrollment was a 1972 policy change to fully remove missionaries from much of the recruiting process.[37] Victor Brown Jr. recalled that when Unified Social Services initiated that policy it led to a dramatic decline in enrollment. He estimated a drop from 5,000 students to 2,100 over the following two years. Brown noted that Kimball was disheartened by the program's decline but respected the bureaucratic lines of authority and did not criticize Brown or otherwise interfere in the program's administration.[38] For the rest of the decade, enrollment rested at around 2,500 students per year.

Previous to this change, the ISPP often served as a proselytizing tool to attract new converts, often with the promise of education or middle-class leisure. Many students and parents who sought out Placement fully realized the ties to the church, but many did not. LDS missionaries frequently enlisted students who ranged from fully converted and prepared for life in the church to those completely unaware of the Mormon faith. Navajo Jimmy Bennally, a former Placement student and missionary in the Southwest Indian Mission, estimated that "ninety percent of the kids were baptized to go on Placement rather than be baptized into the church." On his mission, he explained, "We always had a quota we had to meet of how many kids we had to get on Placement. As a result, we just went out to fill our quota." He continued, "We just signed up kids and baptized them to go on Placement. You'll find that a lot of kids that were on the LDS Placement Program really weren't converted to the church. They just went to get to go to school."[39] Church leaders knew about feigned conversions and opposed such baptisms. In 1967, Kimball resolved to send a letter to all mission presidents discouraging ISPP-motivated baptisms.[40] Still, the exuberance of young missionaries under pressure to meet quotas combined with students' desires for an education and an opportunity to leave the reservation made it difficult to fully eliminate such practices.

Even after the 1972 removal of missionaries from direct involvement as the primary ISPP recruiters, they continued to assist local members in enrolling recent converts. A March 1978 report from the Southwest Indian Mission commented on the energies missionaries invested in "finding and signing up" children for the ISPP, and in June 1979 the mission indicated they had gathered 1,640 applicants over the summer.[41] Despite this continued involvement on a more limited basis, the policy change still cut enrollment and weakened the role of missionaries in program recruitment.

Another ISPP policy change in the early 1970s involved the use of foster parents as voluntary assistants to caseworkers. Such parents worked with other foster parents and children to ensure the smooth operation of the ISPP. This help was essential because the understaffed ISPP assigned a minimum caseload of seventy-five students for each caseworker, causing some loads to climb to nearly one hundred. In contrast, social workers outside of LDS Social Services typically worked with only forty children.[42] To combat this overload, caseworkers enlisted some foster parents into the "Lamanite Assistance Program" where they served as assistant caseworkers. These volunteers did not have formal training, but generally contributed years of experience to parents and children in need of direction. Still, some foster parents complained that the new arrangement made caseworkers even less accessible. Foster mother Kay Cox recalled, "I didn't like the fact that it put just one more person between the caseworker and the family or student. Another problem was that many who served in that capacity had little or no experience with placement." She continued that "many who were called, not knowing what to do, did nothing."[43] Cox commented that many foster parents never saw their caseworkers at all. This surely both contributed to a sense of abandonment among foster parents and eroded the communication of clear program objectives.

Correlation efforts in the 1960s continued to have an impact in the 1970s and touched the Indian programs at several junctions. As mentioned earlier, organizational restructuring in 1969, 1971, and 1974 diminished the influence of Spencer W. Kimball. In the aftermath of those changes, Stewart A. Durrant took over much of this disempowered administrative work as an employee of the Unified Social Services and reported to Carlos Asay of the Seventy who in turn reported to Apostle Boyd K. Packer via the Welfare Committee.[44] Unified Social Services also took over publication of the *Indian Liahona* magazine and a year later terminated the magazine as part of a larger consolidation of the many LDS Church publications.[45] Also in 1972, the church dissolved the Southwest Indian Mission and BYU's Indian branches, and the First Presidency circulated a letter that recommended congregations provide translating and other services to facilitate integration of non-English-speaking peoples. Foreign language classes "may be organized" within English-speaking wards, if necessary.[46] In an unusually candid interview, former Southwest Indian Mission president and founding father of the ISPP Golden Buchanan identified Harold B. Lee as a primary source of opposition to language branches, a position consistent with Lee's better-known support for priesthood correlation.[47] Lee served as an apostle from 1941 to 1972 and then as prophet for a year and a half, during which time the church initiated many of these changes. In 1973, for example, the Indian Seminary Program also began a long-term decline in enrollment that eventually culminated in its termination.[48] Even still, correlation alone could not fully justify the termination of programs once thought divinely inspired, and so began a wave of investigative studies that challenged the ISPP's value.

The earliest indications of the ISPP's shortcomings appeared in reports organized by the Indian Committee in the 1950s. They tracked graduation and dropout rates and generally overlooked the high turnover of students by focusing on the academic achievement of those who remained in the program. These conclusions led Kimball and the committee to increase enrollment to impact more Indian youth. They believed in victory by volume and reinvested in that strategy each year until enrollment climaxed in 1971.[49] To explore concerns about spiritual deviance among Placement students, the Indian Committee conducted a survey of 235 ISPP graduates in 1968. The 165 responses showed that the graduates exhibited positive signs of church allegiance and cultural integration through service in missions, marriages in LDS temples, and the procurement of higher education. However, the committee overlooked that 30 percent of those graduates did not respond to the survey, which may indicate less-thorough conversions. A more complete survey simultaneously sent to 480 branch presidents in the Southwest Indian Mission indicated that 58 percent of then current ISPP students actively participated in church during the summers, 27 percent were "partially active," and 18 percent did not attend any meetings.[50] This report indicated that ISPP graduates matched white Mormons in their religiosity, or at least church attendance.

Academic achievement also emerged as a major point of investigation during the 1970s. A 1970 report found that ISPP students performed well below the minimum BYU general admission standards instituted several years earlier.[51] A 1972 study of BYU Indian students found that those ISPP students who advanced to BYU earned no better grades than American Indian students who did not spend their adolescence in white foster homes.[52] Royce Flandro, coordinator of Indian Student Services at BYU, explained that former ISPP students constituted both the best and worse at the university. He said Placement graduates with four or more years in the ISPP constituted "some of our most outstanding students at Brigham Young University in terms of leadership, academic, and spiritual qualities." However, he also explained that other former ISPP students seemed to "behave as if they were escaping the controls of the foster parent (at last free) and the customs of the Church attendance and activity."[53] One year later, in 1973, BYU professor of sociology Arturo de Hoyos produced a similar study. Because of improving elementary educational standards and resources on reservations, he recommended cutting the youngest children from the ISPP altogether.[54] A 1974 report by three BYU faculty found that after an initial boost the academic achievement of ISPP students progressively declined each year.[55] In aggregate, these studies reported negatively on the ISPP and certainly provided support for those many church leaders who already opposed the program.

In response to ever more vocal criticisms, both internal and external, the church commissioned an independent study of American Indian opinions regarding the Placement Program. The 1979 Wasatch Opinion Research Report polled 783 Indians, including 400 parents of enrolled students, 100 ISPP children, 100 tribal leaders, and 83 LDS college graduates who formerly participated in the ISPP. The report found that 95 percent of parents had a "good" or "very good" attitude about Placement as did 92 percent of current students, 81 percent of former students, and 82 percent of tribal leaders. It examined religious affiliation and found positive attitudes even among 90 percent of non-Mormon parents. The report demonstrated that parents, tribal leaders, and students believed Placement children fit into their Native communities without significant trouble and that most of the respondents did not perceive the program as harmful to the children's identity as Indians. Respondents valued the ISPP for perceived access to superior schools and cross-cultural exposure.[56] Despite the program's apparent failure to elevate academic performance above that of Indians who did not participate, parents and community members remained positive about the program's function. Regardless of religious affiliation, many American Indians generally valued the ISPP as an academic institution and demonstrated no social reservations about its graduates.

The most significant report, however, appeared in draft form in 1982 and was released internally in 1984. At the request of the Presiding Bishopric and Welfare Services and under direction from the Correlation Department, several BYU professors compiled a massive 322-page evaluation of the

Placement Program. At the urging of the Correlation Committee, in 1977 the bishopric requested "hard" data on the impact of participation, and objective measurements of accomplishments related to the program's stated goals "to provide opportunity for the enhancement of Indian [each] child's social, spiritual, cultural, educational, and leadership abilities and experiences."[57] The study explained its own origins in the controversial debates and publicity leading up to the Indian Child Welfare Act and in the church's need to examine accusations about harm caused by removing Indian children from Native homes. Albrecht and Associates interviewed hundreds of students, foster parents, siblings, and caseworkers.

The report found "a positive relationship between the Placement experience and level of education attained," though those "long-term" students contributed most of the significance. Those on Placement for at least four years obtained much more education overall, including bachelor's and even graduate degrees. The program also impacted students' spirituality in the sense of faith and activity in the church. Students were more likely to believe in Jesus Christ, pray before meals, and attend church meetings; however, they were no more likely to believe in the Bible and no less likely to use tobacco—a habit explicitly forbidden by the church but that was extremely common on most reservations. Like education, they found that those with "long term ISPP experience" had increased spirituality. Additionally, former ISPP students were more likely to have bank accounts, hold jobs, live independent of their parents, and attend college or obtain other training and, thus, earn higher wages. This was especially true for those who participated for four or more years. In the social adjustment category, they found that students who were on the Placement Program from four to eight years were more likely to vote in elections, interact in a larger social network, and identify themselves as "happy"; surprisingly, after eight years that rate decreased and less-desirable behaviors emerged, such as a higher likelihood of being arrested. Students enrolled beyond eight years were less likely to claim LDS membership or attend church meetings and more likely to use alcohol, another expressly forbidden item. In presenting these results the report did not speculate as to why the effectiveness of the program declined when students were involved for more than eight years. For whatever reason, the magic window of "success" seemed to be four to eight years of participation.

The report also identified several concerns about the Placement Program. Many respondents identified family stress introduced by participation in the ISPP, particularly white foster siblings who experienced rivalries with Indian foster children. The thirty-six Placement workers who were interviewed expressed another range of concerns and problems with the program, including confusion over its purpose. Was the ISPP intended to focus on spiritual elements, educational opportunities, leadership development, or perhaps even something else? Should they take only the best students who could become leaders, or seek out the most troubled youth to provide them needed resources? One caseworker asked, "Who is placement for, the weak, the strong, any who want to come, or only a select few? Nobody has defined these things." Consequently, caseworkers varied widely in the admission standards they applied, which often created tensions with local branch presidents on the reservations. One caseworker commented:

> We have a foster care program with 3,000 kids, and we don't have anyone that is really over it. There is the Area Welfare Director, the Assistant Commissioner, the Agency Director, the Priesthood leaders, and three Regional Representatives. They all have their input.... There is no single source of direction from the Prophet on down.[58]

The result was that caseworkers often worked independently and responded however they thought best when facing local circumstances.

The confidential report earned immediate notoriety among ISPP administrators, the Presiding Bishopric, apostles, and First Presidency: the audience for whom it was written. Despite the program's success in certain areas, the ecclesiastic authorities who sought to purge Placement and other "special programs" certainly found ample evidence in this report to support those measures. Immediately following the report's formal submission to church leaders, the Placement Program's enrollment again declined and advocates of correlation like Boyd K. Packer moved to terminate the ISPP.

Despite negative reports in the 1970s and early 1980s, the ISPP and the church Indian program as a whole enjoyed one great point of protection, that of Spencer W. Kimball. Though his apostolic authority was outmaneuvered in 1969 by the relocation of the ISPP to the Unified Social Services, Kimball assumed the role of prophet and church president in 1973. Placement administrators hoped his new position as the head of the church would enable the prophet to reemphasize the program they knew he loved. Clare Bishop later recalled,

When Elder Kimball became President, all of a sudden a champion of Indian Placement was in a position again where he could have influence and there was motivation for Social Services to pull the program back together, to begin adhering again to policies and to procedures, to have training for case workers, to have the numbers increased, and to make it a program benefiting many children.[59]

Consistent with that anticipation, the church under Kimball's tenure as president moved to restore some special programs for ethnic groups. In 1977 it introduced the Basic Unit Plan, which repealed former restrictions and permitted ethnic and foreign-language branches to reorganize.[60] A year later the church extended the priesthood to African American males. In terms of the Placement Program, the freefalling enrollment leveled out again during Kimball's presidency. Although it never again increased its enrollment, the ISPP maintained an average of two thousand annual participants until the early 1980s.[61]

Kimball's health declined in the early 1980s, much like the Indian programs he defended. Though Kimball did not pass away until 1985, following the October 1982 General Conference he offered only one additional address to the general population before his passing. It is likely that if he could not make it to biannual general conferences, he probably struggled to participate in his weekly meetings with the apostles as they managed church affairs and programs. Presiding bishop Victor Brown Sr. commented that pressures and tensions increased between himself and the apostles as Kimball's health declined. Some apostles long held suspicions that Kimball and the presiding bishop sought to circumvent the committees chaired by the apostles. As the prophet fell ill, Brown explained, the apostles grew bolder in their assumption of authority.[62] In Kimball's absence, Apostle Boyd K. Packer emerged as the obvious candidate to determine church Indian policies as he served on various committees. He took a leading role in determining the future of the Indian Student Placement Program and the Indian programs at Brigham Young University.[63]

The termination of Brigham Young University's Indian program in the early 1980s further illustrates the resurgence of post-Kimball opposition to ethnic individuality through rapid mainstreaming and the dissolution of group-specific programs. BYU's Indian enrollment peaked at just over five hundred students in the early and mid-1970s but then declined, particularly in the early 1980s.[64] In 1978, Indian Education Department chair John R. Mae-stas announced the creation of a new, broader multicultural program at BYU intended to replace any ethnic-specific programs; Native Americans would no longer constitute an independent organizational identity.[65] Rising admission standards and a reduction in scholarships undercut Indian enrollment, as did the shifting focus from Indian-specific programs to broader multicultural efforts that amalgamated all nonwhite students into a single group.[66]

During the 1979 Indian Week at BYU, Elder Packer gave a keynote address to Placement students, Indian seminary students, and BYU Indian students. His comments expressed frustration at shortcomings of Native Americans and contrasted the successes of the ever-growing Latin American Lamanite population. Packer scolded the Indian audience and indicated that many Indians had "wasted" away their lineage birthright; each needed to recommit themselves to the gospel.[67] The apostle reproved them with example after example of Latin American Lamanites who had fulfilled leadership and activity expectations. He contrasted that success with unimpressive efforts by some American Indians who pleaded for the crutch of Indian wards where lower expectations made church membership more comfortable. To such he exclaimed, "We're not interested in [your] being comfortable. We're interested in your being of service."[68] Packer's speech closed with a final assertion of the Lamanite's noble potential. "You are chosen," he said as he called on them to "move ahead and take your place."[69] That place, according to Packer, was beside their better-achieving Lamanite and white brethren in joint service in the church. Dissolving the Indian student wards was only the first step toward forcing the rapid integration envisioned by Packer and other general authorities.

Packer's assessment was similar in tone to comments made by Apostle A. Theodore Tuttle of the First Presidency in 1968. Speaking of Placement Students nearly a generation earlier, Tuttle had said, "It is only when these young people have succeeded in school, filled honorable missions, married in the temple, and are faithfully giving service to their fellowmen that the efforts of this program can be assessed."[70] Elder Packer looked over the many Indian programs, from BYU to the Indian seminary and the ISPP, and seemed unconvinced of their success.[71]

Over the following five years, the organizational distinctiveness of American Indians at BYU continued to dissolve. The erosion of Indian focused programs began in 1983 when Indian Week became Lamanite Week, featuring Latin American and Polynesian cultures alongside Native American festivities. At the same time, sponsorship shifted from the Tribe of Many Feathers club to the recently organized Multicultural Education Department, which heavily employed both Polynesian and American Indian students for the week's festivities.[72] In 1984, the university began replacing the semiautonomous chairs in Indian Education, Multicultural Education, and International Student Offices with far less empowered "coordinators" who by 1985 took their lead from a newly empowered director over all multicultural programs.[73] That fall, the university reassigned Indian Education faculty to other humanities departments and essentially dismantled any distinct Indian programs at BYU, leaving only a Native American minor operated out of the history department.[74] By 1986, only eighty students registered for the minor and the once thriving program was all but dead.[75] As American Indian programs withered, the university-wide admission standards rose, making the university both less accommodating and less accessible for Indian students. These policies led to a 45 percent decline in Indian enrollment during the mid-1980s.

Terminating the Indian program at BYU proved a controversial move among Lamanites. Though designed to more rapidly integrate all students, many Native Mormons saw it as an attack on Indians ordered by Packer or other apostles. When BYU administrators swore the faculty to silence about the process, it only raised more eyebrows among Lamanites.[76] The former director of Multicultural Programs explained that "a decision was made by the administration to 'mainstream' Indian education."[77] The restructuring undermined the social identity of American Indians at BYU and pushed the remaining Indian students to choose between two racial distinctions: whites and multicultural nonwhites.

In addition to the diminished Native American studies minor, the American Indian Services constituted another remnant of BYU's once massive Indian program. This research and outreach arm of the program once organized studies and demonstration farms across Indian reservations. Former Southwest Indian Mission president Dale Tingey ran the program from 1971 until its closure in 1989.[78] He recalled that Kimball was quite supportive during his apostleship and presidency, as were BYU presidents Wilkinson (1951–1971) and Dallin H. Oaks (1971–1980). In contrast, President Jeffrey R.

Holland (1980–1989) encouraged Tingey to seek independent funding and organize a privately operated equivalent of the program. Tingey did just that. Though BYU terminated the program, it continues today as a private Indian operation located within a hundred feet of campus.[79]

The *Eagle's Eye* magazine constituted the final vestige of BYU's Indian program. Once dedicated to BYU Indians, the magazine followed the trend towards general multicultural representation in the 1980s and 1990s. The Winter 1993 edition featured Black Awareness Week, and during that decade the magazine's pages increasingly featured other ethnic groups as well. By the close of the decade the magazine was characterized by spotlights on black, Hispanic, and other nonwhite professors and students. What originated as an American Indian magazine deteriorated to exhibit only occasional articles related to that population.[80] In effect, this reflects the binary of white and nonwhite that was institutionalized a decade earlier, and in the process it minimizes the cultural distinctiveness of any particular group.

Much as the Indian programs at Brigham Young University suffered a radical decline in the mid-1980s, the Placement Program also faced serious reductions at that time. The first major reduction in Placement Program enrollment occurred just after the 1969 organization of LDS Unified Social Services and before the 1972 ordination of Harold B. Lee as prophet and president. It continued to decline for only a few years until it stabilized at just over two thousand students in the mid-1970s. This stabilization occurred, not coincidentally, following the ordination of long-time Indian program advocate Spencer W. Kimball as prophet and president in December 1973. Kimball surely bolstered the program during the early years of his presidency; however, his declining health likely inhibited his ability to defend it and other Indian programs against the ever-present priesthood correlation movement. The 1982–1984 Presiding Bishopric report, which criticized the ISPP, emerged as Kimball's health all but removed him from church governance and certainly from the oversight of specific programs, such as the ISPP.

In February of 1984, Elder Packer presided over a meeting of the Welfare Committee that directed the Presiding Bishopric and all social services, including the ISPP. One attendee recalled how Packer raised up his hands and held them wide to indicate how much effort the church had put into the Indian program; he then narrowed his hands to indicate the results. By contrast, the apostle explained, other programs excelled on far fewer

resources.[81] Packer then presented a plan to phase out the younger participants from the program. Beginning in the following school year, 1984–
1985, only students in fifth grade or higher could participate, and each year
thereafter that level would rise until no elementary or junior high students
could enroll in the ISPP. In this way, no current students would be forced to
leave the program, but over the succeeding years the program would contract to include only high school students in grades nine through twelve
(generally ages fifteen through eighteen).[82] This offered the twofold benefit of eliminating small children who had access to new alternatives on the
reservation (recalling the concerns and recommendations of DeHoyos's
1973 report) and restricting enrollment to only four years, the fewest years
within the ideal time frame identified by the Bishopric report. Packer laid
out the plan and then, in a twist of irony, he, just as Kimball had decades
earlier, relied on his apostolic authority to insist compliance. The Welfare
Committee members accepted the terms Packer dictated and unanimously
passed the resolution.

The church announced the policy change the following month in a
Deseret News newspaper article.[83] Two months later, *Ensign* magazine featured an interview with ISPP coordinator David Albrecht who attributed the
changes to an unnamed "major research study," presumably the Presiding
Bishopric report. He summarized the report as claiming that students who
participated in the program "had higher grades, were more likely to go
to college, were more active in the church, and were more likely to go on
missions and to be married in the temple." It also found that "four years
seemed to be the optimum time on the program" and that "benefits didn't
necessarily increase with added years."[84] He anticipated that the annually
scaled-back age requirements would perpetuate a 60 percent reduction of
enrollment from 1984 to 1989.[85] Records tracking the declining enrollment
are not available; however, if the enrollment was at about 2,100 before the
policy change, as he recalls, and if Albrecht's prediction of a 60 percent
decline was generally correct, a reasonable estimate projects a loss of some
700 student participants each year.[86]

The dissolution of the entire Indian program, including the Southwest
Indian Mission, Indian seminary, BYU programs, and the declining ISPP
enrollment drew concerns from many Mormon Native Americans, most
notably George P. Lee who then served in the First Quorum of the Seventy.

TABLE 8.2. ELIGIBILITY REQUIREMENTS AND
PROJECTED STUDENT ENROLLMENT, 1979–1989

YEAR	ELIGIBILITY	PROJECTED ENROLLMENT
1979–1980	8 years +	2,100
1980–1981	8 years +	2,100
1981–1982	8 years +	2,100
1982–1983	8 years +	2,100
1983–1984	8 years +	2,100
1984–1985	Grades 5–12	1,900
1985–1986	Grades 6–12	1,700
1986–1987	Grades 7–12	1,450
1987–1988	Grades 8–12	1,150
1988–1989	Grades 9–12	900

*Source: Indian Placement Program Files, 1950–1998, LDS Church
Archives.*

Lee's resistance to these changes culminated in his excommunication on September 1, 1989. His was the first excommunication of a general authority in almost fifty years, and it sent reverberations through the church and particularly the Mormon–American Indian community.

Elder George P. Lee did not have a specific assignment to work with Native Americans, but as a product of the church's Indian program he occasionally spoke at BYU's Indian Week and other LDS activities related to American Indians. He recounted that the apostles discouraged him from focusing his energies on Native Americans and in 1975 explicitly forbade him from speaking on Indian issues at his first General Conference as a member of the Seventy. Nevertheless, his remarks at the conference did center on Native Americans. Standing before the thousands of white onlookers in the Salt Lake Tabernacle, he opened with a bit of Indian humor. He said, "Brothers and Sisters, I finally realize how General Custer must have felt." He then defied his apostolic superiors and continued speaking specifically to Native Americans. "We have a choice heritage," he said as he challenged fellow Indians to "realize that we have no guarantee to the celestial kingdom."[87] Despite his intentions to assert himself as an authority on Indian affairs within the church, his participation was not welcome. In private interviews with an LDS Church historian he expressed frustrations that he enjoyed no access to the First Presidency on Indian matters and did not receive any assignments relating to Indian policy.[88]

Tensions rose between Lee and the church leadership over the following years. Lee's interpretation of the Book of Mormon indicated that the division of Lamanite Israel and gentiles adopted into Israel retained significance in the present days. Lee believed that as converted Gentiles, white Mormons' only responsibility was to bring the gospel to Lamanites who then would take lead of the church. By dissolving the various Indian programs Lee believed the church leaders turned their backs on Lamanites and sought to usurp that role for themselves. Though unknown to the general membership, Lee endured disciplinary actions for several years before his excommunication in September of 1989. According to Lee, the apostles even accused him of practicing polygamy and put him on probation as early as 1986.[89]

In the summer of 1989, Lee submitted a controversial letter to the Quorum of Twelve Apostles. Recalling the specter of the deceased church leader and Indian advocate, the letter began, "Do you think President Kimball approves of your action?"[90] The letter followed with a series of pointed questions about the reduction of Indian programs:

> Who terminated the BYU Indian Education Dept.? ... Who terminated BYU Indian Special Curriculum? ... Who is phasing out BYU American Indian Services? ... Who is phasing out the church's Indian Student Placement Program? ... Who got rid of the Church's 'Indian Committee'? ... Who fired the Indian Seminary teachers and send [sic] them out into the cold? ... Who pulled the full time missionaries off the Navajo and other Indian reservations?[91]

Lee's questions went on for pages, and he boldly accused the apostles of "spiritual and scriptural extermination of Lamanites." Another volley of questions centered on his own estrangement from the church hierarchy, each accusing them of "scheming how to get rid of George P. Lee."[92] The letter finally concluded by pleading for repatriation, though the tone of the letter made it clear that Lee expected the apostles to repent.

Needless to say, the apostles did not enthusiastically accept the criticisms. The apostles gathered for a meeting on September 1, 1989, and requested Lee's attendance. Lee arrived with yet another letter in hand. In it he clarified points of doctrine, again asserting the special role of Lamanites and the only temporary custodial role of white gentiles who joined the church. Lee warned, "In short, you [are] betraying and turning your backs on the very people on whom your own salvation hangs. I cannot be a party to this kind of teaching which runs counter to the Lord's instructions in the scriptures."[93] He charged the apostles with "pride, arrogance, and unrighteous dominion" as well as "love of power, status, position" and even a "love of money."[94] Within ten minutes of the meeting's conclusion, security officers arrived at Lee's office to collect his building keys and church credit card as well as his signed recommend to enter LDS temples.[95] That afternoon, a church spokesperson released a brief statement announcing Lee's excommunication.[96]

In the following days, Lee issued a variety of statements to reporters. He cited "white supremacy" and charged the apostles with apostasy. He said, "It got to the point where I had to follow them or Jesus Christ, and I chose to follow Jesus Christ."[97] In a television interview, he asserted that the apostles were changing the scriptures and "cutting off all Indian projects and programs."[98] He told the *Salt Lake Tribune* that the church hierarchy "have washed their hands of their responsibilities to the Lamanites.... My conscience would not allow me to go on."[99] He widely articulated his grounds for leaving the church; however, the church remained customarily silent on the reasons for Lee's excommunication. Speculation further swirled in 1993 when Lee was charged and convicted on child molestation charges related to events that occurred in 1989.

One week after the excommunication, Apostle M. Russell Ballard and Burke Peterson of the Seventy began a tour of American Indian communities in the Southwest as part of a damage control effort. They spoke to Latter-day Saints in Window Rock and Shiprock over two days.[100] One Navajo recalled, "Generally they said it was not the church's fault and that it was due to George losing his testimony."[101] The church authorities promised the members that the prophet would never lead them astray.[102]

To some listeners, the two men seemed to backpedal on the significance of American Indians within the gospel. One listener recalled, "The

Navajos also wanted to know if the church still considered them to be of the royal blood of Israel, and Bros. Ballard and Peterson stated that the church didn't 'advocate' that position." He surmised that "Navajo LDS members have been told that they are not a chosen people and that their church is a worldwide church, and that it doesn't cater to any ethnic group. Navajos were told that they should take their blinders off and recognize the world-wide status of the church."[103]

Following the dissolution of other Indian programs, in 1992 church leaders determined to phase out the ISPP entirely. Over the course of the program, several states had expressed misgivings about the cost of educating out-of-state children. In 1962, Utah raised these concerns and estimated school district costs at $700 to $1,000 for each of the several hundred Arizona Indians hosted by Utah families.[104] The issue remained quiet for decades until 1989 when Washington County School District in Utah demanded tuition from an unrelated program that relocated Indian youths. Raindancer, Inc., brought troubled Native American teens from New Mexico and Arizona to its dorms and foster homes in southern Utah.[105] These children struggled with drugs, alcohol, and other issues that led the tribal courts to require their participation in Raindancer's recovery program. Federal funding that backed the program restricted its use to behavior modification and did not extend to academic education. Consequently, Raindancer enrolled students in local schools and then augmented that experience with an additional five to six hours of programs each day.[106]

In December 1989, Washington County School District sent a letter to Raindancer, Inc., explaining that the district could refuse admission and/or require tuition for out-of-state students. Concerns about overcrowded schools and the troubled teens hosted by Raindancer inspired the district to establish an enrollment allotment for that youth program, which became effective on January 1, 1990. Thirty-two of Raindancer's thirty-five students could return to classes in January without fees while any additional children would have to pay tuition.[107] Washington County School District demanded some $43,000 total tuition for that year.

Raindancer director Ron Hatch launched a civil rights lawsuit against Superintendent Steven Peterson, the Washington County School Board, and Utah State Office of Education representative (and active Latter-day Saint) Douglas Bates. Hatch charged that the county violated the children's First

Amendment constitutional rights and discriminated against the program while permitting the similar Mormon ISPP students to continue unchallenged. Hatch employed several strategies to try to secure victory. One of the few children expected to pay fees lived in an LDS home that also fostered an ISPP child. The stark contrast and discrimination was obvious as two out-of-state Indian students living in the same home faced different admission standards based solely on the foster program to which they belonged. Hatch also pushed to require Utah to recognize the Navajo Nation's court orders mandating their enrollment in the Utah-based Raindancer program as evidence that the youth were no longer residents of Arizona. Under such logic, Hatch asserted, they were technically considered homeless, so the Federal Homeless Assistance Act required Utah to recognize the children as residents.[108]

Hatch never intended to destroy the LDS Placement Program, or the BIA dorms in Sevier and San Juan counties who similarly served out-of-state Indians. On the contrary, he mistakenly expected that by overt legal comparison his program could also benefit from the strong position of the church in Utah and that all such programs could continue. Nevertheless, local Mormons blamed Hatch for causing the termination of both the BIA programs, which brought in quite a bit of revenue, and the much larger Indian Student Placement Program.[109]

Rather than save Raindancer's program, the litigation sped along the termination of the Placement Program. Former ISPP caseworker Kenneth Brown recalled, "We got dragged into that and we decided we were not going to fight it."[110] It is likely that the case provided an awaited catalyst to finally terminate a program that had been in a long decline. Advocates of the correlation movement surely noticed the redundancy and cost of the ISPP. It was expensive to maintain fifty full-time caseworkers and pay their travel to the reservation three times each year, as well as covering annual medical and dental costs at the reception center, rental buses, and ward welfare budget expenditures for Placement children's needs beyond the foster parents' abilities.[111] Quite a few reports over the preceding twenty years also questioned its effectiveness and contributed to growing opposition.

By December 1990, Utah courts ruled that all programs must be treated equally. In anticipation of the ruling, the BIA announced the closure of dormitories in San Juan and Sevier.[112] However, Douglas Bates indicated the implications to the church much earlier, and private negotiations and lobbying picked up before the court issued its decision. In 1992, the assistant Utah attorney general announced a settlement in which all programs would cease to function free of tuition. While Utah required tuition from students who resided outside of the state for any part of the year, all current students would be permitted to complete their schooling without charge.[113] In January 1992, the agreement was ratified as Utah House Bill 102. It grandfathered in all students enrolled prior to January 1, 1992, but all new out-of-state students would pay district-specific tuitions of around $3,000 per student.[114]

The Indian Student Placement Program seemed to be at its end. Over the prior fifteen years, enrollment had declined steadily. Under Packer's earlier plan, enrollment narrowed to only high school students by 1988, and in 1992 Utah legislation allowed only for existing ISPP students to graduate, which essentially blocked any new enrollment for non-Utah residents fostered in that state. The church made no effort to fortify the ISPP in other states where it could legally continue. It appeared that the Placement Program would simply cease after students who had been grandfathered into the ISPP graduated four years later in 1996. Beyond that, the program's longtime caseworkers and last supportive administrative advocates retired one by one. Clarence Bishop left LDS Social Services in 1993. Harold Brown, who served as the ISPP coordinator (1974–1976), LDS Social Services commissioner (1976–1981, 1987–1996), and director of operation (1981–1985) retired in 1996.[115] A 1998 article by an LDS Church historian said that "by 1996 it was a thing of the past," and a 2008 dissertation drew the same conclusion.[116]

The program, however, did not end in 1996, though it remained a mere shadow of its former self. In 1997, caseworker Kenneth Brown commented, "It's very limited. It will probably go out. We will just have a handful of students next year [1997–1998]. I think there are about twenty or so this year. Half of them graduate next year."[117] Enrollment statistics for the final decade are speculative at best. Nevertheless, the program did continue until 2000 when perhaps the final student, Mary Nelson, graduated from high school.[118] She and others could continue if quietly placed in Utah or any other state without the watchful eye of church headquarters. In effect, the final years of the program returned to its local and unsanctioned origins.

TABLE 8.3. PROJECTED STUDENT ENROLLMENT,
1989–2000

YEAR	ENROLLMENT
1989–1990	700*
1990–1991	500
1991–1992	420*
1992–1993	340*
1993–1994	260*
1994–1995	180*
1995–1996	100*
1996–1997	20
1997–1998	10
1998–1999	5*
1999–2000	1

* Estimates based on consistent decline between known years
*Source: Genevieve De Hoyos, "Indian Student Placement Ser-
vices,"* Encyclopedia of Mormonism, *679; Kenneth Brown, interview, 1997, Snowflake, Arizona, microfilm without pagination,
Church Archives; Kent Parke, phone interview by author, June 8,
2009; Mary Nelson, phone interview by author, July 30, 2009.*

Just as the program began with a Navajo student, Helen John, the program may have finished with a Navajo young woman. Mary Nelson recalled
the family troubles that preceded her enrollment in 1991. "My mother wasn't
there, and neither was my father, so I was raised by my brothers and sisters,"
she explained. Her father had once been a Placement student, and he prevailed upon caseworker Kent Parke to admit his children even though they
were below the age limit accepted at that time: James (eighth grade), Alice
(seventh grade), Michael (sixth grade), and Mary (fifth grade). Like many
caseworkers, Parke thoroughly believed in the program despite its eminent closure and was anxious to take advantage of the grandfather clause
before that window closed. He determined to enroll the family regardless
of their young age, possibly categorizing them in the regular foster system
to avoid any internal questions.[119] Such arrangements were uncommon but

not unheard of, despite internal mandates to restrict enrollment to older children.[120] Parke later only admitted that "promises had been made" to the family.[121] No single family could house all four children, so they were separated in homes across Utah. Mary lived in St. George and relocated to a new family each year until she arrived with her final foster home with parents whom she felt "let me be me." In that home, church attendance was optional, and the heavy pressures of Mormon culture seemed a little lighter.[122]

In the mid-1990s, several caseworkers tried to commemorate the approaching end of the program, but church authorities silenced their efforts. Students in the district overseen by caseworker Dale Shumway suggested a special fireside celebration in Richfield, the birthplace of the program. However, his superiors made it clear that this would not be permitted.[123] Kent Parke, the St. George caseworker who monitored Mary Nelson, independently invited Helen John from Salt Lake City for a meeting of the first and last students. The two exchanged stories and Parke took photographs. Parke then wrote an article about the occasion for an LDS Church magazine, but the editorial board rejected his submission. He recalled that ISPP coordinator Harold Brown explained that the church would not publish the article because it was not sure the program was over.[124] Indeed, the Indian Student Placement Program never was officially terminated, but without students or assigned caseworkers it hardly exists.

The final closure of the ISPP came as the result of a long and complicated series of changes. Rising criticisms of the church's Indian program from internal and external forces, reports that identified faults of the program, increasing educational opportunities on reservations, the passing of Spencer W. Kimball, and the 1992 lawsuit all contributed to the program's unofficial termination. However, at the very center of this policy change was an internal dispute over just how to manage the increasingly international church with a growing nonwhite membership. The solution to that problem rested in the correlation movement. One historian defined it as an effort to "enforce a sense of orthodoxy and obedience" upon the growing membership, whites and nonwhites alike.[125] The incorporation of those new members and their spiritual and social adherence to the doctrine and culture of the American-based church intimately impacted the Indian program. Though once under the protection of Spencer W. Kimball, the various

Indian programs evaporated during his declining years and immediately following his passing.

The Placement Program lingered on beyond other LDS Church Indian programs, possibly insulated by the extensive bureaucracy that evolved to operate the program during the 1960s and 1970s. While new layers of administrators minimized the influence of the most passionate casework-ers, it also institutionalized a massive structure that took time to phase out. The advocacy of Spencer W. Kimball, intermitted as it was by shifting lines of authority and his health, ultimately prolonged the Placement Program. Enrollment reached a plateau during Kimball's highest point of influence, and yet his hands were tied because policy decisions fell to other stewards in the church leadership. As his health declined, advocates of the correla-tion movement filled senior positions, including chair of the Welfare Com-mittee, which oversaw Social Services and the Placement Program. Ranking apostles anxiously trimmed back the many "special programs" that com-plicated a simple authority line and pointed to perceived failures of Amer-ican Indians generally and the Placement Program specifically as grounds to scale back Indian outreach efforts. In seeking to mainstream American Indians, Elder Packer and others worked to erode Indian programs over several decades and notably reduced ISPP enrollment until the 1992 law-suit provided the ideal excuse to close the program altogether. After seve-ral decades of debate, the program quietly faded away. Most Mormon young adults today have never even heard of the program that once dominated the church's attention.

9

CONCLUSION

In 2002, Clare Bishop looked back on the Indian Student Placement Program and estimated that in total some fifty thousand students participated.[1] Former caseworker and ISPP administrator David Albrecht recalled that during the 1980s, just after the program's apex, he calculated that one in twelve Navajos living on the reservation had participated in the ISPP.[2] The Placement Program certainly influenced the lives of many people, particularly when considering the natural and foster parents and siblings, caseworkers, and administrators, not to mention the succeeding generations that also were impacted, though less directly. For some, it provided a positive experience; for others, a culturally destructive mistake. A handful of students and some nonparticipants even repudiated the program as culturally genocidal. As these varied responses demonstrate, the consequences of Placement were multifaceted and remain hotly disputed today. Longtime caseworker Dale Shumway recognized the controversial status of the ISPP. He likened the program to the church's mid-nineteenth-century practice of polygamy, saying, "They were both short term programs of the church that had a definite purpose that were controversial and that had some goals that were different to different people, and a lot of negative, and a lot of positive." In such a politically and socially charged context, he asked, "How do you get a largely spiritual adventure like this quantified or qualified or written about in an honest manner?"[3] It is one thing to chronicle the history of the ISPP from its mid-twentieth-century rise to its decline in the 1980s and 1990s. To convey its meaning to participants, both secular and spiritual, is more difficult. Nevertheless, there are several conclusions that can be drawn about the program's influence on the individuals whose lives the ISPP impacted and its impact on the Mormon Church.

The Placement Program's origins and purposes are steeped in over one hundred years of efforts to convince Native peoples of a Lamanite heritage and prepare them to fulfill a prophetic role as leaders within the church and their Native communities. This policy of colonization began with Book of Mormon and LDS theology that defined Native Americans and white Mormons as Israelites, and sought to reconcile spiritual and cultural differences by converting Indians to the cultural standards of Latter-day Saints. From the middle and late nineteenth-century Indian farms in the Salt Lake Valley and the Washakie colony in northern Utah to the mid-twentieth-century Southwest Indian Mission, Indian seminary, and BYU Indian programs, the Mormon Church long tried to "redeem" American Indians while still granting them some special uniqueness as Lamanites. The Placement Program emerged in this historical and theologically charged background.

A changing national climate also gave context to the Placement Program. In the wake of the culturally sensitive Indian New Deal, a new federal termination policy materialized. Legislators worked to break down tribal affiliations, which they viewed as unnecessary dependencies, and maneuvered to assimilate Native Americans into mainstream America. Following World War II, national highways, markets, and wage economies penetrated the Navajo Reservation. This transformation inspired many living there to seek higher education and more training for their children so that they might interact better with white society. Insufficient school facilities on the reservation led Navajos to either abandon their children's education or seek off-reservation alternatives. Generations of hatred toward the boarding schools operated by the Bureau of Indian Affairs and church organizations led many to seek other alternatives. Tens of thousands of youth turned to the LDS-operated Placement Program. They appreciated the family unit that extended their children's intercultural exposure, and some valued the ISPP for the spiritual instruction they received. Most who enrolled, however, viewed it primarily as a means to obtain education to better survive in the changing world.

The Placement Program's popularity stemmed from its fusion of socio-economic advancement with a theological identity that reassured that potentiality. The ISPP consciously built up students' self-confidence to succeed in that education and traditional American markers of socioeconomic success. One Navajo who participated in the program remarked that "you can't go around singing I am a Child of God and not feel good about yourself."[4] For such students, the Lamanite identity adopted for education and socioeconomic gain also offered faith that even as adults they could enjoy the middle-class leisure they had experienced on Placement.

The adoption or alteration of identities is a common phenomenon. As historian Dave Edmunds explained, tribal identity has "never been fixed in stone," nor has any ethnic identity.[5] Many indigenous identities are relatively new historical constructs; many more have flexed and changed over time. Navajos, for example, shared language and customs for hundreds of years but did not emerge as a single people until their imprisonment at Bosque Redondo between 1864 and 1868.[6] Navajos and other Native communities have adopted imposed tribal categories that emerged from external relations with Europeans, including for the convenience of treaty making and reduction to reservation life.

Pan-Indian identities in particular are modern creations born of boarding school encounters, shared history, intertribal socialization, and political interest. In the early twentieth century, the Red Progressives founded the Society of American Indians. Though initially organized by a non-Indian, the highly educated Native Americans who joined pioneered a new model of Indianness that fused two worlds. They pledged their support to preserve "distinguishing virtues" while promoting Christianity and citizenship through "betterment stations" that mirrored sometimes assimilationist settlement homes for immigrants. These Western-educated Indians forged a bicultural model and held it up as an ideal standard to other Native Americans. Two generations later, protests united disparate Native Americans who rallied behind a new activist identity. Pioneering and confrontational personalities like Clyde Warrior, Lehman Brightman, Dennis Banks, and Clyde Bellecourt championed ethnic pride and public activism. Even still, many Native Americans scorned activist movements as disconnected from reservation communities and, hence, inauthentic.

Like the Red Progressives and Red Power activists, many Placement Program students shared a common vision. Unlike boarding schools, the ISPP encouraged students to learn and share indigenous languages and arts, and students participated in Indian-specific activities from dances to leadership conferences designed to reinforce a group identity centered on education, self-reliance, and religious devotion. Mormon host families, few of whom had direct knowledge of Navajo or other Indian cultures, varied in their understanding or acceptance of foster students' cultural practices, but LDS policy clearly encouraged and celebrated outward, social expressions of tradition. Many students prided themselves as a new generation of Lamanites who fused indigenous and Western cultures to establish a truer model of Indianness. Although in some ways their institutionalized experience resembled boarding school efforts to colonize their parents, their responses also can be likened to Red Progressive and Red Power youths who forged new models of Indianness that openly embraced elements of American culture while retaining some traditions.

Self-confident Lamanites armed with education often exhibited socioeconomic mobility. Placement students proved twice as likely to graduate high school, and they entered college at a younger age than Indians who did not participate in the ISPP.[7] They also were more likely to hold a professional career and ultimately obtained greater economic independence than their peers who remained on a reservation or attended boarding schools.[8] Students in the program valued economic self-reliance and proved more likely than their peers to have a bank account and a professional or managerial occupation.[9] One Navajo explained that while on Placement, he "started to learn a little bit more that my financial stability is not just a paycheck to paycheck thing or a month to month thing." He continued:

> I saw people were able to work but [also] have their money working for them rather than them working for their money.... I am still learning how to do stuff like that, like the markets and the stock exchange, and the investing, and a lot of that type of knowledge, but that opened my view as far as the economic part is concerned.[10]

Mid-century Navajos living in hogans hardly understood the emerging wage-labor markets, let alone financial planning via stocks and bonds. Placement exposed generations of Navajos to such concepts, and many took their new found value and understanding of education and professional careers back to the reservation. In this way the program undeniably empowered Indians.

Some students even believed it was their spiritual or moral duty to return to the reservation and help serve among their native people. While on Placement, Elly Curley wrote a letter to the *Navajo Times*, explaining that "The program has strengthened me to realize that I have a job here on earth. I really have a deep concern for my people and what the future holds for them."[11] Erdman Jake, Navajo, related his foster experience among white Mormons to the raising of Moses among the educated Egyptians, and he shared the prophet's charge to return to his own people with that knowledge:

> I see myself in that same respect. Taken from my people, as Moses was, taught the best education that they could get at the time and then allowed to choose what I needed to choose. As Moses did, he went back to his people to teach them and to do whatever he needed to do with them and I see myself in that respect of being taught, of getting the education and being able to go back, in the future, and to work with my native people and to work with the Indian tribes.[12]

For Jake and others, the Placement experience offered valuable tools that the Navajo Nation required. Former Placement students graduated from Brigham Young University and other colleges and vocational institutes with new skills appropriate to the changing life on reservations.

After the election of Peterson Zah to the Navajo tribal chairmanship in 1982, a deluge of Indian Mormons, including many former Placement students, served in tribal offices and over a dozen held seats on the tribal council. Press Secretary Ray Baldwin Louis, an active Latter-day Saint, venerated the accomplishments of Placement graduates in a 1978 *Navajo Times* article titled "It's Tough to Be a Good Mormon."[13] He wrote about the charge that those students felt to complete their education and lead their communities:

> From such have come young men and women with doctorates, law degrees, bachelor and associate degrees in education, social service, communication, engineering, business administration and many more. They hold prominent positions today with the Navajo Nation, Bureau of Indian Affairs, and Independent companies. They have returned to the reservation and many more are coming back because they know their identity and understand the need of the people.[14]

George P. Lee stood out as the most notable of these graduates. Lee recounted that in the 1970s Peter MacDonald contacted him with an invitation to "groom me to be the next chairman," but Lee said church service required he defer the opportunity, which he unsuccessfully pursued over a decade later in 1989.[15]

As Placement students completed their training and determined their own future course, it remained clear that education constituted only one aspect of the ISPP. It also instilled Western values that superseded traditional views held by Navajos and other Indians. Hogan living and restricted water use from hand-filled reservoirs no longer appeased these children. Relief Society general president Belle Spafford recalled, "One Indian mother said to me, 'I don't know whether I can keep my little girl in the program or not. She comes home and wants salad.'"[16] Most students enjoyed Placement, and when they returned to the reservation, many viewed their former homes in terms of deficiencies.[17]

Western science and culture constituted a major point of comparison for these youth. While on Placement, children learned to appreciate the technology that made mass consumption possible. Upon returning to the reservation, many students obsessed over the lack of cleanliness in their candle-lit, dirt-floor hogans and dilapidated trailer homes. They also missed the fresh produce, television, and other technological conveniences available in their foster homes. Adolescent desires germinated, and as adults, many of these former participants recreated their own space to reflect their mixed Navajo and Western values, either by avoiding the reservation or by consciously working to transform it.

Beyond scientific elements of Western culture, many Placement students also adopted some of the political and philosophical attitudes reflected by their Mormon host families. Former ISPP students rarely participated in Red Power activism. They shared this aversion in common with many reservation-bound Indians who likewise questioned the authenticity of self-aggrandizing urban protestors. Self-identified Lamanites usually looked down on such activist Indians, whom they often termed "militant." Some even equated such activism to the coercive strategies of Satan, who, according to Mormon theology, proposed a premortal plan to withhold human agency and force mankind to behave morally. In much the same way, some believed Red Power activism forced its will upon others and demanded compliance through confrontation.

As some Placement students adopted or deepened their faith in the gospel, as outlined by the church, they internalized yet another element of

Western society: a Judeo-Christian belief system. Quite a few Indian Placement students came from LDS families, but many were members on paper alone and had little to no knowledge of the church. Other student participants came as fresh converts with an equally questionable understanding. Regardless of their degree of preparation, participants in the ISPP incrementally gained a fuller understanding of the theological and cultural tenets of Mormonism. Many also accepted the crowning literary element of the church, the Book of Mormon, as a history of their own people. It reminded them that American Indians held a special place in God's eternal plan, and their Mormon hosts encouraged a variation of the Protestant ethic upon these youths. Just as colonial-era Puritans worked tirelessly to demonstrate their elect status, so, too, did these Indians who internalized LDS values seek education and professional positions as a demonstration of their faith. They regimented their bodies to the tick-tock of clocks and functioned on Western schedules to attain their goals.

Despite the erosion of Native ways and the convenience of assimilation as a descriptive process, it offers neither a complete nor accurate description of the Placement experience. The program certainly created an atmosphere where students engaged in Western culture; however, it also returned them to their reservation homes each summer and encouraged them to eventually serve that community. As much as students may have felt pressured to comply with white Mormon expectations during the school year, they also felt alternate pressures from their Native families and community during the summer months. Each year children and their parents determined whether or not the child would participate in the following school year.

This voluntary nature of the program cannot be overlooked. Native parents and children enjoyed ultimate authority to withdraw at any time, and many exercised that prerogative. Also, Indian children could choose to participate as much or as little in the church's extensive summer programs, and many chose not to participate at all. Some wanted to attend, but felt the weight of their natural family pulling them away from the church. Still others engaged in the church-sponsored activities. During the school year, students likewise made conscious decisions about their degree of participation, though the program mandated minimal participation. The fact that some opted to define themselves as Lamanites, pursue education and professional careers, and adopt much of Western culture does not diminish their decision any more than those who chose to resist and maintain the traditional ways of their parents and Native community.

Many students used their agency to resist and eventually withdraw from the program. They violated foster family and ISPP rules during the school year and avoided Mormon retention efforts in the summer months. Theirs is an equally important story of adolescent development and identity construction that contested Mormon colonization.

Students themselves determined who and what they were and cast a personal interpretation of Lamanite that met their own objectives. For some, a Lamanite identity offered little more than a derogatory term coined by Mormons as a vessel of their racist nineteenth- and twentieth-century perceptions. For others, the term reflected a royal lineage with the potential and responsibility to achieve the spiritual and material goals they sought. In either case, students engaged the cultures around them and sampled each as they saw fit as they created their own worldview.

Outsiders and onlookers often fail to see that agency within the program. Some label it as crudely assimilationist and denounce any participants who do not reject its efforts. Certainly the program did seek to colonize Indians—of that there is no doubt—but that observation cannot discount the experience of its participants. Critics may characterize Mormon Indians who internalize the Lamanite identity in derogatory terms designed to discount their quintessential Indianness. Ironically, however, many of the Western ambitions adopted by Placement students also were shared by non-Mormon tribal leaders who similarly sought to transform the Navajo Nation. What, then, are we to make of these Mormon Indians whose seemingly foreign-born identity shares so much of the same Western values other Native Americans have readily adopted on their own terms? The answer lies in the ever-changing nature of culture.

The old adage that you can never go home again reflects not only the changes of an individual but also those of the home place. In the case of Placement students, they reassessed their values while in Mormon society and over the course of their adolescence and young adulthood. Many stayed away from the reservation even longer as they attended Brigham Young University or other colleges and vocational institutions. When they returned, however, the home they left also had changed. The Navajo Nation pursued its own technological modernization and churned up its lands as it adopted Western notions of industry, production, and consumption. Today it boasts the first tribally controlled community college, established in 1968 and now located at Tsaile, Arizona, and with seven extension campuses; a massive 2,250-megawatt coal-fired power plant at Kayenta, Arizona, completed in 1974; and an active housing authority that spends tens of millions of dollars each year for the construction of new homes and the "modernization" of old ones.[18] The reservation and its inhabitants did not assimilate into Western culture, but rather they selected attributes like formal education and industry and redefined Navajo-ness to include those qualities. Placement students conducted a similar synthesis, and in many ways the Navajo Reservation more resembles them than those who remained isolated in their cultural traditions. In such a context, the selectively constituted culture and identity of former ISPP students is no less authentic than that of Navajos who did not participate in the program.

As natural as the process of cultural change and adaptation may be, it does leave many, including Placement students, with a sincere sense of loss. One former student explained, "We've lost our traditions." She continued:

> We have squaw dances you know, like the last week we had a squaw dance...and there was certain things that was done at the squaw dance, I didn't even know! Why does it happen?...And I don't know what to teach my kids, they ask me, "What is this, mom?" I say, "I really don't know but it's done this way."...I know there is a sacredness about it but I don't understand that. And during the winter time, during the fall and winter, these kids learn....[They] know more about my culture—our culture—than I was taught. Because during the winter and the fall, there's stories that are told, during only the fall and the winter that carries on a tradition of culture. I didn't hear any because I was gone, so I don't know....My parents are close to their seventies now, and my dad gets after me once in a while for not teaching these kids the language. I barely can understand the language but when it comes to actually carrying on a conversation with an elderly, it's hard for me to do....I'm afraid that when I teach my kids I'll teach them the wrong words, so I don't teach them any.[19]

Such comments reveal sincere concerns about a cultural disconnect caused by the ISPP. Another former student commented about "the church's attitude at uplifting Lamanite people." He said, "I think they pushed just a little bit too far. And, you know, when they could have done it in proper phases, you know going to the right places with proper timing. But instead, you know, they got shoved through it."[20] For some, their thoughts about Placement are filled with sadness and resentment.

Many former participants balance this discomfort against the socio-economic gains, spiritual strength, and other benefits of the program. One Navajo woman lamented the loss of language she suffered but was grateful for the family support she gained in her foster home. She said, "If I had never gone I would have never known how a real family is."[21] Orlando Tsosie, Navajo, reflected on the benefits and drawbacks of Placement:

> It was one of the best things that ever happened to me, because I've learned a lot about people, I've learned a lot about myself, I've learned a lot about my culture, I've learned a lot about the educational standpoint, the advantages I have. There is just a bunch of things. I could go on and on about the advantages I've had. But there are also some disadvantages, the disadvantages of staying away from a culture. Being up here nine months out of the year, I lost some of that Navajo language. I can still converse, I can still speak when I have to, and I understand, but I don't feel completely fluent in Navajo. I've forgotten some of the stories my grandmother told me. So the culture aspect, being away from that culture, from eight years old until you're eighteen, kind of takes a toll.[22]

Another former Placement student commented on the cultural drawbacks of the ISPP but remained appreciative because "white culture is encroaching upon us whether we like it or not."[23] She and others believed that at the very least the ISPP gave some support to make that transition.

The ultimate meaning that former students bestowed upon the program is, thus, neither all good nor entirely bad, but rather a complex mixture of feelings. Many former students conclude that it was, despite the cultural loss and social disconnect, a valuable program for which they are appreciative. It has become an integral part of their being, and most would not purge it if they could. The experience—the good and the bad—has become a part of them and their identity.

Today, former Placement students do not gather for reunions, but their shared experience creates a bond through which a community of sorts does exist. Sociologist Armand Mauss likened the program to a personal quest unique to its participants.[24] The journey for refuge features predominantly in Mormon folklore and historical memory and continues in the form of missions served by young adults today.[25] In much the same way, Placement provided students a coming-of-age quest for self-exploration. It tested participants' abilities to traverse cultures and solidified their selected values and self-perceptions. The experience created an anchor or cultural marker to reflect back on as they made later life choices. It continued to weigh on them as they decided what activities they should or should not participate in after Placement, and for many today the Lamanite identity still provides a source of strength. In a sense, the ISPP experience stays with them. One former student who dropped out of church activity after graduating from Placement expressed just this feeling. He said that "there was something about the church that stayed in the back of my mind. Something about it that I always had a place for the church in my heart, even though I went off, quite a ways off on a tangent."[26] He found himself humming LDS hymns and applying lessons learned from his foster family as he went about his daily life. That process of negotiation between Mormon and Native values continues today among the program's graduates and other Indian Latter-day Saints. Each person must decide how and when to participate in Indian and Mormon customs.

Just as ISPP's impact on Indian youth and their interpretation of it reveals mixed results, so too is the program's impact on the church contested. The Placement Program served as the flagship program in the church's broader Indian program. The Southwest Indian Mission, succeeded by the Arizona Holbrook Mission, and ISPP worked together to build a vast population of Navajo Mormons as well as adherents from dozens of other tribes. Though the socioeconomic results of the program proved successful, the spiritual reinforcement it hoped to provide never did fully manifest itself. After decades of invested energies, Mormon activity in the LDS community on the Navajo Reservation never did match that of non-Indian Latter-day Saints living off the reservation, and this shortcoming may suggest at least some degree of failure for the church.

Rather than increase the frequency of devout LDS Indians, the Southwest Indian Mission and the Placement Program instead simply increased the number of baptized Indians who did not necessarily practice the faith. In the 1990s, a Navajo reservation bishop commented, "All the units on the reservation have a lot of members. A lot of them were baptized in the '60s and '70s when the Placement Program was at its peak." He continued, "They have come back and for whatever reason became less-active. Right now in our ward, our membership from headquarters indicates 819 members, but out of that we get as many as 300 coming in at any one time."[27] Another bishop in Tuba City recalled that of the 2,000 baptized members on their ward records, only 200 to 300 attended.[28] Their observations are supported by the bishopric report of the early 1980s. It measured several factors, such as church attendance and personal prayer, and found that only 15 percent of ISPP students demonstrated a "marked increase in spirituality."[29] The Indian program did not succeed in elevating most Indian participants to the expectations of white church members.

Until 1990, the geographically determined congregations divided the Navajo Nation into wards and branches and assigned each to neighboring white-dominated stakes. White church members filled stake leadership positions and even some responsibilities in the Indian wards and branches. Such policies drew the scorn of many Navajos who interpreted the outsiders as unnecessary emblems of the church's distrust. Former placement student Mary Stevens remembered:

> When we were in the Gallup Stake, we'd go to leadership meetings for the Primary and Relief Society. I was in these positions at different times in our branch. When we'd go there, we were always made to feel like, "You're a Lamanite, we'll give you something easier over here. You don't understand."[30]

Stevens believed that church leaders conveyed the message, "You don't really understand a ward level organization kind of thing."[31] The institutionalized dependence of Navajo wards and branches on neighboring white stakes reflected a final symbol of Mormon outreach and colonization.

On September 30, 1990, the church organized the first all-Indian stake, centered on the Navajo Reservation at Chinle, Arizona. It spanned six thousand miles and boasted twelve units, nine of which were led by a Native American bishop or branch president. At several times the size of a typical stake, it encompassed an unprecedentedly massive ten thousand baptized members.[32] Former placement student Ray Mitchell served on the Chinle Stake presidency. He recounted, "It was high time for that to happen because the majority of the time the Navajos, or the Lamanites, were just being entertained. They were just sitting on the sideline letting the Anglo do all the work." He thought, "Now is the time of the Lamanite. I want the Lamanite to go forth and to do their own work, to do the things that they were supposed to do that was prophesied in the scriptures."[33]

Despite this apparent victory, the newly organized stake faced serious problems. While attendance rates in white wards typically ranges widely from 30 to 60 percent, only 10 percent of Latter-day Saints (mostly Indian) in the new Chinle Stake wards and branches attended Sunday services, and less than 5 percent of the adult males attended Sunday priesthood meetings.[34] Such inactivity stifled many of the programs. The handful of active men could hardly complete the home teaching of thousands of marginally interested but technically baptized Indian families.

Many Navajos simply refused to accept leadership responsibilities. President Mitchell explained that "the enthusiasm that the majority of the people had went down, because they didn't want to accept the calling." He continued, "They go to church, yes. They sit in the congregation. They get entertained. They were just being entertained. There's no challenge. So when the time came for them to do something, when they were called, some of them, they didn't want to."[35] Chinle Stake president Itsuo Tano reiterated this concern when he spoke to Indian students at Brigham Young University a week after the stake's organization. Much like Elder Packer's comments a decade earlier, Tano discouraged Lamanites from resting on some prophetic entitlement and instead demanded they lift themselves up and fulfill church expectations. He explained that "being a Lamanite is a great privilege, but, the status of being *chosen* is not a privilege of birth, but of living worthily."[36]

Though many Navajos interpreted the organization of the Chinle Stake as a sign of long-overdue trust from the church hierarchy, it also may exemplify the final extension of the mainstreaming efforts that ultimately terminated the Indian programs. Prior to the organization of the stake on the Navajo Reservation, the church leadership closely managed Navajos by carefully carving the reservation into appendages of neighboring caretaking white stakes. The organization of the Chinle Stake represented one last thrust of disproportionately high attention on Indians because the new stake contained insufficient priesthood leaders to warrant its formation.[37] With this move, however, the church ceased any future special outreach to Native Americans and left the Navajos to prove their merit on their own.

Like any other stake in the world, they would be expected to provide their own leadership and welfare efforts with only limited funds from Salt Lake and no assistance from the neighboring stakes.

The final mainstreaming of Lamanites, as a church-wide policy, also is evident in an Indian conference hosted by Brigham Young University in 1997. Apostle Jeffery R. Holland predicted the final assimilation of Lamanites into the body of the church.[38] In 2009, the church closed its last Lamanite high school in New Zealand. Much as among the Navajo, rumors of Maori failure to live up to LDS expectations permeated the incident. However, when Elder Rolfe Kerr of the Seventy announced the closure, he only said that the school had achieved its objective.[39] With the end of this school, the Lamanites—Navajo, Maori, or other—would no longer be recipients of a particular focus by the Mormon Church. Lamanites would independently model the same spiritual and socioeconomic behaviors expected of white Latter-day Saints.

The decisive value of the Placement Program can then be assessed in several categories. As an institution to heighten allegiance to the church, it seems to have failed, notwithstanding those Indians who increased their greater devotion to the church and its spiritual and cultural standards. As a vehicle of education, the ISPP proved a glowing success. Placement students proved far more likely to obtain higher education, and in the program's earlier years it offered one of the few options for Navajo children to attain an education. Finally, as a mechanism of colonization designed to reframe Indians as Lamanites defined by their scriptural heritage and prophetic future, the program remains disputed. A binary moral valuation of the ISPP remains insufficient, but certainly it impacted the self-perception of many Indians.

Just what it meant to be a Lamanite is dictated to some degree by the Book of Mormon, the church, and Mormon society. LDS theology overtly recrafted Native American heritage in a way that rationalized assimilation. However, as students appropriated that identity and strove for their own goals, educational or otherwise, the label took on different meanings to different people. For some, the Lamanite identity was no more than a colonial trope, and the ISPP simply a device for assimilation. Even some foster parents viewed the program's function as such. Others sought to preserve a semblance of Native traditions and fuse them with the industrious aspects of Western culture to produce some unique character. The program did create a space with definite cultural pressures that certainly weighed heavily on impressionable adolescents, but as students matured they ultimately chose what elements to incorporate into their definition of a Lamanite, and what that meant for them.

The Placement Program created an environment where Native youth operated between Mormon and Indian cultures, particularly as Navajo society underwent a transformation of its own. This unique experience molded young Indians into Lamanites but also empowered them to positively define themselves in the Western terms that increasingly characterized the Navajo Reservation. Though many participants lamented the cultural loss, those who embraced it saw themselves as leaders at the forefront of change and enjoyed exceptional confidence that they were capable of functioning in that new world of Navajo and Western values.

The process of picking and choosing from different cultures, synthesizing, deleting, and ultimately creating something new naturally evokes a sense of cultural gains and losses. Consequently, students look back on their experiences in the ISPP with mixed feelings. Nearly all credit it with forming the adults they became, for better or worse, and most who graduated from the ISPP would not remove that aspect of their personal history if given the opportunity. To term the program a success or failure is far too simplistic, but certainly its impact is significant, and its ramifications are still felt today among Mormons, Indians, and Lamanites.

NOTES

CHAPTER 1: INTRODUCTION

1. Longtime director of the ISPP Clare Bishop estimated that fifty thousand students participated in the program over its tenure. Dale L. Shumway and Margene Shumway, eds., *The Blossoming: Dramatic Accounts of the Lives of Native Americans in the Foster Care Program of the Church of Jesus Christ of Latter-day Saints* (Orem, UT: Granite Press, 2002), x. My own projection from the fragmented historical record rests at between forty-eight and sixty-two thousand.

2. Pierre Bourdieu, *The Logic of Practice* (Stanford: Stanford University Press, 1990), 76–77.

3. Calvin Martin, "Ethnohistory: A Better Way to Write Indian History," *Western Historical Quarterly* 9, no. 1 (January 1978): 41–56.

4. Robert Berkhofer, *The White Man's Indian: Images of the American Indian from Columbus to the Present* (New York: Alfred A. Knopf, 1978).

5. Notable examples that advanced Berkhofer's emphasis are Sherry Smith, *Reimagining Indians: Native Americans through Anglo Eyes, 1800–1940* (New York: Oxford University Press, 2000); Philip Deloria, *Playing Indian* (New Haven: Yale University Press, 1998); Philip Deloria, *Indians in Unexpected Places* (Lawrence: University Press of Kansas, 2004).

6. David Wallace Adams, *Education for Extinction: American Indians and the Boarding School Experience, 1875–1928* (Lawrence: University Press of Kansas, 1995), 100.

7. Adams, *Education for Extinction*, 58.

8. See, for example, the award-winning work by Margaret D. Jacobs, *White Mother to a Dark Race: Settler Colonialism, Materialism, and the Removal of Indigenous Children in the American West and Australia, 1880–1940* (Lincoln: University of Nebraska Press, 2009), 31.

9. J. Edard Chamberlin, "From Hand to Mouth: The Postcolonial Politics of Oral and Written Traditions," in *Reclaiming Indigenous Voice and Vision*, ed. Marie Battiste (Vancouver: UBC Press, 2000), 136.

10. Tsianina Lomawaima, *They Called It Prairie Light: The Story of Chilocco Indian School* (Lincoln: University of Nebraska Press, 1994), 167; Brenda

Child, *Boarding School Seasons: American Indian Families, 1900–1940*
(Lincoln: University of Nebraska Press, 2000), xiii. See also Scott Riney,
The Rapid City Indian School, 1898–1933 (Norman: University of Oklahoma
Press, 1999); Celia Haig-Brown, *Resistance and Renewal: Surviving the Indian
Residential School* (Vancouver: Arsenal Pulp Press, 2006); Clifford E. Trafzer,
Boarding School Blues: Revisiting American Indian Educational Experiences
(Lincoln: University of Nebraska Press, 2006); Clyde Ellis, *To Change Them
Forever: Indian Education at the Rainy Mountain Boarding School, 1893–1920*
(Norman: University of Oklahoma Press, 2008).

11. Elise Boxer, "'To Become White and Delightsome': American Indians and
Mormon Identity" (PhD diss., Arizona State University, 2009); Elise Boxer,
"'The Lamanites Shall Blossom as a Rose': The Indian Student Placement
Program and Mormon Native Identity" (paper presented at the annual
meeting for the Mormon History Association, Layton, Utah, June 8, 2013).

12. Frantz Fanon, *The Wretched of the Earth* (New York: Grove Press, Inc. 1963);
Albert Memmi, *The Colonizer and the Colonized* (New York: Orion Press,
1965). See also Haunani-Kay Trask, *From a Native Daughter: Colonialism and
Sovereignty in Hawai'i* (Honolulu: University of Hawaii Press, 1999); Jennifer
Nez Denetdale, *Reclaiming Diné History: The Legacies of Navajo Chief
Manuelito and Juanita* (Tucson: University of Arizona Press, 2007).

13. In 2007, Western History Association president David Edmunds warned of
"academics [who] have urged that scholarship conform to a new orthodoxy
defined through the rhetoric of post-colonialism." R. David Edmunds,
"Blazing New Trails or Burning Bridges: Native American History Comes of
Age," *Western Historical Quarterly* 39, no. 1 (Spring 2008): 14.

14. James Clifford, *The Predicament of Culture: Twentieth-Century Ethnography,
Literature, and Art* (Cambridge: Harvard University Press, 1988), 338. See
also Barbara L. Voss, *The Archaeology of Ethnogenesis: Race and Sexuality
in Colonial San Francisco* (Berkeley: University of California Press, 2008),
37, for her call for "an understanding of power that moves beyond simple
binaries of oppression and resistance."

15. Craig N. Cipolla, *Becoming Brothertown: Native American Ethnogenesis and
Endurance* (Tucson: University of Arizona Press, 2013), 6, 8.

16. Chamberlin, "From Hand to Mouth," 132, 134.

17. One report estimated a 40 percent student request drop rate plus an
additional 8 percent expulsion rate from 1947 to 1982. Bruce A. Chadwick,
Stan L. Albrecht, and Howard M. Bahr, "Evaluation of an Indian Student
Placement Program," *Social Casework* 17, no. 9 (November 1986): 517.

18. Scholarly works within and without Indian studies have consistently
recognized the formation of valid, functional communities based upon
groups of people recognizing or, put another way, socially constructing
themselves as a community. Benedict Anderson, *Imagined Communities:
Reflections on the Origins and Spread of Nationalism* (London: Verso, 1983);
Fredrik Barth, *Ethnic Groups and Boundaries* (Boston: Little, Brown, 1969);
Morris W. Foster, *Being Comanche: A Social History of an American Indian
Community* (Tucson: University of Arizona Press, 1991).

19. Robert Gottlieb and Peter Booth Wiley, *America's Saints: The Rise of Mormon Power* (New York: G. P. Putnam's Sons, 1984), 158.
20. Clifford, *The Predicament of Culture*, 5–6, 11.
21. Anderson, *Imagined Communities*, 6.
22. The emergence and identification of new identities enjoys a rich historiography that began in part with the study of Native Americans. In 1971, William Sturtevant expanded scholarship challenging monolithic notions of race and introduced the concept of *ethnogenesis* as he traced the appearance of the Seminoles as a distinct group diverging from the Creeks. Since then, anthropologists and historians have worked from the premise that identities are fluid constructs that emerge and submerge. Barbara Voss has pointed to ethnogenesis studies as "a powerful metaphor for the creativity of oppressed and marginalized peoples birthing a new cultural space for themselves amidst their desperate struggle to survive." She continues, "Ethnogenesis might be one way in which the subaltern can 'speak,' even as forces of history and systems of domination seek to exploit or destroy them." While the Lamanite identity has some of the markers of ethnicity, such as a shared narrative of lineal descent, it lacks others, and so ethnogenesis may not fully apply. Even still, that concept of emergence provides a cooperative model to imagine how students could carve out a cultural space, engage colonizing pressures, and not only survive but adapt to something new. Like colonialism, this approach addresses societies in transition but is concerned less with imagined cultural absolutes in conflict and more with individuals' decisions in adopting new and preserving old elements. To understand the creation of Lamanites both lens must be applied, one focused on colonial pressures and the other on individual agency. William C. Sturtevant, "Creek into Seminole," in *North American Indians in Historical Perspective*, ed. Eleanor B. Leacock and Nancy O. Lurie (New York: Random House, 1971), 92–128; Voss, *The Archaeology of Ethnogenesis*, 36–37. See also Ashley Montagu, *Man's Most Dangerous Myth: The Fallacy of Race* (New York: Columbia University Press, 1942).

CHAPTER 2: REIMAGINING ISRAEL
1. See "Proclamation of the Twelve Apostles of the Church of Jesus Christ of Latter-day Saints, New York, April 6, 1845," http://www.utlm.org/onlineresources/proclamationoftwelve.htm.
2. Joseph Smith Jr., *The Book of Mormon: An Account Written by the Hand of Mormon, Upon Plates Taken from the Plates of Nephi* (Palmyra, NY: E. B. Grandin, 1830), 496–97. The modern edition of the Book of Mormon includes over one thousand changes, and in an effort to better reflect the text read by the early Mormons, this book draws quotes directly from the 1830 edition.
3. A more critical assessment of Mormon-Indian relations in Utah evolved several decades ago which characterized Mormons as paternalistic and violent toward Indians. Some such authors include: Floyd O'Neil and Stanford J. Layton, "Of Pride and Politics: Brigham Young as Indian Superintendent," *Utah Historical Quarterly* 46, no. 3 (Summer 1978): 236–50;

Charles S. Peterson, *Take Up Your Mission: Mormon Colonizing Along the Little Colorado River, 1870–1900* (Tucson: University of Arizona Press, 1973), 195–96; Lawrence G. Coates, "Brigham Young and Mormon Indian Policies: The Formative Period, 1836–1851," *BYU Studies* 18, no. 2 (Spring 1978): 428–52; Warren Metcalf, "A Precarious Balance: The Northern Utes and the Black Hawk War," *Utah Historical Quarterly* 57, no. 1 (Winter 1989): 24–35; Ronald W. Walker, "Toward a Reconstruction of Indian Relations, 1847–1877," *BYU Studies* 29, no. 4 (Fall 1989): 23–42; Ronald W. Walker, "Wakara Meets the Mormons, 1848–52: A Case Study in Native American Accommodation," *Utah Historical Quarterly* 70, no. 3 (Summer 2002): 215–37; Marlin K. Jensen, "The Rest of the Story: Latter-day Saints Relations with Utah's Native Americans," *Mormon Historical Studies* 12, no. 2 (Fall 2011): 16–25. Additionally, Sandra Jones issues an excellent discussion of the historiography and how post-1970 revisionist historians began to challenge former notions of exceptionally peaceful Mormon-Indian relations. Sandra Jones, "Saints or Sinners," *Utah Historical Quarterly* 72, no. 1 (2004): 19–46.

4. Quite a few historians have pointed to this literary trend, including Robert Berkhofer, *White Man's Indian*; Reginald Horsman, *Race and Manifest Destiny: The Origins of American Racial Anglo-Saxonism* (Cambridge, MA: Harvard University Press, 1981); Francis Jennings, *Invasion of America: Indians, Colonialism, and the Cant of Conquest* (Chapel Hill: University of North Carolina Press, 1975); Roy Harvey Pearce, *Savages of America: A Study of the Indian and the Idea of Civilization* (Baltimore: Johns Hopkins Press, 1953); Bernard Sheehan, *Savagism and Civility: Indians and Englishmen in Colonial Virginia* (Cambridge: Cambridge University Press, 1980); William Stanton, *Leopard's Spots: A Romance of the White Man's Burden, 1865–1900* (Ridgewood, NJ: Gregg Press, 1967); Ronald Takaki, *Iron Cages: Race and Culture in Nineteenth Century America* (New York: Alfred A. Knopf, 1979).

5. Richard Slotkin, *Regeneration through Violence: The Mythology of the American Frontier, 1600–1860* (Middletown, CT: Wesleyan University Press, 1972); Deloria, *Playing Indian*.

6. The belief that Indians were descendents of the Lost Ten Tribes of Israel surfaced in the earliest European explorations and settlements of America. For a more complete study, see Richard W. Cogley, "'Some Other Kinde of Being and Condition': The Controversy in Mid-Seventeenth-Century England over the Peopling of Ancient America," *Journal of the History of Ideas* 68, no. 1 (January 2007): 35–56. The connections between Joseph Smith's Book of Mormon and that literature are readily found in a variety of texts. See Dan Vogel, *Indian Origins and the Book of Mormon: Religious Solutions from Columbus to Joseph Smith* (Salt Lake City: Signature Books, 1986); Richard L. Bushman, *Joseph Smith and the Beginnings of Mormonism* (Urbana: University of Illinois Press, 1984), 133–37.

7. For a more complete discussion of LDS veneration of Native Americans as lost Israelites, see Vogel, *Indian Origins and the Book of Mormon*.

8. Orson Pratt, "Divine Authority; or, Was Joseph Smith Sent of God?," *Latter-day Saints' Millennial Star* 10, no. 17 (September 1, 1848): 257–60; Parley P. Pratt, "Mormonism Unveiled: Zion's Watchman Unmasked, and Its

Editor, Mr. L. R. Sunderland, Exposed; Truth Vindicated; The Devil Mad, and Priestcraft in Danger!," in *The Essential Parley P. Pratt* (Salt Lake City: Signature Books, 1990), 39.

9. "Hosea Chapter III," *Evening and Morning Star* 1 (July 1832): 6.

10. Smith, *The Book of Mormon*, 499; William Harris, *Mormonism Portrayed: Its Errors and Absurdities Exposed, and the Spirit and Designs of Its Authors Made Manifest* (Warsaw, IL: Sharp & Gamble, 1841), 44.

11. In January of 1836 Smith expressed pleasure in Andrew Jackson's removal policy, noting that through such means the U.S. government would assist in the gathering by pressing the many Indian nations together as a single nation; see Joseph Smith, *History of the Church of Jesus Christ of Latter-day Saints, ed.* B. H. Roberts (Salt Lake City: The Church of Jesus Christ of Latter-day Saints, 1932–51), 2:357.

12. Smith, *The Book of Mormon*, 566–67 [modern Ether 13:7–10].

13. Smith, *The Book of Mormon*, 496–97 [modern 3 Nephi, chapter 20].

14. Parley P. Pratt, *A Voice of Warning and Instruction to All People; or, An Introduction to the Faith and Doctrine of the Church of Jesus Christ of Latter-day Saints, Commonly Called Mormons* (New York: W. Sandford, 1837), 186.

15. Smith, *History of the Church* 2:357–58.

16. G. St. John Stott, "New Jerusalem Abandoned: The Failure to Carry Mormonism to the Delaware," *Journal of American Studies* 21, no. 1 (April 1989): 71, 79; David Pursuitte, *Joseph Smith and the Origins of the Book of Mormon* (Jefferson, NC: McFarland, 1985), 245.

17. Arnold Green, "Gathering and Election: Israelite Descent and Universalism in Mormon Discourse," *Journal of Mormon History* 25, no. 1 (Spring 1999): 200–206; for a broader discussion of American efforts to organize an American Zion centered on Native Americans, see Robert F. Berkhofer Jr., "Model Zions for the American Indian," *American Quarterly* 15, no. 2 (1963): 176–90.

18. Smith, *History of the Church* 1:111–112.

19. *Book of Commandments for the Government of the Church of Christ, Organized According to Law, on the 6th of April, 1830* (Zion [Independence, MO]: W. W. Phelps, 1833), 67 [modern-day Doctrine and Covenants 28]; alternatively, Dan Vogel argues that a driving factor behind Smith's dispatching Cowdery was the latter's growing influence and a desire to remove the potential rival; regardless, such an interpretation does not explain away the mission or undermine the emphasis on Native Americans. Dan Vogel, *Joseph Smith: The Making of a Prophet* (Salt Lake City: Signature Books, 2004), 530.

20. Leland H. Gentry, "Light on the 'Mission to the Lamanites,'" *BYU Studies* 36, no. 2 (1996–1997): 226–28; "History of Parley P. Pratt," *Latter-day Saints' Millennial Star* 26 (1864): 822–25; Michael Marquardt, *The Rise of Mormonism, 1816–1848* (Longwood, FL: Xulon Press, 2005), 256.

21. Pratt's journal explains that after initial suspicion the Delawares grew eager to learn more. Similarly, a letter from Cowdery stated that despite uncertainties, the Indians "were very glad for what I their Brother had told them and they had received it in their hearts." For more information about the party's perceptions of success, see Gentry, "Light on the 'Mission to the Lamanites,'" 227–32; Stanley R. Gunn, *Oliver Cowdery: Second Elder and*

Scribe (Salt Lake City: Bookcraft, 1962), 80; Parley Pratt, *Autobiography of Parley P. Pratt* (Salt Lake City: Deseret Book, 2000), 14–18.

22. Gentry, "Light on the 'Mission to the Lamanites,'" 230; "W. W. Phelps to Brigham Young, Report of Joseph Smith Revelation, July 17, 1831," Revelations Collection, LDS Church Archives; Marquardt, *Rise of Mormonism*, 265.

23. Smith, *History of the Church* 1:182; "Phelps to Young, Report of Joseph Smith Revelation"; David J. Whittaker, "Mormons and Native Americans: A Historical Bibliographical Introduction," *Dialogue: A Journal of Mormon Thought* 18, no. 4 (Winter 1985): 35.

24. For more information on Rigdon's ministry, see Bushman, *Joseph Smith and the Beginnings of Mormonism*, 173–74; Grant Underwood, *The Millenarian World of Early Mormonism* (Urbana: University of Illinois Press, 1993), 25; William Alexander Linn, *The Story of the Mormons* (New York: Russell and Russell, 1963), 59–65; Richard McClellan, "Sidney Rigdon's 1820 Ministry: Preparing the Way for Mormonism in Ohio," *Dialogue: A Journal of Mormon Thought* 36, no. 4 (Winter 2003): 152–59; Eugene Ready, "William Heath Whittsitt: Insights into Early Mormonism" (Master's thesis, Southern Baptist Theological Seminary, 2001); Lloyd Alan Knowles, "The Appeal and Course of Christian Restorationism on the Early Nineteenth Century American Frontier—with a Focus on Sidney Rigdon as a Case Study" (PhD diss., Michigan State University, 2000); F. Mark McKiernan, *The Voice of One Crying in the Wilderness: Sidney Rigdon, Religious Reformer, 1793–1876* (Lawrence, KS: Coronado Press, 1971), ch. 2.

25. Pratt, *Autobiography of Parley P. Pratt*, 52.

26. Bushman, *Joseph Smith and the Beginnings of Mormonism*, 182–83.

27. *Western Reserve Chronicle* (March 3, 1831), as quoted in Richard S. Van Wagoner, *Sidney Rigdon: A Portrait of Religious Excess* (Salt Lake City: Signature Books, 1994), 92.

28. D. Michael Quinn, *Early Mormonism and the Magic World View* (Salt Lake City: Signature Books, 1987).

29. Jesse W. Crosby, Autobiography, undated, Harold B. Lee Library, Brigham Young University, Provo, Utah (hereafter HBLL).

30. J. B. Turner, *Mormonism in All Ages; or, The Rise, Progress, and Causes of Mormonism, with the Biography of Its Author and Founder, Joseph Smith, Junior* (New York: Platt & Peters, 1842), 28.

31. "Undated letter from Ezra Booth," reprinted in E. D. Howe, *Mormonism Unvailed; or, A Faithful Account of that Singular Imposition and Delusion from Its Rise to the Present Time* (Painesville, OH: E. D. Howe, 1834), 184.

32. John Corrill, *A Brief History of the Church of Jesus Christ of Latter-day Saints* (St. Louis: N.p., 1839), 9, 16–17. Similar occurrences are recorded in Henry Caswell, *The Prophet of the Nineteenth Century; or, The Rise, Progress, and Present State of the Mormons, or Latter-Day Saints: To Which Is Appended. An Analysis of The Book of Mormon* (London: Printed for J.G.F. & J. Rivington, 1843), 63–67; and Daniel P. Kidder, *Mormonism and the Mormons: A Historical View of the Rise and Progress of the Sect Self-Styled Latter-Day*

Saints (New York: G. Lane & P. P. Sandford, for the Methodist Episcopal Church, 1842), 71.

33. David Benedict, *A General History of the Baptist Denomination in America* (Boston: N.p., 1813), 2:256, as quoted in Knowles, "The Appeal and Course of Christian Restorationism," 66.

34. Howe, *Mormonism Unvailed*, 105.

35. Deloria explains that mimicry of Indians allowed Americans "to translate texts, images, and ideologies into physical reality.... In doing so, they lived out the cultural ideas that surrounded Noble Savagery as concrete gestures that possessed a physical and emotional meaning," Deloria, *Playing Indian*, 6–7.

36. Fear of a Mormon-Indian alliance, and rumors of Mormon efforts to turn Indians against non-Mormon neighbors, features predominantly in the Latter-day Saints' expulsion from Missouri; Leonard J. Arrington and Davis Bitton, *The Mormon Experience: A History of the Latter-day Saints* (New York: Alfred A. Knopf, 1979), 48; Jared Farmer, *On Zion's Mount: Indians, Mormons, and the American Landscape* (Cambridge, MA: Harvard University Press, 2008), 58–59.

37. W. W. Phelps, "Prospects of the Church," *Evening and Morning Star* 1 (March 1833): 76; W. W. Phelps, "Progress of the Church of the Latter-day Saints," *Evening and Morning Star* 2 (May 1834): 156; W. W. Phelps, "Millenium [*sic*] VIII," *Evening and Morning Star* 2 (August 1834): 177; Oliver Cowdery, "Answer," *Evening and Morning Star* 2 (September 1834): 189.

38. "Millenium [*sic*]," *Messenger and Advocate* 1 (November 1834): 17.

39. "Keokuk's Visit to Nauvoo," *Warsaw Signal* 2 (August 25, 1841), rpt. in Maj. S. H. M. Byers, "Recollections of Slave Days," *Annals of Iowa* 3, no. 4 (April 1897): 283.

40. Section IV of the 1833 *Book of Commandments* included a March 1829 revelation that indicated Smith "has the power to translate the book, and I have commanded him that he shall pretend no other gift, for I will grant him no other gift." However, Section XXXII of the 1835 *Doctrine and Covenants* includes the same revelation but then reads, "And you have a gift to translate the plates; and this is the first gift that I bestowed upon you, and I have commanded you that you should pretend no other gift until my purpose is fulfilled in this; for I will grant unto you no other gift until it is finished." [Joseph Smith,] *A Book of Commandments for the Government of the Church of Christ, Organized According to Law, on the 6th of April, 1830* (Zion [Independence, MO]: W. W. Phelps & Co., 1833), 10; Joseph Smith, *Doctrine and Covenants of the Church of the Latter Day Saints Carefully Selected from the Revelations of God* (Kirtland, OH: F. G. Williams & Co., 1835), 158.

41. Dean C. Jessee, Mark Ashurst-McGee, and Richard L. Jensen, eds., Journals, Vol. 2: 1832–1842, in *Papers of Joseph Smith* (Salt Lake City: Deseret Book Co., 1989), 182, 205–6; organization of councils and committees in Fred Collier and William S. Harwell, *Kirtland Council Minute Book (Salt Lake City: Collier Publishing, 1996)*, 87–90, 159–61, 165; Church of Jesus Christ of Latter-day

Saints, The Doctrine and Covenants of the Church of Jesus Christ of Latter-day Saints (Salt Lake City: Church of Jesus Christ of Latter-Day Saints, 1982), 41:9, 107:60–92, 99–100; Andrew Jensen, *Church Chronology: A Record of Important Events Pertaining to the History of the Church of Jesus Christ of Latter-day Saints*, 2d ed. (Salt Lake City: Deseret News, 1899), xxv; Donald Q. Cannon and Lyndon W. Cook, *Far West Record: Minutes of the Church of Jesus Christ of Latter-day Saints, 1830–1844* (Salt Lake City: Deseret Book Co., 1983), 7, 70–72, 151; Barbara J. Faulring, "Kirtland Revelation Book" (N.p., 1981), HBLL, 84–86; Smith, *History of the Church*, 1:267; Collier and Harwell, *Kirtland Council Minute Book*, 23–29, 70–72, 84–90, 159–61, 165; Doctrine and Covenants 102; "Minutes of a Grand Council, Kirtland, Ohio," Patriarch Blessing Book 2, Church of Jesus Christ of Latter-day Saints Archives, Salt Lake City (hereafter LDS Church Archives).

42. Smith, *A Book of Commandments*, 83.

43. Smith, *Doctrine and Covenants*, 90 (this passage remains unchanged in the modern Doctrine and Covenants 84:33–34).

44. In January 1836, Smith wrote that he believed the U.S. removal policy represented a gathering of sorts for Indians, and he expressed hope that they would become a cohesive single nation. Smith then concluded, "May they all be gathered in peace, and form a happy union among themselves, to which thousands may shout, *Esto Perpetua* [in perpetuity]." Later that year he vaguely defined a separate organization of Lamanites within the larger latter-day gathering. See Smith, *History of the Church*, 2:362.

45. Smith, *History of the Church*, 7: 379; William Clayton, Diary entry for March 1, 1845, in James B. Allen and Thomas G. Alexander, eds., *Manchester Mormons: The Journal of William Clayton, 1840–1842* (Salt Lake City: Peregrine Smith, 1974).

46. Matthew J. Grow and Jeffery Mahas, "'As Soon as We Get Cousin Lemuel Converted I Don't Fear': Mormon Attempts at Indian Alliance in Nauvoo, 1844–1846" (paper presented at the annual meeting of the Western History Association, Newport Beach, California, October 18, 2014). See also Jedediah Rogers, *The Council of Fifty: A Documentary History* (Salt Lake City: Signature Books, 2014).

47. Smith, *A Book of Commandments*; translations accompanied the code names in later editions of Doctrine and Covenants. Other code words (mostly for locations) include Shinelah, Shinelane, Shule, Ozondah, Lan-shine-house, Tahhanes, and Cainhannoch.

48. Pursuitte, *Joseph Smith and the Origins of the Book of Mormon*, 185.

49. Mauss similarly concludes that the 1833 advent of patriarchal blessings was pivotal in the reconfiguration of gentile Mormons as members of Israel in Armand L. Mauss, *All Abraham's Children: Changing Mormon Conceptions of Race and Lineage* (Urbana: University of Illinois Press, 2003), 22; elsewhere, Mauss contends evolving views of Mormons as Israelites functioned in conjunction with the assimilation of British and other peoples in Mauss, "Mormonism's Worldwide Aspirations and Its Changing Concept of Race," *Dialogue: A Journal of Mormon Thought* 34, nos. 3–4 (Fall/Winter 2001): 103–4.

50. For clarity's sake Joseph Smith Sr. will always be identified as such (while his son may be referred to as either Smith Jr. or simply Smith).

51. Joseph Smith Sr., Patriarchal Blessing Book, 1, Historical Department, The Church of Jesus Christ of Latter-day Saints, Salt Lake City, Utah.

52. *Doctrine and Covenants* 103:17.

53. Irene E. Bates and E. Gary Smith, *Legacy Lost: The Mormon Office of Presiding Patriarch* (Urbana: University of Illinois Press, 1996), 17, 39–40; Benjamin F. Johnson, *My Life's Review* (Independence, MO: Zion's Printing & Pub. Co., 1947), 17; Earnest M. Skinner, *Joseph Smith, Sr.: First Patriarch to the LDS Church* (Mesa, AZ: Palmyra Publishing Company, 2002), 95–101; Irene M. Bates, "Patriarchal Blessings and the Routinization of Charisma," *Dialogue: A Journal of Mormon Thought* 26, no. 3 (Fall 1993): 2.

54. Brigham Young, April 8, 1855, in G. D. Watt, ed., *Journal of Discourses: By President Brigham Young and Other Church Leaders* (London: F. D. Richards, 1854–86), 2:268–69; Hosea 7:8 offers the scriptural foundation for this principle.

55. Dean C. Jessee, "The Kirtland Diary of Wilford Woodruff," *BYU Studies* 12, no. 4 (Summer 1972): 388.

56. Milton V. Backman Jr., *The Heavens Resound* (Salt Lake City: Deseret Book Co., 1983), 328; Church Educational System, *Church History in the Fullness of Times: The History of the Church of Jesus Christ of Latter-day Saints* (Salt Lake City: Church of Jesus Christ of Latter-day Saints, 1993), 177; Bates and Smith, *Legacy Lost*, 44; James B. Allen and Glen M. Leonard, *The Story of the Latter-day Saints* (Salt Lake City: Deseret Book, 1976), 110–15.

57. Smith, *History of the Church*, 2:489; Bates and Smith, *Legacy Lost*, 45.

58. Richard L. Jensen, "Transplanted to Zion: The Impact of British Latter-day Saint Immigration upon Nauvoo," *BYU Studies* 31, no. 1 (Winter 1991): 1.

59. Smith, *History of the Church*, 2:357–58.

60. Farmer, *On Zion's Mount*, 58.

61. Edward Partridge, "To the Saints of Christ Jesus Scattered Abroad," *Evening and Morning Star* (June 1832): 2.

62. "W. W. Phelps, To Man," *Evening and Morning Star* (June 1832): 6.

63. "Revelations, September 22–23, 1832," in James R. Clark, *Messages of the First Presidency of the Church of Jesus Christ of Latter-day Saints* (Salt Lake City: Bookcraft, 1966–71), 5:323.

64. Grant Underwood, "Book of Mormon Usage in Early LDS Theology," *Dialogue: A Journal of Mormon Thought* 17, no. 3 (1984): 39.

65. Smith, *The Book of Mormon*, 501 [modern 3 Nephi 21:22–24].

66. Underwood, "Book of Mormon Usage," 39.

67. Oliver Cowdery, "Dear Brother," *Latter Day Saints' Messenger and Advocate* 1 (October 1834): 14; "A Summary," *Latter Day Saints' Messenger and Advocate* 1 (January 1835): 63.

68. Smith, *History of the Church*, 6:401–2.

69. John Lowe Butler, Autobiography, undated, HBLL.

70. Smith, *History of the Church*, 7:401.

71. "This to the Chiefs and all the honorable men among the Senecas and all the Tribes through which we may pass, dated sometime in August 1845," as

quoted in Lawrence G. Coates, "Brigham Young and Mormon Indian Policies: The Formative Period, 1836–1851," *BYU Studies* 18, no. 2 (Spring 1978): 430.

72. Melvin C. Johnson, *Polygamy on the Pedernales: Lyman Wight's Mormon Villages in Antebellum Texas, 1845–1858* (Logan: Utah State University Press, 2006); Davis Bitton, *The Ram and the Lion: Lyman Wight and Brigham Young* (Provo, UT: Foundation for Ancient Research and Mormon Studies, 1997); Jeremy Benton Wight, *The Wild Ram of the Mountain: The Story of Lyman Wight* (Star Valley, WY: Afton Thrift Print, 1996); Lyman Wight, "An Address by Way of an Abridged Account and Journal of My Life From February 1844 up to April 1848 with an Appeal to the Latter Day Saints," HBLL; C. Stanley Banks, "The Mormon Migration to Texas," *Southwestern Historical Quarterly* 49, no. 2 (1945): 233–44.

73. William Clayton, Diary for April 1845 to January 30, 1846, as quoted in Fillerup, *William Clayton's Nauvoo Diaries*, http://www.code-co.com/rcf/mhistdoc/clayton.htm; Smith, *History of the Church* 7:374, 379, 437.

74. Whittaker, "Mormons and Native Americans," 36, italics in original.

75. Farmer, *On Zion's Mount*, 60; Howard A. Christy, "Open Hand and Mailed Fist: Mormon-Indian Relations in Utah, 1847–52," *Utah Historical Quarterly* 46, no. 3 (Spring 1978): 218; Coates, "Brigham Young and Mormon Indian Policies," 430–34.

76. Hosea Stout, Autobiography, vol. 1, HBLL; William Draper, Autobiography, HBLL; Levi Jackman, Autobiography, HBLL.

77. Eliza Dana Gibbs, Autobiography, 1813–1900, Utah State Historical Society, Salt Lake City; William Leany, Autobiography, HBLL; Jackman, Autobiography.

78. Christy, "Open Hand and Mailed Fist," 220–24.

79. Paul Reeve, *Religion of a Different Color: Race and the Mormon Struggle for Whiteness* (New York: Oxford University Press, 2015), 78.

80. "J. W. Gunnison to Martha Gunnison, 1 March 1850," in J. W. Gunnison, *The Mormons* (Philadelphia: J. P. Lippincott & Co., 1860), 147.

81. Jones, "Saints or Sinners," 27.

82. Peter Gottfredson, *History of Indian Depredations in Utah* (Salt Lake City: Skelton Publishing, 1919), 18–19.

83. "Autobiography of Joel Hills Johnson," typescript in HBLL.

84. Cordelia Morley Cox, "Biography of Isaac Morley: A Sketch of the Life of My Father Isaac Morley, One of the Pioneers to Salt Lake Valley in 1848," HBLL.

85. Coates, "Brigham Young and Mormon Indian Policies," 439–40.

86. Fred Gowans and Eugene Campbell, *Fort Supply: Brigham Young's Green River Experiment* (Provo, UT: Brigham Young University Publications, 1976), 17–19; W. M. Jennings, "Carson Valley," *Nevada Historical Society Papers, 1913–1916* (Carson City: Nevada State Printing Office, 1917), 179–80; Wesley R. Law, "Mormon Indian Missions, 1855" (Master's thesis, Brigham Young University, 1959), 2–7; Beverly Beeton, "Teach Them to Till the Soil: An Experiment with Indian Farms, 1850–1862," *American Indian Quarterly* 3, no. 4 (Winter 1977–1978): 299–320; Eugene E. Campbell, *Establishing Zion: The Mormon Church in the American West, 1847–1869* (Salt Lake City: Signature Books, 1988), 113–33.

87. Juanita Brooks, "Indian Relations on the Mormon Frontier," *Utah State Historical Society* 12, nos. 1–2 (January–April 1944): 10.

88. Thomas D. Brown, "Journal of the Southern Indian Mission," in Brooks, "Indian Relations on the Mormon Frontier," 11; James S. Brown, *Giant of the Lord: Life of a Pioneer* (Salt Lake City, Utah: Bookcraft, 1960), 320; Johnson, Autobiography.

89. While many Natives remained in the area for generations, late nineteenth-century polygamy prosecutions disrupted organizational supports from Salt Lake and much of the colony fell to public and local private ownership over succeeding decades. Surprisingly, the ward created in 1890 continued on until 1965 when the church dissolved the remaining ten-member congregation. "Preliminary Summary of Research on the History of Mormon Agricultural Colonization Projects among the North American Indians of the United States from 1830 to 1967," May 1, 1967, p. 2, Brigham Young University Records, 1956–1972, HBLL; Lawrence G. Coates, "Mormons and Social Change Among the Shoshoni, 1853–1900," *Idaho Yesterdays* 15, no. 4 (Winter 1972): 8–11.

90. Johnson, Autobiography; Charles E. Dibble, "The Mormon Mission to the Shoshoni Indians," *Utah Humanities Review* 1, nos. 1–3 (January, April, July, 1947): 53–73, 166–77, 279–93.

91. James S. Brown, *Giant of the Lord: Life of a Pioneer* (Salt Lake City: Bookcraft, 1960), 320; Juanita Brooks, ed., *On the Mormon Frontier: The Diary of Hosea Stout, 1844–1861* (Salt Lake City: University of Utah Press, 1964), 516–17.

92. John R. Young, *Memoirs of John R. Young: Utah Pioneer, 1847* (Salt Lake City: Deseret News Press, 1920), 62; Hubert Howe Bancroft, *History of Utah* (San Francisco: The History Company Publishers, 1889), 278; Gottfredson, *History of Indian Depredations in Utah*, 16–17; Johnson, Autobiography; Brooks, "Indian Relations on the Mormon Frontier," 5.

93. Brooks, "Indian Relations on the Mormon Frontier," 6.

94. Ibid., 6, 8.

95. For a more complete discussion of Mormon adoption of Indian slaves, see Robert M. Muhlestein, "Utah Indians and the Indian Slave Trade: The Mormon Adoption Program and Its Effect on the Indian Slaves" (Master's thesis, Brigham Young University, 1991); Richard D. Kitchen, "Mormon-Indian Relations in Deseret: Intermarriage and Indenture, 1847–1877" (PhD diss., Arizona State University, 2002); Stephen P. Van Hoak, "And Who Shall Have the Children? The Indian Slave Trade in the Southern Great Basin, 1800–1865," *Nevada Historical Quarterly* 41, no. 1 (Spring 1998), 3–25; Brian Q. Cannon, "Adopted or Indentured, 1850–1870: Native Children in Mormon Households," in Ronald W. Walker and Doris R. Dant, eds., *Nearly Everything Imaginable: The Everyday Life of Utah's Mormon Pioneers* (Provo: Brigham Young University Press, 1999), 341–57; Brian Q. Cannon and Richard D. Kitchen, "Indenture and Adoption of Native American Children by Mormons on the Utah Frontier, 1850–1870," *Common Frontiers: Proceedings of the 1996 Conference and Annual Meeting* (North Bloomfield, OH: Association for Living History Farms and Agricultural

Museums, 1997), 131–41; Brooks, "Indian Relations on the Mormon Frontier," 1–48.

96. C. S. Lewis, *Perelandra* (New York: Macmillan, 1944), 3–4.

CHAPTER 3: TURNING TO PLACEMENT

1. Louise Lockard, "New Paper Words: Historical Images of Navajo Language Literacy," *American Indian Quarterly* 19, no. 1 (Winter 1995): 19; Michael J. Warner, "Protestant Missionary Activity Among the Navajo, 1890–1912," *New Mexico Historical Review* 45, no. 3 (July 1970): 213–17.

2. Lomawaima, *They Called It Prairie Light*, 6.

3. Adams, *Education for Extinction*, 44–46, 48.

4. Ibid., 52.

5. Lomawaima, *They Called It Prairie Light*, 4–5.

6. Adams, *Education for Extinction*, 54.

7. Margaret Connell Szasz, *Education and the American Indian: The Road to Self-Determination, 1928–1973* (Albuquerque: University of New Mexico Press, 1974), 10.

8. Adams, *Education for Extinction*, 31.

9. Robert A. Trennert, *The Phoenix Indian School: Forced Assimilation in Arizona, 1891–1935* (Norman: University of Oklahoma Press, 1988), 14.

10. Jacobs, *White Mother to a Dark Race*, 230.

11. Trennert, *The Phoenix Indian School*, 95, 117–18.

12. Frederick Hoxie, *A Final Promise: The Campaign to Assimilate the Indians* (Lincoln: University of Nebraska Press, 2001), 205.

13. *The Statutes at Large of the United States of America*, 26:1014; ibid., 27:635. See also Adams, *Education for Extinction*, 63; Jacobs, *White Mother to a Dark Race*, 163.

14. Robert S. McPherson, Jim Dandy, and Sarah E. Burak, *Navajo Tradition, Mormon Life: The Autobiography and Teachings of Jim Dandy* (Salt Lake City: University of Utah Press, 2012), 94.

15. "Record Number of Navajo Children Attend School, 1954," Window Rock, Director of Navajo Schools, Internal Report, September 1, 1954, Peter Iverson Papers, Labriola Center, Arizona State University, Tempe (hereafter Labriola Center, ASU).

16. U.S. Board of Indian Commissioners, *Annual Report of the Board of Indian Commissioners to the Secretary of the Interior* (Washington, DC: Government Printing Office, 1932).

17. Hoxie, *A Final Promise*, 202–3.

18. Szasz, *Education and the American Indian*, 19.

19. Lewis Meriam, *The Problem of Indian Administration: Report of a Survey Made at the Request of Hubert Work, Secretary of the Interior, and Submitted to Him, February 21, 1928* (Baltimore: John Hopkins Press, 1928), 33–35; Szasz, *Education and the American Indian*, 23.

20. Szasz, *Education and the American Indian*, 24–25, 29, 31–32, 53–54; Lomawaima, *They Called It Prairie Light*, 7.

21. Szasz, *Education and the American Indian*, 63, 109–10.

22. Navajo Tribal Council Resolutions, 1922–1951, Labriola Center, ASU.

23. "E. R. Fryer, General Superintendent, to Commissioner of Indian Affairs, March 23, 1939," Peter Iverson Papers, Labriola Center, ASU; Statute 3645, "An Act to Conserve and Develop Indian Lands and Resources; to Extend to Indians the Right to Form Business and Other Organizations; to Establish a Credit System for Indians; to Grant Certain Rights of Home Rule to Indians; to Provide for Vocational Education for Indians; and for Other Purposes," June 18, 1934, *The Statutes at Large of the United States of American from March 1933 to June 1934: Concurrent Resolutions, Recent Treaties and Conventions, Executive Proclamations to and Agreements, Twenty-First Amendment to the Constitution*, vol. 48, part 1 (Washington, DC: Government Printing Office, 1934), 984–88.

24. Hildegard Thompson, *The Navajos Long Walk for Education: A History of Navajo Education* (Tsaile: Navajo Community College Press, 1975), 74–79; George Sanchez, *The People: A Study of the Navajo* (Washington, DC: United States Indian Service, 1948).

25. Teresa L. McCarty, *A Place to Be Navajo: Rough Rock and the Struggle for Self-Determination in Indigenous Schooling* (Mahwah, NJ: Lawrence Erlbaum Associates, Publishers, 2002), 59.

26. Navajo Tribal Council Resolutions, 1922–1951, Labriola Center, ASU. See also Navajo Tribal Council resolution, July 12, 1945, NAPR, Navajo Area Office, as quoted in Peter Iverson, *Diné: A History of the Navajos* (Albuquerque: University of New Mexico Press, 2006), 191.

27. "Tribal Council Notes, July 10–13, 1945," Peter Iverson Papers, Labriola Center, ASU.

28. Robert W. Young, *The Navajo Yearbook* (Window Rock, AZ: Navajo Agency, 1961), 15.

29. Tribal Council Notes, July 10–13, 1945, Peter Iverson Papers, Labriola Center, ASU.

30. Navajo Tribal Council Resolutions, 1922–1951, Labriola Center, ASU.

31. Young, *The Navajo Yearbook*, 13–14. For a synopsis of Navajo Tribal Council requests from the government, see Chee Dodge, testimony, U.S. Senate, Committee on Indian Affairs, May 12, 1946, Record Group 75, BIA, National Archives, Washington, DC, Central Classified Files, Navajo Area Office; "Chee Dodge, May 20, 1946," in Peter Iverson, *"For Our Navajo People": Diné Letters, Speeches, and Petitions, 1900–1960* (Albuquerque: University of New Mexico Press, 2002), 99; Hearings IAS-0002 (May 14, 1946), PLV-0008 (May 16, 1946), and SAP-0009 (May 16, 17, 20–25, 27, 29, and 30, 1946), LexisNexis. com; NAPR, Navajo Area Office, as quoted in Peter Iverson, *Diné: A History of the Navajos*, 189.

32. Chee Dodge, testimony, U.S. Senate, Committee on Indian Affairs, May 12, 1946, Record Group 75, BIA, National Archives, Washington, DC, Central Classified Files, Navajo Area Office, as quoted in Peter Iverson, *Diné: A History of the Navajos*, 191.

33. J. A. Krug, Secretary of Interior, *The Navajo: A Long-Range Program for Navajo Rehabilitation* (Washington, DC: U.S. Government Printing Office, 1948), 1.

34. House Resolution 4627, "An Act to Authorize an Appropriation for the Immediate Relief of the Navajo and Hopi Indians, and for Other Purposes,"

December 19, 1947, *United States Statutes at Large*, vol. 61, part 1, p. 940; Statute 2734, "An Act to Promote the Rehabilitation of the Navajo and Hopi Tribes of Indians and a Better Utilization of the Resources of the Navajo and Hopi Indian Reservations, and for Other Purposes," April 19, 1950, *United States Statutes at Large*, vol. 64, part 1, pp. 44–47.

35. Thompson, *The Navajos' Long Walk for Education*, 119.

36. Young, *The Navajo Yearbook*, 8.

37. Navajo Tribal Council Resolutions, 1922–1951, Labriola Center, ASU; Tribal Council Notes, February 18–21, 1947, Peter Iverson Papers, Labriola Center, ASU.

38. Tribal Council Notes, February 18–21, 1947, Peter Iverson Papers, Labriola Center, ASU.

39. L. Madison Coombs, *Doorway Toward the Light* (Washington, DC: U.S. Department of the Interior Bureau of Indian Affairs, 1962), 19–20, 47.

40. Thompson, *The Navajos' Long Walk for Education*, 86.

41. Krug, *The Navajo: A Long-Range Program for Navajo Rehabilitation*, 7.

42. John Birch, "Helen John: The Beginnings of Indian Placement," *Dialogue: A Journal of Mormon Thought* 18, no. 4 (1985): 120.

43. Golden Buchanan, "The 'Outing' Program as It Has Developed," Indian Committee Correspondence, 1941–1952, LDS Church Archives, Salt Lake City, Utah.

44. Ibid., 121.

45. Helen Rose John Hall, interview by Neil J. Birch, 1978, Salt Lake City, typescript, p. 3, James Moyle Oral History Program, Church Archives.

46. Like other communities, the town of Sevier hosted several congregations, or wards, and several of these units are organizationally gathered together as a stake, which is led by a stake president and his two counselors which constitute a presidency.

47. Golden Buchanan, interview, October 13, 1966, as quoted in Clarence Bishop, "Indian Placement: A History of the Indian Student Placement Program of the Church of Jesus Christ of Latter-day Saints" (Master's thesis, University of Utah, 1967), 30–31.

48. George Albert Smith, *Conference Report*, April 1950, 184–85; Spencer W. Kimball, *Conference Report*, April 1951, 175–78; Spencer W. Kimball, *Conference Report*, April 1949; all online at gospelink.com. Also David Flake, "History of the Southwest Indian Mission," unpublished manuscript, HBLL, 119.

49. E. L. Kimball & A. E. Kimball, *Spencer Kimball: Twelfth President of the Church of Jesus Christ of Latter-day Saints* (Salt Lake City: Bookcraft, 1977), 237; see also LeGrand Richards, "Blessings and Promises to the Lamanites," *Indian Liahona* 8, no. 1 (January/February 1971): 3.

50. Birch, "Helen John: The Beginnings of Indian Placement," 124–25. See also Bishop, "Indian Placement," 31–32.

51. Birch, "Helen John: The Beginnings of Indian Placement," 124–25.

52. Thelma S. Buchanan, interview by William G. Hartley, Salt Lake City, 1976, typescript, p. 4, James Moyle Oral History Program, Church Archives.

53. Bishop, "Indian Placement," 34.

54. Birch, "Helen John: The Beginnings of Indian Placement," 128.

55. Bishop, "Indian Placement," 34.

56. Golden R. Buchanan to President Flake, Southwest Indian Mission, Richfield, UT, August 1, 1949, Indian Committee Correspondence, 1941–1952, Church Archives.

57. Golden Buchanan to Mrs. Constance W. Deer, August 2, 1949, Indian Committee Correspondence, 1941–1952, Church Archives.

58. Bishop, "Indian Placement," 38–39.

59. Golden Buchanan, "The 'Outing' Program as It Has Developed," Indian Committee Correspondence, 1941–1952, Church Archives; see also Belle Spafford to Heber C. Kimball, December 8, 1949, Indian Committee Correspondence, 1941–1952, Church Archives.

60. Elder M. H. Kunz, Office Elder, Southwest Indian Mission to Golden R. Buchanan, July 28, 1949, Indian Committee Correspondence, 1941–1952, Church Archives; Rob Gwilliam to Golden Buchanan, Shiprock, New Mexico, August, 3, 1949, Indian Committee Correspondence, 1941–1952, Church Archives.

61. Buchanan, "The 'Outing' Program as It Has Developed."

62. Ben Tsosie to Dear Sir, September 24, 1951, Gallup, Indian Committee Correspondence, 1941–1952, Church Archives.

63. Buchanan, "The 'Outing' Program as It Has Developed."

64. Dale Shumway interview by author, June 18, 2009, Orem, Utah.

65. Thompson, *The Navajos' Long Walk for Education*, 141–42.

66. Rhonda J. Lee, interview by Jim M. Dandy, April 10, 1991, typescript, p. 3, Redd Center, HBLL.

67. "An Even Chance," *Fort Defiance (AZ) Diné Baa-Hani* 11, no. 7, February 1971.

68. Geraldine Taylor Lindquist, "The Indian Student Placement Program as a Means of Increasing the Education of Children of Selected Indian Families" (Master's thesis, Utah State University, 1974), 34.

69. "Wasatch Research Opinion Report, 1979," 59, Church Archives.

70. Andrew Hamilton, "Their Indian Guests," *Saturday Evening Post*, September 17, 1960.

71. Donna Deyhle, "Empowerment and Cultural Conflict: Navajo Parents and the Schooling of Their Children," *Journal of Qualitative Studies in Education* 4, no. 4 (1991): 286.

72. Jennifer Ludden, "Navajo Indians and Mormons Remember Their Involvement in Program Placing Indian Children with Mormon Families," National Public Radio, January 23, 2005, transcript available online at Lexisnexis.com.

73. Shumway and Shumway, *The Blossoming*, 50.

74. McPherson, Dandy, and Burak, *Navajo Tradition, Mormon Life*, 96.

75. Ibid., 80.

76. Ronald Singer, interview by Odessa Neaman, June 14, 1990, Provo, Utah, typescript, pp. 5–6, LDS Native American Oral History Collection Project, Charles Redd Center for Western History (hereafter Redd Center), L. Tom Perry Special Collections, HBLL.

77. Donald Mose, interview by Jim M. Dandy, November 6, 1990, Provo, Utah, 1990, typescript, p. 2, LDS Native American Oral History Collection Project, Redd Center, HBLL.
78. Krug, *The Navajo: A Long-Range Program*, 1.
79. Ibid.
80. Shumway and Shumway, *The Blossoming*, 166.
81. Donald L. Fixico, *Termination and Relocation: Federal Indian Policy, 1945–1960* (Albuquerque: University of New Mexico Press, 1986), 139.
82. Shumway and Shumway, *The Blossoming*, 220. Pamela Polacca similarly explained, "My sister, she went on Placement, like I said. Lots of things from placement program, lot of you know, goodies and stuff like that, and presents and whatnot! I thought all people up there were rich and everything else." Pamela Polacca [pseudonym], interview by Tona Hangen, July 30, 1991, Ganado, Arizona, typescript, p. 3, in author's files.
83. Beth Wood, "The LDS Indian Placement Program: An Educational System that Works," *Window Rock (AZ) Navajo Times*, September 28, 1978.
84. Rhonda J. Lee interviewed by Jim M. Dandy, April 10, 1991, typescript, p. 4, LDS Native American Oral History Collection Project, Redd Center, HBLL.
85. Wasatch Research Opinion Report, 1979, 59, Church Archives.
86. Ibid., 33.
87. Walter D. Atene, interview by Jim M. Dandy, Provo, Utah, November 3, 1990, typescript, p. 5, LDS Native American Oral History Collection Project, Redd Center, HBLL.
88. Ludden, "Navajo Indians and Mormons Remember."
89. Ibid.
90. Emery Bowman, interview by Deborah Lewis, January 27, 1990, typescript, p. 11, LDS Native American Oral History Collection Project, Redd Center, HBLL.
91. Rosie Tsosie-Bingham, phone interview by author, June 11, 2009.
92. Geraldine M. Goenett, "The Placement Program in My Life," *Indian Liahona* (July/August 1971): 23.
93. McCarty, *A Place to Be Navajo*, 56.

CHAPTER 4: THE INSTITUTIONAL RISE OF THE INDIAN STUDENT PLACEMENT PROGRAM, 1947–1972

1. Spencer W. Kimball to Ernest L. Wilkinson, October 8, 1963, Wilkinson Presidential Papers, BYU; Ernest L. Wilkinson and Leonard J. Arrington, *Brigham Young University: The First One Hundred Years* (Provo, UT: Brigham Young University Press, 1976), 3:519.
2. Bishop, "Indian Placement," 38.
3. Callings are church assignments executed by most actively participating Mormons.
4. The First Presidency is the office held by the president/prophet of the church and his two counselors.
5. Spencer W. Kimball, Chairman, Indian Relations Committee of the Church of Jesus Christ of Latter-day Saints, to President George Albert Smith, Salt Lake City, Utah, August 25, 1949, in Bishop, "Indian Placement," 38.

6. Golden R. Buchanan, interview, vol. 2, p. 12, typescript, James Moyle Oral History Program, Church Archives.
7. Miles Jensen, interview by Gordon Irving, May 18, 1983, pp. 7, 9, James Moyle Oral History Program, Church Archives.
8. Ibid.; Bishop, "Indian Placement," 35, 39.
9. Belle Spafford, interview by Jill Mulvay Derr, 1975–1976, Salt Lake City, typescript, p. 220, Church Archives.
10. Spafford to Kimball, Dec. 8, 1949, Indian Committee Correspondence, 1941–1952, Church Archives.
11. Spafford, interview, 220.
12. Ibid.
13. Bishop, "Indian Placement," 40.
14. Miles Jensen, interview by Clarence Bishop, November 17, 1966, in Bishop, "Indian Placement," 39.
15. Shumway and Shumway, *The Blossoming*, 27.
16. Bishop, "Indian Placement," 38–39.
17. Miles Jensen, dictation, December 13, 1973, typescript, p. 7, James Moyle Oral History Program, Church Archives; Miles Jensen, interview, in Bishop, "Indian Placement," 39; Clarence Bishop, interview by Loretta L. Hefner, 1979, James Moyle Oral History Program, Church Archives.
18. Spencer W. Kimball, "The Navajo...His Predicament," *Improvement Era* 51, no. 2 (February 1948): 76–78, 120.
19. Spencer W. Kimball, "The Navajo...His Predicament," *Improvement Era* 51, no. 4(April 1948): 212.
20. Ibid., 252.
21. Spencer W. Kimball, *Conference Report, April, 1949*, online at gospelink.com.
22. Jensen, dictation, 3.
23. Ibid., 6.
24. Ibid.
25. Ibid., 4; see also Shumway and Shumway, *The Blossoming*, 28.
26. Jensen, dictation, 6.
27. The eventual attorney for the program, Thomas Quentin Cannon, recalled: "And it was real touchy for a long, long time. Not all of the Brethren were agreed on the wisdom of the program.... [One questioned,] 'Is it fair for us to take these youth out of their own culture and bring them here?' [T]hat question was raised a thousand times and gone over. It always seemed to me that the sisters were more concerned about that than the Brethren. The Brethren wanted to do good. They wanted to raise the standard of these people. It was really one brother in the Quorum, and not very far up in the Quorum then, that was the big proponent of it. How far the support went up above him I have no idea, because the negotiations were between that particular brother and the Relief Society presidency, rather than between the First Presidency and the Relief Society Presidency. We had to be extremely careful under the circumstances." Thomas Quentin Cannon, interview by Loretta L. Hefner, 1979, Salt Lake City, typescript, p. 13, James Moyle Oral History Program, Church Archives.

28. Bishop, "Indian Placement," 42–44.
29. Jensen, dictation, 4–5.
30. Ibid., 6.
31. Ibid.
32. First Presidency to the Presidents of the Following Stakes: Sevier, South Sevier, North Sevier, Gunnison, South Sanpete, North Sanpete, and Moroni, August 10, 1954, Salt Lake City, Church Archives.
33. Miles Jensen, interview, April 27, 1979, microfilm without pagination, reference OH 641, James Moyle Oral History Program, Church Archives.
34. John Farr Larson, Director of the Bureau of Services for Children, Utah State Department of Public Welfare, to Belle S. Spafford, Salt Lake City, Utah, April 16, 1954, as quoted in Bishop, "Indian Placement," 44.
35. Bishop, "Indian Placement," 46.
36. Jensen, interview, 1983, pp. 4–5.
37. Margaret McPherson Keller, interview by Loretta L. Hefner, 1979, Salt Lake City, Utah, typescript, p. 1, James Moyle Oral History Program, Church Archives.
38. Bishop, "Indian Placement," 49.
39. Spencer W. Kimball, "The Expanded Indian Program," *Improvement Era* 59, no. 12 (December 1956): 938.
40. Ibid.; LDS Social Services, July 2, 1956, Meeting Minutes, Indian Placement Program Files, 1950–1998, Church Archives; Bishop, "Indian Placement," 50; Jensen, dictation, 7.
41. Bishop, "Indian Placement," 47–48; *Report to Relief Society General Board of Reception Center of Indian Students Held at Richfield, Utah, August 21, 22, 23, 24 of 1956 by L.D.S. Relief Society Social Service and Child Welfare*, in Bishop, "Indian Placement," 52.
42. Kimball, "The Expanded Indian Program," 938.
43. Letter from David O. McKay, Stephen L. Richards, and J. Reuben Clark Jr. of the First Presidency of the Church of Jesus Christ of Latter-day Saints, Salt Lake City, Utah, June 27, 1955, in Bishop, "Indian Placement," 54–55.
44. Ibid., 52–53.
45. D. Michael Quinn, "I-Thou vs. I-It Conversions: The Mormon 'Baseball Baptism' Era," *Sunstone Magazine* 16, no. 7 (December 1993): 30–44.
46. Larry Denetsosi [pseudonym], interview by Tona Hangen, August 5, 1991, Page, Arizona, typescript, pp. 3–4, in author's files.
47. Shumway and Shumway, *The Blossoming*, 179–80.
48. Ibid., 242.
49. Southwest Indian Mission Annual Historical Reports, 1978–1980, Church Archives.
50. Stewart and Wiley, "Cultural Genocide," 84.
51. Erdman Jake, interview by Jenny M. Smith, May 8, 1999, Salt Lake City, Utah, typescript without pagination, Jenny M. Smith's Indian Student Placement Program Oral Histories, Special Collections and Archives, Merrill-Cazier Library, Utah State University, Logan (hereafter USU).
52. Jimmy N. Bennally, interview by Odessa Neaman, July 18, 1990, Provo, Utah, typescript, p. 3, LDS Native American Oral History Project, Redd Center, HBLL.

53. Rex Richard Ashdown, interview by Loretta L. Hefner, 1979, Ogden, Utah, typescript, p. 5, James Moyle Oral History Program, Church Archives.
54. Teddy Redhouse [pseudonym], interview by Tona Hangen, March 12, 1991, typescript, p. 7, in author's files.
55. Indian Committee Minutes, December 4, 1956, Church Archives.
56. These mass baptism enrollees only represented a minute percentage of total students (4 percent in 1954, 6 percent in 1955, and 3 percent in 1956). Most placement students were then the children of Indian parents baptized well before the prospects of the ISPP.
57. Indian Committee Minutes, February 5, 1957, Church Archives.
58. Jensen dictation, 10–11.
59. Ibid., 8.
60. Spafford, interview, 223–24.
61. Indian Committee Minutes, December 4, 1956, Church Archives.
62. Jensen, interview, 1983, p. 11.
63. Indian Committee Minutes, January 8, 1957, and May 9, 1958, Church Archives; Keller, interview, 8.
64. Attendees included: Relief Society president Belle Spafford, Margaret Keller, and Miles Jensen of the LDS General Relief Society; Director John Farr Larson and LaMar Andrus of the Utah State Department of Public Welfare; Commissioner Fen Hildreth and Ann Bracken of the Arizona Department of Public Welfare; Dr. Robert Hansen of the U.S. Department of Health, Education and Welfare; Ruth Bartlett and Bess William representing the U.S. Children's Bureau; Bea Erickson from the welfare department of the Window Rock Navajo Agency; BIA welfare division representatives Lois McVey, Florence Miller, and Beatrice L. Erickson; and Navajo Tribal Council representatives Samuel Billison and Mr. Natoni.
65. *Indian Student Placement Program: Report Given March 19, 1957, at Kanab, Utah*, Indian Placement Program Files, 1955–1960, Church Archives.
66. Indian Committee Minutes, May 9, 1958, Church Archives.
67. Billison served on the Tribal Council, and later as vice chairman, followed by an impressive but failed campaign for the chairmanship in 1970.
68. Indian Committee Minutes, May 9, 1958, Church Archives.
69. Spafford, interview, 223–24; Bishop, "Indian Placement," 59, 60; Keller, interview, 8.
70. For a more complete discussion of termination policy and Watkins's role therein, see R. Warren Metcalf, *Termination's Legacy: The Discarded Indians of Utah* (Lincoln: University of Nebraska Press, 2002).
71. Indian Committee Minutes, May 9 and June 10, 1958, Church Archives.
72. Ibid., May 9, 1958; Bishop, "Indian Placement," 60–63.
73. Indian Committee Minutes, November 12, 1957, Church Archives
74. Ibid.
75. Ibid., August 11, 1958; Bishop, "Indian Placement," 65–67.
76. Indian Committee Minutes, May 9, June 10, June 23, and September 9, 1958, Church Archives.
77. Indian Committee Minutes, May 9, 1958, Church Archives.
78. Bishop, "Indian Placement," 38–39, 53, 68.

79. Spencer W. Kimball to Ernest L. Wilkinson, October 8, 1963, Wilkinson Presidential Papers, Brigham Young University; see also Wilkinson and Arrington, *Brigham Young University: The First One Hundred Years*, 3:519.

80. Jensen, interview, April 27, 1979.

81. Indian Committee Minutes, July 3, 1958, Church Archives.

82. In June 1958, the Relief Society hired Charlie Steward as an additional caseworker; other additions to the staff included Robert Gwilliam as an administrative assistant to Keller in June 1959, Glen VanWagenen as a caseworker over central Utah in January 1960, and Melvin Farnsworth to replace Charlie Steward in April 1960. Fred Richards and Rolin Davis joined the staff in 1960, helping to drop the 1957–1958 caseload of over one hundred students per caseworker down to just seventy. Bishop, "Indian Placement," 69–70. Indian Committee Minutes, February 24 and September 11, 1959, Church Archives.

83. The mass baptism and independent placement issues rose again in May 1958 when the committee learned that Mormons in California baptized some 695 Indian children and placed them in LDS foster homes without any licensed authority. Again in September, the committee received word of independent placements. Kimball resolved to send letters to mission presidents and bishops outlining the legal restrictions on unsanctioned foster placements. In March 1960 the committee learned of several more placements in Snowflake, Arizona. In July 1960 Bob Gwilliam echoed Kimball's concerns to reception center volunteers and staff, explaining that the church could lose its license if independent placements continued. Indian Committee Minutes, May 9 and September 9, 1958; March 15, 1960; and July 28, 1961, Church Archives.

84. Bishop, "Indian Placement," 73–75.

85. "Indian Student Placement Program," *Shiprock (AZ) Navajo Times*, December 27, 1961.

86. Keller, interview; Bishop, "Indian Placement," 77; Indian Committee Minutes, January 16, 1964, Church Archives; Newsletter: LDS Indian Student Placement Program, March 1964, HBLL.

87. Bishop, "Indian Placement," 72–73; Doyle L. Green, "Southwest Indian Mission," *Improvement Era* 58, no. 4 (April 1955): 233; Indian Committee Minutes, August 11, 1959, Church Archives.

88. Iverson, *Diné*, 191–96; Jessie L. Embry, "Lamanite/Indian Branches," unpublished manuscript, p. 8, Armand Mauss Papers, Utah State Historical Society, Salt Lake City, Utah (hereafter Mauss Papers); Edward Kimball and Andrew Kimball, *Spencer W. Kimball: Twelfth President of the Church of Jesus Christ of Latter-day Saints* (Salt Lake City: Bookcraft, 1977), 236–41; Jensen, interview, 1983.

89. Iverson, *Diné*, 211–13; Iverson, *"For Our Navajo People,"* 257; Paul Jones, inaugural address, Window Rock, Arizona, January 1959, Special Collections, University of Arizona Library, Tucson; 1955 inaugural address found in Spencer W. Kimball, *Conference Report*, October 1956, p. 53.

90. Keller, interview, 8.

91. Indian Committee Minutes, August 11 and September 9, 1958, Church Archives.
92. S. Fox to Paul Jones, September 24, 1958, Indian Placement Program Files, Church Archives.
93. Orville Gunther to Paul Jones, September 9, 1958, Indian Placement Program Files, Church Archives.
94. Mrs. Hazel Lincoln to Paul Jones, [n.d.], Indian Placement Program Files, Church Archives.
95. Indian Committee Minutes, September 11, 1959, Church Archives.
96. Keller, interview, 8.
97. Raymond Nakai, inaugural address, April 13, 1963, Peter Iverson Papers, Labriola Center, Arizona State University, Tempe, Arizona; see also Raymond Nakai, "Will We Meet the Challenge?," *Journal of American Indian Education* 4, no. 1 (October 1964): 10–12.
98. The April 1963 committee minutes explain: "It appears that some members of the [Navajo] Education Committee, Mr. John Y. Begaye Director of the Department of Health, Education and Welfare, and Mr. Martin did not understand our Program and were drawing conclusions about the Program such as the following: 'If those white people are going to take the Indian children out of the Indian culture and adopt them, then they should be responsible for the total education of these children, therefore, the students are not eligible for Navajo scholarships because when they are adopted into white families they lose their rights as Navajos.'" Indian Committee Minutes, April 16, 1963, Church Archives.
99. "Clarence Bishop to Chairman Raymond Nakai, April 22, 1965," *Shiprock (AZ) Navajo Times,* May 6, 1965, p. 4.
100. Nakai was accompanied by Vice Chairman Nelson Damon; Councilmen Frank Luther, Wilson Halona, and John Brown; Youth Corps representative Robert Melvin; tribal scholarship committee member Sandy Town; and director of tourism Charles Damon. "Bishop to Nakai," 4; Clarence Bishop, Mauray Payne, and Dale Shumway to Foster Parents, Salt Lake City, September 30, 1965, HBLL; "They Like What They Saw," *Salt Lake City Church News,* October 23, 1965.
101. "They Like What They Saw"; Keller, interview; Felt to Taylor, September 16, 1965, Institute of American Indian Services and Research, Records, 1956–1972, Special Collections, HBLL; "Indian Leaders Visit Church Headquarters," *Indian Liahona* 3, no. 1 (Winter 1965/66): 1.
102. Indian Committee Minutes, July 29, 1969, Church Archives; Clarence R. Bishop, Executive Director, to Elder Spencer W. Kimball, Aptos, California, July 30, 1969, Indian Committee Minutes, Church Archives; Spencer W. Kimball, "Of Royal Blood," *Ensign* 1, no. 7 (July 1971): 7.
103. The Relief Society transferred veteran Placement caseworker Glen VanWagenen to Arizona to supervise the ISPP there, allowing agency director Miltenberger to direct other social programs. Typically, VanWagenen reported directly to Bishop, who regularly attended Indian Committee meetings with Spencer W. Kimball and other Indian

program leaders of the Indian seminaries and the BYU Indian program. The Indian Committee expanded placement into Arizona through a bureaucratic system that ostensibly existed with a separate leadership; however, Kimball's longstanding interest led him to regularly exercise ecclesiastical authority in order to play a central role in both Utah and Arizona. Indian Committee Minutes, September 22, 1964, Church Archives; see also Bishop, "Indian Placement," 86; Paul E. Felt, "I Remember When," bound manuscript, p. 106, HBLL; Indian Committee Minutes, February 20, 1962, Church Archives; see also Bishop, "Indian Placement," 82; Letter to President Belle S. Spafford, Relief Society General Board, from First Presidency of the Church of Jesus Christ of Latter-day Saints, Salt Lake City, Utah, May 10, 1962, Church Archives; Letter from Six Stake Presidents, February 11, 1962, Church Archives; Bishop, "Indian Placement," 77–82.

104. Indian Committee Minutes, September 22, 1964, Church Archives.

105. The Arizona Agency opened in the summer of 1962 and immediately worked to build up the Placement Program. The first reception center operated in Phoenix, but then moved to a tri-stake building in Mesa. After the first year, the program expanded farther south to Tucson and also started recruiting students from outside the Southwest, particularly in the northern plains. Initially, some school districts complained about the arrival of out-of-state students and the cost of education; however, caseworkers generally resolved such incidents by providing evidence of legal foster care arrangements. Bishop, "Indian Placement," 84–85, 89.

106. Bishop, "Indian Placement," 86–87; Indian Committee Minutes, April 22, 1964, Church Archives.

107. In the spring of 1965 Bishop transferred Utah caseworker Harry Smith to Canada to direct the forty-eight students who enrolled in the 1965–1966 school year. The Canadian program followed the Arizona model and functioned legally through a board of directors with Walker as chairman. Indian Committee Minutes, May 11, 1965; Bishop, "Indian Placement," 87–88.

108. Indian Committee Minutes, August 10, 1965, Church Archives.

109. Ibid., November 9, 1965.

110. Bishop, "Indian Placement," 79–80, 93–95, 99–100.

111. Ibid., 101–2.

112. Ibid., 108; "Student Enrollment: School Year 1966–67," HBLL.

113. Dale Tingey, interview by author, June 18, 2009, Provo, Utah, in author's files.

114. Dale Shumway, interview.

115. Boyd K. Packer, "Manual of Policies and Procedures for the Administration of Indian Seminaries of the Church of Jesus Christ of Latter-day Saints" (PhD diss., Brigham Young University, 1962), 29; "Enrollment in LDS Indian Seminary, 1957–1967," Brigham Young University Records, 1958–1972, HBLL; "Lamanite Handbook for the Church of Jesus Christ of Latter-day Saints, December 1, 1968," 12, HBLL; Richards, "Blessings and Promises to the Lamanites," 4.

116. "Seminary Program Teaches About Home and Gospel," *Salt Lake City Church News*, September 9, 1967.

117. "Sign-Ups Are as Good as Baptisms," [n.d.], Southwest Indian Mission, Manuscript History and Historical Reports, HBLL.

118. Ibid.

119. E. Bruce Preece, "Mormon Missionary Work Among the Indians of North America in the Twentieth Century," July 14, 1965, unpublished manuscript, 7–8, 16–17, HBLL; Southwest Indian Mission, Historical Reports.

120. "Four Indian Programs of the Church of Jesus Christ of Latter-day Saints, 1965," Brigham Young University Records, 1958–1972, HBLL.

121. Spencer W. Kimball, "The Day of the Lamanite Is Now," *Improvement Era* 71, no. 8 (August 1968): 37; Kimball, "Of Royal Blood," 6.

122. Melvin A. Lyman, *Out of Obscurity into Light* (Salt Lake City, Albany Book, 1985), 124, 153; J. Thomas Fyans, "The Lamanites Must Rise in Majesty and Power," *Ensign* 6, no. 5 (May 1976): 12; R. Lanier Britsch, "The Church in the South Pacific," *Ensign* 6, no. 2 (February 1976): 19; "Lamanite Handbook," 14–15; Tereapii Solomon, "Towards an Educational Analysis of Māori and Pacific Island Student Achievement at the Church College of New Zealand," *MAI Review*, no. 1 (2007): 1; Tereapii Solomon, "Intern Research Report 8: Towards an Educational Analysis of Māori and Pacific Island Student Achievement at the Church College of New Zealand," *MAI Review*, no. 1 (2007): 4. See also Keith R. Oaks, "Church Elementary and Secondary Education," unpublished report, March 8, 1971, p. 4, Mauss Papers.

123. "Lamanite Handbook," 22. "Words of Wisdom from Lamanite Leaders," *Indian Liahona* (July/August 1971): 16; Harold C. Brown, "What Is a Lamanite?," *Ensign* 2, no. 9 (September 1972): 62–64.

124. Brown, "What Is a Lamanite?," 62; Mauss, *All Abraham's Children*, 134–42; Spencer W. Kimball, "Our Paths Have Met Again," *Ensign* 5, no. 12 (December 1975): 2; Dean L. Larsen, "Mingled Destinies: The Lamanites and the Latter-day Saints," *Ensign* 5, no. 12 (December 1975): 8; Lane Johnson, "Who and Where Are the Lamanites?" *Ensign* 5, no. 12 (December 1975): 15; Lawrence Cummins, "Elder George Lee: 'I Owe Every Opportunity to the Lord,'" *Ensign* 5, no. 12 (December 1975): 26; Carlos L. Pedraja, "Carlos L. Pedraja: 'I Didn't Go to Russia,'" *Ensign* 5, no. 12 (December 1975): 29; "Larry EchoHawk: Someone's Concerned about Me," *Ensign* 5, no. 12 (December 1975): 20.

125. Kimball, "Of Royal Blood," 5–6.

126. Richards, "Blessings and Promises to the Lamanites," 4.

127. Spencer W. Kimball, "Church Growth and Lamanite Involvement" (speech, Brigham Young University, November 7, 1972).

CHAPTER 5: THE PLACEMENT EXPERIENCE: ENTERING MORMON HOMES AND COMMUNITIES

1. Spencer W. Kimball to Fred N. Spackman, May 21, 1957, Harold B. Lee Papers, Church Archives; see also Wilkinson and Arrington, *Brigham Young University: The First One Hundred Years*, 3:506.

2. Elizabeth Pickett, "Conflicts Between Generations May Be Reason for Juvenile Delinquency," *Window Rock (AZ) Navajo Times*, March 22, 1979; Child, *Boarding School Seasons*, 1–3; Szasz, *Education and the American Indian*, 8–15.

3. For example, Melissa Lichai [pseudonym], interview by Tona Hangen, August 6, 1991, Page, Arizona, typescript, p. 4, in author's files.
4. Harold C. Brown, "Learning the Best of Both Worlds' Cultures," *Ensign* 5, no. 12 (December 1975): 22; Hearing before the United States Senate Select Committee on Indian Affairs, Ninety-Fifth Congress, First Session on S. 1214, August 4, 1977 (Washington, DC: U.S. Government Printing Office, 1977), 209.
5. "Natural Parent Guide, The LDS Indian Student Placement Program, June 1968," HBLL; "LDS Indian Student Placement Program: Policies Regarding Requirements and Responsibilities," [n.d.], HBLL.
6. Arizona Holbrook Mission Records, 1970–1983, Church Archives.
7. Gwen Roessel [pseudonym], interview by Tona Hangen, August 5, 1991, LeChee, Arizona, typescript, p. 12, in author's files. The blessingway is one of the two core ritual sets outlined in Navajo philosophy. It is delivered through prayerful songs intended to fortify an individual. The blessingway contains a series of rites that practitioners draw from in order to restore one's balance and harmony, which constitutes the ultimate aspiration of Navajo philosophy. The ritual may serve as a prophylactic or a restorative function that is offered as often as needed, but also quite commonly in conjunction with major life events, such as puberty and childbearing. John R. Farella, *The Main Stalk: A Synthesis of Navajo Philosophy* (Tuscon: University of Arizona Press, 1984), 32; Maureen Trudelle Schwartz, *Molded in the Image of Changing Woman: Navajo Views on the Human Body and Personhood* (Tucson: University of Arizona Press, 1997), 99, 127, 160; Robert McPherson, *Dineji Na'Nitin: Navajo Traditional Teachings and History* (Boulder: University Press of Colorado, 2012), 74.
8. Lenora Tsosie, autobiographical sketch, June 19, 2009, typescript, no pagination, in author's files.
9. George P. Lee, *Silent Courage* (Salt Lake City: Deseret Book Co., 1987), 106.
10. Tsosie, autobiographical sketch.
11. Ibid.
12. Ludden, "Navajo Indians and Mormons Remember."
13. Lee, *Silent Courage*, 106–7.
14. Tsosie, autobiographical sketch.
15. Lee, *Silent Courage*, 111–13.
16. Kimball, "The Expanded Indian Program," 938.
17. Lee, *Silent Courage*, 116; Margaret Wauneka [pseudonym], interview by Tona Hangen, August 9, 1991, Tuba City, Arizona, typescript, pp. 5–6, in author's files.
18. Lee, *Silent Courage*, 114.
19. Kimball, "The Expanded Indian Program," 937–40.
20. Minutes of the Indian Student Placement Committee, November 12, 1957, Church Archives.
21. Kimball, "The Expanded Indian Program," 937–40.
22. Lee, *Silent Courage*, 117.
23. Clarence R. Bishop, "Foster Parent Orientation Meeting, August 28, 1963, Phoenix Arizona," American Indian Research Services, HBLL.

24. Ibid.
25. Roessel, interview, 4.
26. Lee, *Silent Courage*, 118–19.
27. Ronald Singer, interview by Odessa Neaman, January 14, 1990, typescript, p. 9, LDS Native American Oral History Project, Redd Center, HBLL.
28. Bishop, interview, 1979.
29. Ludden, "Navajo Indians and Mormons Remember."
30. Emma Woods [pseudonym], interview by Tona Hangen, August 10, 1991, Coalmine Mesa, Arizona, typescript, p. 2, in author's files.
31. Roessel, interview, 5.
32. Lee, *Silent Courage*, 122–23.
33. "A Father: 'Six + one = six,'" 1, no. 1 *Ensign* (January 1971): 28.
34. Shumway and Shumway, *The Blossoming*, 170.
35. Lee, *Silent Courage*, 126; Wauneka, interview, 25.
36. Keith H. Basso, *Wisdom Sits in Places: Landscape and Language Among the Western Apache* (Albuquerque: University of New Mexico, 1996), xv.
37. Klara Bonsack Kelley and Harris Francis, *Navajo Sacred Places* (Bloomington: Indiana University Press, 1994), 2.
38. Lee, *Silent Courage*, 128.
39. For example, see ibid., 126; Woods, interview, 2.
40. Polacca, interview, 17–18.
41. Sarah Tso [pseudonym], interview by Tona Hangen, July 18, 1991, Provo, Utah, typescript, p. 4, in author's files.
42. Lilly Chester [pseudonym], interview by Tona Hangen, August 6, 1991, Page, Arizona, typescript, p. 7, in author's files; Dorothy Schimmelpfennig's 1971 dissertation charged that such discontent served as a major characteristic of the Placement Program. She argues that students felt controlled in every aspect of their lives and keenly used the program to access better education while resisting cultural impositions of the program. Most students, she contends, resisted assimilation. Dorothy Schimmelpfennig, "A Study of Cross-Cultural Problems in the L.D.S. Indian Student Placement Program in Davis County" (PhD diss., University of Utah, 1971).
43. Shumway and Shumway, *The Blossoming*, 111.
44. Lee, *Silent Courage*, 128.
45. Shumway and Shumway, *The Blossoming*, 170.
46. Latricia Charley, correspondence with author, November 16, 2009.
47. Ludden, "Navajo Indians and Mormons Remember."
48. Orlando Tsosie, interview by Jenny M. Smith, April 13, 1999, Logan, Utah, typescript, p. 3, Jenny M. Smith's Indian Student Placement Program Oral Histories, Special Collections, Merrill-Cazier Library, Utah State University, Logan, Utah (hereafter USU).
49. Charley, correspondence with author.
50. 1 Nephi 12:23.
51. Mormons were not alone in this conflation of cultural and spiritual expectations along a perceived linear progression that placed white society and Native American societies at opposite ends. Robert Berkhofer explained that "Christianity and civilization were unified in the minds of

missionaries." Berkhofer, "Model Zions for the American Indian," 188; J. F. Freedman, "The Indian Convert: Theme and Variation," *Ethnohistory* 12, no. 2 (1965): 125.

52. Dean Larsen, *You and the Destiny of the Indian* (Salt Lake City: Bookcraft, 1966), 13.

53. See also Whittaker, "Mormons and Native Americans," 34–44; Thomas W. Murphy, "Imagining Lamanites: Native Americans and the Book of Mormon" (PhD diss., University of Washington, 2003), 3; "Changes in Book of Mormon about Indians Causes Stir," Associated Press State & Local Wire, November 10, 2007.

54. 2 Nephi 5:20–21.

55. Alma 3:6; see also Mormon 5:15.

56. In 1981 the church changed the phraseology in the Book of Mormon from "white and delightsome" to "pure and delightsome," citing mistakenly ignored changes that Smith initiated in the 1840 edition. "Mormons No Longer Promise 'White' Skin to Indians," *Los Angeles Times*, September 30, 1981; Douglas Campbell, "'White' or 'Pure': Five Vignettes," *Dialogue: A Journal of Mormon Thought* 29, no. 4 (1996): 131–35.

57. Ludden, "Navajo Indians and Mormons Remember."

58. 2 Nephi 30:6; see also 3 Nephi 2:15–16.

59. Charles S. Peterson, "The Hopis and the Mormons, 1858–73," *Utah Historical Quarterly* 39, no. 2 (Spring 1971): 179–94; Rex C. Reeve Jr. and Galen L. Fletcher, "Mormons in the Tuba City Area," in *Regional Studies in Latter-day Saint Church History: Arizona*, ed. H. Dean Garret and Clark V. Johnson (Provo: Brigham Young University Press, 1989), 133–58. See also Scott Christensen, *Sagwitch: Shoshone Chieftain, Mormon Elder, 1822–1887* (Logan: Utah State University Press, 1999), 21–23, and Matthew Cowley and Wilford Woodruff, *Wilford Woodruff, Fourth President of the Church of Jesus Christ of Latter-day Saints, History of His Life and Labors as Recorded in His Daily Journals* (Salt Lake City: Bookcraft, 1986), 521–27.

60. John Dart, "'Curse' Idea Upsets Some Indian Mormons: But Many Are Converted Despite Dark-Skin Teachings," *Los Angeles Times*, February 10, 1979; also reprinted in *Window Rock (AZ) Navajo Times*, March 1, 1979.

61. Charles Wilkinson, *Fire on the Plateau: Conflict and Endurance in the American Southwest* (Washington, DC: Island Press, 1999), 60; "Mormons Altering Indian Prophecy," *New York Times*, October 1, 1981.

62. Gottlieb and Wiley, *America's Saints*, 174.

63. Spencer W. Kimball, *Conference Reports*, October 1960. See also Dart, "'Curse' Idea Upsets Some Indian Mormons."

64. Spencer W. Kimball, "The Day of the Lamanite," *Improvement Era* 63, no. 12 (December 1960): 922–23.

65. Eddie Brown, interview by author, April 27, 2009, Tempe, Arizona, in author's files.

66. Dart, "'Curse' Idea Upsets Some Indian Mormons."

67. Camille Bedoni [pseudonym], interview by Tona Hangen, August 11, 1991, Tuba City, Arizona, typescript, p. 15, in author's files.

68. Newsletter, LDS Placement Program, May 1968 (Salt Lake City: Church Indian Committee, 1968), HBLL.
69. Tommy Holtsoi [pseudonym], interview by Tona Hangen, August 5, 1991, Page, Arizona, typescript, pp. 12–13, in author's files.
70. Kimball, "The Expanded Indian Program," 938.
71. "LDS Indian Student Placement Program: Policies Regarding Requirements and Responsibilities," [n.d.], HBLL.
72. As quoted in Molly Ivins, "Mormons' Aid to Indian Children Preserved by New Law," *New York Times*, December 26, 1978.
73. Indian Student Placement Services Evaluation Study Summary Report prepared by Presiding Bishopric Research and Evaluation Services, May 1982, draft with no pagination, Mauss Papers.
74. Ibid.
75. Bishop, "Foster Parent Orientation Meeting."
76. Tim B. Heaton, Kristen L. Goodman, and Thomas B. Holman, "In Search of a Peculiar People: Are Mormon Families Really Different?," in Cornwall, Heaton, and Young, *Contemporary Mormonism*, 87–117.
77. Ibid., 97, 100.
78. Jan Shipps, "Making Saints: In the Early Days and the Latter Days," in *Contemporary Mormonism: Social Science Perspectives*, ed. Marie Cornwall, Tim B. Heaton, and Lawrence A. Young (Urbana: University of Illinois Press, 1994) 74–75.
79. Indian Committee Minutes, June 12, 1962, Church Archives.
80. *Foster Parent Guide*, 1965, p. 14, HBLL.
81. Erdman Jake, interview.
82. Melanie Sonni [pseudonym], interview by Tona Hangen, August 4, 1991, Page, Arizona, typescript, p. 5, in author's files.
83. Julius Ray Chavez, interview by Odessa Neaman, June 27, 1990, typescript, p. 9, Redd Center, HBLL; see also Roessel, interview, 11; Bedoni, interview, 16.
84. Anaba Becenti [pseudonym], interview by Jenny M. Smith, May 8, 1999, Salt Lake City, typescript, p. 5, Jenny M. Smith's Indian Student Placement Program Oral Histories, USU.
85. Polacca, interview, 6.
86. Beth Wood, "The LDS Indian Placement Program: An Educational System that Works," *Window Rock (AZ) Navajo Times*, September 28, 1978.
87. For example, see Roessel, interview, 7; Polacca, interview, 10; Sonni, interview, 4; "Indian Son," *Indian Liahona* (May/June 1971): 12. See also U.S. Senate, Hearing, 211, 458.
88. U.S. Senate, Hearing, 453; Bishop, "Indian Placement," 71.
89. Indian Committee Minutes, December 2, 1958, Church Archives; See also Bishop, "Indian Placement," 71.
90. U.S. Senate, Hearing, 204.
91. Dale Shumway, interview by author, June 18, 2009, Orem, Utah.
92. "A Father: 'Six + one = six,'" 29.
93. Celina Jake, interview by Jenny M. Smith, May 5, 1999, Ogden, Utah, typescript, p. 5, Jenny M. Smith's Indian Student Placement Program Oral Histories, USU.

94. Bishop, "Indian Placement," 107; see also Lenora Tsosie, autobiographical sketch; Bedoni, interview, 5; Shumway and Shumway, *The Blossoming*, 52.
95. Chavez, interview, 9.
96. Tso, interview, 2–3.
97. Roberta Bennally [pseudonym], interview by Tona Hangen, July 31, 1991, Ganado, Arizona, typescript, p. 8, in author's files.
98. Becenti, interview, 5.
99. Ibid.
100. Charley, correspondence; S. Fox to Paul Jones, September 24, 1958, Indian Placement Program Files, Church Archives; Chavez, interview, 9–10; Steamboat Branch Manuscript History, Aug. 13, 1969, Church Archives.
101. Shumway and Shumway, *The Blossoming*, 171.
102. Ibid., 74, 159, 189, 213; Kimball, "The Expanded Indian Program," 938; Chavez, interview, 11; Loretta Chino, Email correspondence, June 2009.
103. Shumway and Shumway, *The Blossoming*, 197.
104. Emily Benedek, *Beyond the Four Corners of the World: A Navajo Woman's Journey* (Norman: University of Oklahoma Press, 1998), 128.
105. Kay H. Cox, *Without Reservation* (Salt Lake City: Bookcraft, 1980), 4–5.
106. Dale Shumway, interview.
107. S. Fox to Paul Jones, September 24, 1958, Indian Placement Program Files, Church Archives.
108. "A Father: 'Six + one = six,'" 29.
109. Mary Helen Powell, "Room for Calvin," *Ensign* 3, no. 5 (May 1973): 61–62; Andrew Hamilton, "Their Indian Guests," *Saturday Evening Post*, September 17, 1960.
110. Janice Kapp Perry, "Shared Son," *Ensign* 10, no. 10 (October 1980): 44.
111. Shumway and Shumway, *The Blossoming*, 171.
112. Erdman Jake, interview.
113. Wauneka, interview, 13.
114. Cathy Bankhead, telephone interview by Lynette A. Riggs, October 25, 2006, as quoted in Lynette A. Riggs, "The Church of Jesus Christ of Latter-day Saints' Indian Student Placement Service: A History" (PhD diss., Utah State University, 2008), 159; M. Smith, "Beyond the Statistics: Indian Experiences in the Indian Student Placement Program" (Master's thesis, Utah State University, 2003), 28.
115. Indian Student Placement Services Evaluation Study Summary Report prepared by Presiding Bishopric Research and Evaluation Services, May 1982 [Draft with no pagination], Mauss Papers.
116. U.S. Senate, Hearing, 457.
117. J. A. Reyner, *Teaching American Indian Students* (Norman: University of Oklahoma Press, 1992), 16.
118. Dale Shumway, interview.
119. Cox, *Without Reservation*, 4.
120. Shumway and Shumway, *The Blossoming*, 197.
121. Ibid., 159; see also Becenti, interview, 6; Nora Begay, interview by Sam Myers, October 27, 1975, Provo, Utah, typescript, p. 9, Listening to Indians,

New York Times Oral History Program, Labriola Center, ASU; Orlando Tsosie, interview, 6.

122. Cox, *Without Reservation*, 4.
123. Chavez, interview, 10.
124. Celina Jake, interview, 3, 5.
125. Roessel, interview, 5; Erdman Jake, interview; Lee, *Silent Courage*, 147–48; Shumway and Shumway, *The Blossoming*, 159.
126. Orlando Tsosie, interview, 6.
127. Emery Bowman, interview by Deborah Lewis, January 27, 1990, Provo, Utah, typescript, pp. 15–16, LDS Native American Oral History Collection Project, Redd Center, HBLL.
128. Chavez, interview, 10.
129. Shumway and Shumway, *The Blossoming*, 74.
130. Donald Mose, interview by Jim M. Dandy, November 6, 1990, Provo, Utah, typescript, p. 6, LDS Native American Oral History Project, Redd Center, HBLL. See also Tsosie, autobiographical sketch.
131. Singer, interview, 10.
132. Andrew Hamilton, "Their Indian Guests," *Saturday Evening Post*, September 17, 1960.
133. Becenti, interview, 6; Erdman Jake, interview; Aneta Whaley, interview by Jim M. Dandy, November 15, 1990, Provo, Utah, typescript, pp. 7–8, LDS Native American Oral History Collection Project, Redd Center, HBLL.
134. Polacca, interview, 9.
135. Bedoni, interview, 10.
136. Tsosie, autobiographical sketch.
137. Lee, *Silent Courage*, 143–44.
138. Tsosie, autobiographical sketch.
139. Shumway and Shumway, *The Blossoming*, 213; see also the experiences of Frankie Gilmore, Allen Goatson, Roy Talk, and Jim Dandy in Shumway and Shumway, *The Blossoming*, 197, 189, 159, 74.
140. For example, see the experiences related in the interviews with Julius Chavez, Anaba Becenti, Lenora Tsosie, Ronald Singer, and Loretta Chino.
141. Indian Student Guide (Salt Lake City: LDS Social Services, Church of Jesus Christ of Latter-day Saints, May 1973), 2, HBLL.
142. For example, see Erdman Jake, interview; Celina Jake, interview, 2.
143. Benedek, *Beyond the Four Corners of the World*, 124–35.
144. Chino, correspondence.
145. Holtsoi, interview, 3.
146. Benedek, *Beyond the Four Corners of the World*, 124–35.
147. Chadwick, Albrecht, and Bahr, "Evaluation of an Indian Student Placement Program," 517.
148. Vanta Quintero, "My Happiest Year," *Relief Society Magazine* 52, no. 10 (October 1965): 734.
149. Roberta Bennally, interview, 5.
150. Schimmelpfennig, "A Study of Cross-Cultural Problems."
151. Charles Ainsworth, interview by Armand Mauss, May 15, 1986, Mauss Papers.

152. Dale Shumway, interview.
153. Cox, *Without Reservation*, 48–49.
154. Ibid., 83.
155. Hamilton, "Their Indian Guests."
156. Indian Student Guide, 4–5.
157. Chadwick, Albrecht, and Bahr, "Evaluation of an Indian Student Placement Program," 517.
158. For example, see Buchanan to Mr. & Mrs. Howela Polacca (parents), March 15, 1950, Indian Committee Correspondence.
159. ISPP Evaluation Study Summary Report.
160. Indian Committee Minutes, October 2, 1956.
161. Ibid., May 19, 1959.
162. Lee, *Silent Courage*, 124–35.
163. Ibid.
164. "Larry Tracy to Elder Packer, Elder Richards, Elder Kimball," Indian Committee Scrapbook, 1964, Church Archives.
165. Indian Committee Scrapbook.
166. Tona Hangen, "A Place to Call Home: Studying the Indian Placement Program," *Dialogue: A Journal of Mormon Thought* 30, no. 1 (1997): 63.
167. Philip Deloria, "Comment: Navajo Religious Encounters in the Twentieth Century," speech presented at the Organization of American Historians Conference, Seattle, Washington, March 27, 2009, in author's files.
168. Lacee A. Harris, "To Be Native American—and Mormon," *Dialogue: A Journal of Mormon Thought* 18, no. 4 (1985): 147–52.
169. Lee, *Silent Courage*, 162.
170. Irene Stewart and Doris Ostrander Dawdy, eds., *A Voice in Her Tribe: A Navajo Woman's Own Story* (Socorro, NM: Ballen Press, 1980), 33.
171. Buchanan, interview in Church Archives, as quoted in Gottlieb and Wiley, *America's Saints*, 166.
172. Beth Wood, "The Mormons and Indian Child Placement: Is Native Culture Being Destroyed?," *San Fransisco Wassaja* (March 1979): 7.
173. Benedek, *Beyond the Four Corners of the World*, 125–26, 129.
174. Nadine Sosie [pseudonym], interview by Tona Hangen, 1991, Utah, typescript, p. 8, in author's files.
175. Ibid., 9.
176. Ludden, "Navajo Indians and Mormons Remember."
177. For example, Julius Chavez commented, "You need to keep your head on straight and not lean too much one way or not lean too much the other way, but remain in the middle, learning good from both sides. You can use tools that you know from both sides." Chavez, interview, 12.
178. Christopher B. Balme, *Decolonizing the Stage: Theatrical Syncretism and Post-Colonial Drama* (Oxford: Clarendon Press, 1999), 8–11; Charles Stewart and Rosalind Shaw, *Syncretism/Anti-Syncretism: The Politics of Religious Synthesis* (New York: Routledge, 1994), 6–9.
179. Munro S. Edmonson, "Nativism, Syncretism, and Anthropological Science," in *Nativism and Syncretism*, ed. Munro S. Edmonson et al. (New Orleans: Middle America Research Institute, Tulane University, 1960), 192.

180. Ibid., 193.
181. Orlando Tsosie, interview, 15.

CHAPTER 6: THE PLACEMENT EXPERIENCE: BECOMING A LAMANITE
1. Spencer W. Kimball, "Lamanite Dreams May Be Fulfilled: Excerpts from October 1959 Conference Address, Elder Spencer W. Kimball," *Indian Liahona* 2, no. 4 (Fall 1964): 2–3.
2. Kimball, "Church Growth and Lamanite Involvement."
3. Larsen, *You and the Destiny of the Indian*; Arturo De Hoyos, *The Old and the Modern Lamanite* (Provo: Brigham Young University Press, 1970); Harris, "To Be Native American—and Mormon"; Mauss, *All Abraham's Children*; Boxer, "'To Become White and Delightsome.'"
4. Woods, interview, 7.
5. Benedek, *Beyond the Four Corners of the World*, 126.
6. Shumway and Shumway, *The Blossoming*, 251.
7. Lee, *Silent Courage*, 159–60.
8. Redhouse, interview, 4.
9. One 1973 study of Indian children in southern Utah found that Placement children enjoyed a more positive self-image than non-LDS Indians. Donald R. Lankford, William G. Matterfis, and Carolyn Carter Stueroke, "Paiute Indian Youth: The Values, Vocational Aspirations and Expectations of the Paiute Indian Youth Living in Southern Utah" (Master's thesis, University of Utah, 1973).
10. There is an obvious parallel here to the phenomenon of "ascetic Protestantism" in Protestant America. Max Weber, *The Protestant Ethic and Spirit of Capitalism* (Mineola, NY: Dover Publications, 2003), chapter 5 *passim*.
11. Gottlieb and Wiley, *America's Saints*, 168.
12. There may be some irony in the authorship of this manual. Howard Rainer, himself a Taos Pueblo, was also a product of the church Indian program and among the faculty at BYU. He illustrates the complex claims to Indianness encapsulated in this Lamanite trope that claimed authenticity through the historicity of the Book of Mormon. Howard T. Rainer, "American Indian Self-Image Workshop Manual" (Provo, UT: BYU American Indian Services and Research Center, [n.d]).
13. Holtsoi, interview, 13–14.
14. Ludden, "Navajo Indians and Mormons Remember."
15. Lynn Lilliston, "Southland Homes Aiding Indian Youths' Education," *Los Angeles Times*, September 10, 1969.
16. Spencer W. Kimball, speech to Indian students and missionaries, January 5, 1965, L. Tom Perry Special Collections, HBLL.
17. Lee, *Silent Courage*, 148.
18. For example, see Carole Croxton, interview by author, November 18, 2008, Phoenix, Arizona; Verenda Rainer and Ray and Nona Slim comments in Giles H. Florence Jr., "'The Best of Both Worlds,'" *Ensign* 20, no. 1 (January 1990): 59.
19. Sosie, interview, 16.

20. Kent Begay, correspondence with author, June 4, 2009, in author's files. See also Shumway and Shumway, *The Blossoming*, 97.
21. Ray Louis, "BYU Publication Denies Charges of Cultural Genocide in Off-Reservation Indian Education Programs," BYU *Universe*, reprinted in *Window Rock (AZ) Navajo Times*, June 20, 1974; Ramona Nez, interview by Sam Myers, October 25, 1975, Provo, Utah, typescript, p. 11, Listening to Indians, New York Times Oral History Program, Labriola Center, ASU.
22. Carole Sue Tsosie, interview by Georgia J. Brown, May 12, 1971, Brea, California, typescript draft, pp. 30–31, Center for Oral and Public History, California State University–Fullerton.
23. Kimball, "The Expanded Indian Program," 940.
24. Shumway and Shumway, *The Blossoming*, 172. See similar accounts from Kathy Watchman and Julius Chavez in U.S. Senate, Hearing, 459; Chavez, interview, 8.
25. Polacca, interview, 6; Bedoni interview, 7; Janice Kapp Perry, "Shared Son," *Ensign* 10, no. 10 (October 1980): 44.
26. The church launched the Family Home Evening program in 1965 and instructed families to gather on Monday evenings (or another night if necessary) to develop family bonds and build spiritual strength. Allen and Leonard, *The Story of the Latter-day Saints*, 599.
27. U.S. Senate, Hearing, 455.
28. Ibid., 461.
29. Tso, interview, 7; Polacca, interview, 7; see also Allen Goatson's comments in Shumway and Shumway, *The Blossoming*, 189; See also Laura Brown's comments in Ludden, "Navajo Indians and Mormons Remember."
30. Shumway and Shumway, *The Blossoming*, 221.
31. Chavez, interview, 10.
32. Richards, "Blessings and Promises to the Lamanites," 3–4; "A Latter-day Saint First," *Indian Liahona* (Spring 1966): 8; Bessie Spencer, "My Feelings of Being a Navaho," *Indian Liahona* 8, no. 2 (March/April 1971): 28.
33. Kimball, "Lamanite Dreams May Be Fulfilled," 2–3.
34. Stella Mosqueda Numkena, "For Indian Leaders," *Indian Liahona* 8, no. 5 (September/October 1971): 13.
35. Erdman Jake, interview.
36. Emery Bowman, interview, 18.
37. Chino, correspondence.
38. John L. Hart, "Former LDS Placement Students Hold Reunion," *Eagle's Eye* 13, no. 7 (November 1981): 4; Wilson Yazzie Deschine, interview by Matthew K. Heiss, April 30, 1992, Window Rock, Arizona, typescript, pp. 2–3, James Moyle Oral History Program, Church Archives.
39. Rhonda J. Lee, interview, 4.
40. Indian Student Guide, 2.
41. Carole Sue Tsosie, interview, 23.
42. "Lamanite Handbook," 38.
43. Ibid.

44. Singer, interview, 11.
45. "If You Have an Indian Student in Your Class, the Following Guidelines and Insights May Be of Help to You," [n.d.], HBLL.
46. Tsosie, autobiographical sketch.
47. Shumway and Shumway, *The Blossoming*, 205.
48. A. Theodore Tuttle, "Student Placement Program," *Improvement Era* (August 1968): 43.
49. Cox, *Without Reservation*, 16.
50. Newsletter, LDS Placement Program, October 1964.
51. Ibid.
52. Indian Student Placement Service Yearly Calendar, [n.d.], HBLL.
53. Emery Bowman, interview, 11.
54. Tso, interview, 7.
55. Harold C. Brown "Learning the Best of Both Worlds' Cultures," *Ensign* 5, no. 12 (December 1975): 22; U.S. Senate, Hearing, 204, 210.
56. Dale Shumway, interview.
57. LDS Social Services Indian Student Placement Services: Monthly Progress Report, Miles Jensen, Indian Student Placement Program, Church Archives.
58. Dale Shumway, interview.
59. Talk Given by Betty Redhouse in Sacrament Meeting at Fairfield, Utah, February 14, 1960, Church Archives.
60. Golden Buchanan, "The 'Outing' Program as It Has Developed," [n.d.], Indian Committee Correspondence, 1941–1952; Indian Committee Minutes, January 8, 1957, Church Archives.
61. Bruce R. McConkie, "Caste System," in McConkie, *Mormon Doctrine* (Salt Lake City: Bookcraft, 1966), 107–8.
62. "Spencer W. Kimball to 'Dear Brother,' Salt Lake City, May 19, 1962," in James D. Matthews, "A Study of the Cultural and Religious Behaviors of the Navaho Indians which Caused Animosity, Resistance, or Indifference to the Religious Teachings of the Latter-day Saints" (Master's thesis, Brigham Young University, 1968), Appendix; Spencer W. Kimball, *The Teachings of Spencer W. Kimball* (Salt Lake City: Deseret Books, 1982), 302.
63. Bishop, "Indian Placement," 70.
64. For example, see Sharon Mearbrick's comments in Ludden, "Navajo Indians and Mormons Remember"; see also Rosie Tsosie-Bingham, phone interview by author, June 11, 2009, in author's files; Carole Sue Tsosie, interview, 36; Singer, interview, 11.
65. Indian Committee Minutes, January 8, 1957, Church Archives.
66. Miles Jensen Reports, 1954–1955, Indian Student Program Files, Church Archives.
67. Ibid.
68. Indian Committee Minutes, January 9, 1959, Church Archives.
69. Ibid., December 15, 1959.
70. Ibid., February 16 and March 15, 1960.
71. Ibid., June 15, 1961.
72. Indian Student Guide, 2.

73. Indian Student Placement Service Yearly Calendar; Dale Shumway, interview; see also Lichai, interview, 5–6; Shumway and Shumway, *The Blossoming*, 172.

74. Roessel, interview, 7.

75. Cox, *Without Reservation*, 46.

76. Tso, interview, 6.

77. Whaley, interview, 7–8.

78. Erdman Jake, interview.

79. Stephanie Chiquito, interview by Jim M. Dandy, April 11, 1991, Provo, Utah, typescript, p. 4, LDS Native American Oral History Project, Redd Center, HBLL.

80. Glen E. VanWagenen, interview by Loretta L. Hefner, 1979, Salt Lake City, typescript, p. 7, James Moyle Oral History Program, Church Archives.

81. "Conferences Convene for Youth of the Church," *Eagle's Eye* 9, no. 6 (June 1978): 7.

82. "LDS Young People Confer at Center," *Window Rock (AZ) Navajo Times*, June 20, 1962; "Indian Youth Conference Set for Window Rock," *Window Rock (AZ) Navajo Times*, June 6, 1962; "Southwest Indian Mission Youth Conference," *Indian Liahona* 1, no. 3 (Summer 1963): 6–7.

83. Bishop, "Indian Placement," 98.

84. "Report to Indian Committee of Youth Conference, April 27, 1963, by the Indian Student Placement Program of the Church of Jesus Christ of Latter-day Saints," as quoted in Bishop, "Indian Placement," 98.

85. Indian Committee Minutes, April 8, 1965.

86. E. Mauray Payne, "Indian Youth Conference," *Indian Liahona* 2, no. 3 (Summer 1964): 2.

87. ISPP Newsletter, March 1964.

88. Payne, "Indian Youth Conference," 2; ISPP Newsletter, May 1964.

89. ISPP Newsletter, May 1965.

90. Indian Committee Minutes, June 8, 1965.

91. ISPP Newsletter, April 1966.

92. ISPP Newsletter, March 1967.

93. Shumway and Shumway, *The Blossoming*, 172.

94. ISPP Newsletter, March 1968.

95. Dorothy O. Rea, "All-Indian Youth Conference Held at BYU," *Indian Liahona* 5, no. 3 (Summer 1968): 19.

96. "All-Lamanite Youth Conference Held at BYU," *Indian Liahona* 6, no. 4 (July/August 1969): 27.

97. "Regional Lamanite Youth Conferences," *Indian Liahona* 7, no. 4 (July/August 1970): 26–27; see also "All-Lamanite Youth Conferences," *Indian Liahona* 7, no. 4 (July/August 1970): 29.

98. "Programs and Policies Newsletter," *Ensign* 1, no. 5 (May 1971): 76; "Lamanite Leadership Youth Conference," *Indian Liahona* 8, no. 4 (July/August 1971): 13.

99. Spencer W. Kimball, "Of Royal Blood," *Ensign* 1, no. 7 (July 1971): 7.

100. "Words of Wisdom from Lamanite Leaders," 16; Kimball, "Of Royal Blood," 3.

101. "Words of Wisdom from Lamanite Leaders," 16.

102. "Lamanite Leadership Awards," *Indian Liahona* 8, no. 4 (July/August 1971): 24.
103. "Lamanite Leadership Youth Conference," 20.
104. Becenti, interview, 7.
105. Shipps, "Making Saints," 74–75; see also the experiences of Clayton Long, Ralph Begay, and Romero Brown in Shumway and Shumway, *The Blossoming*, 108, 126, 149.
106. Lindquist, "The Indian Student Placement Program," 32–33; Chadwick, Albrecht, and Bahr, "Evaluation of an Indian Student Placement Program," 518.
107. Woods, interview, 9.
108. A variety of studies argue this point. For a full exploration of that assessment, see the following works: Clarence R. Bishop, "An Evaluation of the Scholastic Achievement of Selected Indian Students Attending Elementary Public Schools of Utah" (Master's thesis, Brigham Young University, 1960); Linda O. Wilson, "Changes in Scholastic Achievement and Intelligence of Indian Children Enrolled in a Foster Placement Program" (Master's thesis, Brigham Young University, 1973); Bert P. Cundick, Linda Wilson, and Douglas K. Gottfredson, "Changes in Scholastic Achievement and Intelligence of Indian Children Enrolled in a Foster Placement Program," *Developmental Psychology* 10, no. 6 (1974): 815–20; Lindquist, "The Indian Student Placement Program"; David R. Willmore, "A Comparative Study of the Religiosity of Navajo High School Students in Four Different School Settings" (PhD diss., Brigham Young University, 1974); George P. Lee, "A Comparative Study of Activities and Opinions of Navajo High School Graduates among Four Selected School Models" (PhD diss., Brigham Young University, 1975).
109. Lankford, Matterfis, and Stuercke, "Paiute Indian Youth," 55.
110. Mauss, *All Abraham's Children*, 134.
111. Ibid.
112. Harris, "To Be Native American—and Mormon," 143.
113. Leslie Ellis, correspondence with Lynette Riggs, July 26, 2009, as quoted in Riggs, "The Church of Jesus Christ of Latter-day Saints' Indian Student Placement Service," 153.
114. Behe Reck, correspondence with Lynette Riggs, July 26, 2006, as quoted in Riggs, "The Church of Jesus Christ of Latter-day Saints' Indian Student Placement Service," 168–69.
115. Ron Wipple to Brother [George] Lee, [n.d.], Placement Program files, Church Archives.
116. For examples, see Schimmelpfennig, "A Study of Cross-Cultural Problems"; Hangen, "A Place to Call Home"; Wauneka, interview.
117. Indian Committee Minutes, November 6, 1956; see also minutes from June 10, 1958.
118. Ludden, "Navajo Indians and Mormons Remember."
119. "Lamanite Youth Speaks," 39.
120. "Statement of Robert W. Barker, Special Counsel to the Church of Jesus Christ of Latter-day Saints," March 9, 1978, Indian Child Welfare Act of 1978, S. 1214 to Establish Standards for the Placement of Indian Children in Foster or Adoptive

Homes, to Prevent the Breakup of Indian Families, and for Other Purposes, Hearings before the Subcommittee on Indian Affairs and Public Lands of the Committee on Interior and Insular Affairs, House of Representatives, Ninety-Fifth Congress, Second Session (February 9 and March 9, 1978), 172.

121. J. Lynn Lee, "Mormon Defense," *San Francisco Wassaja*, April 1979.

122. Indian Student Guide, 5–6.

123. Bishop, interview.

124. Lee, *Silent Courage*, 152.

125. Carletta Yellowjohn, interview by Odessa Neaman, July 10, 1990, Provo, Utah, typescript, p. 6, LDS Native American Oral History Project, Redd Center, HBLL.

126. Cox, *Without Reservation*, 6.

127. Begay, correspondence.

128. Lee, *Silent Courage*, 152–53.

129. Chavez, interview, 13.

130. Emery Bowman, interview, 11.

131. Shumway and Shumway, *The Blossoming*, 90; Roessel, interview, 6; Bennally, interview, 10; Stewart and Dawdy, *A Voice in Her Tribe*, 11; Coombs, *Doorway Toward the Light*, 29–30.

132. Benedek, *Beyond the Four Corners of the World*, 125.

133. Lee, *Silent Courage*, 154.

134. Edwardo Zondajas, interview, Redd Center, HBLL; see also Wauneka, interview, 16.

135. Tso, interview, 4.

136. Paul Felt to Steward Durrant, August 8, 1967, Brigham Young University Institute of American Indian Studies Records, 1956–1972, HBLL.

137. Mitchel Kalauili, interview by Matthew K. Heiss, 1992, Tuba City, Arizona, typescript, pp. 8–9, James Moyle Oral History Program, Church Archives.

138. Lee, *Silent Courage*, 165.

139. Sosie, interview, 8.

140. Brian Begay [pseudonym], interview by Tona Hangen, July 18, 1991, Provo, Utah, typescript, p. 7, in author's files.

141. Lee, *Silent Courage*, 149.

142. Beth Wood, "The LDS Indian Placement Program: An Educational System that Works," *Window Rock (AZ) Navajo Times*, September 28, 1978.

143. Benedek, *Beyond the Four Corners of the World*, 125.

144. Loretta Chino, email correspondence with author, June 2009.

145. Sosie, interview, 9.

146. Becenti, interview, 7; see also Wauneka, interview, 20.

147. "Councilmen Comment on Mormon Placement Program," *Fort Hall (ID) Sho-Ban News*, January 23, 1985.

148. Lee, *Silent Courage*, 164.

149. "Hal L. Taylor, Southwest Indian Mission President to Mr. James Mathews, August 15, 1967," in Matthews, "Cultural and Religious Behaviors of the Navaho Indians," Appendix.

150. Natural Parent Guide, The LDS Indian Student Placement Program, June 1968, HBLL.

151. Indian Student Guide, 6.
152. Ibid.
153. Ludden, "Navajo Indians and Mormons Remember."
154. Indian Committee Minutes, May 18, 1966.
155. Indian Student Guide, 6.
156. Ibid.
157. Lee, *Silent Courage*, 167.
158. Cox, *Without Reservation*, 9.
159. Ibid., 11.
160. Benedek, *Beyond the Four Corners of the World*, 125.
161. Shumway and Shumway, *The Blossoming*, 98.
162. Redhouse, interview, 5.
163. Shumway and Shumway, *The Blossoming*, 221.
164. Sosie, interview, 7–8.
165. Ibid., 13–14.
166. Chino, correspondence.
167. Presiding Bishopric Research and Evaluation Services, Indian Student Placement Program Services Evaluation Study Summary Report, May 1982, draft, p. 221, Church Archives.
168. John P. Livingstone, *Same Drum, Different Beat: The Story of Dale T. Tingey and American Indian Services* (Provo, UT: Religious Studies Center, Brigham Young University, 2003), 75.
169. Lichai, interview, 7; See also Allen Watchmen's account in Shumway and Shumway, *The Blossoming*, 205–6.
170. "Leadership Opportunities Through Day Camp," *Indian Liahona* 8, no. 1 (January/February 1971): 31.
171. "Chinle Branch, Manuscript History, 1965–1983," no pagination, Church Archives.
172. Ibid.
173. "Sawmill Branch, Manuscript History," April 1969; July 12–13 and 18, 1969; and August 21, 1969, Church Archives.
174. Chester, interview, 6.
175. For example, see Steamboat Branch, Manuscript History, August 13, 1969, Church Archives.
176. Chino, correspondence.
177. Hal L. Taylor, "Summer Activities Are Successful," *Indian Liahona* 2, no. 4 (Fall 1964): 6.
178. "LDS Young People Confer at Center," *Window Rock (AZ) Navajo Times*, June 20, 1962; "Indian Youth Conference Set for Window Rock," *Window Rock (AZ) Navajo Times*, June 6, 1962; "Southwest Indian Mission Youth Conference," 6–7.
179. "Youth Conference Held at Tuba City," *Indian Liahona* 6, no. 6 (November/December 1969): 29.
180. "Lamanite Youth Attend Conference," *Indian Liahona* 7, no. 3 (May/June 1970): 33.
181. "Southwest Indian Mission Youth Conference," *Indian Liahona* 7, no. 6 (November/December 1970): 32.

182. Bishop Klien Rollo, "Southern Indian Regional Basketball Tournament," *Indian Liahona* 3, no. 4 (Summer 1966): 2.

183. Steamboat Branch, Manuscript History, July 24–25, 1969, Church Archives.

184. "Mormon Church in Navajoland: 20,000 Strong and Growing Fast," *Window Rock (AZ) Navajo Times*, July 27, 1978.

185. Clarence Bishop, phone interview with Lynette Riggs, October 4, 2004, as quoted in Riggs, "Indian Student Placement Service: A History," 173.

186. Ludden, "Navajo Indians and Mormons Remember."

CHAPTER 7: RIVAL IDEOLOGIES AND RIVAL INDIANS

1. Office of Indian Education Programs, BIA, *Report on BIA Education: Excellence in Indian Education through Effective Schools Process* (Washington, DC: Government Printing Office, 1988), 7; Hildegard Thompson, *The Navajos' Long Walk for Education: A History of Navajo Education* (Tsaile: [Navajo Community College Press], 1975), 127.

2. Ethel G. Young, "Navajo Children Seek Education," *Window Rock (AZ) Navajo Times*, January 1961.

3. Statute 2317, "An Act Relating to the Construction of School Facilities in Areas Affected by Federal Activities, and for Other Purposes," September 23, 1950, *United States Statutes at Large Containing the Laws and Concurrent Resolutions Enacted During the Second Session of the Eighty-First Congress of the United States of America, 1950–1951…*, vol. 64, part 1 (Washington, DC: Government Printing Office, 1952), 967–69; House Resolution 7940, "An Act to Provide Financial Assistance for Local Educational Agencies in Areas Affected by Federal Activities, and for Other Purposes," September 30, 1950, ibid., vol. 64, part 1, p. 1100.

4. Thompson, *The Navajos' Long Walk for Education*, 137; Young, *Navajo Yearbook*, 19.

5. The Chinle Boarding School opened in 1960 with space for one thousand Navajos in grade eight and above. It boasted thirty-four classrooms, a library, and special facilities such as a science lab, materials shop class, and a home economics classroom, as well as furnished bedrooms, private lockers, and community rooms for dorm students. "New Look in Education," *Window Rock (AZ) Navajo Times*, September 1960.

6. Thompson, *The Navajos' Long Walk for Education*, 147–49.

7. Ibid., 150.

8. U.S. Department of the Interior Bureau of Indian Affairs, *Report to the Senate Appropriations Committee on the Navajo Bordertown Dormitory Program by the Commissioner of Indian Affairs, February, 1965* (Washington, DC: Government Printing Office, 1965), 4–5.

9. "Youth Conference Opens with Flourish," *Window Rock (AZ) Navajo Times*, December 6, 1961.

10. Ibid.

11. Keeyah Sanford Begay, "The Navajo Youth Speaks: Education," *Window Rock (AZ) Navajo Times*, January 24, 1962.

12. "Letter to Parents of Off-Reservation Pupils," *Window Rock (AZ) Navajo Times*, April 1960.

13. Raymus Lee, "Navajo Youth Speaks: Recreation," *Window Rock (AZ) Navajo Times*, January 17, 1962.

14. "Boy Scouts," *Window Rock (AZ) Navajo Times*, November 1959. Mormons played a notable role in this movement—encouraged by Southwest Indian Mission president J. Edwin Baird—and by 1963 Mormon missionaries filled scoutmaster and/or assistant scoutmaster positions in some forty troops on the reservation. "Scouting and Youth Activities in the Indian Mission," *Indian Liahona* 1, no. 4 (Fall 1963): 11; see also "Scouting in the Southwest Indian Mission," Special Collections, HBLL.

15. "Fourteen Teams in Youth Leagues," *Window Rock (AZ) Navajo Times*, August 4, 1960; "Recreation Is a Great Need on the Reservation," *Window Rock (AZ) Navajo Times*, March 22, 1979.

16. "Tribal Council Supports Scouting for Navajo Youth," *Window Rock (AZ) Navajo Times*, January, 1960.

17. "Youth Government Model," *Eagle's Eye* 12, no. 1 (January 1980): 8; "Youth Affairs Office Programs Designed to Aid Youth," *Window Rock (AZ) Navajo Times*, August 2, 1979.

18. "Summer Student," *Window Rock (AZ) Navajo Times*, September 20, 1961.

19. "Indian Youth Uniquely Suited for Peace-Corps," *Window Rock (AZ) Navajo Times*, November 22, 1962.

20. Office of Navajo Economic Opportunity to the Advisory Committee of the Navajo Tribal Council, "A History and Semi-Annual Report: History, 1965 to 1968, Report, June through November, 1967," Labriola Center, Arizona State University.

21. Nancy Niere, "Crystal YCC Is More than a Summer Job," *Window Rock (AZ) Navajo Times*, August 2, 1979.

22. Broderick H. Johnson, ed., *Stories of Traditional Navajo Life and Culture* (Tsaile, Navajo Nation, AZ: Navajo Community College Press, 1977), 275; Young, *Navajo Yearbook*, 133; Garrick Bailey and Roberta Glenn Bailey, *A History of the Navajos: The Reservation Years* (Santa Fe: School of American Research Press, 1986), 264.

23. Young, *Navajo Yearbook*, 137.

24. Johnson, *Stories of Traditional Navajo Life and Culture*, 185–87.

25. *Window Rock (AZ) Navajo Times*, September 1960.

26. "Tribal Officials Break Ground for Shopping Center," *Window Rock (AZ) Navajo Times*, May 31, 1979; "Navajos Break Ground for Shopping Center," *Eagle's Eye* 18, no. 1 (Summer 1985): 3.

27. Deescheeny Nez Tracy lamented, "Modern conveniences give more leisure time today, and the people have become lazy," in Johnson, *Stories of Traditional Navajo Life and Culture*, 165. See also Kit Miniclier, "Stores Cater More to Navajos than Tourists," *Los Angeles Times*, July 28, 1986; see also Colleen O'Neill, *Working the Navajo Way: Labor and Culture in the Twentieth Century* (Lawrence: University Press of Kansas, 2005).

28. "Navajo Fair Queen Plans," *Window Rock (AZ) Navajo Times*, August 2, 1961; "Navajo Tribal Beauty Contest," *Window Rock (AZ) Navajo Times*, September 1960.

29. Johnson, *Stories of Traditional Navajo Life and Culture*, xi.

30. Ibid., 70–72, 158, 159, 165, 200, 227, 265; Nancy Niere, "Teenage Pregnancy Is 'Epidemic,'" *Window Rock (AZ) Navajo Times*, August 9, 1979.
31. Johnson, *Stories of Traditional Navajo Life and Culture*, 159.
32. Anne and Ken Mazlen, "Genocide in Navajo Land," *Akwesasne Notes*, September 1971.
33. Jimmie C. Begay, "Nature: The Core of Navajo Religion," *Window Rock (AZ) Navajo Times*, May 31, 1979.
34. "Chairman and Vice Chairman Speak," *Window Rock (AZ) Navajo Times*, May 6, 1965.
35. Abe Plummer et al., Ramah Navajo High School Evaluation 1971–1972, Research and Evaluation Report Series No. 05-A, unpublished report (May 1972), Educational Resource Information Center (ERIC) database, ED128128, p. 6, available online at: http://files.eric.ed.gov/fulltext/ED128128.pdf. See also Joal H. Spring et al., Ramah Navajo High School Evaluation 1972–1973 (May 1973), Research and Evaluation Report Series No. 05-B, Final Report, unpublished report, Educational Resource Information Center (ERIC) database, ED128129, available online at: http://files.eric.ed.gov/fulltext/ED128129.pdf.
36. "Ramah Navajos Start Own School," *Fort Defiance (AZ) Diné Baa-Hani*, April 1970.
37. "Ramah School: An Experiment in Education," *San Francisco Wassaja: A National Newspaper of Indian America*, September 1972; see also "Ramah Navajos Start Own School."
38. Thompson, *The Navajos' Long Walk for Education*, 177.
39. "Dibe Yazhe Ha Bitiin Olta: New Community Controlled School," *Diné Baa-Hané*, July 7, 1972; "Towards Greater Community Control at Rock Point," *Diné Baa-Hané*, July 7, 1972.
40. Thompson, *The Navajos' Long Walk for Education*, 177.
41. Johnson, *Stories of Traditional Navajo Life and Culture*, 177–78.
42. Ibid., 216.
43. Ibid., 189.
44. Clyde Warrior, "'Which One Are You?' Five Types of Young Indians," *ABC: Americans Before Columbus* 2, no. 4 (December 1964).
45. "Special Message to the Congress on Indian Affairs, July 8, 1970," *Public Papers of the Presidents of the United States: Richard Nixon, 1970* (Washington, DC: Government Printing Office, 1971), 566–67.
46. Brown, interview.
47. "Broken Treaties Trail Leads to D.C.: While Americans Vote Pan-Am Natives Ask for Justice," *Fort Defiance (AZ) Diné Baa-Hané*, October/November 1972.
48. "'Native People Get Divine Guidance to Ask Mormons for One Million Dollars," *Akwesasne Notes*, Late Autumn 1972; "Broken Treaties Trail Leads to D.C.," 6.
49. "Broken Treaties Trail Leads to D.C.," 6; "Native People Get Divine Guidance," 11.
50. "Native People Get Divine Guidance," 11.
51. "Mormons Assure Indian Militants on Aid by Church," *New York Times*, April 9, 1973; "Indians Plan to March Against Mormon Event," *Los Angeles Times*, April 8, 1973; "Locked Gates Meet March on Temple," *Salt Lake Tribune*, April

9, 1973; "Indians Ask Mormons for $1 Million Annually," *Los Angeles Times*, April 9, 1973.

52. "Indians Ask Mormons for $1 Million Annually," 22.

53. Church of Jesus Christ of Latter-day Saints, "Press Release: Statement on Indians, April 8, 1973," Armand Mauss Papers, Utah State Historical Society, Salt Lake City, Utah.

54. "Church Replies to Indian 'Challenges,'" *Salt Lake City Deseret News*, April 9, 1974; "Mormons' Program for Indians Stirs Controversy in Utah," *Washington Post*, April 26, 1974.

55. "American Indian Movement Group Continues Vigil at Temple Square," *Salt Lake City Deseret News*, April 5, 1974; "Church Replies to Indian 'Challenges.'"

56. "80 Indians Protest at Temple Square," *Salt Lake Tribune*, April 7, 1974.

57. "Indians Give LDS 7 'Challenges,'" *Salt Lake Tribune*, April 8, 1974.

58. "Mormons' Program for Indians Stirs Controversy in Utah."

59. "Church Replies to Indian 'Challenges.'"

60. Rainer, "An Analysis of Attitudes Navajo Community Leaders Have," 126.

61. Becenti, interview, 8.

62. Redhouse, interview, 4.

63. Lynne Hollisten, "Indian Education at BYU is finest in U.S.," *Salt Lake City Deseret News*, June 4, 1977. See also Paul E. Felt to President Hal Taylor and President J. Edwin Baird, June 15, 1965, Provo, Utah, HBLL; Letter from Paul E. Felt to President Ernest L. Wilkinson, January 3, 1967, titled: "Memorandum: A Brief Summary of BYU's Efforts to Educate the Indian," Brigham Young University, Institute of American Indian Studies, Records, 1956–1972, Special Collections, HBLL; Paul E. Felt to President J. Edwin Baird, December 29, 1964, Brigham Young University Institute of American Indian Studies Records, 1956–1972, HBLL; Lynne Hollisten, "Indian Education at BYU Is Finest in U.S.," *Salt Lake City Deseret News*, June 4, 1977.

64. Mark Stevens, "Utah University Gives American Indians a Chance to Learn," *Christian Science Monitor*, February 25, 1980.

65. Virgus C. Osborne, "An Appraisal of the Education Program for Native Americans at Brigham Young University, 1966–1974" (PhD diss., University of Utah, 1975), 60–61.

66. Ezequiel C. Sanchez, letter to the editor, *Window Rock (AZ) Navajo Times*, October 7, 1976.

67. For more information on romanticized notions of Manuelito, see Denetdale, *Reclaiming Diné History.*

68. Paul E. Felt, Director of Indian Affairs, BYU, to Elder Spencer W. Kimball, April 14, 1966, Brigham Young University Institute of American Indian Studies Records, 1956–1972, HBLL.

69. Ibid.

70. Paul E. Felt to Spencer W. Kimball, April 16, 1966, Ibid.

71. Ibid.

72. John Rainer, "Note on Uses of Lamanite Identity," Mauss Papers, Utah State Historical Society, Salt Lake City, Utah.

73. Ibid.

74. Ibid.

75. William Hartley, interview, August 29, 1985, Armand Mauss Papers, Utah State Historical Society; Eddie Brown, interview.

76. John R. Maestas, "Indian Week Keynote Address: Freeing Ourselves to Soar," *Eagle's Eye* 6, no. 4 (April 1976): 4.

77. Robert Raleigh, "Elder George P. Lee: Navajo General Authority Speaks on Self-Image, Discipline," *Eagle's Eye* 18, no. 2 (Winter 1985/1986): 21.

78. John R. Maestas, interview, Provo, Utah, October 27, 1975, Listening to Indians, New York Times Oral History Program, no. 85, Labriola Center, ASU.

79. Paul Felt, "The Promised Restoration: What and Why, June 9, 1964," in The Book of Mormon, the Lamanite, and Prophetic Destiny (unpublished collection of Paul Felt speeches, 1964), 14, HBLL.

80. Mark E. Petersen, *Children of Promise, The Lamanites: Yesterday and Today* (Salt Lake City: Bookcraft, 1981), 56.

81. Dave Clemens, "Mormon Tells of NIYC Views," *Provo (UT) Daily Universe*, May 1, 1972.

82. "Stanley Snake Elected NIYC President," *Eagle's Eye* 2, no. 5 (March 1972): 1. See also Stanley Snake, "BYU Indians Meet with AIM Leader," *Eagle's Eye* 3, no. 5 (January 1973): 1. Editorial, *Eagle's Eye* (April 1974): 2.

83. "And They Shall Blossom As Roses—Oh Really," *Eagle's Eye* 3, no. 2 (November 1972): 4; "Editorial," *Eagle's Eye* 4, no. 4 (April 1974): 2; Larry Schurz, editor, "Purpose of Eagle's Eye," *Eagle's Eye* 10, no. 1 (September 1978): 2.

84. Lawrence E. Cummins, "Hope for the American Indian?" *Ensign* 1, no. 7 (July 1971): 14.

85. Dennis Banks and Richard Erdoes, *Ojibwa Warrior: Dennis Banks and the Rise of the American Indian Movement* (Norman: University of Oklahoma, 2005), 110.

86. Brian Kelly, "Student Power at Santaquin," *New Era* 1, no. 1 (January 1971): 38–41.

87. Jeffrey L. Simmons, "Militancy and the Church," *Eagle's Eye* 7, no. 3 (March 1973): 2.

88. Ibid.

89. Rondo S. Hammon, Coordinator, Indian Student Services, to Royce Flandro, January 6, 1972, in L. Robert Webb, "An Examination of Certain Aspects of the American Indian Education Program at Brigham Young University: A Study Conducted by Robert Webb," 1972, Appendix C, HBLL.

90. "Boyd K. Packer to BYU Students During Indian Week, 1979," 10, Armand Mauss Papers.

91. Joane Nagel, *American Indian Ethnic Renewal: Red Power and the Resurgence of Identity and Culture* (New York: Oxford University Press, 1996), 169–73.

92. "Miss Indian America Warns Youth Against Militants," *Brigham Young University Today* (August 1971): 17.

93. Maestas, interview.

94. Ibid.

95. Rainer, "American Indian Self-Image Workshop Manual."

96. "Indian Panel on Alcoholism Is Moving Office to Denver," *New York Times*, September 13, 1972.

97. Victor Selam, "Don't Sit Under the Apple Tree," *Fort Defiance (AZ) Diné Baa-Hani*, October 19, 1971.

98. Ibid.

99. "Apples Control Schools," *Fort Defiance (AZ) Diné Baa-Hani*, September 12, 1970.

100. Daniel M. Cobb and Loretta Fowler, eds., *Beyond Red Power: American Indian Politics and Activism since 1900* (Santa Fe: School for Advanced Research Global Indigenous Politics, 2007).

101. Gottlieb and Wiley, *America's Saints*, 164.

102. Laura Briggs, *Somebody's Children: The Politics of Transracial and Transnational Adoption* (Durham, NC: Duke University Press, 2012), 72.

103. W. Blyer, "The Destruction of American Indian Families," in *The Destruction of American Indian Families*, ed. S. Unger (New York: Association on American Indian Affairs, 1977), 2–3.

104. Mary Crow Dog, *Lakota Woman* (New York: HarperCollins, 1990), 16–17.

105. David Fanshel, *Far from the Reservation: The Transracial Adoption of American Indian Children* (Metuchen, NJ: Scarecrow Press, 1972).

106. Bertram Hirsch, "Keynote Address," in *The Indian Child Welfare Act, the Next Ten Years: Indian Homes for Indian Children, Conference Held at UCLA Faculty Center, August 22–24, 1990*, ed. Troy R. Johnson (American Indian Studies Center, University of California, 1991), 23–24.

107. "Social Genocide," *Akwesasne Notes*, Early Summer 1974. See also "Why Must You Adopt Our Children?" *San Francisco Wassaja*, February 1977.

108. "Losing a Nation by Adoptions," *Akwesasne Notes*, Early Spring 1977.

109. "Mormons Steal Indian Children," *Warpath*, 1970, p. 6, HBLL; "Mormons Refuse to Release Navajo Baby," *Fort Defiance (AZ) Diné Baa-Hani*, June/July 1970.

110. Schimmelpfennig characterizes herself as a fifth-generation Mormon, and her graduate study prompted her to "look beyond the borders of Mormondom" to recognized the trauma inflicted by its Placement Program. Dorothy Schimmelpfennig, correspondence, November 30, 2007, in author's files.

111. Schimmelpfennig, "A Study of Cross-Cultural Problems," 35.

112. David Hill et al. "Declaration to the Mormon Church," leaflet statement of April 11, 1974, as quoted in Rainer, "An Analysis of Attitudes Navajo Community Leaders Have," 32–33.

113. American Academy of Child Psychology, "The Placement of American Indian Children: The Need for Change," adopted January 15, 1975, as quoted in Indian Child Welfare Act of 1977, U.S. Senate, Hearing, 110–21.

114. Steven Unger, ed., *The Destruction of American Indian Families* (New York: Association of American Indian Affairs, 1977).

115. "Social Genocide," 40.

116. "Secretariat to Administrator of the Interstate Compact on the Placement of Children, June 4, 1976," in U.S. Senate, Hearing, 464–65.

117. "Secretariat to Administrator of the Interstate Compact on the Placement of Children, June 4, 1976," in U.S. Senate, Hearing, 464–65; U.S. Senate, Hearing, 212, 435.
118. Ibid., 464–65.
119. Statute 1214, "An Act to Establish Standards for the Placement of Indian Children in Foster or Adoptive Homes, to Prevent the Breakup of Indian Families, and for Other Purposes," November 8, 1978, *United States Statutes at Large*, vol. 92, part 3, pp. 3069–78; Suzanne Garner, "The Indian Child Welfare Act: A Review," *Wicazo Sa Review* 9, no. 1 (Spring 1993): 48; Eve P. Smith and Lisa A. Merkel-Holguin, *A History of Child Welfare* (New Brunswick, NJ: Transaction Publishers, 1996), 269.
120. See *Arizona Dept. of Economic Security v. Mahoney* (1975) which explored parental rights severed between Indian mother and child on grounds of abandonment, neglect, and insufficient support; *Wisconsin Potawatomies v. Houston* (1973) challenge by Potawatomies to establish the tribe's right to determine custody of three orphaned children living off the reservation; *Wakefield v. Little Light* (1975) finding for birth mother and adoption of *Williams v. Lee* position that states may only intercede "where essential tribal relations were not involved and where rights of Indians would not be jeopardized"; and *Moore v. East Cleveland* (1977) which offered protection of extended family lifestyle from unwarranted intrusions by social workers; sanctity of the family extends to multigenerational family common to Indian communities.
121. U.S. Senate, Hearing, 567.
122. Ibid., 445.
123. *Fisher v. District Court* 424 U.S. 382 (1976).
124. Unger, *The Destruction of American Indian Families*, 85–86. See also Briggs, *Somebody's Children*, 84; Colleen Keane, "'Where Have All the Children Gone?' Controversy over Native Child Placement by Mormon Church," *Wassaja: The Indian Historian*, September/October 1982.
125. U.S. Senate, Hearing, 169–74.
126. Ibid., 192. Catholic Social Services representative Sister Mary Clare Ciulla also expressed her organization's resistance to any requirement that a young mother publically expose her otherwise secret effort to adopt-out her child without her own parents' involvement.
127. Ibid., 193.
128. Raleigh, "Elder George P. Lee," 20; "Mormons Appoint Navajo as Mission President," *Window Rock (AZ) Navajo Times*, May 22, 1975; "'Effective Leadership is Colorblind,' Ganado College President Declares," *Window Rock (AZ) Navajo Times*, April 25, 1974.
129. U.S. Senate, Hearing, 198.
130. Ibid., 195–207.
131. "Statement of Robert W. Baker, Special Counsel to the Church of Jesus Christ of Latter-day Saints," March 9, 1978, Indian Child Welfare Act of 1978 Hearings, 159–72.
132. Indian Child Welfare Act of 1978 Hearings, 79, 110.

133. Ibid., 111–12.

134. Statute 1214, *United States Statutes at Large*, vol. 92, part 3, pp. 3069–78; for a more complete study of the Indian Child Welfare Act, see Russel Lawrence Barsh, "The Indian Child Welfare Act of 1978: A Critical Analysis," *Hastings Law Journal* 31 (July 1980): 1287–1336.

135. Manuel P. Guerrero, "Indian Child Welfare Act of 1978: A Response to the Threat to Indian Culture Caused by Foster and Adoptive Placements of Indian Children," *Indian Law Review* 51, no. 1 (1979): 55.

136. Molly Ivins, "Mormons' Aid to Indian Children Preserved by New Law," *New York Times*, December 26, 1978; see also Rupert Costo, "The Mormon Church," *San Francisco Wassaja*, January/February 1979; Beth Wood, "The Mormons and Indian Child Placement: Is Native Culture Being Destroyed," *San Francisco Wassaja*, March 1979.

137. Martin D. Topper, "'Mormon Placement': The Effects of Missionary Foster Families on Navajo Adolescents," *Ethos* 7, no. 2 (Summer 1979): 142–60.

138. Abe Weisburd, "Indian Welfare: Mormons Exempted," *New York Guardian*, January 10, 1979; Stewart and Wiley, "Cultural Genocide," 152; Ivins, "Mormons' Aid to Indian Children Preserved by New Law"; Keane, "'Where Have all the Children Gone?'"

139. John Dart, "Indians Hope to Shift Mormon View of Their Skin Color," *Akwesasne Notes*, May 23, 1979; "Is the Placement Program Legal? Doing the LDS Sidestep," *Akwesasne Notes*, Winter 1978; Weisburd, "Indian Welfare: Mormons Exempted"; Wood, "The Mormons and Indian Child Placement."

140. Robert Gottlieb and Peter Wiley, "The Kids Go Out Navaho, Come Back Donny and Marie," *Los Angeles Magazine* (December 1979): 138–46.

141. George P. Lee, "The Mormon Student Placement Program," March 1980.

142. Stewart and Wiley, "Cultural Genocide," 82, 84, 152.

143. Keane, "'Where Have All the Children Gone?'"; "Cultural Thuggery: Native Culture Is the Loser to Missionaries and Non-Indian 'Tribes'," *Akwesasne Notes*, January 31, 1984; Michele Cutschall, "Lamanite Generation In Rapid City," *Rapid City Indian Country Today*, April 25, 1984; Vine Deloria, "Mormons Think Indians Are Dumb," *Rapid City Indian Country Today*, May 2, 1984; "Mormons to Modify Indian Youth Adoption Programs," *Rapid City Indian Country Today*, February 13, 1985; T. R. Reid, "Mormon-Navajo Adoption Fight Settled; White Couple Keeps Indian Child; Biological Mother Retains Rights," *Washington Post*, October 30, 1987; Ivins, "Mormons' Aid to Indian Children Preserved by New Law."

144. Cutschall, "Lamanite Generation in Rapid City." See also Thomas B. Rosenstiel, "Whites Adopt Navajo: Sovereignty on Trial in Custody Case," *Window Rock (AZ) Navajo Times*, February 11, 1987; Reid, "Mormon-Navajo Adoption Fight Settled"; Katherine M. Griffin, "Girl's Guardian Parents Forge Rare Kinship with Navajo Birth Mother," *Los Angeles Times*, May 15, 1988; Katherine M. Griffin, "Navajo Court to Rule: Girl in Custody Battle Arrives at Reservation," *Los Angeles Times*, April 16, 1988.

CHAPTER 8: DECLINE OF THE PLACEMENT PROGRAM, 1972–2000

1. Spencer W. Kimball to "Dear Brother," Salt Lake City, May 19, 1962, in Matthews, "Cultural and Religious Behaviors of the Navaho Indians," Appendix.

2. Jessie L. Embry, *In His Own Language: Mormon Spanish Speaking Congregations in the United States* (Provo, UT: Charles Redd Center for Western Studies, Brigham Young University, 1997), 59.

3. Ibid., 60.

4. President Paul E. Felt to Thomas S. Monson, September 9, 1972, Correspondence, Institute of American Indian Research and Services, Brigham Young University, HBLL; Felt, "I Remember When," 115.

5. First Presidency to BYU Stakes, Circular Letter, Sept. 28, 1972, Church Archives; First Presidency Circular Letter, October 10, 1972, Church Archives.

6. The irony of this policy change is that it occurred just as federal Indian policy transitioned in the opposite direction and began to support funding and programs to strengthen tribal institutions and Native peoples.

7. Lucile C. Tate, *Boyd K. Packer: A Watchman on the Tower* (Salt Lake City: Bookcraft, 1995), 131.

8. Ibid., 131–33, 162–64, 174, 181.

9. Richard O. Cowan, *The Church in the Twentieth Century* (Salt Lake City: Bookcraft, 1985), 169.

10. L. Brent Goates, *Harold B. Lee: Prophet and Seer* (Salt Lake City: Bookcraft, 1985), 363.

11. Cowan, *The Church in the Twentieth Century*, 312; Gottlieb and Wiley, *America's Saints*, 60.

12. Tate, *Boyd K. Packer*, 249; Philip L. Barlow, "Shifting Ground and the Third Transformation of Mormonism," in *Perspectives in American Religion and Culture*, ed. Peter W. Williams (Malden, MA: Blackwell, 1999), 149–50.

13. Tate, *Boyd K. Packer*, 136.

14. Ibid., 250.

15. For the purposes of this chapter, the General Welfare Committee and Executive Welfare Committee are glossed together as the Welfare Committee, though in truth the two meetings rotated with slight variances in membership. Barlow, "Shifting Ground and the Third Transformation of Mormonism," 150–51; David Albrecht, interview by author, June 17, 2009, Salt Lake City, Utah; Harold Brown, phone interview by author, July 30, 2009.

16. As quoted by Lee in "Lee Condemns Church Leaders," *Ogden (UT) Standard-Examiner*, September 2, 1989; also stated by Packer's good friend Dale Tingey who recalled Packer felt, "I don't have any special calling" for Indians, Dale Tingey, interview.

17. Indian Committee Minutes, June 8, 1965, and May 18, 1966, Church Archives; "Status Report on Indian Seniors, 1970," Indian Placement Program Records, 1955–1960, Church Archives.

18. Kimball and Kimball, *Spencer W. Kimball: Twelfth President of the Church*, 377–78.

19. Victor Brown Jr., interview, August 2, 1977, reference OH 373, James Moyle Oral History Program, Church Archives.

20. Garth L. Mangum and Bruce D. Blumell, *The Mormons' War on Poverty: A History of LDS Welfare, 1830-1990* (Salt Lake City: University of Utah Press, 1993), 193.

21. "Placement Program Part of Unified Social Services," *Indian Liahona* 7, no. 2 (March 1970): 28; M. Dallas Burnett, "Lamanites and the Church," *Ensign* 1, no. 7 (July 1971): 11.

22. Clarence Bishop, phone interview by author, July 15, 2009, in author's files; Albrecht, interview.

23. "Divisions of the Indian Program and Their Objectives," undated, Brigham Young University Records, Institute of American Indian Studies, HBLL. The report is undated, but contextual remarks suggest it was written between 1966 and 1969.

24. *Salt Lake City Church News*, February 27, 1971.

25. Ibid.

26. Clarence Bishop, interview, 1979, p. 7.

27. Ibid., 5.

28. Garth and Blumell, *The Mormons' War on Poverty*, 195.

29. Victor Brown, "An Overview of Church Welfare Services," *Ensign* 5, no. 11 (November 1975): 113; Bishop, interview, 2009.

30. Albrecht, interview; Brown, "An Overview of Church Welfare Services," 113.

31. Albrecht, interview; Victor L. Brown Sr., interview, 1985, pp. 8, 17.

32. Victor L. Brown Sr., interview, 1985, pp. 17, 28-29.

33. David O. McKay, Diary, May 30, 1967, as quoted in Gregory A. Prince and Wm. Robert Wright, *David O. McKay and the Rise of Modern Mormonism* (Salt Lake City: University of Utah Press, 2005), 156.

34. Shumway, interview.

35. Bishop, interview, 1979.

36. Shumway, interview.

37. "LDS Alter Indian Policy," *Salt Lake City Deseret News*, March 9, 1984.

38. Victor Brown Jr., interview, August 2, 1977, reference OH 373, Church Archives.

39. Jimmy N. Bennally, interview by Odessa Neaman, July 18, 1990, Provo, Utah, typescript, p. 3, LDS Native American Oral History Project, Charles Redd Center for Western History, HBLL. Victor Brown Jr. also commented that quotas drove enrollment until the 1972 policy change. Victor Brown Jr., interview, 1997.

40. Indian Committee Minutes, August 29, 1969, Church Archives.

41. "Southwest Mission History," Church Archives; Southwest Indian Mission, Historical Reports, 1978-1980; Arizona Holbrook Mission Records, 1970-1983.

42. Ibid.

43. Cox, *Without Reservation*, 74.

44. Mauss, *All Abraham's Children*, 98.

45. Barlow, "Shifting Ground and the Third Transformation of Mormonism," 150; Daniel F. Littlefield Jr. and James W. Parins, *American Indian and Alaska*

Native Newspapers and Periodicals, 1925–1970 (New York: Greenwood Press, 1986), 190.

46. First Presidency Letter, October 10, 1972, as quoted in Richard O. Cowan and Wilson K. Andersen, "The Living Church: The Unfolding of the Programs and Organization of the Church of Jesus Christ of Latter-day Saints during the Twentieth Century (Provo: Brigham Young University, undated manuscript [1971]), 477, HBLL.

47. Golden Buchanan, interview by William G. Hartley, April 1975, typescript, pp. 122–24, James Moyle Oral History Program, Church Archives.

48. Chris L. Jones, "Seminary for Six-Year-Olds," *Ensign* 5, no. 12 (December 1975): 21–22.

49. Indian Student Placement Program, 1959–1960, report, Indian Student Placement Program Records, 1955–1960, Church Archives.

50. Indian Committee Minutes, April 5, 1968, Church Archives.

51. Status Report on Indian Seniors, 1970, Indian Placement Program Records, 1955–1960, Church Archives.

52. Webb, "An Examination of Certain Aspects of the American Indian Education Program," 31, 61.

53. Rondo S. Hammon, Coordinator, Indian Student Services, to Royce Flandro, January 6, 1972, in Webb, "An Examination of Certain Aspects of the American Indian Education Program," Appendix C.

54. Herbert Yazzie, "Eagle's Eye Motivates Placement Students," *Eagle's Eye* 17, no. 3 (March 1985): 16–17.

55. Cundick, Wilson, and Gottfredson, "Changes in Scholastic Achievement," 815–20.

56. Wasatch Research Opinion Report, 1979, pp. 16, 21, 33, 125, Church Archives.

57. ISPP Evaluation Study Summary Report.

58. Ibid.

59. Bishop, interview, 1979.

60. Embry, "Lamanite/Indian Branches," 10.

61. David Albrecht, Placement Coordinator from 1982 through 1990, recalled that enrollment remained stagnant at two thousand students for many years. However, enrollment drastically declined no later than 1984. See Albrecht, interview; "A Conversation About Changes in the Indian Student Placement Service," *Ensign* 15, no. 10 (October 1985): 76.

62. Victor L. Brown Sr., interview, 1985, p. 34.

63. Quorum of Seventy member George P. Lee, excommunicated for teaching false doctrine about the role of Native Americans, claimed that Elder Boyd K. Packer was in charge of Lamanite programs after Kimball's death. See "Lee Condemns Church Leaders," *Ogden (UT) Standard-Examiner,* September 2, 1989.

64. Osborne, "An Appraisal of the Education Program," 39.

65. John R. Maestas, "New BYU Multi-Cultural Program Includes Indians," *Eagle's Eye* 10, no. 2 (October 1978): 1.

66. John Powless, letter to the editor, *Provo (UT) Daily Herald,* October 23, 1989.

67. "Boyd K. Packer to BYU Students During Indian Week, 1979," 8, Armand Mauss Papers.

68. Ibid.
69. "Boyd K. Packer to BYU Students During Indian Week, 1979," 13, Armand Mauss Papers.
70. Tuttle, "Student Placement Program," 43.
71. Mauss argues that the church was successful at education, but that was not its goal; the programs were failing to make self-perpetuating good Mormons who would raise up a succeeding generation of good Mormons. See Mauss, *All Abraham's Children*, 95–96.
72. "Indian Week Becomes Lamanite Week," *Eagle's Eye* 15, no. 2 (December 1983): 16.
73. Janice White Clemmer, "Native American Studies Programs," *Wicazo Sa Review* 2, no. 2 (Autumn 1986): 20.
74. Ibid.; Telephone interview with Janice W. Clemmer [former scholar with IAIS], by Armand Mauss, May 26, 1999, Armand Mauss Papers.
75. Clemmer, "Native American Studies Programs," 21.
76. Janice W. Clemmer, interview.
77. Stirling Adams, "'Y' Turns Back on Indian Education Program," *Student Review: BYU's Unofficial Magazine* 2, no. 8 (October 21, 1987): 1.
78. Powless, letter to the editor.
79. Tingey, interview.
80. "Black Awareness Week, 1993," *Eagle's Eye* 25, no. 1 (Winter 1993): 8.
81. Albrecht, interview; David A. Albrecht to Matthew Garrett, August 17, 2015.
82. "LDS Alter Indian Policy," *Salt Lake City Deseret News*, March 9, 1984.
83. Ibid.
84. "A Conversation About Changes in the Indian Student Placement Service," 76.
85. Ibid.
86. Albrecht recalled that enrollment was a little over two thousand for quite a few years during his administration. Albrecht,.
87. George P. Lee, "My Heritage Is Choice," *Ensign* 5, no. 11 (November 1975): 100.
88. William Hartley, interview; "Mormons Name Indian," *Los Angeles Times*, October 11, 1975. The entire multivolume interview appeared in Church Archives holdings in 2013 but remains inaccessibly "closed to research."
89. Patrick Christian, *Provo (UT) Daily Herald*, September 14, 1989.
90. George P. Lee, Letter 1, presented to the First Presidency and the Twelve, 1989, p. 2, Special Collections, Marriott Library, University of Utah, Salt Lake City.
91. Ibid., 2–4.
92. Ibid., 2–6, 12.
93. George P. Lee, Letter 2, Presented to the First Presidency and the Twelve, September 1, 1989, pp. 2–4, 8, Special Collections, Marriott Library, University of Utah, Salt Lake City.
94. Ibid., 19.
95. "Mormons Try to Soften Impact of Indian Leader's Forced Exit," *Spokesman-Review Spokane Chronicle*, September 10, 1989.
96. "LDS Church Announces Seventy Excommunicated," *Provo (UT) Daily Herald*, 1 September 1989, p. BA1.

97. "Lee Condemns Church Leaders," *Ogden (UT) Standard-Examiner*, September 2, 1989.

98. Ibid.

99. "Mormon Officials Excommunicate General Authority: Indian Calls Leaders Racist, Is Charged with Apostasy," *Salt Lake Tribune*, September 2, 1989.

100. "Church Explains Excommunication to Navajos as Lee Seeks a Rebirth," *Salt Lake City Deseret News*, September 9, 1989.

101. Ibid.

102. "Mormons Try to Soften Impact of Indian Leader's Forced Exit," *Spokesman-Review Spokane Chronicle*, September 10, 1989.

103. Powless, letter to the editor.

104. Indian Committee Minutes, September 18, 1962, Church Archives.

105. Marrianne Funk, "Settlement May Spell End of Two Programs," *Salt Lake City Deseret News*, September 30, 1992.

106. "Suit Seeks to Have 3 Navajo Students Admitted to School," *Salt Lake City Deseret News*, December 27, 1990.

107. Ibid.

108. Ibid.

109. Katherine Kapos, "Law to Cut School Funds for Out-of-State Minorities," *Salt Lake Tribune*, May 5, 1992; Reed L. Madsen, "Sevier Says Loss of Funds for Indian Education Would Cost Economy $1.2 Million," *Salt Lake City Deseret News*, January 29, 1992; Ron Hatch, phone interview by author, June 17, 2009.

110. Kenneth Brown, interview, 1997, Snowflake, Arizona, microfilm without pagination, reference OH 1619, James Moyle Oral History Program, Church Archives.

111. Dale Shumway, interview; Presiding Bishopric, Victory L. Brown, H. Bruke Peterson, J. Richard Clarke, to all stake, mission, and district presidents, bishops and branch presidents in the Western United States and Western Canada, February 28, 1979, Arizona Holbrook Mission Records, 1970–1983, Church Archives.

112. Marrianne Funk, "Settlement May Spell End of Two Programs," *Salt Lake City Deseret News*, September 30, 1992.

113. "Suit Seeks to Have 3 Navajo Students Admitted to School."

114. Kapos, "Law to Cut School Funds for Out-of-State Minorities"; Funk, "Settlement May Spell End of Two Programs."

115. Bishop, interview, 2009; Harold Brown, interview.

116. Lynette A. Riggs, "Indian Student Placement Service," 1; James B. Allen, "The Rise and Decline of the LDS Indian Student Placement Program, 1947–1996," in *Mormons, Scripture, and the Ancient World: Studies in Honor of John L. Sorenson*, ed. Davis Bitton (Provo: Foundation for Ancient Mormon Research and Studies, 1988), 85–119.

117. Kenneth Brown, interview, 1997, Snowflake, Arizona, microfilm without pagination, Reference OH 1619, Church Archives.

118. Kent Parke, phone interview by author, June 8, 2009.

119. Genevieve De Hoyos, "Indian Student Placement Services," *Encyclopedia of Mormonism*, 679; Kenneth Brown, interview; Parke, interview; Mary Nelson, phone interview by author, July 30, 2009, in author's file.

120. Harold C. Brown, interview.
121. Parke, interview.
122. Nelson, interview.
123. Dale Shumway, interview.
124. Parke, interview.
125. Peter Wiley, "The Lee Revolution and the Rise of Correlation," *Sunstone* 10, no. 1 (January 1985): 21.

CHAPTER 9: CONCLUSION
  1. Shumway and Shumway, *The Blossoming*, x. My own projection from the fragmented historical record rests at between 48,000 and 62,000.
  2. Albrecht, interview.
  3. Dale Shumway, interview.
  4. Redhouse, interview, 3.
  5. R. David Edmunds, "Moving with the Seasons, Not Fixed in Stone: The Evolutions of Native American Identity," in *Reflections on American Indian History*, ed. Albert Hurtado (Norman: University of Oklahoma Press, 2008), 37. See also Richard Alba and Victor Nee, *Remaking the American Mainstream: Assimilation and Contemporary Immigration* (Cambridge: Harvard University Press, 2003).
  6. Iverson, *Diné*, 64, 133–34.
  7. Bruce A. Chadwick and Stan L. Albrecht, "Mormons and Indians: Beliefs, Policies, Programs, and Practices," in *Contemporary Mormonism: Social Science Perspectives*, ed. Marie Cornwall, Tim B. Heaton, and Lawrence A. Young (Urbana: University of Illinois Press, 1994), 295. George P. Lee's dissertation thesis found that just 51.7 percent of former ISPP students lived on reservation and that 34.7 percent lived in urban areas. Lee, "A Comparative Study of Activities and Opinions," 121.
  8. Chadwick, Albrecht, and Bahr, "Evaluation of an Indian Student Placement Program," 518–19; Geraldine Taylor Lindquist, "The Indian Student Placement Program as a Means of Increasing the Education of Children of Selected Indian Families" (Master's thesis, Utah State University, 1974), 32–33.
  9. Chadwick, Albrecht, and Bahr, "Evaluation of an Indian Student Placement Program," 518–19.
 10. Orlando Tsosie, interview, 7.
 11. Elly Curley, letter to the editor, *Window Rock (AZ) Navajo Times*, October 12, 1978.
 12. Erdman Jake, interview.
 13. Gottlieb and Wiley, *America's Saints*, 169.
 14. Ray Baldwin Louis, "'It's Tough to Be a Good Mormon,'" *Window Rock (AZ) Navajo Times*, October 5, 1978.
 15. Lee, *Silent Courage*, 333–34.
 16. Spafford, interview, 222.
 17. Chadwick, Albrecht, and Bahr, "Evaluation of an Indian Student Placement Program," 519, 521.
 18. U.S. Department of Interior, National Park Service, "Environmental Assessment for the Navajo Generating Station Water Intake Project,

March 2005," ii, http://www.srpnet.com/about/pdfx/ngsintake.pdf; U.S. Department of Housing and Urban Development, Indian Housing Block Grant (IHBG) Annual Performance Report, 2009, Document 5 Navajo Housing Authority, 2009.

19. Wauneka, interview, 17–19.
20. Holtsoi, interview, 15.
21. Sonni, interview, 4.
22. Orlando Tsosie, interview, 8–9.
23. Wauneka, interview, 29.
24. Armand L. Mauss, "Refuge and Retrenchment: The Mormon Quest for Identity," in Cornwall, Heaton, and Young, *Contemporary Mormonism*, 25.
25. Keith Parry, "The Mormon Missionary Companionship," in Cornwall, Heaton, and Young, *Contemporary Mormonism*, 182–206.
26. Holtsoi, interview, 4.
27. Arnold Dinet Yazzie, interview by Michael N. Landon and Matthew K. Heiss, 1997, Window Rock, Arizona, microfilm, pp. 8–9, James Moyle Oral History Program, Church Archives.
28. Kalauili, interview, 8–9.
29. Presiding Bishopric, Summary Report.
30. Mary Jean Stevens, interview by Matthew K. Heiss in Crystal, New Mexico, 1992, typescript, p. 11, James Moyle Oral History Program, Church Archives.
31. Ibid.
32. Richard Kennedy, "First Native American Stake Organized: The Organization of the Chinle Arizona Stake Is a Landmark Event for LDS Native Americans," *Eagle's Eye* 24, no. 2 (Spring 1992): 15.
33. Ray Robert Mitchell, interview by Matthew K. Heiss, 1992, Tuba City, Arizona, typescript, p. 4, James Moyle Oral History Program, Church Archives.
34. "Proposed Chinle Arizona Stake Stats as of August 12, 1990," Church Archives.
35. Mitchell, interview, 5.
36. Kennedy, "First Native American Stake Organized," 15.
37. "Proposed Chinle Arizona Stake Statistics, of August 12, 1990," Church Archives.
38. Mauss, *All Abraham's Children*, 103.
39. David Eames, "Mormons Admit Closure of Church College Will Be a Loss," *New Zealand Herald*, June 30, 2006.

BIBLIOGRAPHY

BOOKS, ARTICLES, DISSERTATIONS, AND GOVERNMENT DOCUMENTS

Adams, David Wallace. *Education for Extinction: American Indians and the Boarding School Experience, 1875–1928.* Lawrence: University Press of Kansas, 1995.

Adams, Stirling. "'Y' Turns Back on Indian Education Program." *Student Review: BYU's Unofficial Magazine* 2, no. 8 (October 21, 1987): 1, 16.

Adams, William Y. *Shonto: A Study of the Role of the Trader in a Modern Navaho Community.* Washington, DC: U.S. Government Print Office, 1963.

Alba, Richard, and Victor Nee. *Remaking the American Mainstream: Assimilation and Contemporary Immigration.* Cambridge: Harvard University Press, 2003.

Alexander, Thomas G. *Mormonism in Transition: A History of the Latter-day Saints, 1890–1930.* Urbana: University of Illinois Press, 1986.

Allen, James B. "The Rise and Decline of the LDS Indian Student Placement Program, 1947–1996." In Bitton, *Mormons, Scripture, and the Ancient World.* Provo: Foundation for Ancient Mormon Research, 1998, 85–119.

Allen, James B., and Thomas G. Alexander, eds. *Manchester Mormons: The Journal of William Clayton, 1840–1842.* Salt Lake City: Peregrine Smith, 1974.

Allen, James B., and Glen M. Leonard. *The Story of the Latter-day Saints.* Salt Lake City: Deseret Book Company, 1976.

"All-Lamanite Youth Conferences." *Indian Liahona* 7, no. 4 (July/August 1970): 29–33.

"All-Lamanite Youth Conference Held at BYU." *Indian Liahona* 6, no. 4 (July/August 1969): 27.

Amerman, Steve. "Making an Indian Place in Urban Schools: Native American and Education in Phoenix, 1941–1984." PhD diss., Arizona State University, 2002.

Anderson, Benedict. *Imagined Communities: Reflections on the Origins and Spread of Nationalism.* London: Verso, 1983.

Anderson, Nels. "The Mormon Family." *American Sociological Review* 2, no. 5 (October 1937): 601–8.

"And They Shall Blossom As Roses—Oh Really." *Eagle's Eye* 3, no. 2 (November 1972): 4.

Arrington, Leonard J. "The Mormons and the Indians: A Review and Evaluation." *The Record* 31 (1970): 4–29.

Arrington, Leonard J., and Davis Bitton. *The Mormon Experience: A History of the Latter-Day Saints.* New York: Alfred A. Knopf, 1979.

Backman, Milton V., Jr. *The Heavens Resound.* Salt Lake City: Deseret Book Co., 1983.

Bailey, Garrick, and Roberta Glenn Bailey. *A History of the Navajos: The Reservation Years.* Santa Fe: School of American Research Press, 1986.

Balme, Christopher B. *Decolonizing the Stage: Theatrical Syncretism and Post-Colonial Drama.* Oxford: Clarendon Press, 1999.

Bancroft, Hubert Howe. *History of Utah.* San Francisco: The History Company Publishers, 1889.

Banks, C. Stanley. "The Mormon Migration to Texas." *Southwestern Historical Quarterly* 49, no. 2 (1945): 233–44.

Banks, Dennis, and Richard Erdoes. *Ojibwa Warrior: Dennis Banks and the Rise of the American Indian Movement.* Norman: University of Oklahoma, 2005.

Barclay, LeRoi Gardner, Jr., et al. "A Study of the Graduates of the Indian Student Placement Program of the Church of Jesus Christ of Latter-Day Saints." Master's Thesis, University of Utah, 1972.

Barlow, Philip L. "Shifting Ground and the Third Transformation of Mormonism." In Williams, *Perspectives on American Religion and Culture,* 140–53.

Barsh, Russel Lawrence. "The Indian Child Welfare Act of 1978: A Critical Analysis." *Hastings Law Journal* 31 (July 1980): 1287–1336.

Barth, Fredrik. *Ethnic Groups and Boundaries.* Boston: Little, Brown, 1969.

Basso, Keith H. *Wisdom Sits in Places: Landscape and Language Among the Western Apache.* Albuquerque: University of New Mexico, 1996.

Bates, Irene M. "Patriarchal Blessings and the Routinization of Charisma." *Dialogue: A Journal of Mormon Thought* 26, no. 3 (Fall 1993): 1–29.

Bates, Irene M., and E. Gary Smith. *Legacy Lost: The Mormon Office of Presiding Patriarch.* Urbana: University of Illinois Press, 1996.

Beeton, Beverly. "Teach Them to Till the Soil: An Experiment with Indian Farms, 1850–1862." *American Indian Quarterly* 3, no. 4 (Winter 1977–1978): 299–320.

Benedek, Emily. *Beyond the Four Corners of the World: A Navajo Woman's Journey.* Norman: University of Oklahoma Press, 1998.

Benedict, David. *A General History of the Baptist Denomination in America.* 2 vols. Boston: N.p., 1813.

Bennett, Kay. *Kaibah: Recollections of a Navajo Girlhood.* Los Angeles: Westernlore Press, 1964.

Berkhofer, Robert F., Jr. "Model Zions for the American Indian." *American Quarterly* 15, no. 2 (1963): 176–90.

———. *The White Man's Indian: Images of the American Indian from Columbus to the Present.* New York: Alfred A. Knopf, 1978.

Binney, Judith. *The Legacy of Guilt: A Life of Thomas Kendall.* Auckland, New Zealand: Oxford University Press, 1968.

Birch, John. "Helen John: The Beginnings of Indian Placement." *Dialogue: A Journal of Mormon Thought* 18, no. 4 (1977): 119–29.

Bishop, Clarence R. "An Evaluation of the Scholastic Achievement of Selected Indian Students Attending Elementary Public Schools of Utah." Master's thesis, Brigham Young University, 1960.

———. "Indian Placement: A History of the Indian Student Placement Program of the Church of Jesus Christ of Latter-day Saints." Master's thesis, University of Utah, 1967.

Bitton, Davis, ed. *Mormons, Scripture, and the Ancient World: Studies in Honor of John L. Sorenson.* Provo: Foundation for Ancient Mormon Research, 1998.

———. *The Ram and the Lion: Lyman Wight and Brigham Young.* Provo, UT: Foundation for Ancient Research and Mormon Studies, 1997.

"Black Awareness Week, 1993." *Eagle's Eye* 25, no. 1 (Winter 1993): 8–9.

Blackhawk, Ned. *Violence over the Land: Indians and Empires in the Early American West.* Cambridge: Harvard University Press, 2006.

Blyer, W. "The Destruction of American Indian Families." In *The Destruction of American Indian Families,* edited by S. Unger, 1–11. New York: Association on American Indian Affairs, 1977.

Bourdieu, Pierre. *The Logic of Practice.* Stanford: Stanford University Press, 1990.

Boxer, Elise. "'To Become White and Delightsome': American Indians and Mormon Identity." PhD diss., Arizona State University, 2009.

———. "'The Lamanites Shall Blossom as a Rose': The Indian Student Placement Program and Mormon Native Identity." Paper presented at the annual meeting for the Mormon History Association, Layton, Utah, June 8, 2013.

Briggs, Laura. *Somebody's Children: The Politics of Transracial and Transnational Adoption.* Durham, NC: Duke University Press, 2012.

Britsch, R. Lanier. "The Church in the South Pacific." *Ensign* 6, no. 2 (February 1976): 19–27.

———. *Unto the Islands of the Sea: A History of the Latter-day Saints in the Pacific.* Salt Lake City: Deseret Book, 1986.

Brooks, James. *Captives and Cousins: Slavery, Kinship and Community in the Southwest Borderlands.* Chapel Hill: University of North Carolina, 2002.

Brooks, Juanita, ed. "Indian Relations on the Mormon Frontier." *Utah Historical Quarterly* 12, nos. 1–2 (January–April 1944): 1–48.

———. *On the Mormon Frontier: The Diary of Hosea Stout, 1844–1861.* 2 vols. Salt Lake City: University of Utah Press, 1964.

Brown, Douglas Summers. *The Catawba Indians: The People of the River.* Colombia: University of South Carolina Press, 1966.

Brown, Harold C. "Learning the Best of Both Worlds' Cultures." *Ensign* 5, no. 12 (December 1975): 22–23.

———. "What Is a Lamanite?" *Ensign* 2, no. 9 (September 1972): 62–64.

Brown, James S. *Giant of the Lord: Life of a Pioneer.* Salt Lake City: Bookcraft, 1960.

Brown, Victor. "An Overview of Church Welfare Services." *Ensign* 5, no. 11 (November 1975): 113.

Burder, George. *The Welch Indians.* London: T. Chapman, 1797.

Burnett, M. Dallas. "Lamanites and the Church." *Ensign* 1, no. 7 (July 1971): 11–12.

Bush, Lester E., Jr. "The Spaulding Theory Then and Now." *Dialogue: A Journal of Mormon Thought* 4, no. 4 (Autumn 1977): 40–69.

Bushman, Richard L. *Joseph Smith and the Beginnings of Mormonism.* Urbana: University of Illinois Press, 1984.

Byers, S. H. M. "Recollections of Slave Days." *Annals of Iowa* 3, no. 4 (April 1897): 277–83.

Campbell, Douglas. "'White' or 'Pure': Five Vignettes." *Dialogue: A Journal of Mormon Thought* 29, no. 4 (1996): 119–35.

Campbell, Eugene E. *Establishing Zion: The Mormon Church in the American West, 1847–1869.* Salt Lake City: Signature Books, 1988.

Cannon, Brian Q. "Adopted or Indentured, 1850–1870: Native Children in Mormon Households." In Walker and Dant, *Nearly Everything Imaginable,* 341–57.

Cannon, Brian Q., and Richard D. Kitchen. "Indenture and Adoption of Native American Children by Mormons on the Utah Frontier, 1850–1870." *Common Frontiers: Proceedings of the 1996 Conference and Annual Meeting,* 131–41. North Bloomfield, OH: Association for Living History Farms and Agricultural Museums, 1997.

Cannon, Donald Q., and Lyndon W. Cook. *Far West Record: Minutes of the Church of Jesus Christ of Latter-day Saints, 1830–1844.* Salt Lake City: Deseret Book Co., 1983.

Carlton, Richard, et. al. *Education, Change and Society: A Sociology of Canadian Education.* Toronto: Gage Educational Pub., 1977.

Caswell, Henry. *The Prophet of the Nineteenth Century; or, The Rise, Progress, and Present State of the Mormons, or Latter-Day Saints: To Which Is Appended, An Analysis of the Book of Mormon.* London: Printed for J.G.F. and J. Rivington, 1843.

Chadwick, Bruce A., and Stan L. Albrecht. "Mormons and Indians: Beliefs, Policies, Programs, and Practices." In Cornwall, Heaton, and Young, *Contemporary Mormonism,* 287–309.

Chadwick, Bruce A., Stan L. Albrecht, and Howard M. Bahr. "Evaluation of an Indian Student Placement Program." *Social Casework* 17, no. 9 (November 1986): 515–24.

Chamberlin, J. Edard. "From Hand to Mouth: The Postcolonial Politics of Oral and Written Traditions." In *Reclaiming Indigenous Voice and Vision,* edited by Marie Battiste, 124–41. Vancouver: UBC Press, 2000.

Child, Brenda J. *Boarding School Seasons: American Indian Families, 1900–1940.* Lincoln: University of Nebraska Press, 1998.

Christensen, Scott. *Sagwitch: Shoshone Chieftain, Mormon Elder, 1822–1887.* Logan: Utah State University Press, 1999.

Christy, Howard A. "Open Hand and Mailed Fist: Mormon-Indian Relations in Utah, 1847–52." *Utah Historical Quarterly* 46, no. 3 (Spring 1978): 216–35.

Church Educational System. *Church History in the Fullness of Times: The History of the Church of Jesus Christ of Latter-day Saints.* Salt Lake City: Church of Jesus Christ of Latter-day Saints, 1993.

Church of Jesus Christ of Latter-day Saints. *2005 Church Almanac.* Salt Lake City: Deseret Morning News, 2004.

Churchill, W., and N. S. Hill, Jr. "Indian Education at the University Level: An Historical Survey." *Journal of Ethnic Studies* 7, no. 3 (Fall 1979): 43–58.

Cipolla, Craig N. *Becoming Brothertown: Native American Ethnogenesis and Endurance.* Tucson: University of Arizona Press, 2013.

Clark, James R. *Messages of the First Presidency of the Church of Jesus Christ of Latter-day Saints.* 6 vols. Salt Lake City: Bookcraft, 1966–1971.

Clemmer, Janice White. "Native American Studies Programs." *Wicazo Sa Review* 2, no. 2 (Autumn 1986): 19–23.

Clifford, James. *The Predicament of Culture: Twentieth-Century Ethnography, Literature, and Art.* Cambridge: Harvard University Press, 1988.

Coates, Lawrence G. "Brigham Young and Mormon Indian Policies: The Formative Period, 1836–1851." *BYU Studies* 18, no. 2 (Spring 1978): 428–52.

———. "Mormons and Social Change among the Shoshone, 1853–1900." *Idaho Yesterday* 15, no. 4 (Winter 1972): 3–11.

Cobb, Daniel M., and Loretta Fowler. *Beyond Red Power: American Indian Politics and Activism since 1900.* Santa Fe: School for Advanced Research Global Indigenous Politics, 2007.

Cogley, Richard W. "'Some Other Kinde of Being and Condition': The Controversy in Mid-Seventeenth-Century England over the Peopling of Ancient America." *Journal of the History of Ideas* 68, no. 1 (January 2007): 35–56.

Collier, Fred, and William S. Harwell. *Kirtland Council Minute Book. Salt Lake City: Collier Publishing, 1996.*

Conference Report of the Church of Jesus Christ of Latter-day Saints. Salt Lake City: Church of Jesus Christ of Latter-day Saints, 1890, 1897.

"Conferences Convene for Youth of the Church." *Eagle's Eye* 9, no. 6 (June 1978): 7.

"A Conversation About Changes in the Indian Student Placement Service." *Ensign* 15, no. 10 (October 1985): 76.

Coombs, L. Madison. *Doorway Toward the Light.* Washington, DC: U.S. Department of the Interior Bureau of Indian Affairs, 1962.

Cornwall, Marie, Tim B. Heaton, and Lawrence A. Young, eds. *Contemporary Mormonism: Social Science Perspectives.* Urbana: University of Illinois Press, 1994.

Corbett, Pearson H. *Jacob Hamblin, the Peacemaker.* Salt Lake City: Deseret News Press, 1952.

Corrill, John. *A Brief History of the Church of Jesus Christ of Latter-day Saints.* St. Louis: N.p., 1839.

Cowan, Richard O. *The Church in the Twentieth Century.* Salt Lake City: Bookcraft, 1985.

Cowan, Richard O., and Wilson K. Andersen. "The Living Church: The Unfolding of the Programs and Organization of the Church of Jesus Christ of Latter-day Saints during the Twentieth Century." Provo, UT: Brigham Young University, undated manuscript [1971].

Cowger, Thomas. *The National Congress of American Indians: The Founding Years.* Lincoln: University of Nebraska Press, 1999.

Cowley, Matthew, and Wilford Woodruff. *Wilford Woodruff: Fourth President of the Church of Jesus Christ of Latter-day Saints: History of His Life and Labors as Recorded in His Daily Journals.* Salt Lake City: Bookcraft, 1964.

Cox, Kay H. *Without Reservation*. Salt Lake City: Bookcraft, 1980.

Crow Dog, Mary. *Lakota Woman*. New York: HarperCollins, 1990.

Cuch, Forrest, ed. *A History of Utah's American Indians*. Salt Lake City: Utah State Division of Indian Affairs, 2000.

Culmsee, Carlton. *Utah's Black Hawk War: Lore and Reminiscences of Participants*. Logan: Utah State University Press, 1973.

Cummins, Lawrence E. "Elder George Lee: 'I Owe Every Opportunity to the Lord.'" *Ensign* 5, no. 12 (December 1975): 26–27.

———. "Hope for the American Indian?" *Ensign* 1, no. 7 (July 1971): 14.

Cundick, Bert P., Linda Wilson, and Douglas K. Gottfredson. "Changes in Scholastic Achievement and Intelligence of Indian Children Enrolled in a Foster Placement Program." *Developmental Psychology* 10, no. 6 (1974): 815–20.

De Hoyos, Arturo. *The Old and the Modern Lamanite*. Provo, UT: Brigham Young University Press, 1970.

Decker, Peter R. *"The Utes Must Go!" American Expansionism and the Removal of a People*. Golden, CO: Fulcrum Publishing, 2004.

Deloria, Philip. *Indians in Unexpected Places*. Lawrence: University Press of Kansas, 2004.

———. *Playing Indian*. New Haven: Yale University Press, 1998.

Deloria, Vine. *Custer Died for Your Sins: An Indian Manifesto*. New York: Macmillan Company, 1969.

Denetdale, Jennifer Nez. *Reclaiming Diné History: The Legacies of Navajo Chief Manuelito and Juanita*. Tucson: University of Arizona Press, 2007.

Deyhle, Donna. "Empowerment and Cultural Conflict: Navajo Parents and the Schooling of Their Children." *Journal of Qualitative Studies in Education* 4, no. 4 (1991): 277–97.

Dibble, Charles E. "The Mormon Mission to the Shoshoni Indians." *Utah Humanities Review* 1, no. 1 (January 1947): 53–73.

———. "The Mormon Mission to the Shoshoni Indians." *Utah Humanities Review* 1, no. 2 (April 1947): 166–77.

———. "The Mormon Mission to the Shoshoni Indians." *Utah Humanities Review* 1, no. 3 (July 1947): 279–93.

"Larry EchoHawk: Someone's Concerned about Me." *Ensign* 5, no. 12 (December 1975): 29–30.

Edmonson, Munro S. "Nativism, Syncretism, and Anthropological Science." In *Nativism and Syncretism*, edited by Munro S. Edmonson et al., 180–204. New Orleans: Middle America Research Institute, Tulane University, 1960.

Edmunds, R. David. "Blazing New Trails or Burning Bridges: Native American History Comes of Age." *Western Historical Quarterly* 39, no. 1 (Spring 2008): 6–15.

———. "Moving with the Seasons, Not Fixed in Stone: The Evolutions of Native American Identity." In *Reflections on American Indian History*, edited by Albert Hurtado, 32–57. Norman: University of Oklahoma Press, 2008.

Ellis, Clyde. *To Change Them Forever: Indian Education at the Rainy Mountain Boarding School, 1893–1920*. Norman: University of Oklahoma Press, 2008.

Embry, Jessie L. *In His Own Language: Mormon Spanish Speaking Congregations in the United States*. Provo, UT: Charles Redd Center for Western History, Brigham Young University, 1997.

Fanshel, David. *Far from the Reservation: The Transracial Adoption of American Indian Children*. Metuchen, NJ: Scarecrow Press, 1972.

Fanon, Frantz. *The Wretched of the Earth*. New York: Grove Press, Inc., 1963.

Farella, John R. *The Main Stalk: A Synthesis of Navajo Philosophy*. Tuscon: University of Arizona Press, 1984.

Farmer, Jared. *On Zion's Mount: Indians, Mormons, and the American Landscape*. Cambridge, MA: Harvard University Press, 2008.

"A Father: 'Six + one = six.'" *Ensign* 1, no. 1 (January 1971): 27–29.

Felt, P. E., and S. L. Tyler. "The Institute of American Indian Studies at Brigham Young University." *BYU Studies* 6, no. 1 (1964): 52–54.

Fixico, Donald L. *The American Indian Mind in a Linear World: American Indian Knowledge and Traditional Knowledge*. New York: Routledge, 2003.

———. *Termination and Relocation: Federal Indian Policy, 1945–1960*. Albuquerque: University of New Mexico Press, 1986.

———. *The Urban Indian Experience in America*. Albuquerque: University of New Mexico Press, 2000.

Florence, Giles H., Jr. "'The Best of Both Worlds.'" *Ensign* 20, no. 1 (January 1990): 58–62.

Foreman, Grant. "Missionaries of the Latter Day Saints Church in Indian Territory." *Chronicles of Oklahoma* 13, no. 2 (June 1935): 196–213.

Foster, Morris W. *Being Comanche: A Social History of an American Indian Community*. Tucson: University of Arizona Press, 1991.

Foucault, Michel. *Discipline and Punish: The Birth of the Prison*. New York: Pantheon Books, 1977.

Freedman, J. F. "The Indian Convert: Theme and Variation." *Ethnohistory* 12, no. 2 (1965): 113–28.

Fyans, J. Thomas. "The Lamanites Must Rise in Majesty and Power." *Ensign* 6, no. 5 (May 1976): 12–13.

Garner, Suzanne. "The Indian Child Welfare Act: A Review." *Wicazo Sa Review* 9, no. 1 (Spring 1993): 47–51.

Garret, H. Dean, and Clark V. Johnson, eds. *Regional Studies in Latter-day Saint Church History: Arizona*. Provo, UT: Brigham Young University Press, 1989.

Gentry, Leland H. "Light on the 'Mission to the Lamanites.'" *BYU Studies* 36, no. 2 (1996–1997): 227–34.

George, Dan. "My People, the Indians." *Dialogue: A Journal of Mormon Thought* 18, no. 4 (1985): 130–32.

Gibbons, Helen. *Saint and Savage*. Salt Lake City: Deseret Book Company, 1965.

Goates, L. Brent. *Harold B. Lee: Prophet and Seer*. Salt Lake City: Bookcraft, 1985.

Goffman, Erving. *Asylums: Essays on the Social Situation of Mental Patients and Other Inmates*. Chicago: Aldine Publishing Company, 1961.

Gottfredson, Peter. *History of Indian Depredations in Utah*. Salt Lake City: Shelton Publishing Company, 1919.

Gottlieb, Robert, and Peter Wiley. *America's Saints: The Rise of Mormon Power.* New York: G. P. Putnam's Sons, 1984.

———. "The Kids Go Out Navaho, Come Back Donny and Marie." *Los Angeles Magazine* (December 1979): 135–45.

Gowans, Fred, and Eugene Campbell. *Fort Supply: Brigham Young's Green River Experiment.* Provo, UT: Brigham Young University Publications, 1976.

Green, Arnold. "Gathering and Election: Israelite Descent and Universalism in Mormon Discourse." *Journal of Mormon History* 25, no. 1 (Spring 1999): 195–228.

Green, Doyle L. "Southwest Indian Mission." *Improvement Era* 58, no. 4 (April 1955): 233–35.

Grow, Matthew J., and Jeffery Mahas. "'As Soon as We Get Cousin Lemuel Converted I Don't Fear': Mormon Attempts at Indian Alliance in Nauvoo, 1844–1846." Paper presented at the annual meeting of the Western History Association, Newport Beach, California, October 18, 2014.

Guerrero, Manuel P. "Indian Child Welfare Act of 1978: A Response to the Threat to Indian Culture Caused by Foster and Adoptive Placements of Indian Children." *Indian Law Review* 51, no. 1 (1979): 55–77.

Gunn, Stanley R. *Oliver Cowdery: Second Elder and Scribe.* Salt Lake City: Bookcraft, 1962.

Gunnison, J. W. *The Mormons.* Philadelphia: J. P. Lippincott & Co., 1860.

Haig-Brown, Celia. *Resistance and Renewal: Surviving the Indian Residential School.* Vancouver, BC: Arsenal Pulp Press, 2006.

Hall, Gerald. "A Weekend Foster Parent Program Designed to Aid in the Development, Education, and Instruction of the Latter-day Saint Indian Youth Attending Federal Boarding Schools." PhD diss., Brigham Young University, 1970.

Hamilton, Andrew. "Their Indian Guests." *Saturday Evening Post*, September 17, 1960.

Hangen, Tona J. "A Place to Call Home: Studying the Indian Placement Program." *Dialogue: A Journal of Mormon Thought* 30, no. 1 (1977): 53–69.

Harris, Lacee A. "To Be Native American—and Mormon." *Dialogue: A Journal of Mormon Thought* 18, no. 4 (Winter 1985): 143–52.

Harris, William. *Mormonism Portrayed: Its Errors and Absurdities Exposed, and the Spirit and Designs of Its Authors Made Manifest.* Warsaw, IL: Sharp & Gamble, 1841.

Hart, John L. "Former LDS Placement Students Hold Reunion." *Eagle's Eye* 13, no. 7 (November 1981): 4.

Hartley, William G. "The Seventies in the 1880s: Revelations and Reorganizing." *Dialogue: A Journal of Mormon Thought* 16, no. 1 (1983): 62–88.

Heaton, Tim B., Kristen L. Goodman, and Thomas B. Holman. "In Search of a Peculiar People: Are Mormon Families Really Different?" In Cornwall, Heaton, and Young, *Contemporary Mormonism*, 87–117.

Hirsch, Bertram. "Keynote Address." In *The Indian Child Welfare Act, the Next Ten Years: Indian Homes for Indian Children, Conference Held at UCLA Faculty*

Center, August 22–24, 1990, edited by Troy R. Johnson, 23–24. Los Angeles: American Indian Studies Center, University of California, 1991.

Horsman, Reginald. *Race and Manifest Destiny: The Origins of American Racial Anglo-Saxonism*. Cambridge: Harvard University Press, 1981.

Howe, E. D. *Mormonism Unvailed; or, A Faithful Account of that Singular Imposition and Delusion from Its Rise to the Present Time*. Painesville, OH: E. D. Howe, 1834.

Hoxie, Frederick. *A Final Promise: The Campaign to Assimilate the Indians*. Lincoln: University of Nebraska Press, 2001.

"Indian Leaders Visit Church Headquarters." *Indian Liahona* 3, no. 1 (Winter 1965/1966): 1.

"Indian Week Becomes Lamanite Week." *Eagle's Eye* 15, no. 2 (December 1983): 15–16.

Iverson, Peter. *Diné: A History of the Navajos*. Albuquerque: University of New Mexico, 2002.

———. *"For Our Navajo People": Diné Letters, Speeches, and Petitions, 1900–1960*. Albuquerque: University of New Mexico Press, 2002.

———. *"We Are Still Here": American Indians in the Twentieth Century*. Wheeling: Harlan Davidson, 1998.

Jacobs, Margaret D. *White Mother to a Dark Race: Settler Colonialism, Materialism, and the Removal of Indigenous Children in the American West and Australia, 1880–1940*. Lincoln: University of Nebraska Press, 2009.

Jennings, Francis. *Invasion of America: Indians, Colonialism, and the Cant of Conquest*. Chapel Hill: University of North Carolina Press, 1975.

Jennings, W. M. "Carson Valley." *Nevada Historical Society Papers, 1913–1916*. Carson City: Nevada State Printing Office, 1917.

Jensen, Andrew. *Church Chronology: A Record of Important Events Pertaining to the History of the Church of Jesus Christ of Latter-day Saints*. 2nd ed. Salt Lake City: Deseret News, 1899.

———. *Encyclopedic History of the Church of Jesus Christ of Latter-day Saints*. Salt Lake City: Deseret News Pub. Co., 1941.

Jensen, Marlin K. "The Rest of the Story: Latter-day Saints Relations with Utah's Native Americans." *Mormon Historical Studies* 12, no. 2 (Fall 2011): 16–25.

Jensen, Richard L. "Transplanted to Zion: The Impact of British Latter-day Saint Immigration upon Nauvoo." *BYU Studies* 31, no. 1 (Winter 1991): 77–87.

Jessee, Dean C. "The Kirtland Diary of Wilford Woodruff." *BYU Studies* 12, no. 4 (Summer 1972): 365–99.

Jessee, Dean C., Mark Ashurst-McGee, and Richard L. Jensen, eds. *Papers of Joseph Smith. Vol. 2, 1832–1842*. Salt Lake City, UT: Deseret Book Co, 1989.

Johnson, Benjamin F. *My Life's Review*. Independence, MO: Zion's Printing and Pub. Co., 1947.

Johnson, Broderick H., ed. *Stories of Traditional Navajo Life and Culture*. Tsaile, Navajo Nation, AZ: Navajo Community College Press, 1977.

Johnson, Lane. "Who and Where Are the Lamanites?" *Ensign* 5, no. 12 (December 1975): 14–15.

Johnson, Melvin C. *Polygamy on the Pedernales: Lyman Wight's Mormon Villages in Antebellum Texas, 1845–1858*. Logan: Utah State University Press, 2006.

Jones, Chris L. "Seminary for Six-Year-Olds." *Ensign* 5, no. 12 (December 1975): 21–22.

Jones, Sondra. "Saints or Sinners." *Utah Historical Quarterly* 72, no. 1 (2004): 19–46.

Josephy, Alvin M., Joane Nagel, and Troy R. Johnson. *Red Power: The American Indians' Fight for Freedom*. Lincoln: University of Nebraska, 1999.

Kelley, Klara Bonsack, and Harris Francis. *Navajo Sacred Places*. Bloomington: Indiana University Press, 1994.

Kelly, Brian. "Student Power at Santaquin." *New Era* 1, no. 1 (January 1971): 38–41.

Kennedy, Richard. "First Native American Stake Organized: The Organization of the Chinle Arizona Stake Is a Landmark Event for LDS Native Americans." *Eagle's Eye* 24, no. 2 (Spring 1992): 15–16.

Kidder, Daniel P. *Mormonism and the Mormons: A Historical View of the Rise and Progress of the Sect Self-Styled Latter-Day Saints*. New York: G. Lane and P. P. Sandford, for the Methodist Episcopal Church, 1842.

Kimball, Edward L. *Lengthen Your Stride: The Presidency of Spencer W. Kimball*. Salt Lake City: Deseret Book, 2005.

Kimball, Edward L., and Andrew E. Kimball. *Spencer W. Kimball: The Early and Apostolic Years*. Salt Lake City: Deseret Book, 2006.

———. *Spencer W. Kimball: Twelfth President of the Church of Jesus Christ of Latter-day Saints*. Salt Lake City: Bookcraft, 1977.

Kimball, Spencer W. "Church Growth and Lamanite Involvement." Speech given at Brigham Young University, November 7, 1972.

———. *Conference Report, April, 1949*. Online at gospelink.com.

———. "The Day of the Lamanite." *Improvement Era* 63, no. 12 (December 1960): 922–25.

———. "The Day of the Lamanite Is Now." *Improvement Era* 71, no. 8 (August 1968): 37–38.

———. "The Expanded Indian Program." *Improvement Era* 59, no. 12 (December 1956): 937–40.

———. "Lamanite Dreams May Be Fulfilled: Excerpts from October 1959 Conference Address, Elder Spencer W. Kimball." *Indian Liahona* 2, no. 4 (Fall 1964): 2–3.

———. "The Navajo…His Predicament." *Improvement Era* 51, no. 2 (February 1948): 76–80.

———. "The Navajo…His Predicament." *Improvement Era* 51, no. 4 (April 1948): 210–12.

———. "Our Paths Have Met Again." *Ensign* 5, no. 12 (December 1975): 2–7.

———. "Of Royal Blood." *Ensign* 1, no. 7 (July 1971): 3–7.

———. *The Teachings of Spencer W. Kimball*. Salt Lake City: Deseret Books, 1982.

Kitchen, Richard. "Mormon-Indian Relations in Deseret: Intermarriage and Indenture, 1847–1877." PhD diss., Arizona State University, 2002.

Knowles, Lloyd Alan. "The Appeal and Course of Christian Restorationism on the Early Nineteenth Century American Frontier—with a Focus on Sidney Rigdon as a Case Study." PhD diss., Michigan State University, 2000.

Krug, J. A. *The Navajo: A Long-Range Program for Navajo Rehabilitation.* Washington, DC: U.S. Government Printing Office, 1948.

"Lamanite Leadership Awards." *Indian Liahona* 8, no. 4 (July/August 1971): 24.

"Lamanite Leadership Youth Conference." *Indian Liahona* 8, no. 4 (July/August 1971): 13–20.

"Lamanite Youth Attend Conference." *Indian Liahona* 7, no. 3 (May/June 1970): 33.

"Lamanite Youth Speaks." *Improvement Era* 71, no. 8 (August 1968): 39.

Lankford, Donald R., William G. Matterfis, and Carolyn Carter Stueroke. "Paiute Indian Youth: The Values, Vocational Aspirations and Expectations of the Paiute Indian Youth Living in Southern Utah." Master's thesis, University of Utah, 1973.

Larsen, Dean L. *American Indians Today.* Provo: Brigham Young University, 1965.

———. "Mingled Destinies: The Lamanites and the Latter-day Saints." *Ensign* 5, no. 12 (December 1975): 8–14.

———. *You and the Destiny of the Indian.* Salt Lake City: Bookcraft, 1966.

Larson, Nadine. *Listen to the Song of Israel: The Missionary Labors of George R. Bloomfield.* Privately printed, 1960.

Law, Wesley R. "Mormon Indian Missions, 1855." Master's thesis, Brigham Young University, 1959.

"Leadership Opportunities Through Day Camp." *Indian Liahona* 8, no. 1 (January/February 1971): 31.

Lee, George P. "A Comparative Study of Activities and Opinions of Navajo High School Graduates among Four Selected School Models." PhD diss., Brigham Young University, 1975.

———. "My Heritage Is Choice." *Ensign* 5, no. 11 (November 1975): 100–101.

———. *Silent Courage: An Indian Story.* Salt Lake City: Deseret Book Company, 1987.

Lee, Jerry. "A Study of the Influence of the Mormon Church on the Catawba Indians of South Carolina, 1882–1975." Master's thesis, Brigham Young University, 1976.

Lewis, C. S. *Perelandra.* New York: Macmillan, 1944.

Lindquist, Geraldine Taylor. "The Indian Student Placement Program as a Means of Increasing the Education of Children of Selected Indian Families." Master's thesis, Utah State University, 1974.

Linn, William Alexander. *The Story of the Mormons.* New York: Russell and Russell, 1963.

Little, James A. *Jacob Hamblin.* Salt Lake City: Deseret News Publishing Co., 1909.

Littlefield, Daniel F., Jr., and James W. Parins. *American Indian and Alaska Native Newspapers and Periodicals, 1925–1970.* New York: Greenwood Press, 1986.

Livingstone, John P. *Same Drum, Different Beat: The Story of Dale T. Tingey and American Indian Services.* Provo, UT: Religious Studies Center, Brigham Young University, 2003.

Lobo, Susan, ed. *American Indians and the Urban Indian Experience*. Los Angeles: American Indian Studies Center, University of California, 1998.

Lockard, Louise. "New Paper Words: Historical Images of Navajo Language Literacy." *American Indian Quarterly* 19, no. 1 (Winter 1995): 17–30.

Logue, Larry M. "Modernization Arrested: Child Naming and the Family in a Utah Town." *The Journal of American History* 74, no. 1 (June 1987): 131–38.

Lomawaima, Tsianina. *They Called It Prairie Light: The Story of Chilocco Indian School*. Lincoln: University of Nebraska Press, 1994.

Ludden, Jennifer. "Navajo Indians and Mormons Remember Their Involvement in Program Placing Indian Children with Mormon Families." National Public Radio, January 23, 2005. Transcript available online at Lexisnexis.com.

Ludlow, Daniel H., ed. *Encyclopedia of Mormonism*. New York: MacMillian, 1992.

Lyman, Melvin A. *Out of Obscurity into Light*. Salt Lake City: Albany Book, 1985.

Madsen, Brigham D. *The Northern Shoshoni*. Caldwell, ID: Caxton Printers, 1980.

Maestas, John R. "Indian Week Keynote Address: Freeing Ourselves to Soar." *Eagle's Eye* 6, no. 4 (April 1976): 4.

——. "New BYU Multi-Cultural Program Includes Indians." *Eagle's Eye* 10, no. 2 (October 1978): 1–2.

Mangum, Garth L., and Bruce D. Blumell. *The Mormons' War on Poverty: A History of LDS Welfare, 1830–1990*. Salt Lake City: University of Utah Press, 1993.

Marquardt, Michael. *The Rise of Mormonism, 1816–1848*. Longwood, FL: Xulon Press, 2005.

Martin, Calvin. "Ethnohistory: A Better Way to Write Indian History." *Western Historical Quarterly* 9, no. 1 (January 1978): 41–56.

Matthews, James D. "A Study of the Cultural and Religious Behaviors of the Navaho Indians which Caused Animosity, Resistance, or Indifference to the Religious Teachings of the Latter-day Saints." Master's thesis, Brigham Young University, 1968.

Mauss, Armand L. *All Abraham's Children: Changing Mormon Conceptions of Race and Lineage*. Urbana: University of Illinois Press, 2003.

——. *The Angel and the Beehive: The Mormon Struggle with Assimilation*. Urbana: University of Illinois Press, 1994.

——. "Mormonism's Worldwide Aspirations and Its Changing Concept of Race." *Dialogue: A Journal of Mormon Thought* 34, nos. 3–4 (Fall/Winter 2001): 103–33.

——. "Refuge and Retrenchment: The Mormon Quest for Identity." In Cornwall, Heaton, and Young, *Contemporary Mormonism*, 24–42.

——. "Sociological Perspectives on the Mormon Subculture." *Annual Review of Sociology* 10 (1984): 437–60.

May, Dean L., and Reid L. Neilson. *The Mormon History Association's Tanner Lectures: The First Twenty Years*. Urbana: University of Illinois, 2006.

McCarty, Teresa L. *A Place to Be Navajo: Rough Rock and the Struggle for Self-Determination in Indigenous Schooling*. Mahwah, NJ: Lawrence Erlbaum Associates, Publishers, 2002.

——. "Bilingual-Bicultural Education in a Navajo Community." PhD diss., Arizona State University, 1984.

McClellan, Richard. "Sidney Rigdon's 1820 Ministry: Preparing the Way for Mormonism in Ohio." *Dialogue: A Journal of Mormon Thought* 36, no. 4 (Winter 2003): 153–54.

McConkie, Bruce R. *Mormon Doctrine.* Salt Lake City: Bookcraft, 1966.

McKiernan, F. Mark. *The Voice of One Crying in the Wilderness: Sidney Rigdon, Religious Reformer, 1793–1876.* Lawrence, KS: Coronado Press, 1971.

McPherson, Robert. *Dineji Na'Nitin: Navajo Traditional Teachings and History.* Boulder: University Press of Colorado, 2012.

McPherson, Robert S., Jim Dandy, and Sarah E. Burak. *Navajo Tradition, Mormon Life: The Autobiography and Teachings of Jim Dandy.* Salt Lake City: University of Utah Press, 2012.

Memmi, Albert. *The Colonizer and the Colonized.* New York: Orion Press, 1965.

Meriam, Lewis. *The Problem of Indian Administration: Report of a Survey Made at the Request of Hubert Work, Secretary of the Interior, and Submitted to Him, February 21, 1928.* Baltimore: Johns Hopkins Press, 1928.

Metcalf, R. Warren. "A Precarious Balance: The Northern Utes and the Black Hawk War." *Utah Historical Quarterly* 57, no. 1 (Winter 1989): 24–35.

———. *Termination's Legacy: The Discarded Indians of Utah.* Lincoln: University of Nebraska Press, 2002.

Milner, Clyde A., II, and Floyd A. O'Neil. *The Churchmen and the Western Indians, 1820–1920.* Norman: University of Oklahoma Press, 1985.

"Miss Indian America Warns Youth Against Militants." *Brigham Young University Today* (August 1971): 17.

Montagu, Ashley. *Man's Most Dangerous Myth: The Fallacy of Race.* New York: Columbia University Press, 1942.

Morgan, Brandon. "Educating the Lamanites: A Brief History of the LDS Indian Student Placement Program." *Journal of Mormon History* 35, no. 4 (Fall 2009): 191–217.

Muhlestein, Robert M. "Utah Indians and the Indian Slave Trade: The Mormon Adoption Program and Its Effect on the Indian Slaves." Master's thesis, Brigham Young University, 1991.

Murphy, Thomas W. "Imagining Lamanites: Native Americans and the Book of Mormon." PhD diss., University of Washington, 2003.

Nagel, Joane. *American Ethnic Renewal: Red Power and the Resurgence of Identity and Culture.* New York: Oxford University Press, 1996.

Nasatir, Abraham P. *Before Lewis and Clark: Documents Illustrating the History of the Missouri, 1785–1804.* St. Louis: St. Louis Historical Documents Foundation, 1952.

Nakai, Raymond. "Will We Meet the Challenge?" *Journal of American Indian Education* 4, no. 1 (October 1964): 10–16.

"Navajos Break Ground for Shopping Center." *Eagle's Eye* 18, no. 1 (Summer 1985): 3.

Neff, Andrew. *History of Utah, 1847–1869.* Salt Lake City: Deseret News Press, 1940.

Nixon, Richard. *Public Papers of the Presidents of the United States: Richard Nixon, 1970.* Washington, DC: Government Printing Office, 1971.

Numkena, Stella Mosqueda. "For Indian Leaders." *Indian Liahona* 8, no. 5 (September/October 1971): 13.

Office of Indian Education Programs, Bureau of Indian Affairs. "Report on BIA Education: Excellence in Indian Education through Effective Schools Process." Washington, DC: Government Printing Office, 1988.

O'Neil, Floyd, and Stanford J. Layton. "Of Pride and Politics: Brigham Young as Indian Superintendent." *Utah Historical Quarterly* 46, no. 3 (Summer 1978): 236–50.

O'Neill, Colleen. *Working the Navajo Way: Labor and Culture in the Twentieth Century.* Lawrence: University Press of Kansas, 2005.

Osborne, Virgus C. "An Appraisal of the Education Program for Native Americans at Brigham Young University, 1966–1974." PhD diss., University of Utah, 1975.

Packer, Boyd K. "Manual of Policies and Procedures for the Administration of Indian Seminaries of the Church of Jesus Christ of Latter-day Saints." PhD diss., Brigham Young University, 1962.

Parman, Donald L. *The Navajo and the New Deal.* New Haven: Yale University Press, 1976.

Parry, Keith. "The Mormon Missionary Companionship." In Cornwall, Heaton, and Young, *Contemporary Mormonism*, 182–206.

Pavlik, Steve. "Of Saints and Lamanites: An Analysis of Navajo Mormonism." *Wicaso Sa Review* 8, no. 1 (Spring 1992): 21–30.

Payne, E. Mauray. "Indian Youth Conference." *Indian Liahona* 2, no. 3 (Summer 1964): 2–3.

Pearce, Roy Harvey. *Savages of America: A Study of the Indian and the Idea of Civilization.* Baltimore: Johns Hopkins Press, 1953.

Pedraja, Carlos L. "Carlos L. Pedraja: 'I Didn't Go to Russia.'" *Ensign* 5, no. 12 (December 1975): 29.

Perry, Janice Kapp. "Shared Son." *Ensign* 10, no. 10 (October 1980): 42–44.

Petersen, Mark E. *Children of Promise, The Lamanites: Yesterday and Today.* Salt Lake City: Bookcraft, 1981.

Peterson, Charles S. "The Hopis and the Mormons, 1858–1873." *Utah Historical Quarterly* 39, no. 2 (Spring 1971): 179–94.

———. *Take Up Your Mission: Mormon Colonizing Along the Little Colorado River, 1870–1900.* Tucson: University of Arizona, 1973.

Peterson, John Alton. *Utah's Black Hawk War.* Salt Lake City: University of Utah Press, 1998.

Phelps, W. W., ed. *Book of Commandments for the Government of the Church of Christ, Organized According to Law, on the 6th of April, 1830.* Zion [Independence, MO]: W. W. Phelps, 1833.

"Placement Program Part of Unified Social Services." *Indian Liahona* 7, no. 2 (March/April 1970): 28.

Poll, Richard D. *Utah's History.* Logan: Utah State University, 1989.

Powell, Mary Helen. "Room for Calvin." *Ensign* 3, no. 5 (May 1973): 61–62.

Pratt, Orson. "Divine Authority; or, Was Joseph Smith Sent of God?" *Latter-day Saints' Millennial Star* 10, no. 17 (September 1, 1848): 257–60.

BIBLIOGRAPHY 317

Pratt, Parley P. *Autobiography of Parley P. Pratt*. Salt Lake City: Deseret Book, 2000.

———. *The Essential Parley P. Pratt*. Salt Lake City: Signature Books, 1990.

———. *A Voice of Warning and Instruction to All People; or, An Introduction to the Faith and Doctrine of the Church of Jesus Christ of Latter-day Saints, Commonly Called Mormons*. New York: W. Sandford, 1837.

Prince, Gregory, and Wm. Robert Wright. *David O. McKay and the Rise of Modern Mormonism*. Salt Lake City: University of Utah Press, 2005.

"Programs and Policies Newsletter." *Ensign* 1, no. 5 (May 1971): 76.

Pursuitte, David. *Joseph Smith and the Origins of the Book of Mormon*. Jefferson, NC: McFarland, 1985.

Quinn, D. Michael. *Early Mormonism and the Magic World View*. Salt Lake City: Signature Books, 1987.

———. "Ezra Taft Benson and Mormon Political Conflicts." *Dialogue: A Journal of Mormon Thought* 26, no. 2 (Summer 1993): 1–87.

———. "I-Thou vs. I-It Conversions: The Mormon 'Baseball Baptism' Era." *Sunstone Magazine* 16, no. 7 (December 1993): 30–44.

———. *J. Reuben Clark: The Church Years*. Provo, UT: Brigham Young University Press, 1983.

———. *The Mormon Hierarchy: Extensions of Power*. Salt Lake City: Signature Books, 1997.

———. *The Mormon Hierarchy: Origins of Power*. Salt Lake City: Signature Books, 1994.

Quintero, Vanta. "My Happiest Year." *Relief Society Magazine* 52, no. 10 (October 1965): 733–35.

Rainer, Howard T. "American Indian Self-Image Workshop Manual." Provo, UT: BYU American Indian Services and Research Center, n.d.

———. "An Analysis of Attitudes Navajo Community Leaders Have Toward a Religion Sponsored Program Based upon Membership of that Faith and Amount of Information Attained." Master's thesis, Brigham Young University, 1976.

Raleigh, Robert. "Elder George P. Lee: Navajo General Authority Speaks on Self-Image, Discipline." *Eagle's Eye* 18, no. 2 (Winter 1985/1986): 20–21.

Rea, Dorothy O. "All-Indian Youth Conference Held at BYU." *Indian Liahona* 5, no. 3 (Summer 1968): 19–20.

Ready, Eugene. "William Heath Whittsitt: Insights into Early Mormonism." Master's thesis, Southern Baptist Theological Seminary, 2001.

Reeve, Paul W. *Religion of a Different Color: Race and the Mormon Struggle for Whiteness*. New York: Oxford University Press, 2015.

Reeve, Rex C., Jr., and Galen L. Fletcher. "Mormons in the Tuba City Area." In Garret and Johnson, *Regional Studies in Latter-day Saint Church History: Arizona*, 133–58.

"Regional Lamanite Youth Conferences." *Indian Liahona* 7, no. 4 (July/August 1970): 26–27.

Reyner, J. A. *Teaching American Indian Students*. Norman: University of Oklahoma Press, 1992.

Richards, LeGrand. "Blessings and Promises to the Lamanites." *Indian Liahona* 8, no. 1 (January/February 1971): 3–4.

———. "A Latter-day Saint First." *Indian Liahona* 3, no. 1 (Spring 1966): 8.

Riggs, Lynette A. "The Church of Jesus Christ of Latter-day Saints' Indian Student Placement Service: A History." PhD diss., Utah State University, 2008.

Riney, Scott. *The Rapid City Indian School, 1898–1933.* Norman: University of Oklahoma Press, 1999.

Roberts, B. H. *A Comprehensive History of the Church.* 6 vols. Salt Lake City: Deseret Book Co., 1959.

Rogers, Jedediah. *The Council of Fifty: A Documentary History.* Salt Lake City: Signature Books, 2014.

Roessel, Robert A., Jr. *Navajo Education in Action: The Rough Rock Demonstration School.* Chinle, AZ: Navajo Curriculum Center Rough Rock Demonstration School, 1977.

Rollo, Bishop Klien. "Southern Indian Regional Basketball Tournament." *Indian Liahona* 3, no. 4 (Summer 1966): 2.

Rosenfelt, Daniel. "Indian Schools and Community Control." *Stanford Law Review* 25, no. 4 (April 1973): 489–550.

Rousselot, John H. "Civil Rights: Communist Betrayal of a Good Cause." *American Opinion* 7 (February 1964): 1–11.

Said, Edward. *Orientalism.* New York: Pantheon Books, 1978.

Sanchez, George. *The People: A Study of the Navajo.* Washington, DC: United States Indian Service, 1948.

Schimmelpfennig, Dorothy Jensen. "A Study of Cross-Cultural Problems in the L.D.S. Indian Student Placement Program in Davis County." PhD diss., University of Utah, 1971.

Schurz, Larry, ed. "Purpose of Eagle's Eye." *Eagle's Eye* 10, no. 1 (September 1978): 2.

Schwartz, Maureen Trudelle. *Molded in the Image of Changing Woman: Navajo Views on the Human Body and Personhood.* Tucson: University of Arizona Press, 1997.

"Scouting and Youth Activities in the Indian Mission." *Indian Liahona* 1, no. 4 (Fall 1963): 11.

Sekaquaptewa, Helen. *Me and Mine: The Life Story of Helen Sekaquaptewa.* Tucson: University of Arizona Press, 1969.

Sheehan, Bernard. *Savagism and Civility: Indians and Englishmen in Colonial Virginia.* Cambridge: Cambridge University Press, 1980.

Shipps, Jan. "Making Saints: In the Early Days and the Latter Days." In Cornwall, Heaton, and Young, *Contemporary Mormonism,* 64–84.

Shumway, Dale L., and Margene Shumway, eds. *The Blossoming: Dramatic Accounts of the Lives of Native Americans in the Foster Care Program of the Church of Jesus Christ of Latter-day Saints.* Orem, UT: Granite Press, 2002.

Simmons, Jeffrey L. "Militancy and the Church." *Eagle's Eye* 7, no. 3 (March 1973): 2.

Skinner, Earnest M. *Joseph Smith, Sr.: First Patriarch to the LDS Church.* Mesa, AZ: Palmyra Publishing Company, 2002.

Slotkin, Richard. *Regeneration Through Violence: The Mythology of the American Frontier, 1600–1860.* Middletown, CT: Wesleyan University Press, 1973.

Smith, Eve P., and Lisa A. Merkel-Holguin. *A History of Child Welfare.* New Brunswick, NJ: Transaction Publishers, 1996.

Smith, Joseph, Jr. *A Book of Commandments, for the Government of the Church of Christ, Organized According to Law, on the 6th of April, 1830.* Zion [Independence, MO]: W. W. Phelps and Co., 1833.

———. *The Book of Mormon: An Account Written by the Hand of Mormon, Upon Plates Taken from the Plates of Nephi.* Palymyra, NY: E. B. Grandin, 1830.

———. *Doctrine and Covenants of the Church of Jesus Christ of Latter Day Saints: Carefully Selected from the Revelations of God, and Compiled by Joseph Smith Junior, Oliver Cowdery, Sidney Rigdon, Frederick G. Williams.* Kirtland, OH: F. G. Williams & Co., 1835.

———. *History of the Church of Jesus Christ of Latter-day Saints, edited by B. H. Roberts.* 7 vols. Salt Lake City: The Church of Jesus Christ of Latter-day Saints, 1932–1951.

Smith, Joseph, Sr. *Patriarchal Blessing Book.* Vol. 1. Salt Lake City: The Church of Jesus Christ of Latter-day Saints, Historical Department, 1833.

Smith, M. "Beyond the Statistics: Indian Experiences in the Indian Student Placement Program." Master's thesis, Utah State University, 2003.

Smith, Paul Chaat, and Robert Allen Warrior. *Like a Hurricane: The Indian Movement from Alcatraz to Wounded Knee.* New York: New Press, 1996.

Smith, Robert. "Relationships between Foster Home Placement and Later Acculturation Patterns of Selected American Indians." Master's thesis, Utah State University, 1968.

Smith, Sherry. *Reimagining Indians: Native Americans through Anglo Eyes, 1800–1940.* New York: Oxford University Press, 2000.

Snake, Stanley. "BYU Indians Meet with AIM Leader." *Eagle's Eye* 3, no. 5 (January 1973): 1.

Solomon, Tereapii. "Towards an Educational Analysis of Māori and Pacific Island Student Achievement at the Church College of New Zealand." *MAI Review,* no. 1 (2007): 14–31.

"Southwest Indian Mission Youth Conference." *Indian Liahona* 1, no. 3 (Summer 1963): 6–7.

"Southwest Indian Mission Youth Conference." *Indian Liahona* 7, no. 6 (November/December 1970): 32.

Spencer, Bessie. "My Feelings of Being a Navaho." *Indian Liahona* 8, no. 2 (March/April 1971): 28.

Spicer, Edward. *Cycles of Conquest: The Impact of Spain, Mexico, and the United States on the Indians of the Southwest, 1533–1960.* Tucson: University of Arizona Press, 1973.

"Stanley Snake Elected NIYC President." *Eagle's Eye* 2, no. 5 (March 1972): 1.

Stanton, William. *Leopard's Spots: A Romance of the White Man's Burden, 1865–1900.* Ridgewood, NJ: Gregg Press, 1967.

Stegner, Wallace. *Mormon Country.* Lincoln: University of Nebraska Press, 1972.

Stewart, Charles, and Rosalind Shaw. *Syncretism/Anti-Syncretism: The Politics of Religious Synthesis.* New York: Routledge, 1994.

Stewart, Irene, and Doris Ostrander Dawdy, eds. *A Voice in Her Tribe: A Navajo Woman's Own Story.* Socorro, NM: Ballen Press, 1980.

Stewart, Jon, and Peter Wiley. "Cultural Genocide." *Penthouse Magazine* 12, no. 10 (June 1981): 80–84.

Stott, G. St. John. "New Jerusalem Abandoned: The Failure to Carry Mormonism to the Delaware." *Journal of American Studies* 21, no. 1 (April 1987): 71–85.

Sturtevant, William C. "Creek into Seminole." In *North American Indians in Historical Perspective*, edited by Eleanor B. Leacock and Nancy O. Lurie, 92–128. New York: Random House, 1971.

Szasz, Margaret Connell. *Education and the American Indian: The Road to Self-Determination Since 1928*. Albuquerque: University of New Mexico Press, 1974.

Takaki, Ronald. *Iron Cages: Race and Culture in Nineteenth Century America*. New York: Alfred A. Knopf, 1979.

Tate, Lucile C. *Boyd K. Packer: A Watchman on the Tower*. Salt Lake City: Bookcraft, 1995.

Taylor, Graham D. *The New Deal and American Indian Tribalism: the Administration of the Indian Reorganization Act, 1934–45*. Lincoln: University of Nebraska Press, 1980.

Taylor, Hal L. "Summer Activities Are Successful." *Indian Liahona* 2, no. 4 (Fall 1964): 6–7.

Thompson, Hildegard. *The Navajos' Long Walk for Education / Diné Nizaagóó Iiná Bíhoo'aah Yíkanaaskai: A History of Navajo Education / Diné Óhoot'aahii Baa Hane'*. Tsaile, Navajo Nation, AZ: Navajo Community College Press, 1975.

Topper, Martin D. "'Mormon Placement': The Effects of Missionary Foster Families on Navajo Adolescents." *Ethos* 7, no. 2 (Summer 1979): 142–60.

Trafzer, Clifford E. *Boarding School Blues: Revisiting American Indian Educational Experiences*. Lincoln: University of Nebraska Press, 2006.

Trask, Haunani-Kay. *From a Native Daughter: Colonialism and Sovereignty in Hawai'i*. Honolulu: University of Hawaii Press, 1999.

Trennert, Robert A. *The Phoenix Indian School: Forced Assimilation in Arizona, 1891–1935*. Norman: University of Oklahoma Press, 1988.

Turner, J. B. *Mormonism in All Ages; or, The Rise, Progress, and Causes of Mormonism, with the Biography of Its Author and Founder, Joseph Smith, Junior*. New York: Platt & Peters, 1842.

Tuttle, A. Theodore. "Student Placement Program." *Improvement Era* 71, no. 8 (August 1968): 42–43.

Underwood, Grant. "Book of Mormon Usage in Early LDS Theology." *Dialogue: A Journal of Mormon Thought* 17, no. 3 (1984): 35–74.

——. *The Millenarian World of Early Mormonism*. Urbana: University of Illinois Press, 1993.

——. *Pioneers in the Pacific: Memory, History, and Cultural Identity among the Latter-day Saints*. Provo, UT: Religious Studies Center, Brigham Young University, 2005.

——. *Voyages of Faith: Explorations in Mormon Pacific History*. Provo, UT: Brigham Young University, 2000.

Unger, Steven, ed. *The Destruction of American Indian Families*. New York: Association of American Indian Affairs, 1977.

United States Statutes at Large. Vol. 26 (1889–1891), vol. 27 (1891–1893), vol. 48 (1933–1934), vol. 61 (1947), vol. 64 (1950). Washington, DC: Government Printing Office.

U.S. Board of Indian Commissioners. *Annual Report of the Board of Indian Commissioners to the Secretary of the Interior.* Washington, DC: Government Printing Office, 1932.

U.S. Department of Housing and Urban Development. *Indian Housing Block Grant (IHBG) Annual Performance Report, 2009.* Washington, DC: Navajo Housing Authority, 2009.

U.S. Department of the Interior, Bureau of Indian Affairs. *Report to the Senate Appropriations Committee on the Navajo Bordertown Dormitory Program by the Commissioner of Indian Affairs, February, 1965.* Washington, DC: Government Printing Office, 1965.

U.S. Department of Interior, National Park Service. "Environmental Assessment for the Navajo Generating Station Water Intake Project, March 2005," ii. Washington, DC: Government Printing Office, 2005.

U.S. House of Representatives. *Hearings before the Subcommittee on Indian Affairs and Public Lands of the Committee on Interior and Insular Affairs, House of Representatives, Ninety-Fifth Congress, Second Session, February 9 and March 9, 1978.* Washington, DC: U.S. Government Printing Office, 1981.

U.S. Senate. *Hearing before the United States Senate Select Committee on Indian Affairs, Ninety-Fifth Congress, First Session on S. 1214, August 4, 1977.* Washington, DC: U.S. Government Printing Office, 1977.

Van Dyne, Larry A. "Navajos, Stressing Heritage, Claim Nation's Only Indian College." *The Chronicle of Higher Education* 8 (May 1972): 1–31.

Van Hoak, Stephen P. "And Who Shall Have the Children? The Indian Slave Trade in the Southern Great Basin, 1800–1865." *Nevada Historical Quarterly* 41, no. 1 (Spring 1998): 3–25.

Van Wagoner, Richard S. *Sidney Rigdon: A Portrait of Religious Excess.* Salt Lake City: Signature Books, 1994.

Vogel, Dan, ed. *Early Mormon Documents.* 5 vols. Salt Lake City: Signature Books, 1995–2003.

——. *Indian Origins and the Book of Mormon: Religious Solutions from Columbus to Joseph Smith.* Salt Lake City: Signature Books, 1986.

——. *Joseph Smith: The Making of a Prophet.* Salt Lake City: Signature Books, 2004.

Voss, Barbara L. *The Archaeology of Ethnogenesis: Race and Sexuality in Colonial San Francisco.* Berkeley: University of California Press, 2008.

Walker, Ronald. "Seeking the 'Remnant': The Native American during the Joseph Smith Period." *Journal of Mormon History* 19, no. 1 (Spring 1933): 1–33.

——. "Toward a Reconstruction of Indian Relations, 1847–1877." *BYU Studies* 29, no. 4 (Fall 1989): 23–42.

——. "Wakara Meets the Mormons, 1848–52: A Case Study in Native American Accommodation." *Utah Historical Quarterly* 70, no. 3 (Summer 2002): 215–37.

Walker, Ronald, and Doris R. Dant, eds. *Nearly Everything Imaginable: The Everyday Life of Utah's Mormon Pioneers.* Provo, UT: Brigham Young University Press, 1999.

Walker, Ronald W., David J. Whittaker, and James B. Allen. *Mormon History.* Urbana: University of Illinois Press, 2001.

Warner, Michael J. "Protestant Missionary Activity Among the Navajo, 1890–1912." *New Mexico Historical Review* 45, no. 3 (July 1970): 209–32.

Warrior, Clyde. "Which One Are You? Five Types of Young Indians." *ABC: Americans Before Columbus* 2, no. 4 (December 1964): 1.

Watt, G. D., ed. *Journal of Discourses: By President Brigham Young and Other Church Leaders.* 26 vols. Salt Lake City: [Deseret Book], 1966.

Weber, Max. *The Protestant Ethic and Spirit of Capitalism.* Mineola, NY: Dover Publications, 2003.

Whittaker, David J. "Mormons and Native Americans: A Historical and Bibliographical Introduction." *Dialogue: A Journal of Mormon Thought* 18, no. 4 (Winter 1985): 33–64.

Wight, Jeremy Benton. *The Wild Ram of the Mountain: The Story of Lyman Wight.* Star Valley, WY: Afton Thrift Print, 1996.

Wight, Lyman. "An Address by Way of an Abridged Account and Journal of My Life from February 1844 up to April 1848 with an Appeal to the Latter Day Saints." Salt Lake City: Wight Trust Publishers, 1989.

Wiley, Peter. "The Lee Revolution and the Rise of Correlation." *Sunstone* 10, no. 1 (1985): 18–22.

Wilkinson, Charles. *Fire on the Plateau: Conflict and Endurance in the American Southwest.* Washington, DC: Island Press, 1999.

Wilkinson, Ernest L., and Leonard J. Arrington. *Brigham Young University: The First One Hundred Years.* Vol. 3. Provo, UT: Brigham Young University Press, 1976.

Williams, Peter W., ed. *Perspectives on American Religion and Culture.* Malden, MA: Blackwell, 1999.

Willmore, David R. "A Comparative Study of the Religiosity of Navajo High School Students in Four Different School Settings." PhD diss., Brigham Young University, 1974.

Wilson, Linda O. "Changes in Scholastic Achievement and Intelligence of Indian Children Enrolled in a Foster Placement Program." Master's thesis, Brigham Young University, 1973.

Wright, Lyle O. *Survival of Public Schools: Strengthening Navajo Education.* Window Rock, AZ: Navajo Division of Education, 1975.

Yazzie, Herbert. "Eagle's Eye Motivates Placement Students." *Eagle's Eye* 17, no. 3 (March 1985): 16.

Young, John R. *Memoirs of John R. Young: Utah Pioneer, 1847.* Salt Lake City: Deseret News Press, 1920.

Young, Robert W. *The Navajo Yearbook.* Window Rock, AZ: Navajo Agency, 1961.

"Youth Conference Held at Tuba City." *Indian Liahona* 6, no. 6 (November/December 1969): 29.

"Youth Government Model." *Eagle's Eye* 12, no. 1 (January 1980): 8.

Manuscripts and Collections

Arizona Holbrook Mission Records, 1970–1983. Church Archives.

Bishop, Clarence R. "Foster Parent Orientation Meeting, August 28, 1963, Phoenix Arizona." American Indian Research Services, L. Tom Perry Special Collections, Harold B. Lee Library, Brigham Young University.

Brigham Young University Institute of American Indian Studies Records, 1956–1978. L. Tom Perry Special Collections, Harold B. Lee Library, Brigham Young University.

Buchanan, Golden R. Interview. Bound typescript. 5 volumes. The James Moyle Oral History Program, Church Archives.

Butler, John Lowe. Autobiography. Undated. L. Tom Perry Special Collections, Harold B. Lee Library, Brigham Young University.

Cox, Cordelia Morley. "Biography of Isaac Morley: A Sketch of the Life of My Father Isaac Morley, One of the Pioneers to Salt Lake Valley in 1848." L. Tom Perry Special Collections, Harold B. Lee Library, Brigham Young University.

Crosby, Jesse W. Autobiography. Undated. L. Tom Perry Special Collections, Harold B. Lee Library, Brigham Young University.

Deloria, Philip. "Comment: Navajo Religious Encounters in the Twentieth Century." Speech presented at the Organization of American Historians Conference, Seattle, Washington, March 27, 2009. In author's files.

Doris Duke Oral History Project. Special Collections, Willard J. Marriott Library, University of Utah, Salt Lake City.

Draper, William. Autobiography. L. Tom Perry Special Collections, Harold B. Lee Library, Brigham Young University.

Embry, Jessie L. "Lamanite/Indian Branches." Unpublished manuscript. Armand Mauss Papers, Utah State Historical Society, Salt Lake City.

"Enrollment in LDS Indian Seminary, 1957–1967." Brigham Young University Records, 1958–1972. L. Tom Perry Special Collections, Harold B. Lee Library, Brigham Young University.

Faulring, Barbara J. "Kirtland Revelation Book." N.p., 1981. L. Tom Perry Special Collections, Harold B. Lee Library, Brigham Young University.

Felt, Paul E. The Book of Mormon, the Lamanite, and Prophetic Destiny. Unpublished collection of Paul Felt speeches, 1964. L. Tom Perry Special Collections, Harold B. Lee Library, Brigham Young University.

Felt, Paul E. "I Remember When." Bound manuscript. L. Tom Perry Special Collections, Harold B. Lee Library, Brigham Young University.

Flake, David. "History of the Southwest Indian Mission." Unpublished manuscript. L. Tom Perry Special Collections, Harold B. Lee Library, Brigham Young University.

The Gamalih: Southwest Indian Newsletter. L. Tom Perry Special Collections, Harold B. Lee Library, Brigham Young University.

Gibbs, Eliza Dana. Autobiography, 1813–1900. Utah State Historical Society, Salt Lake City, Utah.

H. Michael Marquardt Papers. Special Collections, J. Willard Marriott Library, University of Utah, Salt Lake City.

Indian Committee Correspondence, 1941–1952. LDS Church Archives, Salt Lake City, Utah.

Indian Committee Scrapbook, 1964. LDS Church Archives.

Indian Placement Program Files, 1950–1998. LDS Church Archives.

Indian Student Guide. LDS Social Services, Church of Jesus Christ of Latter-day Saints, May 1973. L. Tom Perry Special Collections, Harold B. Lee Library, Brigham Young University.

Indian Student Placement Committee, Minutes. LDS Church Archives.

Indian Student Placement Program Records, 1955–1960. LDS Church Archives.

Indian Student Placement Services Evaluation Study Summary Report Prepared by Presiding Bishopric Research and Evaluation Services. May 1982. Draft with no pagination. Armand Mauss Papers, Utah State Historical Society, Salt Lake City.

Indian Student Placement Service Yearly Calendar, [n.d.]. L. Tom Perry Special Collections, Harold B. Lee Library, Brigham Young University.

Institute of American Indian Services and Research. Records, 1956–1972. L. Tom Perry Special Collections, Harold B. Lee Library, Brigham Young University.

Jackman, Levi. Autobiography. L. Tom Perry Special Collections, Harold B. Lee Library, Brigham Young University.

Jenny M. Smith's Indian Student Placement Program Oral Histories. Special Collections and Archives, Merrill-Cazier Library, Utah State University, Logan.

Jensen, Miles. Dictation, December 13, 1973. Typescript, James Moyle Oral History Program. LDS Church Archives.

Jensen, Miles. Reports, 1954–1955. Indian Student Placement Program Files, Church Archives.

Johnson, Joel Hills. Autobiography. Typescript. L. Tom Perry Special Collections, Harold B. Lee Library, Brigham Young University.

Jones, Paul. Inaugural address, 1959. Special Collections, University of Arizona Library, Tucson.

Lamanite Handbook for the Church of Jesus Christ of Latter-day Saints, December 1, 1968. L. Tom Perry Special Collections, Harold B. Lee Library, Brigham Young University.

LDS Indian Student Placement Program: Policies Regarding Requirements and Responsibilities, [n.d.]. L. Tom Perry Special Collections, Harold B. Lee Library, Brigham Young University.

LDS Native American Oral History Collection Project. Charles Redd Center for Western History, L. Tom Perry Special Collections. Harold B. Lee Library, Brigham Young University.

Leany, William. Autobiography. L. Tom Perry Special Collections, Harold B. Lee Library, Brigham Young University.

Listening to Indians: The New York Times Oral History Program. Labriola Center, Arizona State University, Tempe, Arizona.

Minutes of the Indian Student Placement Committee. LDS Church Archives.

Nakai, Raymond. Inaugural address, April 13, 1963. Peter Iverson Papers, Labriola Center, Arizona State University, Tempe.

Natural Parent Guide. The LDS Indian Student Placement Program, June 1968. L. Tom Perry Special Collections, Harold B. Lee Library, Brigham Young University.

Navajo Tribal Council Resolutions, 1922–1951. Labriola Center, Arizona State University, Tempe.

Newsletters, LDS Indian Student Placement Program. L. Tom Perry Special Collections, Harold B. Lee Library, Brigham Young University.

Oaks, Keith R. "Church Elementary and Secondary Education." Unpublished report, March 8, 1971. Armand Mauss Papers, Utah State Historical Society, Salt Lake City.

Peter Iverson Papers. Labriola Center, Arizona State University, Tempe.

Preece, E. Bruce. "Mormon Missionary Work Among the Indians of North America in the Twentieth Century." July 14, 1965. Unpublished manuscript. L. Tom Perry Special Collections, Harold B. Lee Library, Brigham Young University.

"Preliminary Summary of Research on the History of Mormon Agricultural Colonization Projects among the North American Indians of the United States from 1830 to 1967." May 1, 1967. Brigham Young University Records, 1956–1972. L. Tom Perry Special Collections, Harold B. Lee Library, Brigham Young University.

Presiding Bishopric Research and Evaluation Services, Indian Student Placement Program Services Evaluation Study Summary Report, May 1982. LDS Church Archives.

"Record Number of Navajo Children Attend School, 1954." Window Rock, Director of Navajo Schools, Internal Report, September 1, 1954. Peter Iverson Papers, Labriola Center, Arizona State University, Tempe.

Records, 1956–1959: BYU Indian Education Program. L. Tom Perry Special Collections, Harold B. Lee Library, Brigham Young University.

Research on Anglo-Ephraim. Armand Mauss Papers, Utah State Historical Society, Salt Lake City.

Research on Indians. Armand Mauss Papers, Utah State Historical Society, Salt Lake City.

Revelations Collection. LDS Church Archives.

Southwest Indian Mission Annual Historical Reports, 1978–1980. LDS Church Archives.

Southwest Indian Mission, Manuscript History and Historical Reports, 1942–1977. L. Tom Perry Special Collections, Harold B. Lee Library, Brigham Young University.

Statement by the President Making Public a Report on the Needs of the Navajo Indians, December 2, 1947. Public Papers of the Presidents, Harry S Truman, 1945–1953, Harry S. Truman Library and Museum, http://trumanlibrary.org/.

Steamboat Branch Manuscript History, August 13, 1969. LDS Church Archives.

Stout, Hosea. Autobiography. Vol. 1. L. Tom Perry Special Collections, Harold B. Lee Library, Brigham Young University.

Stucki, Larry R. "Mormonism: The Restorer or Destroyer of the 'True' Heritage of the American Indians." Typescript, 1979. L. Tom Perry Special Collections, Harold B. Lee Library, Brigham Young University.

Tribe of Many Feathers and Sons of Ammon, Correspondence and Reports, 1965–1967. L. Tom Perry Special Collections, Harold B. Lee Library, Brigham Young University, Provo, Utah.

Tsosie, Lenora. Autobiographical sketch, June 19, 2009. Typescript, no pagination, in author's files.

Wasatch Research Opinion Report, 1979. LDS Church Archives.

Webb, L. Robert. "An Examination of Certain Aspects of the American Indian Education Program at Brigham Young University: A Study Conducted by Robert Webb." 1972. Appendix C. L. Tom Perry Special Collections, Harold B. Lee Library, Brigham Young University.

Wilkinson Presidential Papers. L. Tom Perry Special Collections, Harold B. Lee Library, Brigham Young University, Provo, Utah.

INDEX

Abourezk, James, 194, 195, 197, 198, 199, 201
acculturation, and placement experiences of ISPP students, 92, 109. *See also* assimilation; colonization
activism. *See* American Indian Movement; National Indian Youth Council; Red Power movement; United Native Americans
Adair, James, 14
Adams, David Wallace, 4, 39–40
adoption, of Native American children by white families, 192–201, 294n120, 294n126. *See also* Indian Child Welfare Act
advertising, of ISPP, 78
African-Americans: and ideological rifts in civil rights movements, 191; and 1978 repeal of priesthood restrictions, 105, 221
agency: of ISPP students in context of colonization, 9–10, 242; and postcolonialism as approach to histories of boarding schools, 5
Ahkeah, Sam, 78
Akwesasne Notes (newspaper), 176, 193, 201, 202
Albrecht, David, 225, 235, 298n61, 299n86

American Academy of Child Psychology, 193–94
American Indian Movement (AIM), 179, 181–83, 190
American Indian Policy Review Commission, 195
American Indian Services (Brigham Young University), 223
American Indian Studies program (University of California), 179
Americans Before Columbus (newsletter), 179
Anderson, Mad Bear, 182
Argentina, and Lamanite identity, 88
Arizona, expansion of ISPP into, 82–83, 84, 272n103, 272n105
Arizona Department of Public Welfare, 71
Arizona Holbrook Mission, 207, 245
Arizona Relief Society Social Services, 83
Arnold, Mildred, 72
Ashdown, Rex, 69
Ashton, Marvin J., 211
assimilation: LDS theology and rationalization of, 248; and placement experiences of ISPP students, 110–11, 121, 126, 241; and Red Power activism at Brigham Young University,

186–87; and shift in Indian policy of LDS Church in 1970s, 207. *See also* acculturation; colonization; resistance

Association on American Indian Affairs (AAIA), 193, 195

Atene, Walter, 54

authenticity: and concepts of identity, 9; Lamanite identity and claims to Indianness, 130, 170, 187, 191, 203, 240, 281n12; and self-determination movement, 171, 184. *See also* culture

Avery, Amy, 48

Baird, J. Edwin, 289n14

Ballard, M. Russell, 228–29

Banks, Dennis, 189, 191, 237

Baptist Church, and frontier revivals in 1830s, 18

baptism, of ISPP students, 64, 67, 68–71, 77, 215, 270n83

Barker, Robert W., 200

Barsh, Russel Lawrence, 295n134

Basic Unit Plan (1977), 221

Basso, Keith, 101

Bates, Douglas, 230–31

Beatty, Willard, 43

Bedonie, Ella, 112, 118, 119, 124, 131–32, 156, 159

Begay, Anna, 68

Begay, Kent, 135, 155

Begay, Maybell, 53–54, 101, 103, 114, 136, 149

Begay, Nora Mae, 110–11, 191

Bellecourt, Clyde, 237

Bellecourt, Vernon, 181, 182, 183, 191

Bellson, Sam, 71

Bennally, Jimmy, 69, 215

Bennally, Roberta, 119

Berkhofer, Robert F., Jr., 4, 251n5, 255n17, 275–76n51

BIA. *See* Bureau of Indian Affairs

biculturalism: and avoidance of cultural conflict by ISPP students, 125; and summer release of ISPP students to reservations, 160. *See also* culture; "two worlds" model

Billison, Samuel, 72–73, 74, 80, 269n67

Bishop, Clare, 78, 82–84, 99, 134, 145, 154, 167, 211–12, 214, 220–21, 235, 251n1

Bishop, Clarence R., 77, 97–98, 108, 231, 272n107, 285n108

Black Hawk War (1865), 31

Black Power nationalism, 180

Blatchford, Paul, 177

Blood Reserve (Alberta), 83

boarding schools: and colonization as federal policy, 4; Mormon worship services at, 86; Navajo experiences with and motives for participation in ISPP, 52–53; Pratt's model of, 40–42; view of ISPP as alternative to, 7–8, 236

Book of Mormon: changes in modern edition of, 253n3, 276n56; concepts of Nephites/Lamanites and skin color in, 104, 105; historicity of and claims to Indianness, 281n12; and history of Mormon Indian theology and policy, 11–12, 128, 129, 241; on Native Americans and gathering, 14–15

Boone, DuWaine, 54, 137, 163

Bosque Redondo, and Navajo history, 237

Boston Tea Party, 13

Bourdieu, Pierre, 3

Bowman, Emery, 116, 139, 142, 155

Boxer, Elise, 5

Boyce, George, 45

Boy Scouts, 92, 141, 173, 289n14

Brigham Young University, 67, 86, 184–86, 202, 210, 217–18, 221–24

Brightman, Lehman, 179, 180, 189, 191, 237

Brooks, Juanita, 262n95

Brown, Eddie, 181

Brown, Harold C., 88, 197, 199, 213, 214, 231, 233

Brown, James S., 32, 33

Brown, John, 82

Brown, Kenneth, 230, 231

Brown, Laura, 54

Brown, Victor, Jr., 212, 213–15, 297n39

Brown, Victor, Sr., 212–13, 221

Buchanan, Golden, 47–48, 49, 50–51, 58, 60–61, 78, 123–24, 143, 216

Buchanan, Thelma, 50

bureaucratization (of ISPP), 211–16. *See also* correlation movement

Bureau of Indian Affairs (BIA): and boarding schools, 42; and child removal centered on adoption by white families, 192–94; criticism of ISPP by, 70, 71, 73; and expanded educational facilities for Navajos in 1950s to 1970s, 172, 176–77; and livestock reductions on Navajo reservation in 1930s, 36–37

Burson, Carnes, 185

Butler, John, 28

Cagey, Elizabeth, 200

California, and ISPP, 83

Campbellites, 10, 17, 24

Canada, expansion of ISPP into, 82, 83, 84, 272n107

Cannon, Brian Q., 261n95

Cannon, Thomas Quentin, 65, 267n27

Carlisle Indian School, 39–40

Carry-the-Kettle Reserve (Saskatchewan), 83

caseworkers (ISPP): acculturation and meetings of with foster parents, 109; and admission process, 93–94; and average caseload, 270n82; and end of ISPP, 233; foster parents as voluntary assistants to, 215–16; and matching of children with foster parents, 98, 99; and recruitment of foster parents, 108; and students as informal assistants, 141–42; visits of to foster parents

and students, 142; visits of to students during summers on reservation, 161

Caswell, Henry, 256n32

Catawba, 86

Central America, and Lamanite identity, 88, 206

Central Navajo Branch, 86

Chamberlin, J. Edard, 5

Charley, Latricia, 103

Charley, Rosie, 102

Chavez, Julius Ray, 110, 112, 115, 116, 280n177

Cheyenne, 39, 196

Cheyenne-Arapaho Indian School (Oklahoma), 86

children, adoption of Native American by white families, 192–201, 294n120, 294n126. *See also* Indian Child Welfare Act; students

Children's Primary Hospital (Salt Lake City), 97

Child Welfare League of America, 192–94

Chilocco Boarding School (Oklahoma), 86

Chinle Boarding School, 288n5

Chinle Stake, 246–48

Chino, Loretta, 118–19, 139, 159

Chippewa, 28

Chiquito, Stephanie, 146

church, use of term in context, xi. *See also* Baptist Church; Episcopal Church; Methodist Church; Mormons and Mormonism; Presbyterian Church

Church News, 211

Cipolla, Craig, 5

civil rights movements, and African-Americans, 191. *See also* Red Power movement

Clark, Dorothy, 140

Clark, Edward, 68

Clark, William, 16

class. *See* socioeconomics

Clifford, James, 5, 9

code names, and Israelite identity of early Mormons, 22, 27, 258n47

Cody, Ernestine, 153–54

Cogley, Richard W., 254n6

Collier, John, 43, 44

colonization, and colonialism: and academic history of term *colonialism*, 3; and conclusions on impact of ISPP, 248; and establishment of ISPP, 57; and experiences of ISPP students in foster homes, 92, 126–27; and hostility between Red Power activists and LDS Church, 183–84, 187; and Lamanite identity and concept of ethnogenesis, 253n22; and Lamanite identity of ISPP students, 130, 135, 168, 236; as theme in history of ISPP, 2–10. *See also* postcolonialism

Comanche, 39

Committee for Lamanites and Other Cultures, 206

Concurrent House Resolution 108 (1953), 195–96

correlation movement: explanation of, 64; Packer's influence on LDS policy of, 208–12; and termination of ISPP, 204, 205, 216–20, 224, 230, 233, 234. *See also* bureaucratization

Corrill, John, 18

Council of Fifty, 21

Cowdery, Oliver, 16, 17, 20, 26–27, 255n19, 255n21

Cowley, Matthew, 48–49, 78

Cox, Kay, 120, 141, 216

criticisms, of ISPP: and closure of program, 233; and controversy on adoption, 202; and cultural differences, 119, 198; illness of Kimball and opposition within LDS to Indian programs, 205; and Kanab Conference, 71, 73–74; and Lamanite identity, 8, 10; and Presiding Bishopric Report,

224; and study by LDS of Native American opinions on program, 218

Crow Dog, Mary, 182, 192–93

cultural evolution theory, and history of education for Native Americans, 39

culture: differences in and experiences of ISPP students in foster homes, 100–104; Mormonism and Lamanite identity of ISPP students, 135; Navajos and integration of non-Navajo ideas and practices, 167–68, 242–43. *See also* acculturation; assimilation; authenticity; biculturalism; colonization; "two worlds" model

Cummins, Richard, 16, 17

Cundick, Bert P., 285n108

Curley, Elly, 239

Curley, Malcolm, 174

Dana, Lewis, 21, 28

Dandy, Jim, 41, 53, 116

Davis, Roger, 46

Davis, Rolin, 270n82

Delaware (tribe), 16, 17, 255n21

delinquency, and placement experiences of ISPP students, 120

Deloria, Philip, 13, 123, 251n5, 257n35

demography, changes in and church emphasis on role of Indians, 24

Denetdale, Jennifer Nez, 291n67

Derrida, Jacques, 4

Deseret News, 225

Destruction of American Indian Families, The (1977), 194

Dick, John, 178

Diné Baa-Hani (newspaper), 176

discipline, recommended approach for ISPP foster parents, 120

Dodge, Chee, 45, 78, 263n31

Dunham, Jonathan, 28

Durrant, Stewart A., 216

Eagle's Eye (student newspaper), 185, 189–90, 224
Economic Development Administration, 175
Economic Opportunity Act (1964), 178
Edmunds, David, 237, 252n13
education: access to on Navajo reservation in 1950s, 171–73; and community college on Navajo reservation, 243; and conclusions on results of ISPP, 248, 299n71; history of on Navajo reservation and events leading to establishment of ISPP, 36–57. *See also* schools; students; teachers
elect: and identity of Mormons as latter-day Israelites, 12; and Mormon concept of gathering, 16, 18, 19, 25, 26–27; and status of Native Americans in Mormon theology, 19, 21, 27, 241
Elementary and Secondary Education Act (1964), 178
Ellis, Leslie, 152
enrollment, in ISPP: in Arizona, Canada, Idaho, and Utah in 1960–1971, 84; decline of in 1970s and 1980s, 214–15, 225, 231, 232, 298n61, 299n86; and end of church Indian programs, 234; and estimates of total participation, 251n1
Ensign (magazine), 87, 225
Episcopal Church, 38
Erickson, Bea, 73
Euro-Americans: fascination with and mimicry of Indians in late colonial and early republic eras, 13, 257n35; ideological transition of LDS Church emphasis from Indians to in 1830s, 27; Mormon Indian policy in Utah and views of Native Americans by, 34; redefinition of gathering to include, 24–27; use of term in context, xi

Evans, Nancy, 52
Evening and Morning Star (newspaper), 14, 19, 26
excommunication, of George P. Lee, 226, 227, 228, 298n63
extracurricular activities. *See* leisure; schools; social activities; sports

family. *See* children; marriage; parents; siblings
Family Home Evening (FHE), 136–37, 282n26
Fanon, Frantz, 5
Farnsworth, Melvin, 270n82
federal government: and beginnings of education policy in 1819, 36; and boarding schools as force for colonization, 4; and policy of self-determination in 1960s and 1970s, 178, 180, 296n6; and policy of termination and national integration in 1950s, 73, 236; and removal policy of Andrew Jackson, 255n11, 258n44. *See also* Bureau of Indian Affairs; Indian Child Welfare Act
Federal Homeless Assistance Act, 230
Felt, Paul, 186, 188, 207
First Presidency, 28, 59, 60, 63–65, 209–10, 213, 216, 220, 222, 227, 266n4, 267n27
Flandro, Royce, 190, 217–18
food, and placement experiences of ISPP students, 101
Fort Sill Boarding School (Oklahoma), 86
Foster, Beverly, 136
foster parents (ISPP): acculturation and meetings of with caseworkers, 109; and admission process, 93–94; author's parents as, 1–2; caseworkers and matching of children with, 98, 99; caseworkers and recruitment of, 108; and household chores by ISPP students, 111–12; and

independent placements, 270n83; introduction of students to, 98–99; and letter-writing campaign in support of program, 80–81; and orientation meetings, 97–98; recommended approach to discipline by, 120; turnover rate among, 120; visits of caseworkers to, 142; visits of natural parents to homes of, 110; visits to reservations by during summers, 161–63; as voluntary assistants to caseworkers, 215–16; and wards, 139–40. *See also Natural Parent Guide*

Foucault, Michel, 4

friendships, and experiences of ISPP students in public schools, 117

Gadianton Robbers, and Lamanites, 31

Gaston, Charity Ann, 38

gathering: and Mormon Indian theology, 14–16; redefinition of to include Euro-Americans, 24–27

gender: and division of roles in Mormon households, 108; LDS youth curriculum and separation by, 141

George, Bobby, 196–97

Georgia, and ISPP, 83

Gibbs, Eliza, 30

Gilbert, Sidney, 17

Gilmore, Frankie, 112, 115

Goenett, Geraldine, 55

"Go My Son" (song), 164, 185

Goshutes, 31

Gottfredson, Douglas K., 285n108

Grant, Ulysses S., 38

Great Britain, and Mormon missions, 24

Green, Arnold, 15, 16

Guatemala, and Lamanite identity, 88

Gulleckson, Bud, 106–7

Gunnison, John, 31

Gunther, Orville, 81

Gwilliam, Robert, 270n82–83

habitus, and colonization, 3

Hale, Jim, 44–45

Hall, Kenneth Woolsey, 50

Hampton Normal and Agricultural Institute (Virginia), 39

Hansen, Robert F., 65, 72, 97

Harris, Lacee, 151–52

Harris, Martin, 20

Haskell Boarding School (Kansas), 86

Hatch, Carl, 45

Hatch, Ron, 229–30

Higher Education Facilities Act (1964), 178

Hildreth, Fen, 82

Hildreth, Fred, 71

Hill, David, 182, 183

history, Mormon theology and interpretation of Navajo, 133–34

Holiday, Maeta, 163

Holland, Jeffrey R., 223–24, 248

Holm, Agnes, 56–57

Holtsoi, Tommy, 119, 133–34

homesickness, and placement experience of ISPP students, 118–19

Hoover, Herbert, 42

House Concurrent Resolution 108 (1954), 73

Howard, Frankie, 82

Howe, E. D., 18

Hoyos, Arturo de, 218

Hualapai, 70

Hunsaker, Don, 167

Hyde, Orson, 24, 33

Idaho, and ISPP, 83, 84

identity: construction of Mormon as latter-day Israelite, 12–13, 20; historiography on emergence and identification of new, 253n22; and Native American history, 237; of ISPP students as Lamanites, 8–9, 126, 128–68, 242; and "two worlds" model, 122–26. *See also* authenticity; Indianness; self

imitation. *See* mimicry

Improvement Era (magazine), 61
Indian, use of term in context, xi.
   See also Indianness; Native
   Americans
Indian Adoption Program (IAP),
   192–94
Indian Child Welfare Act (1978), 170,
   192–201, 203
Indian Committee: expanded
   geographic role of in 1960s, 206;
   and institutional history of ISPP
   during 1950s and 1960s, 65–66,
   67, 70–72, 74–77; and selection
   criteria for ISPP students, 120–
   21; shortcomings of ISPP in
   reports of, 217; and socials for
   ISPP students, 143–45; and
   youth conferences, 148. *See also*
   Lamanite Committee
Indian Education Act (1972), 178
Indian Liahona (magazine), 137–39, 216
Indianness: authenticity and claims
   to, 281n12; ISPP and new notion
   of, 166–67; struggle to define on
   Navajo reservation, 170
Indian Self-Determination and Education Assistance Act (1975), 178
Indian Seminary Program, 85–86, 217
Indian Student Guide (ISPP 1973), 118,
   120, 139–40, 145, 161
Indian Student Placement Program
   (ISPP): conclusions of about
   influence on individuals and
   on Mormon Church, 235–49;
   decline of from 1972 to 2000,
   204–34; establishment and
   institutional history of, 58–90;
   history of education on Navajo
   reservation and events leading to
   establishment of, 36–57; history
   of Mormon Indian theology and
   policy as background for, 11–35;
   impact of self-determination
   movement in 1960s and 1970s on,
   169–203; introduction to themes
   emphasized in history of, 2–10;

motivations for participation
   in, 8, 53–54, 55–56, 75, 206;
   participation of author's parents
   in, 1–2; placement experiences of
   students and exposure to identity
   as Lamanite, 128–68; placement
   experiences of students entering
   Mormon homes and communities,
   91–127; use of terms for, xi–
   xii. *See also* bureaucratization;
   caseworkers; criticisms;
   enrollment; foster parents;
   reception centers; students
Indian Youth Conference, 146–47, 149
institutionalization, of ISPP in 1950s,
   58–90
Intermountain Indian School (Utah),
   85
Interstate Compact Administration
   (ICA), 194–95
ISPP. *See* Indian Student Placement
   Program
Israelites: construction of Mormon
   identity as, 12–13, 20, 22, 258n49;
   Euro-American recasting of
   Indians as, 13–14
Ivins, Antoine R., 65

Jackson, Andrew, 255n11, 258n44
Jacobs, Margaret D., 40, 251n8
Jake, Celina, 115–16
Jake, Erdman, 69, 109–10, 114, 139,
   145–46, 239
James, Harry, 52–53
Jensen, Celia, 61, 66
Jensen, Miles, 60, 61, 62, 63–64, 65, 69,
   71, 72, 77, 96, 144
John, Clarence, 47
John, Helen, 47–48, 49–50, 233
John, Ruth, 49–50
Johnson, Broderick H., 175
Johnson, Joel Hills, 31, 32
Johnson, Lyndon, 174
Jones, Paul, 75, 78, 79–80, 81, 172, 173,
   203
Jones, Sondra, 254n3

Keller, Margaret, 65–66, 72, 79–80, 81
Kennedy, John F., 172
Keokuk (Sac Chief), 20
Kerr, Rolfe, 248
Kidder, Daniel P., 256–57n32
Kimball, Heber C., 24
Kimball, Spencer W.: and church elimination of Spanish American Mission, 206; and establishment of ISPP, 48–49; on foster parents, 107; illness of and dismantling of Indian programs by church, 205, 233–34; and institutional organization of ISPP, 58, 59–60, 61–62, 65, 71, 72, 75, 76, 78, 83, 87, 89, 90, 272n103; and Lamanite identity in Mormon theology and functions of ISPP, 128, 130, 134, 135, 137–38, 143–45, 149; on noncompliant ISPP students, 120; on responsibility to Lamanites, 91; on skin color, 105–6; role of as prophet and church president, 220–21
Kiowa, 39
Kirtland Safety Society Bank, 24
Kitchen, Richard D., 261n95
Krug, Julius, 45, 47, 53

Lamanite Committee, 206, 211. See also Indian Committee
Lamanite Generation (dance troupe), 185
Lamanites: and Book of Mormon, 104, 132; colonization and Mormon theology on, 6, 8–9, 253n22; early Mormon missions to, 16–17, 28; identification of Pacific Islanders and Latin Americans as, 87–88; ISPP and new identity of ISPP students as, 126, 128–68, 242; LDS view of as empowerment ideology, 93, 130–68, 242; mainstreaming of as church-wide policy, 248; Red Power activism and opposition to as identity, 186–87, 189, 191, 202–3, 240; and termination of Indian program at BYU, 223; use of term, xi
landscape. See place
Lankford, Donald R., 281n9
LaPointe, Faye, 200
Larsen, Dean, 104
Larson, John Farr, 65, 71, 72, 77
Latin America, view of peoples of as Lamanites, 87–88, 206
Latter-day Saints, use of term, xi. See also Mormons and Mormonism
LDS Social Services, 212, 216
Leach, Robert E., 194–95
Leany, William, 30
Lee, George P.: on Book of Mormon, 132; as example of influence of ISPP on individuals, 239–40; excommunication of, 226, 227, 228, 298n63; on Mormons and Indian Child Welfare Act, 197–99, 201–2; on placement experience as ISPP participant, 94, 95, 96–97, 98, 100, 101, 102, 117, 121, 123, 134, 150, 155–58, 160–62, 285n108, 301n7; and Red Power activism in 1970s, 182, 187; resistance to dissolution of Indian programs, 225–28, 298n63
Lee, Harold B., 181, 208, 209, 214, 216–17
Lee, Ida, 148
Lee, Lynn, 154
Lee, Rhonda J., 50–51, 54, 139
leisure, and placement experience of ISPP students, 112. See also social activities; sports
Leupp, Francis, 40–41, 42
letter-writing campaign, in support of ISPP, 80–81
Lewis, C. S., 35
Lincoln, Hazel, 81
Littell, Norman M., 79, 173, 203
Long Range Navajo-Hopi Rehabilitation Act (1950), 174
Los Angeles Times, 105

Louis, Ray Baldwin, 239
Lukachukai Demonstration School, 177
Lumbe (North Carolina), 165
Lummi/Marrieta Reservation (Washington), 86

MacDonald, Peter, 82, 149, 173, 239–40
Maestas, John R., 187, 188, 191, 222
manuals, to instruct Indians in proper standards of Mormon life, 133. *See also Indian Student Guide; Natural Parent Guide*
Manuelito (Navajo chief), 185, 291n67
"many," implications of term, xii
Maori (New Zealand), 248
marriage: between Mormons and Native Americans in early Utah, 33; ISPP students and Mormon attitudes on race, 143–44. *See also* polygamy
Martin, Calvin, 3
Matterfis, William G., 281n9
Mauss, Armand, 87, 151, 245, 258n49, 299n71
McKay, David O., 62, 67, 213
medical exams, and ISPP admission process, 96–97
Memmi, Albert, 5
Menominee, 28
Meriam Report (1928), 42
Messenger and Advocate (newspaper), 19, 27
Metcalf, R. Warren, 269n70
Methodist Church, 38
Mexico, and Lamanite identity, 88
mimicry, of Native Americans: by early Mormon converts, 18; and romanticized view of Indians by Euro-Americans, 13, 257n35
missionaries, and ISPP as proselytizing tool, 67–71, 215
Missouri, and history of Mormonism, 21, 257n36
Mitchell, Ray, 246–47
Momaday, N. Scott, 9

Montclair, Roy, 118
Morgan, Lewis Henry, 38–39
Mormons and Mormonism: bureaucratic reform agenda and dismantling of ISPP in 1980s, 204–5, 233–34; colonization and outreach programs to Lamanites, 6–7; conclusions about impact of ISPP on, 235–49; and correlation movement, 209–11, 216, 220, 233; history of Indian theology and policy of as background to ISPP, 11–35; motivations for participation in early years of ISPP, 55–56; official approval and incorporation of ISPP by, 63, 89; opposition to self-determination movement of 1960s and 1970s, 170–203; placement experiences of ISPP students and exposure to identity as Lamanites, 128–68; placement experiences of ISPP students and unique characteristics of subculture, 104–9; use of term, xi. *See also* baptism; Book of Mormon; excommunication; Indian Committee; Lamanites; missionaries; Relief Society; theology; wards
Mose, Donald, 53, 116
"most," implications of term, xii
Muckelshoot Reservation (Washington), 86
Muhlestein, Robert M., 261n95
Multicultural Education Department (Brigham Young University), 223
Mute, Carle, 45
Mutual Improvement Association, 140, 165
Nakai, Raymond, 81–82, 147, 148, 177, 203
National Council of American Indians, 180
National Indian Education Association, 193

National Indian Youth Council (NIYC), 179

Native American(s): and Book of Mormon on Lamanites, 128–29; and federal policy of self-determination in 1960s and 1970s, 169–203; history of Mormon theology and policy on as background to establishment of ISPP, 11–35; Lamanite identity and experiences of ISPP students, 128–68; and noble savage imagery, 13, 24, 27, 257n35; pan-Indian identities and history of, 237; resistance of Mormon Native Americans to church dissolution of Indian programs, 225–26; use of term, xi. *See also* Catawba; Cheyenne; Chippewa; Delaware; Indianness; Kiowa; Lumbe; Menominee; Navajo; Nez Perce; Omaha; Onondaga; Pawnee; Ponca; Potawatomie; Puyallup; Red Power movement; Seneca; Shawnee; Shoshone; Sioux; Southern Paiute; Utes; Wyandot; Yakima

Native American Church, 75

Natural Parent Guide (1968 ISPP), 93–94, 109, 161

Nauvoo (Illinois), 20, 23, 24, 27, 28, 30

Navajo: blessingway ritual and philosophy of, 274n7; conflicts among Red Power activists, Mormon Lamanites, and reservation-bound groups in 1970s, 169–203; experiences of as ISPP students entering Mormon homes and communities, 91–127; history of education on reservation and events leading to establishment of ISPP, 36–57, 236; identity and history of, 237; and institutionalization of ISPP, 58–86; integration of non-Navajo ideas and practices into culture of, 167–68, 242–43; Mormon

theology and interpretation of history of, 133–34; present status of Mormonism on reservation, 245–46; and summers of ISPP students on reservation, 156–65. *See also* Native American(s)

Navajo Emergency Education Program (NEEP), 172

Navajo-Hopi Long Range Act (1950), 46

Navajo Times, 171, 175, 176, 201, 239

Navajo Tribal Scholarship Program, 78

Navajo Youth Conference (New Mexico, 1960), 172–73

Nelson, Alice, 232

Nelson, Floyd, 134

Nelson, James, 232

Nelson, Mary, 231–33

Nelson, Michael, 232

Nephites, and Mormon theology, 6, 104, 105

Nevada, and ISPP, 83

New Deal, 236

New Era (magazine), 189

"New Lamanites," 87

New Left, and Red Power activism, 179

New York Times, 202

New Zealand, and Lamanites, 88, 248

Nez Perce, 165

Nixon, Richard, 180

noble savage, and images of Native Americans, 13, 24, 27, 257n35

Oaks, Dallin H., 223

Office of Navajo Economic Opportunity, 174

Office of Youth Affairs, 173–74

Ohio, and history of Mormonism, 17–18

Oklahoma, and ISPP, 83

Omaha (tribe), 30, 156

Onondaga, 16

Oregon, and ISPP, 83

Orientalism, and academic discourse on Native Americans and colonization, 4

orientation (ISPP), for foster parents, 97–98

other, and views on Native Americans
by early Mormons, 34
outing programs, 49, 57, 58, 59, 61. *See
also* Indian Student Placement
Program (ISPP)

Pacific Islands and Latin American
Religious Education Program, 87
Pacific Isles: and Lamanite identity,
88, 129, 206; Mormon missions
to, 87
Packer, Boyd K., 65, 85, 148, 190, 205,
207–10, 221, 222, 224–25, 234,
298n63
Paiute Moapa Reservation (Nevada),
86
parents (of ISPP students), visits of to
foster homes, 110. *See also* foster
parents
Parke, Kent, 232–33
Partridge, Edward, 20, 26
paternalism, and views on Native Americans by early Mormons, 35, 56
patriarchal blessings, and Israelite
identity of early Mormons, 22–23,
27
Pawnee, 30
Peace Corps, 174
Penthouse (magazine), 202
Perry, Janice Kapp, 113
Peru, and Lamanite identity, 88
Petersen, Mark E., 63, 64, 65, 70–71,
77, 188
Peterson, Burke, 228–29
Peterson, Ziba, 16
peyote, and Native American church, 75
Phelps, W. W., 26
physical environment, and cultural
differences, 103–4
place, cultural differences and
constructions of, 101
Polacca, Pamela, 266n82
policy. *See* federal government
politics. *See* federal government;
Indian Child Welfare Act; Red
Power movement

polygamy: comparison of controversial
status of ISPP to debate on, 235;
and marriages between Mormons
and Native Americans in early
Utah, 33
Ponca, 30
postcolonialism, and academic
discourse on colonization and
Native Americans, 5
postmodernism, and academic
discourse on colonization and
Native Americans, 4
Potawatomie, 294n120
poverty: and barriers to education
on Navajo reservation, 44, 46;
Bishop on Navajo culture and,
167; Kimball on living conditions
on Navajo reservation, 62; and
motivations for participation
in ISPP, 8, 53–54, 55, 75, 206;
and Packer on church missions
in South America, 208; and
protests by AIM activists, 182; and
recruitment of students for ISPP,
85; and slave trade in early Utah,
34. *See also* socioeconomics
Pratt, Orson, 14
Pratt, Parley P., 15, 16, 29, 32, 255n21
Pratt, Richard Henry, 39–40
Presbyterian Church, 38
Presiding Bishopric Report (1982–
1984), 224, 225
primitivism, and noble savage image
of Native Americans, 13
privacy, and cultural differences
between Navajo reservation and
ISPP foster homes, 102
protests, and Native American
activism in 1960s and 1970s, 179,
181, 189, 237
Public Law 80-390 (1947), 46
Public Law 280 (1953), 195–96
Public Laws 815 and 874 (1950), 172
Pursuitte, David, 15, 16
Puyallup, 200

Quillayute Reservation (Washington), 86
Quinn, D. Michael, 67
Quintero, Vanta, 119

race: and caste system in Mormon theology, 143; and concept of ethnogenesis, 253n22; ISPP and Mormon concerns about interracial social activities, 143–44, 145. See also African-Americans; Euro-Americans; Maori; Native American(s); skin color; white
Raindancer, Inc., 229–30
Rainer, Howard, 281n12
Rainer, John, 186–87
Ramah Navajo High School, 177
reception centers, for ISPP, 66–67, 74, 83, 272n105
Reck, Behe, 152
recreation. See Boy Scouts; leisure; social activities; sports
Redhouse, Betty, 143
Redhouse, Teddy, 70, 132–33, 163, 184
Red Power movement: and political activism in 1960s and 1970s, 179; and self-identified Lamanites, 170, 240. See also American Indian Movement
Red River War (1875), 39
Redstone, George, 182, 183
Reeve, Paul, 30–31
Relief Society: and institutional history of ISPP, 60, 72, 77, 78; and professionalization of church welfare system, 210
religion. See church; Mormons and Mormonism; rituals; spirituality; theology
resistance: to adoption of Native American children by white families, 193; and American Indian activism in 1960s and 1970s, 179; to boarding schools in context of colonization, 4, 5, 7, 10,

36, 41–42; of Indians to Mormon settlement in Salt Lake Valley, 30, 31–32, 35; to Lamanite identity, 151–52; Navajo tribal to ISPP, 82; placement experience of ISPP students and assimilation, 119–21. See also agency
Rhoads, Charles J., 43
Rice Boarding School (Arizona), 42
Richards, Fred, 270n82
Richards, LeGrand, 166
Richards, Willard, 24
Rigdon, Sidney, 17
rituals: of advancement in Mormon church and community, 108–9; and blessingway in Navajo philosophy, 274n7; and Navajo rites of passage, 156
Riverside Boarding School (Oklahoma), 86
road construction, on Navajo reservation, 174–75
Rolling Thunder, 182
Romanticism, and noble savage image of Native Americans, 13, 34
Romney, Marion G., 208
Roosevelt, Franklin, 43
Ryan, W. Carson, 43

Said, Edward, 4, 5
Salt Lake Tribune, 228
Samoa, Mormon missions to and Lamanite identity, 87, 88
Saturday Evening Post, 117, 120
Schimmelpfennig, Dorothy, 193, 275n42, 293n110
schools: and history of education on Navajo reservation, 38, 43, 46; opening of public on Navajo reservation in 1970s, 177–78; placement experiences of ISPP students and public, 114–18. See also boarding schools; education; social activities; sports; students; teachers
Scott, John, 31
Seixas, Joseph, 22

Selam, Victor, 191

self, Mormon theology and sense of, 148. *See also* identity

self-determination: and controversy on adoption, 170, 192–96; and expansion of education on Navajo reservation, 171–74, 177–79; federal policy of, 178, 180, 296n6; impact of on ISPP, 171, 194–203; LDS interpretation of, 170–71, 183–90, 191; and Red Power activism, 170–71, 179–84, 191–92; and socioeconomic changes on Navajo reservation, 174–75

Sells, Cato, 41, 42

seminary classes, and ISPP students, 140–41

Seneca, 16, 28, 259n71

Shawnee, 16

Sherman Institute (California), 46

Shipps, Jan, 108–9

Shoshone, 7, 32, 86, 154, 261n89

Shoshone Duckwater Reservation (Nevada), 86

Shumway, Charles, 28, 51

Shumway, Dale, 85, 111, 113, 119–20, 142, 233, 235

siblings, and placement experiences of ISPP students, 92, 112, 114, 136

Simpson, Robert L., 212

Singer, Lewis J., 53, 116–17, 182

Singer, Ronald, 53, 99, 140

Sioux, 30

skin color, and Mormon theology, 104–6, 276n56

slavery and slave trade, and history of Mormons in Utah, 33–34, 261n95

Slotkin, Richard, 13

Smith, Dan, 132

Smith, Ethan, 14

Smith, George Albert, 48–49, 62, 78–79

Smith, Harry, 272n107

Smith, Joseph: and Andrew Jackson's removal policy, 255n11, 258n44; and Israelite-sounding code names, 22; Mormon Indian

theology and concept of gathering, 15, 16, 25–26; and missions to Indians, 17; and organizational structure of church, 20–21; and shift in relations with Native Americans in 1840s, 27–28; and temple blessings, 23

Smith, Joseph, Sr., 22, 23, 259n50

Smith, Joseph Fielding, 68

Smith, Sherry, 251n5

Snake, Stanley, 188–89

social activities, and placement experiences of ISPP students, 143–45

Society of American Indians, 237

socioeconomics: changes in on Navajo reservation in 1950s and 1960s, 174–75; and conclusions on influence of ISPP on individuals, 238. *See also* poverty

Sohsy, Rose Denette, 52, 99–100, 104, 125, 153, 161

"some," implications of term, xii

South America: and Lamanite identity, 88, 129; Mormon missions to, 86–87

Southern Paiute, 7

Southwest Indian Mission, 60, 69, 146–47, 156–57, 165–66, 206–7, 215, 216, 245

South Wing, 182

space, and cultural differences in placement experiences of ISPP students, 102

Spafford, Belle, 60, 65, 71, 73, 75, 105, 148, 240

Spider Rock (Arizona), 101

spirituality, as motivation for Navajo participation in ISPP, 54

sports: and placement experiences of ISPP students, 145–46; and recreational activities as proselytizing tools, 67, 68–69, 112, 118, 136, 147

Steens, Mary, 246

Steward, Charlie, 270n82

Stewart, Irene, 123

Stott, John, 15, 16

Student Guide. See Indian Student Guide

students (ISPP): baptism of, 64, 67, 68–71, 77, 215, 270n83; conclusions about influence of ISPP on, 235–49; placement experiences of in entering Mormon homes and communities, 91–127; placement experiences of and exposure to new identity as Lamanite, 8–9, 128–68

Stueroke, Carolyn Carter, 281n9

Sturtevant, William, 253n22

summers, of ISPP students on reservations, 2, 76, 94, 113, 130, 153, 159–68, 173, 241, 242

syncretism, and placement experience of ISPP students, 125–26

Talayumptewa, David, 141

Talk, Roy, 115

Tano, Itsuo, 247

teachers, and experiences of ISPP students in public schools, 115

technological innovations, and placement experiences of ISPP students, 100–101, 240

temple blessings, and Israelite identity of early Mormons, 23–24, 27

Thackara, Eliza, 38

theology: history of Mormon Indian theology and policy as background to ISPP, 11–35, 236; Lamanites and Nephites in Mormon, 6; and rationalization of colonization, 248. *See also* Book of Mormon; Mormons and Mormonism

Third Supplemental Appropriations Act of 1948, 46

Thompson, Hildegard, 171–72

time, and cultural differences between ISPP students and foster homes, 102–3

Tindale, S., 28

Tingley, Dale, 85, 223–24

Tintic War (1856), 31

Title XI Education Amendments Act (1978), 178

Tonga, and Lamanites, 88

Topper, Martin, 201

Tracy, Deescheeny Nez, 176, 289n27

Tracy, Larry, 121

Trail of Broken Treaties March (1972), 181

Tribe of Many Feathers (Brigham Young University club), 185, 186, 223

Trudell, John, 182

Truman, Harry S., 45–46

Tsosie, Ben, 51

Tsosie, Caroline Sue, 135, 140

Tsosie, Lenora, 94, 95

Tsosie, Orlando, 116, 125, 244

Tsosie-Bingham, Rosie, 55

Turner, Frederick Jackson, 3

Tuttle, A. Theodore, 65, 149, 222

"two worlds" model: and authenticity in Native American scholarship, 9; and boarding schools, 93; and cultural conflicts on Navajo reservation in 1960s and 1970s, 176; and George P. Lee, 198; and placement experiences of ISPP students, 93, 122–26, 176; and Society of American Indians, 237; and summer visits of ISPP foster parents to Navajo reservation, 162. *See also* biculturalism

Udall, Stewart L., 172

Umatilla Reservation (Oregon), 86

Unified Social Services, 211, 216

United Native Americans (UNA), 179

University of California, 179

Uruguay, and Lamanite identity, 88

Utah: enrollment from in ISPP from 1960 to 1971, 84; Mormon arrival in and changes in perception of Native Americans, 30–32,

253–54n3; slavery and slave trade in early, 33–34
Utes, 7, 31, 33, 152

Valdez, Marta, 88
Valentine, Robert, 42
Vancouver Island Reserve (British Columbia), 83
Van Hoak, Stephen P., 261n95
VanWagenen, Glen, 71, 146, 270n82, 271–72n103
Villalobos, Jamie, 87–88
Vogel, Dan, 254n7, 255n19
voluntary nature, of ISPP, 241–42
Voss, Barbara L., 252n14, 252n22

Wakara (Ute chief), 31, 32
Walker War (1853), 31
wards: and foster families, 139–40; institutionalized dependence of Navajo units on neighboring white stakes, 246
Warrior, Clyde, 179, 180, 237
Wasatch Research Opinion Report, 52, 218
Washakie colony (Utah), 33
Washington, and ISPP, 83
Washington County School District (Utah), 229–30
Washington Post, 202
Wassaja (newspaper), 193, 201–2
Watchman, Alvin, 140–41
Watkins, Arthur, 72, 73
Weber, Max, 281n10
Western Historical Quarterly, 3
Western History Association, 3
Whaley, Aneta, 145

white, use of term in context, xi. See also Euro-Americans
Whitmer, David, 20
Whitmer, Peter, 16
Whitney, Newel K., 17
Wight, Lyman, 17, 28–29
Wilkinson, Ernest, 186, 223
Williams, Arlene Nofchissey, 185
Willmore, David R., 285n108
Wilson, Linda O., 285n108
Wood, Beth, 201
Woodruff, Wilford, 23
work ethic, and Lamanite identity, 133
Works Progress Administration, 43
World War II, Navajo participation in, 37, 44, 57
Wounded Knee II (1973), 179
Wyandots, 16

Yakima, 165
Yazzie, Calvin, 136
Yazzie, Mabel, 54, 124
Yellowjohn, Carletta, 154
Young, Brigham, 7, 21, 23, 29, 30–31, 32, 33
Young, Phineas H., 28
Young, S. Dilworth, 65
youth conferences, for ISPP students, 147–51, 164
Youth Conservation Corps, 174
youth programs, in Navajo communities during 1960s, 173–74

Zah, Peterson, 239
Zondaja, Edwardo, 156